# Money and Politics
# in the United States

# Money and Politics in the United States

## Financing Elections in the 1980s

Edited by
MICHAEL J. MALBIN

AMERICAN ENTERPRISE INSTITUTE
FOR PUBLIC POLICY RESEARCH
Washington, D.C.

CHATHAM HOUSE PUBLISHERS, INC.
Chatham, New Jersey

MONEY AND POLITICS IN THE UNITED STATES:
Financing Elections in the 1980s

CHATHAM HOUSE PUBLISHERS, INC.
Box One, Chatham, New Jersey 07928

PUBLISHER: Edward Artinian
COVER DESIGN: Daryl Urig
COMPOSITION: Chatham Composer
PRINTING AND BINDING: Hamilton Printing Company

LIBRARY OF CONGRESS CATALOGING IN PUBLICATION DATA
Main entry under title:

Money and politics in the United States.

    Includes bibliographical references and index.
    1. Campaign funds--United States--Addresses, essays,
lectures.    I. Malbin, Michael J.
JK1991.M73  1984      324.7'8'0973    84-2900
ISBN 0-934540-23-3

Manufactured in the United States of America
10  9  8  7  6  5  4  3  2  1

# Contents

# Tables

# Figures

MONEY AND POLITICS IN THE UNITED STATES

MICHAEL J. MALBIN

# Introduction

As anybody who bought this book must know, it costs money to communicate ideas beyond one's immediate circle. Political campaigning in a representative democracy necessarily involves communication; candidates must persuade people to vote for them. Once, political communication could be done face to face at little cost, but that option is not available in most places today. So, someone must pay for the costs of democracy—but who? In countries with strong party systems, the costs are borne by the party. In other countries, state-owned television picks up much of the tab. But in the United States, with its thousands of elected officials, relatively weak party loyalties, and candidate-centered politics, campaign funds must be raised and spent largely by the candidates themselves. Most candidates hate raising money, but know they have to do it. They also know that the legal rules governing their funding will affect their campaigns' structures, will guide their strategy, and will influence the role and structure of the parties and interest groups that want to support or oppose them.

This book is about how the extensive changes made in finance laws during the 1970s have affected, and will affect, political campaigns in the United States. Three chapters focus on specific campaigns: Herbert E. Alexander studies the 1980 presidential election, Gary C. Jacobson the congressional elections of 1980 and 1982, and Ruth S. Jones the state campaigns for governor and state legislature and ballot issues. Three other chapters concentrate on organizational developments: David Adamany discusses political parties, Theodore J. Eismeier and Philip H. Pollock III the structure and organization of political action committees (PACs), and Margaret Ann Latus the ideological PACs. One chapter, by Richard Smolka, cuts across the terrain covered by the other six to survey major court cases of the 1970s and 1980s that could have dramatic consequences in future elections. The final chapter, by me, looks ahead to future research and the potential impact of proposals for further changes in the law.

These essays do not share a common thesis, nor even agree on all major points, but they teach some common lessons. Some findings may be consistent with what passes for conventional wisdom about campaign finance, but virtually every essay points to at least one major conclusion either unanticipated by the authors of the laws or that runs counter to popular belief.

Alexander builds upon studies he has conducted on every presidential race since 1960. He details the fund-raising and spending strategies of the major Democratic and Republican candidates in the prenomination period, and of Ronald Reagan, Jimmy Carter, and John Anderson during the 1980 general election campaign. During the prenomination period, Alexander shows how contribution and spending limits "had a significant impact on campaign strategies and, one suspects, outcomes." During the general election, the two major-party candidates each received a $29.4 million grant from the federal treasury. Despite this, any account of the presidential race that looked only at the candidates' direct spending would miss almost half the picture. When party expenditures, coordinated spending by organized labor, and independent spending are included, President Carter's campaign amounted to $53.9 million and Reagan's to $64.3 million. Significantly, for a public funding system that was supposed to curtail overall spending, much of the money spent in behalf of each major candidate was not subject to legal limits. After providing details on the major candidates' sources of funds and their spending strategies, and on John Anderson's financial difficulties, Alexander concludes by offering some proposals for refining the law.

Gary Jacobson's chapter on congressional elections, like Alexander's, carries forward research the author has conducted in the past. In many respects, Jacobson finds the two most recent elections following trends that developed in the 1970s. The level of spending continued to increase, money continued to mean more for challengers than for incumbents, and the political environment months ahead of election day continued to influence the strategic decisions of potentially serious nonincumbents in ways that would later affect fundraising and election results. Two other elements of the 1980 and 1982 elections represented departures from the past. The first was the growing importance of political action committees (PACs), particularly ideological committees that concentrated independent expenditures in a few key races. The second was the role of the Republican party. Political scientists have been writing for years about the declining role of parties in American politics. Jacobson argues that because of Republican fund-raising and organizational efforts, the situation may be reversing. At least part of the GOP's congressional election success in 1980, and part of its ability to hold down midterm losses in 1982, may be traced directly to the efforts of the national Republican party organization.

The roles of parties and PACs are described in greater detail in the next three chapters. David Adamany's essay on political parties is appropriately the longest one in this book. It used to be commonly assumed that the campaign laws of the 1970s were contributing to the demise of political parties.[1] By the end of the decade, the contrary argument began to appear. The Republican party's organizational and fund-raising successes, it was said, meant that the laws were helping rebuild strong party organizations—albeit professionalized, nationalized organizations that differed in fundamental ways from strong parties of old.[2] Adamany's view is similar to the second of these two arguments, but more complex. He describes the Republican party's organizational strengths of 1980 in some detail, followed by a parallel description of the much weaker organization on the Democratic side. The 1982 election saw continued growth for the GOP and the beginnings of what may be a significant imitative effort on the part of Democrats. So far, Adamany's position is similar to the "law makes the party stronger" thesis—particularly given his controversial view that the law's contribution and expenditure limits actually favor parties over other organizations. But his conclusions qualify this thesis considerably. For one thing, Adamany says it remains to be seen whether Democrats, given their class base, structure, and issue positions, can ever match the Republican effort. Second, Adamany sees PACs, whose growth the law also encouraged, as serious competitors to parties. Finally, he questions whether party financial strength does now, or will ever, mean a party that is significantly better able to influence the policy positions taken by its officeholders.

If PACs in some respects may be organizational competitors to political parties, that does not mean that all PACs—or even all business PACs or all labor PACs—act monolithically. Nevertheless, there has been a great deal of simplistic writing in the past ten years that seems to begin from such an assumption. Theodore J. Eismeier and Philip H. Pollock III dispel the monolith myth convincingly in their chapter on PAC organization and strategy. They begin by setting out some of the standard assumptions about PACs: PACs portend the nationalization of campaign finance, their growth bodes ill for the fortunes of challengers, and typical PAC strategy is designed to maximize legislative access and influence. Then, through an analysis of 1980 data, the authors show each of these assumptions to be false: The typical PAC is a small operation, is based somewhere outside Washington, gives a substantial share of its money to nonincumbents, and follows a "remarkably unsophisticated" giving strategy if the aim of the strategy is to maximize legislative influence. But even this sweeping portrait is too generalized. The authors show that within each of the major PAC categories, political strategies vary with organizational characteristics. Specific characteristics studied include the size of PAC budgets; the presence or absence of a Washington office; and, for business PACs, some differences among industries. While the conclusions are too rich to be summarized here, one remarkable finding bears some emphasis: Across all PAC categories, an increase in budget size means a disproportionately large increase in the amount of money given to challengers and open-seat candidates. The implication is that although PACs as a whole may give more to incumbents than to challengers or open-seat candidates, the growth and maturation of large PACs may end up producing more money for nonincumbents and thus enhancing competitiveness. While the findings "hardly make [the authors] panglossian about the PAC phenomenon," they do "cast some doubt on a few of the most publicized fears about PACs."

Margaret Ann Latus continues the examination of political action committees with an essay that focuses on ideological PACs. After providing an overview and presenting data for independent expenditures by PACs on congressional elections, Latus turns to a close examination of ten ideological PACs. The PACs she has chosen include four large multi-issue PACs (two liberal and two conservative) and three pairs of single-issue PACs, one liberal and one conservative each on defense policy, gun control, and abortion. She describes each PAC's organization and then examines the ways in which each chooses to influence elections. From her description, it seems clear that if any PACs come close to performing the full range of electoral functions performed by a party—from candidate recruitment and training to framing and publicizing issues, providing financial and technical support, and mobilizing voters—it is among ideological PACs that one must look. Interestingly, Latus finds many strong parallels in the tactics followed by, and resources available to, most of the liberal and conservative groups in her study.

When it comes to assessing the groups' impact, Latus argues that they were neither as important in 1980, nor as unimportant in 1982, as they have been generally portrayed. More important than specific wins or losses, however, may be the influence these PACs have on the democratic process. Here, Latus cautions against accepting the cries of "doomsayers" at face value. "Considering the paucity of information most voters have about congressional candidates, ideological PACs may be enhancing democratic representation. . . . Quite possibly, while some of the activities of ideological PACs may be cause for concern, others may prove to be positive influences in American politics."

After the detailed consideration of federal elections, and their organizational environment, the book turns to an examination of state campaign finance by Ruth S. Jones. As Jones shows, many of the patterns affecting national politics are in evidence at the state level—at least in the minority of states that publish election receipts and expenditures. As at the federal level, the cost of campaigning has increased much faster than the rate of inflation for both statewide and legislative offices. "In recent years," Jones writes, "the average cost of a legislative seat has doubled or tripled in almost every state for which there are records." Funding sources have changed along with costs. Individual contributions continue to form the backbone of campaign finance in state elections, as they do in federal races. PAC funds have increased markedly, although state PAC development lags behind organizational changes at the national level. As in every other area relating to state campaign finance, future patterns will undoubtedly be shaped by the wide variations in state law. In general, however, "it appears that PACs intend to regularize if not institutionalize their role in state elections."

Parties played a smaller financial role in state elections than individuals or PACs, but their role still was significant. "In fact, there was an increase over past years of party activity and party money in state campaigns in 1980." Public money, the fourth major source of campaign funding, is potentially available in only 17 states. Its effect varies with the nature of the funding or check-off mechanism, with whether money goes to parties or candidates, and if it goes to candidates, with the specific office funded and the contribution and expenditure limits that may or may not come with accepting public money.

Jones next turns her attention to state ballot-issue campaigns. Advocates of the initiative and referendum generally argue that these devices facilitate individual, grass-roots, citizen participation. Contrary to these expectations, Jones's review of the financial data shows that the sources of money for these campaigns tend to be "(1) a very few, large contributors, (2) who are highly organized groups rather than single individuals, and (3) who frequently represent out-of-state interests." We will have to wait for further analyses, of course, to see whether the patterns of 1980 and 1982 continue in future ballot-issue and state office campaigns. Jones concludes her essay, however, by noting that such analyses may become less possible in the future as state after state curtails its budget for public disclosure. The situation, she says, "is deplorable. . . . If money indeed talks, it will be extremely difficult in the future to determine whose voices are being heard in state elections."

The final two chapters return to a national focus. Richard Smolka examines cases of the late 1970s and early 1980s to see how the courts have implemented campaign acts in the light of the constitutional rules the Supreme Court articulated in 1976 in *Buckley* v. *Valeo* (described below). The cases examined include ones that upheld unlimited independent expenditures in the 1980 presidential election, permitted unlimited contributions to draft committees for undeclared candidates, prevented the FEC from requiring disclosure from unpopular political parties, and limited FEC inquiries into press activities even if the activities incidentally benefit or hinder a candidate's campaign. In each case, the courts limited the law's application because of a conflict with the First Amendment. The result, according to Smolka, is a patchwork law that "has not limited the impact of money in campaigns nor diminished to any appreciable extent the appearance of potential corruption. . . . The long-range prospect is for more legislation, litigation, and lack of coherent public policy. . . . Unless the First Amendment is redefined, the likelihood of successful, comprehensive, campaign finance regulation is as remote as ever."

The final essay, by me, picks up where Smolka left off. It begins with a review of the attempts reformers have made since *Buckley* v. *Valeo* to limit the role of interest groups. Four basic approaches were on the table when this book was written: simple limitations on the amount of money a candidate may accept from PACs, public financing coupled with limits on both a candidate's expenditures and PAC receipts, enhancing the role of political parties, and providing for a kind of public financing without spending limits in the form of liberalized tax credits. Each approach is examined for potentially unintended consequences, then three basic assumptions underlying the desire to limit PACs are explored in detail. They are (1) that the proportional importance of special interests is something new to American elections, (2) that PAC contributions influence legislation, and (3) that the electoral role of interest groups can be reduced significantly by limiting their direct contributions to candidates.

The next section is less reactive in tone. It begins with the observation that the exact effects of contribution limits will vary with individual organizations, depending on the organization's own view of its maintenance needs. From this perspective, it suggests how one might begin to examine and understand the needs, and likely reactions, of different kinds of PACs. "Legislative proposals designed to curb PACs in fact would affect groups differentially in ways we cannot foresee," the section concludes, "but that undoubtedly would be related to a PAC's or parent group's own organizational needs. If those needs require political involvement, then political involvement there will be."

The final section departs from the consequences of reform to look at more basic questions, leading ultimately to a brief review of the purposes of elections and representation. The section begins by considering whether the formal organization of interest-group giving through PACs helps stifle competition by favoring incumbents, and whether the PAC phenomenon helps lobbying either indirectly (by helping interest groups organize for other lobbying activities) or directly (through the effect of PACs and contemporary campaign fund raising on members of Congress). In each case, the answer is mixed and ambiguous. To mention just one, early PAC contributions seem on balance to help some incumbents solidify their positions, but late contributions are very important to promising challengers. This conclusion is important for the remaining pages, when I make some of my own recommendations for the future. Depending on one's perspective, and the exact question one is trying to answer, the electoral role of interest groups can be seen partly to further and partly to impede the purpose of elections. But the potentially harmful effects seem to stem from sources that are more basic, and less subject to control, than campaign contributions. For that reason, a regulatory strategy based on limits is not likely to achieve its intended effect. Instead, I advocate increasing the role of parties to act as a counterweight to interest-group fractionalization, and public financing without spending limits to increase competition by making it easier for challengers to raise money early in their campaigns. Any other approach might serve to "make a few regulators feel good for a while—but only until they glance backward at the unintended consequences of some past reforms and realize that they are looking at their own future."

The book concludes with an appendix, co-authored by Thomas W. Skladony and me, that contains 27 tables of selected campaign finance data from 1974 through 1982. Most of the tables update ones that appeared in the American Enterprise Institute's *Vital Statistics on Congress, 1982* by Norman J. Ornstein, Thomas E. Mann, Michael J. Malbin, and John F. Bibby. Two new tables look at 1982 PAC contributions not only by candidate status but also by election outcomes. Three other new tables look at the timing of PAC and non-PAC contributions by candidate status and party. Data from *Vital Statistics* that simply duplicated material in the main text of this book were omitted. Our aim in providing these tables is to make the book useful for reference as well as for teaching and reading.

## The Campaign Laws

Some readers may not be familiar with the federal campaign finance laws enacted during the 1970s. What follows is a brief summary of their major provisions.[3]

Until 1971, most federal law relating to campaign finance was codified in the Corrupt Practices Act of 1925,[4] which required disclosure of receipts and expenditures by candidates for the Senate and House of Representatives. But the law did not apply to political committees set up by a candidate nor to presidential and vice-presidential candidates. The 1925 act put spending ceilings on "interstate committees," but presidential candidates evaded the limit by setting up more than one committee in their name. The same device was used to circumvent the $5000 limit on contributions by individuals imposed by the 1940 Hatch Act,[5] as there was no limit on the number of committees candidates could set up, each being eligible to receive $5000.

The Corrupt Practices Act was repealed by the Federal Election Campaign Act (FECA) of 1971.[6] The new act had three major provisions: (1) It significantly tightened disclosure and reporting requirements for all candidates for federal office as of April 7, 1972; (2) it limited the amounts of money candidates could spend on media advertising; and (3) it limited the amount a candidate and his immediate family could contribute to his own campaign. At about the same time, the Revenue Act of 1971[7] allowed taxpayers to claim 50 percent credits of up to $12.50, or deductions of up to $50.00, for political contributions, and allowed taxpayers to check a box on their tax forms in order to place a dollar of their taxes in a fund for presidential and vice-presidential candidates. The 1971 law contained provisions directing how these funds were to be disbursed, but these were to be changed before they were ever implemented.

The FECA Amendments of 1974[8] probably represented the most sweeping set of campaign finance law changes ever adopted in the United States, if not in the world. The 1974 law

- limited the amount individuals could contribute to federal candidates to $1000 per election (primary, general election, or runoff) and a cumulative total of $25,000 per year
- retained the 1971 limit on contributions by candidates to their own campaigns
- limited to $1000 the amount an individual could spend independently to influence an election (such spending is termed an "independent expenditure")
- limited what candidates could spend to get elected
- amended a 1940 Hatch Act provision prohibiting contributions from federal contractors to make it clear that contractors could form PACs
- limited PAC contributions to $5000 per candidate per election, with no cumulative limit
- limited expenditures by political parties on behalf of a candidate (over and above contributions) to $10,000 per candidate for the House in

general elections, $20,000 or two cents per eligible voter, whichever was greater in general elections for the Senate, and two cents per voter in the presidential general election

- established formulas for disbursing public funds to match contributions of up to $250 for presidential candidates in prenomination contests
- used flat grants to cover the full expenses of the conventions of the two major parties and the major presidential general election campaigns, with proportional formulas for postelection grants to qualified candidates of minor parties
- required candidates of major parties who choose to accept flat grants for general elections to forgo private financing and limit their expenditures to the amount of the grant (regulations later permitted candidates to raise money privately to pay for the cost of complying with the law)
- created an independent, six-member Federal Election Commission (FEC)
- strengthened disclosure and closed previous legal loopholes by requiring any federal candidate to establish a single central campaign committee through which all contributions and expenditures would have to be reported

The 1974 law was immediately attacked as unconstitutional. Within days after it went into effect on January 1, 1975, a coalition spanning the political spectrum filed a case that came to be known as *Buckley* v. *Valeo*. The Supreme Court's decision in that case, handed down a little more than a year later on January 30, 1976,[9] held unconstitutional the limits on campaign spending, independent expenditures, and contributions by a candidate to his or her own campaign, along with the method by which the FEC was appointed. The Court upheld disclosure, public financing, and the limits on individual, PAC, and party contributions. The Court also upheld the spending limits imposed on a candidate as a condition for accepting public financing.

Since *Buckley* v. *Valeo* effectively put the FEC out of business in the middle of a presidential election campaign, Congress was forced in 1976 to pass yet another set of amendments to the FECA.[10] It could have simply reconstituted the FEC along lines suggested by the Court, but Congress decided to use the occasion to address a number of other issues. The 1976 law

- limited individual contributions to political parties to $20,000 per year and to other political committees to $5000 per year
- limited contributions to political parties by PACs to $15,000 per year
- increased the amount that the Democratic and Republican Senate campaign committees could contribute to Senate candidates from $5000 per election to $17,500 per year
- limited to $50,000 the amount of their own money that presidential candidates who were publicly financed could spend to support their own campaign
- reversed an FEC ruling on PACs that appeared to allow labor and business PACs to proliferate in a way that effectively might have destroyed the PAC contribution limits

The 1976 and 1978 elections led many members of Congress to seek still further changes in the law. Several attempts were made to enact partial public financing of congressional elections, coupled with limits on congressional campaign expenditures, but these failed repeatedly in the House, where they faced the opposition of most Republicans and many senior Democrats.

One important campaign finance bill did pass in 1979.[11] Largely noncontroversial, the bill attempted to respond to criticisms that the legislation of 1974 and 1976 created excessive paperwork while stifling a great deal of local volunteer activity by parties and other groups. The most important provisions of the 1979 act

- reduced the maximum numbers of reports to be filed by House and Senate candidates
- exempted candidates from filing disclosure statements if they do not receive or spend more than $5000
- permitted state and local parties to spend unlimited amounts for campaign materials (such as bumper stickers or brochures) for distribution by volunteers
- permitted unlimited expenditures by state and local parties for registration and get-out-the-vote drives for the presidential ticket (the provision was silent about volunteers, but FEC regulations say that although professionals may be used to train people to use phone banks, volunteers must do the actual telephoning)
- raised the disclosure threshold from $100 to $200 for contributions and expenditures and from $100 to $250 for independent expenditures
- increased from $2 million to $3 million the 1974 base, before inflation adjustments, for public funds given to major political parties for national nominating conventions
- doubled the threshold for reporting expenditures made by volunteers on travel and home entertainment in support of a candidate (from $500 to $1000) or political party (from $1000 to $2000)

The law has changed in many other important ways since 1979, but through regulation and court cases, not through legislation. The statutory provisions described above, therefore, represent the state of the law in effect at the time of the elections covered by this volume.

## Notes

1. See, for example, *Report by the Campaign Finance Study Group of The Institute of Politics, John F. Kennedy School of Government, Harvard University, to the Committee on House Administration* (Washington, D.C.: U.S. House of Representatives, May 1979).
2. Xandra Kayden, "The Nationalizing of the Party System," in *Parties, Interest Groups and Campaign Finance Laws,* ed. Michael J. Malbin (Washington, D.C.: American Enterprise Institute, 1980), 257-82.
3. For a more complete history, see Herbert E. Alexander, *Financing the 1980 Election* (Lexington, Mass: Heath, 1983), 491-508. The descriptions that follow are based on Alexander's summaries.
4. 43 Stat. 1053, ch. 368, sec. 301-19.
5. 54 Stat. 772.
6. P.L. 92-225.
7. P.L. 92-178.
8. P.L. 93-443.
9. 424 U.S.1 (1976).
10. P.L. 94-283.
11. P.L. 96-187.

HERBERT E. ALEXANDER

# 1. Making Sense About Dollars in the 1980 Presidential Campaigns

The 1980 presidential election was the most expensive in the nation's history. It cost $275 million to elect a President. This figure includes money spent on prenomination and general election campaigns by presidential candidates, by their committees and political parties, and by independent committees and individuals in their behalf, as well as on the national conventions. The total represents some $115 million more than was spent in 1976 to elect a President. Given a 35 percent rise in the Consumer Price Index in the intervening years, the sums spent in 1980 represent an increase of about $60 million in constant terms of value over amounts spent in 1976. Approximately one-third of that increase, however, was caused by much greater spending by independent candidates, notably John Anderson, and by certain minor-party candidates.

Of the $275 million total, some $106 million was spent during the prenomination period: $70.6 million by Republicans and $35.7 million by Democrats. Approximately $10 million was spent to finance the parties' national nominating conventions. About $142 million was spent on behalf of major-party, minor-party, and independent general election candidates.

The record-breaking expenditures lend credence to veteran California politician Jesse Unruh's oft-quoted adage: "Money is the mother's milk of politics." In 1980, although money was essential to nurture the campaigns, and was an important factor in the election equation, it did not determine many outcomes. John Connally's failure to be nominated, despite large amounts of early money, is a notable example. If primary and caucus results are the measure, the party nominations reflected the popular will. The size and breadth of the Reagan victory in the general election, and Republican gains to control the Senate, indicate that factors other than money played key roles.

The largest contributor to the 1980 prenomination and general election campaigns was the U.S. government, which supplied about 37 percent—some $100.6 million—of the $275 million spent. These funds came from voluntary check-off contributions that about 35 million taxpayers make each year by earmarking a dollar each on their federal income tax forms for the Presidential Election Campaign Fund. The check-off receipts are aggregated over a four-year period, but the payoff is made only in the election year. The public funds in 1980 were divided into about $29.7 million in matching funds for the Republican and Democratic candidates seeking nomination, some $8.1 million for the major parties to hold their nominating conventions, and $58.8 million for Reagan and Carter in the general election. In addition, independent candidate John Anderson qualified for $4.2 million in postelection public funding by getting 6.5 percent of the vote (5 percent is necessary to qualify). After 1980 election year payouts were made, approximately $80 million remained in the fund to be carried over to the 1984 presidential elections. It is estimated that an additional $140 million will be raised through the check-off system in the intervening years.[1]

Although public funds were provided to major-party general election candidates in both 1976 and 1980, the 1980 general election was distinguished by significantly greater spending and a greater variety of sources of funds. In fact, the expanded sources from which money was spent for or in behalf of the presidential campaigns is as newsworthy as the high levels of spending. To some observers this is further evidence of a desirable pluralism long thought characteristic of American politics. To others, particular sources of presidential campaign funds represent a threat to the spirit of the campaign finance reforms enacted in the 1970s.

## Prenomination Campaigns

As in 1976, in 1980 federal matching funds provided an important source of income in campaigns for major-party nomination. About 29 percent of the $106.3 million spent by those candidates came from matching funds accepted by ten eligible candidates (see tables 1.1 and 1.2).[2] John Connally, whose fundraising success qualified him to receive the government matching subsidies, did not request public funding; Ben Fernandez and Harold Stassen did not qualify for public funds. Thus, of the ten candidates accepting public funds, some 27.8 percent of their receipts came from the government. To compare 1980 experience with 1976, federal matching funds in the earlier year provided $23.7 million to 15 qualifying candidates, comprising 30.5 percent of their expenditures, which totaled $72.3 million.[3]

Additional money was spent by three candidates seeking minor-party nominations for President, none qualifying for matching funds: Edward Clark ($1 million) and William Hunscher ($100,000) contesting for the Libertarian party nomination; and Andrew Pulley ($120,000) seeking the Socialist Workers party nomination.

### CONTRIBUTION AND SPENDING LIMITS

Despite the amounts of money raised by the major candidates for presidential nomination, the candidates experienced difficulty meeting the financial obligations of conducting their campaigns. A $1000 contribution in the midst of the 1980 primary season was worth only about $641 when compared with the buy-

TABLE 1.1.

PRENOMINATION RECEIPTS AND EXPENDITURES OF MAJOR REPUBLICAN CONTENDERS, 1980

(IN MILLIONS)

| Candidate | Adjusted Receipts | Individual Contributions | PAC Contributions | Matching Funds | Adjusted Disbursements |
|---|---|---|---|---|---|
| Anderson[a] | $ 6.6 | $ 3.9 | $.02 | $ 2.3 | $ 6.5 |
| Baker | 7.1 | 4.2 | .13 | 2.5 | 7.0 |
| Bush | 16.7 | 10.9 | .13 | 5.7 | 16.7 |
| Connally | 12.7 | 11.6 | .20 | – | 12.7 |
| Crane | 5.2 | 3.5 | .00 | 1.9 | 5.2 |
| Dole | 1.4 | .9 | .05 | .4 | 1.4 |
| Fernandez | .3 | .2 | .00 | – | .3 |
| Reagan | 21.4 | 13.8 | .29 | 6.3 | 20.7 |
| Stassen | .1 | .0 | .00 | – | .1 |
| TOTAL | $71.5 | $49.0 | $.82 | $19.1 | $70.6 |

SOURCE: FEC news release, November 15, 1981, includes contributions and expenditures reported from January 1, 1978 through December 31, 1980. Matching funds and adjusted disbursements revised through March 1982.

a. The Anderson Republican prenomination campaign transferred $713,000 of this amount to his independent campaign.

TABLE 1.2.
PRENOMINATION RECEIPTS AND EXPENDITURES OF MAJOR DEMOCRATIC CONTENDERS, 1980
(IN MILLIONS)

| Candidate | Adjusted Receipts | Individual Contributions | PAC Contributions | Matching Funds | Adjusted Disbursements |
|---|---|---|---|---|---|
| Brown | $ 2.7 | $ 1.7 | $.04 | $ .9 | $ 2.7 |
| Carter | 18.6 | 12.9 | .46 | 5.0 | 18.5 |
| Kennedy[a] | 12.3 | 7.8 | .23 | 4.1 | 12.3 |
| LaRouche | 2.1 | 1.6 | .01 | .5 | 2.2 |
| TOTAL | $35.7 | $24.0 | $.74 | $10.5 | $35.7 |

SOURCE: FEC news release, November 15, 1981, includes contributions and expenditures reported from January 1, 1978 through December 31, 1980. Matching funds and adjusted disbursements revised through March 1982.

a. Draft-Kennedy totals of $538,454 were in addition to the authorized committees noted in table, expended prior to Kennedy's announcement of candidacy.

ing power of $1000 in 1975 when the limit went into effect. Further, the low individual contribution limit served to increase the length of prenomination campaigns because candidates needed to put their fund-raising organizations in place early in 1979 in order to obtain "seed money" to get their campaigns rolling. Finally, although the individual contribution limit went far toward eliminating very large donations, the limit enhanced the importance and potential influence of fund raisers who had access to lists of contributors or membership groups.

Like the federal election law's contribution limit, the law's expenditure limits on candidates accepting public funding also had a significant impact on campaign strategies and, one suspects, outcomes. The overall prenomination spending limit forced campaigns to centralize control of spending and plan carefully when and where to spend available money. The limit made for rigid campaign organizations and procedures and reduced flexibility and spontaneity.

For the 1980 campaigns, expenditures chargeable to the limits could not exceed $14,720,000 for all headquarters, primaries, caucuses, and convention costs, plus 20 percent overage for fund-raising expenses, equaling $2,944,000; thus total costs of $17,664,000, plus unlimited compliance costs relating to legal, accounting, and bookkeeping expenses, were allowed. Only Reagan, Bush, and Carter approached these limits.

In addition, the law provided state-by-state expenditure limits, in amounts ranging in 1980 from $294,400 in New Hampshire to $3,880,192 in California. The total of the state limits far exceeded the $14.7 million overall limit, so candidates could not spend up to the limit in each state and had to choose where to spend.

Patterns of spending in the prenomination period reflect the schedule of primaries and caucuses, with emphasis on seeking early and decisive success. Despite low expenditure limits in key early states, such as Iowa ($489,881) and New Hampshire ($294,000), candidate organizations focused a disproportionate amount of time, energy, and money planning on making a showing that would trigger new financial and related support and would create a psychological impact that could be built upon to sustain the candidate through the remaining season of delegate selection and preference primaries culminating with nomination at the convention. Amounts of money spent in early states do not reflect the attention given by campaign staffs to winning in them.

With mandated limits, both overall and state-by-state, requiring careful decision making as to allocations and timing, the centralization of authority in spending is essential. Consideration also must be given to future fund raising as a function of expected spending needs.

The Reagan campaign illustrates the need to control spending. Through March 31, 1980, when only 11 of the 36 Republican contests had been held, the Reagan committee reported having spent a little more than $11 million, 75 percent of the expenditures subject to the limit. The committee was forced to cut its monthly payroll in half[4] and tighten financial controls.[5] If former

President Ford had become a candidate in March, as he considered doing, or Bush or another candidate had been able to challenge Reagan's lead more consistently through the winter and spring, Reagan would have had major problems in staying within the limit and remaining in a competitive spending position.

The state-by-state limits, which vary according to a state's voting-age population, also affected strategic decisions in the campaigns. Candidates felt the need to do well in early contests, which customarily are assigned more importance by the news media than the number of delegates at stake would warrant. The low spending ceilings in early contests in less populous states forced the candidates to budget tightly. One candidate, John Connally, chose to reject public funding in order to avoid the state limits. More than one candidate resorted to subterfuge to get around the limits in the hope of gaining an early advantage, for example, stopping overnight during a primary campaign in a state bordering on the primary state so that the cost of accommodations could be counted against the other state's limits, or arranging flights during a primary campaign to pass through cities outside the primary state and thus making them interstate trips, which do not fall under the primary state's spending limit.

Despite such subterfuges, Reagan, Carter, and Kennedy exceeded state limits in New Hampshire, Carter and Kennedy exceeded them in Iowa, and Carter also did so in Maine.[6] Each campaign organization was fined by the FEC for the violations. (Recommendations regarding the various limitations are made in the conclusion of this chapter.)

The spending limits, particularly state limits, enhanced the potential effectiveness of independent expenditures, especially in early primary states with low spending ceilings. Such expenditures seemed to work to the advantage of candidates attractive to organizations and individuals willing and able to mount independent spending campaigns in behalf of the candidates. The Fund for a Conservative Majority spent more than $60,000 in New Hampshire in behalf of Ronald Reagan when his campaign was approaching the state's $294,000 spending limit.[7] The fund also spent more than $80,000 in the Texas primary, and $600,000 in all to help Reagan.[8]

## CANDIDATES' MEDIA EXPENDITURES
Television coverage of campaigns—or the lack of such coverage—played an important part in prenomination campaign strategies. Although Reagan, Carter, and Connally were rebuffed by the three networks in their efforts to buy program time late in 1979 and early in 1980, the major contenders all spent a significant percentage of their campaign treasuries on local television advertising. In addition, campaign strategies were devised to attract free network or local station coverage.

In deciding not to accept public funds, John Connally made clear that television was a prominent factor.[9] Connally believed that only ample television exposure could project him into a competitive position vis-à-vis front-runner Reagan. When the national networks refused to sell him 30-minute seg-

ments of prime time in November and December 1979, Conn
strategy to buy the attention he sought in the primary states. Bu
lion spent directly on Connally's advertising did not bring him th
tories he sought.

TABLE 1.3.

MEDIA EXPENDITURES DURING THE PRENOMINATION PERIOD
OF THE 1980 PRESIDENTIAL CAMPAIGN

| Candidate | | Media | Production | Media as % of Total Adjusted Disbursements |
|---|---|---|---|---|
| Bush | Air time | $3,750,000 | $730,500 | 29.2 |
| | Print | 388,300 | | |
| Kennedy | | 1,017,250 | 805,100 | 14.8 |
| Connally | | 1,900,000[a] | n/a | 15.0 |
| Carter | | 3,562,700 | 652,350 | 22.8 |
| Reagan | | 3,000,000[a] | n/a | 14.5 |
| Brown | | 345,500 | 45,000 | 14.4 |
| | Television | 670,000 | | |
| Baker | Radio | 160,000 | 281,500 | 16.7 |
| | Newspapers | 58,000 | | |
| Anderson | | 1,274,570[a] | n/a | 19.6 |
| TOTAL | | $16,126,320[b] | $2,514,450[b] | 20.7 |

SOURCE: Citizens' Research Foundation.
  a.  Media amount not separated for production costs. In some cases, production subsumed in media figure; in others, in consultant's fees not isolatable.
  b.  Amount not certain because production costs not ascertained in three cases.

Television advertising did not result in success for most of the other candidates either. A listing of media spending is shown in table 1.3. Although some production costs and media breakdowns are not available, the table reveals that not more than 20 percent of prenomination expenditures went to the media. The wise use of television time particularly remains an important ingredient of winning, yet losers often outspend winners in this category. Senator Howard Baker spent $325,000 in the New England primaries, but he was forced to drop from the running in early March. President Carter far outspent Senator Kennedy in the March 25 New York primary, but Kennedy scored an upset victory by a wide margin. Although Carter stayed ahead of Kennedy in the polls and throughout the early primary season, his media experts spent more than $3.5 million on 30- and 60-second spot announcements and five-minute programs, compared with Kennedy's $1 million. Gerald Rafshoon, Carter's media adviser, stated the purpose was to give Carter "a presence" in the state primaries while allowing the President to remain in the White House to concentrate on the Iranian hostage crisis, above the hurly-burly of the campaign trail.[10]

## CAMPAIGN DEBT REDUCTION

All this spending on media helped produce sizable debts for most of the leading candidates. When the primary season ended, the losing Republican presidential candidates banded together with Ronald Reagan to help pay off the losers' campaign debts. Former candidates Baker, Connally, Dole, Crane, and Fernandez joined Reagan as hosts of a series of four "presidential unity dinners." Former candidate George Bush lent his name to the fund-raising dinners, though his campaign did not seek a share in the dinner proceeds, preferring instead to pay off its estimated $300,000 debt directly, which it did through mail solicitations.[11] At the time the unity dinners were announced late in May, Connally's deficit was estimated at close to $1.5 million.[12] Baker's deficit as of May 19 was $890,586, Crane's was $398,057, and Dole's was $113,000.[13] With the exception of Connally, the dinner co-hosts sought to use the money they raised through the dinners to qualify for additional matching funds until their deficits were paid off.

The first of the dinners, a $500-a-plate affair held in Beverly Hills on June 13, brought in gross receipts of $550,000, a substantial portion of which went for production of a 30-minute television show aired on CBS on June 21 that served as a fund-raising appeal. The meager proceeds—about $200,000—were divided among the various candidates, but the broadcast costs were higher. Winning candidate Reagan, whose campaign paid only 1 percent of the cost of the program, benefited from the exposure and from the endorsement of those he had defeated.[14] The program was not counted as an in-kind contribution to the Reagan campaign because it was reported to the FEC as part of a joint fund-raising operation by the unsuccessful Republican candidates to reduce their campaign debts. Unity dinners brought in a total of $1.4 million for distribution to the candidates.

Losing candidates also used a variety of other approaches to pay off their campaign debts. Like George Bush, Howard Baker used direct mail with good results.[15] John Connally wanted to sell donated artworks through an art dealer with the sale exempt from the contribution limits, much as the sale of leftover campaign materials is exempt.[16] Adverse FEC and IRS rulings severely limited the potential effectiveness of Connally's novel approach.[17]

On the Democratic side, Kennedy ended with a debt of $2.2 million, including bills of $600,000 received in August 1980 from the national convention, the national headquarters, and many states. Carter ended with a debt of $650,000, half of it incurred by the campaign and half by the fund-raising effort. The Kennedy and Carter campaigns agreed to hold three unity dinners in late 1980. Only one dinner was held, and the distribution of the proceeds created a controversy among the principals and the FEC. Because the gross income did not reach levels above which it was agreed that Carter could split the proceeds, Kennedy received the net profit, and Carter received only earmarked funds amounting to a few thousand dollars. One Carter concert raised only $60,000 and cost $58,000. A September 1981 dinner for Carter grossed

$64,890 and netted $33,500, which was allocated to four different funds, leaving a debt of $637,000 in early 1982, with more than half that amount owed to media consultant Jerry Rafshoon.

The Kennedy debts were whittled down to about $520,000 by August 1981. Money to pay off debts came from one unity dinner with Carter, other Kennedy dinners and events, PAC contributions, mostly from labor PACs, of about $50,000, artwork sales of $50,000, direct mail proceeds of $168,000, rebates of deposits, and $650,000 in matching funds. But continuing expenses were being incurred. With three major exceptions, one involving a suit for full payment, most remaining debtors settled for one-third on bills of $5000 or more, 40 percent on bills from $1500 to $4999, and 50 percent on less than $1500. In all, however, some $1.7 million in debts were paid off dollar for dollar.

Governor Jerry Brown paid off his $600,000 campaign debt with the proceeds from a number of private fund-raising events.

## General Election Campaigns

Conceptually, there were in the 1980 major-party presidential contest three different and parallel general election campaigns. The first campaign was completely within the control of the major-party nominees and their campaign organizations. Legally limited, the "controlled campaign" was mostly subsidized by public funds supplemented by privately raised national party spending in support of the presidential ticket.

The second campaign had no legal spending limits. It was partly outside the control of the candidate and his campaign organization, but it could be, and frequently was, coordinated with the candidate and his campaign organization. This campaign included unlimited spending by state and local party committees and by labor unions, corporations, associations, and others, both through their treasuries and through their political action committees (PACs). During 1980 the Federal Election Commission was criticized for not giving precise guidance regarding various coordinated activities — party and nonparty — and for not defining affiliated committees and determining whether their activities were an influence on the election. Privately raised compliance funds also were unlimited.

The third campaign was funded by independent expenditures, in which individuals or groups were legally able to spend unlimited amounts for or against candidates, but had to do so without consultation or collaboration with the candidate or his campaign. The widespread use of independent expenditures was controversial in 1980 and was the subject of various complaints and lawsuits.

These three explicit presidential campaigns were supplemented by less obvious and more subtle efforts (to be recounted later), including an expensive Republican media campaign, "nonpartisan" group activities focusing on issues closely related to the campaigns, and a number of uses of incumbency to benefit the occupant of the White House, Jimmy Carter. It is not legitimate to include among campaign expenditures the costs of campaign coverage by the media; presidential debates and forums; and other nonpartisan, bipartisan, or joint events surrounding the presidential campaigns, however these events were financed. But these factors affect the political environment as much as the three campaigns enumerated, and help make the presidential selection process, in all its phases, the greatest and most pervasive information event every four years in the nation's experience.

## SOURCES OF FUNDS

During the general election period, major-party candidates Ronald Reagan and Jimmy Carter each benefited from a patchwork of funds amounting to more than $60 million for Reagan and $50 million for Carter, as illustrated in table 1.4. Each received $29.4 million in public funds from the Presidential Election Campaign Fund. That amount was supplemented by money raised privately by the national party committees—since 1974 free of the need to raise money for their national nominating conventions. In 1980 each national party committee was allowed to spend $4.6 million of such funds in conjunction with the presidential campaign, making a possible $34 million to be directly controlled by the presidential campaign. The Republican National Committee had no difficulty in raising the $4.6 million and spending $4.5 million of it in the thick of the campaign. The Democratic National Committee fell short by some $600,000.[18]

TABLE 1.4.
SOURCES OF FUNDS IN 1980 GENERAL ELECTION, MAJOR-PARTY CANDIDATES
(IN MILLIONS)

| | Sources of Funds | Reagan | Carter |
|---|---|---|---|
| **Limited Campaign** | | | |
| Candidate controlled | Federal grant | $29.2 | $29.4 |
| | National party | 4.5 | 4.0 |
| **Unlimited Campaigns** | | | |
| | State and local party | 15.0 | 4.0 |
| | Labor[a] | 1.5 | 15.0 |
| Candidate can | Corporate/association[a] | 1.5 | — |
| coordinate | Compliance | 1.5 | 1.5 |
| | Transition planning | .5 | — |
| Independent of candidate | Independent expenditures[b] | 10.6 | .03 |
| TOTAL | | $64.3 | $53.93 |

SOURCE: Citizens' Research Foundation.
  a.  Components of these amounts include internal communications costs (both those reported, in excess of $2000 as required by law, and those unreported, for $2000 or less), registration and get-out-the-vote drives, overhead, and related costs.
  b.  Does not include amounts spent against Carter ($209,781) or Reagan ($47,868).

By accepting public funds for their general election campaigns, Ronald Reagan and Jimmy Carter were prohibited from raising private funds from individuals or political action committees. The candidates, however, were permitted to raise money directly for their compliance costs—costs incurred in complying with the law, including certain bookkeeping, public reporting, and legal disbursements—totaling $1.6 million each. They also were permitted to help raise money for national and state party committees and to help themselves and others erase prenomination campaign debts. In addition, Reagan raised money during the campaign to pay costs of planning for the transition period from election day until the inauguration (which also included private fund raising not noted in table 1.4).

In addition to funds directly under their control, both major-party candidates benefited from considerable spending, some coordinated with their campaigns and some independent of them. Reagan had a substantial direct and indirect spending advantage, but Carter was able to coordinate more spending in his behalf while also enjoying the advantages of incumbency.

## GRASS-ROOTS PARTY ACTIVITY

There was considerable grass-roots activity because state and local party committees could spend unlimited amounts of money for the presidential ticket as long as the spending was related to volunteer participation. Acting on criticism after the 1976 election in which the existing law inhibited local activity, Congress amended the Federal Election Campaign Act in 1979 to permit widespread dissemination of banners, pins, bumper stickers, handbills, brochures, posters, leaflets, yard signs, party tabloids, and buttons. More important, the 1979 FECA amendments allowed state and local party spending on volunteer-operated voter registration and get-out-the-vote drives, including the use of phone banks.

Republican party committees, fully behind the Reagan-Bush ticket and better financed than their Democratic counterparts, spent some $15 million on such volunteer activity and material. About $2.8 million was raised at a party-sponsored event held in Texas in mid-September 1980, which included appearances by candidate Reagan and his running mate as well as other party luminaries.[19] The money raised by state and local party committees was used in part to fund the program called Commitment '80, which included the efforts of a reported 800,000 volunteers nationwide, who manned phone banks and conducted door-to-door canvasses in voter identification and turnout programs.[20] Not all this money was reported federally because some expenditures were made by state party accounts.

Despite the 1979 amendments, the Carter campaign was not able to count on a similar level of support from Democratic state and local party committees. Both Carter and his running mate, Walter Mondale, spoke at events designed to raise money for the party committees, but the committees were able to spend only about $4 million for volunteer efforts. A major reason for the relatively low amount was the sometimes intense competition for available dollars among various state and local party committees, the DNC, the Carter-Mondale Compliance Fund, a Unity Dinner Committee that sought to pay off Carter's and Kennedy's primary campaign debts, and other fund raising, mainly by Kennedy and Governor Brown, to pay off primary debts. In 1981 the Democratic National Committee agreed to assume about $580,000 of the general election debt left from the Carter-Mondale campaign. Much of this amount would have been paid by the DNC as part of its $4.6 million, had the money been available.

The organizational spending by state and local party committees was a notable development. Those interested in strengthening the political parties saw it as a major step in the direction of encouraging more grass-roots voluntary activity. Although the national parties, particularly the RNC, were deeply involved in stimulating such activity, the implementation in spending the money was handled at state and local levels, giving a boost to party activities (and others involved in Commitment '80). Getting national and state and party committees to coordinate their efforts obviously helps strengthen the parties. One analysis, in fact, has recommended encouraging state and local party committees still further by removing all limits on their activities not only in presidential but also in congressional campaigns, to spur more local volunteer activity that conceivably could counter the growing impact of independent expenditures on campaigns.[21]

### ADDITIONAL COORDINATED SPENDING
The Carter forces pointed out still more spending that benefited Reagan, including $8.5 million spent by the Republican National Committee on "anti-Democrat" television advertising urging voters to "Vote Republican. For a Change" and elect "the Republican team," and additional funds spent by "nonpartisan" evangelical and New Right groups attacking the Carter administration. Republicans in their turn pointed to the incalculable value of the perks of office available to Carter and, they say, expertly used by him: the media attention that goes to a sitting President, high-ranking administration officials making political speeches in the President's behalf, and the use of government spending programs to benefit the incumbent's campaign.

Though Carter did not receive much from independent committees, labor spending for Carter-Mondale helped make up the difference. Studies indicate that for the November 1976 election, organized labor spent some $11 million on internal communication with union members and their families, on membership and voter registration and get-out-the-vote drives coordinated to benefit the Carter-Mondale ticket, and on overhead and other costs.[22] In 1980, due in large part to inflation, such labor spending was even greater in dollar terms, reaching $15 million; most of it supported Carter, however reluctantly. Of the $15 million, some $1.3 million in pro-Carter communication costs were reported.[23] The Teamsters and a few other unions supported Reagan in amounts totaling about $1.5 million. The business community generally supported Reagan, but corporate expenditures directed to employees, stockholders, and their families and intended to benefit Reagan did not approach those of labor favoring Carter-Mondale.

INDEPENDENT EXPENDITURES

In addition to benefiting from funds directly under the control of his campaign and from money spent in his behalf by state and local party committees that coordinated their spending with the campaign committee, Ronald Reagan attracted substantial independent expenditures—about $10.6 million—while Carter received only $27,773. According to the 1976 Supreme Court decision in *Buckley* v. *Valeo,* individuals or committees cannot be prohibited from spending money independently as long as the activity is carried out without consultation or collaboration with candidates or their campaigns.[24] This noncooperation, the Court held, prevents independent expenditures from violating the spirit and intention of the federal law's spending and contribution limits. Some supporters of the reform laws question this concept and seek legislation that would decrease the attractiveness of independent expenditures.

Early in the general election campaign, exaggerated estimates suggested independent committees would raise $50 million to $70 million to help Reagan.[25] Financial expectations were later lowered because groups seeking to make independent expenditures competed with one another for available dollars and because some of them were newly organized and lacked the ongoing fundraising capability of permanent committees. For example, at the national level, the Republican National Committee, Republican Senatorial Campaign Committee, and National Republican Congressional Committee combined grossed some $112.3 million in 1979-80 for their 1980 campaign efforts.[26] It was unrealistic to expect that independent support for Reagan could approximate in a few months what the long-established national Republican committees, with their proven lists of contributors and their regular appeals, had achieved over the course of the years. In addition, lawsuits brought by the Carter-Mondale Committee, Common Cause, and the Federal Election Commission, questioning the legality of such expenditures and the independence of the committees proposing to make them, chilled some early independent activity and diverted some funds to legal battles.

Complaints to the FEC and litigation were used widely to achieve political goals in 1980.[27] The Carter-Mondale Reelection Committee joined with the Democratic National Committee to file a complaint with the FEC charging the self-styled independent committees actually were working in concert with the Reagan campaign. In addition, the Carter campaign sent a letter to television stations across the country warning them that any sales of time to independent groups supporting Ronald Reagan could raise serious legal questions. When the FEC failed to respond favorably, the Carter committee went to court. (Common Cause, a nonpartisan group, sued the independent expenditure committees on different grounds, in a suit that the FEC opposed in favor of its own suit.)

This litigation and its results are reported in chapter 7 in this volume. The political aspects described here merely indicate the uses of complaints and litigation as strategies to harm opponents by invoking the law and suggesting that violations are occurring.[28] Each step in these disputes is reported in the media, with unknown political impact. But one can assume the plaintiffs are satisfied that the publicity is helpful to their causes. Of course, changes or clarifications in the law often are mandated in FEC answers to complaints or by the courts, and constitutional principles may be enhanced in the process.

Independent expenditures were of major significance in the 1980 presidential campaigns. A compilation by the Federal Election Commission reveals that independent spending in 1980 exceeded $16 million.[29] About $13.7 million of that amount was spent to influence various presidential campaigns, some $12.9 million promoting presidential candidates and $812,886 spent to defeat certain candidates.

Table 1.5 lists independent expenditures in the campaigns for presidential nomination and election. In both periods, Reagan was the heavy favorite of independent spenders, but most of the money was spent in the general election. As noted earlier in table 1.4, some $10.6 million was spent independently for Reagan after his nomination, and only $47,868 against; whereas only $27,773 was spent favoring Carter, while $209,781 was spent in opposition to him. Negligible amounts were spent for or against John Anderson in the general election period.

There is no sure measure of the effectiveness of independent expenditures. Both individuals and committees spent money independently, much more, of course, by political committees than by individuals.[30] And independent spending by political committees was the more controversial, particularly spending by committees established for helping Reagan in the general election. Independent expenditures generally were controversial; the total amounts were significant, and those in the presidential campaigns led to litigation that reached the U.S. Supreme Court. The main consequence of their use in 1980 was to demonstrate the violability of strict expenditure limits in prenomination and general election campaigns, a subject explored at length in the concluding section of this chapter.

### CANDIDATE EXPENDITURES: MEDIA

More than half the money controlled by the Carter and Reagan campaigns in the general election was spent on mass media advertising. For example, the Carter campaign spent $20.5 million: $15.8 million for television, $2.6 million for radio, and the remainder for print media and production costs.

The initial Carter TV ads sought to portray the candidate as calm and hard-working—able to shoulder the heavy demands of the Presidency. Once ads emphasizing Carter's positive qualities had made their appeal to shaky sup-

TABLE 1.5.

INDEPENDENT EXPENDITURES RELATING TO CANDIDATES FOR PRESIDENT, 1980

| Candidates | Prenomination[a] | | | General Election | | | Total |
| | Expenditures For | Expenditures Against | Subtotal | Expenditures For | Expenditures Against | Subtotal | |
| --- | --- | --- | --- | --- | --- | --- | --- |
| Reagan | $1,643,468 | 0 | $1,643,468 | $10,602,589 | $47,868 | $10,650,457 | $12,293,925 |
| Kennedy | 77,189 | 491,161 | 568,350 | 0 | 0 | 0 | 568,350 |
| Carter | 18,096 | 35,830 | 53,926 | 27,773 | 209,781 | 237,554 | 291,480 |
| Connally | 288,032 | 0 | 288,032 | 0 | 0 | 0 | 288,032 |
| Anderson | 196,354 | 0 | 196,354 | 3,084 | 2,635 | 5,719 | 202,073 |
| Others[b] | 68,466 | 25,611 | 94,077 | 7,505 | 0 | 7,505 | 101,584 |

GRAND TOTALS  $13,745,444

SOURCE: FEC Index of Independent Expenditures, 1979-80, November 1981.

a. The prenomination period ends, and the general election period begins, on different dates for each candidate. Prenomination expenditures are funds spent on or before April 24, 1980 for Anderson, July 15, 1980 for Republican candidates, and August 14, 1980 for Democratic candidates.

b. Includes expenditures for and against Baker, Brown, Bush, Clark, and Pulley; also expenditures were made for and against Ford, Haig, Jackson, Kemp, and Simon, who were not declared candidates.

porters and undecided voters, a second series of ads sought to discredit Reagan.[31] The Carter campaign also ran some anti-Anderson commercials in states where Anderson was thought to have significant support.[32]

The Reagan campaign spent $16.8 million on mass media advertising and production, including about $10.8 million on television, $1.5 million for radio, $2.2 million in newspapers, and $2.3 million on production. The Reagan media campaign strategy, based in large measure on data gathered from extensive surveys and computer simulations, focused on the candidate's abilities as an electronic media communicator and featured Reagan talking directly to the audience about his approach to solving what he perceived as the nation's problems.[33] During the last ten days of the campaign, some $6 million was poured into Reagan media advertising in targeted states and communities.

TABLE 1.6.
REAGAN-BUSH COMMITTEE MEDIA EXPENDITURES

| | Expenditures (in millions)[a] | | |
| | Gross | Net | Percentage Difference |
| --- | --- | --- | --- |
| Television | | | |
| Network TV | $7,581 | $6,444 | 44.3 |
| Spot TV | 5,158 | 4,384 | 30.2 |
| Subtotal | 12,739 | 10,828 | 74.5 |
| Radio | | | |
| Network radio | 344 | 292 | 2.0 |
| Spot radio | 1,417 | 1,204 | 8.3 |
| Subtotal, broadcast | 14,500 | 12,324 | 84.8 |
| Print | | | |
| National magazine | 265 | 225 | 1.5 |
| Local newspapers | 2,345 | 1,992 | 13.7 |
| Subtotal, print | 2,610 | 2,217 | 15.2 |
| GRAND TOTAL | $17,110 | $14,541 | 100.0 |

SOURCE: Information provided by Campaign '80.
  a. Does not include $2.25 million in production costs. Net figures, which represent those actually paid by the committee, exclude the customary 15 percent advertising agency fee.

Table 1.6 depicts the Reagan general election media campaign, provided by the Campaign '80 organization, an in-house advertising agency assembled for the purpose and disbanded after the election. The differences between gross and net figures is 15 percent, the fee normally charged by traditional advertising agencies for their services, covering overhead plus profit. Because Campaign '80 was in-house, the only charges beyond air time mounted to $2.252 million for production, editing, dubbing, and related costs. These were basic operating costs, there was no profit, and accordingly the Reagan campaign accrued considerable savings not possible if the work had gone to a regular advertising agency. Hence the gross figures are for comparison and a gauge to actual savings for the campaign.

Both major-party candidates also sought to make use of free television time. Here Carter held an advantage over his opponent because as the incumbent he attracted media attention by fulfilling the responsibilities of his office. In addition to free coverage on national and local news programs of his "town meetings" and election campaign rallies, Carter received full network coverage of his news conference on September 18 and news coverage of other noncampaign activities such as receiving foreign heads of state and signing important bills.

In refusing to join Reagan and John Anderson in a nationally televised debate sponsored by the League of Women Voters and holding out for a one-on-one debate with Reagan, Carter took a calculated risk: that whatever loss of esteem he might suffer in the eyes of the electorate would be less damaging than the loss of votes he might suffer if Anderson, who was thought to appeal to some of the same constituencies, were to make a strong showing in the same forum as the incumbent. When Carter finally did participate in a one-on-one debate with Reagan shortly before the election, it proved, by most accounts, to have decreased his chances of winning the election.[34]

The Reagan campaign organized many activities to invite coverage on the evening news. Crowd events, such as noon rallies or strolls through ethnic neighborhoods, were scheduled to allow time for films to be edited for slots on the national news. The campaign also sought free air time to reply to statements President Carter made at the opening of his news conference on September 18, but the networks characterized the conference as a legitimate news event exempt from the so-called equal time regulations.[35]

On September 21, Reagan debated independent candidate John Anderson in a televised broadcast carried nationwide on prime time by NBC and CBS. Reagan gambled that he would make a good showing against Anderson and that the electorate would think poorly of Carter for having rejected the invitation to debate. Both gambles paid off. Later in the campaign, Reagan realized that although he could not command the media attention that Carter could as the incumbent, participation in a televised debate — at no cost to his campaign — would give him more exposure than he could possibly buy. The strategy paid off, and the October 28 Reagan-Carter debate is considered to have boosted Reagan's chances of success.[36]

OTHER CANDIDATE EXPENDITURES

While media expenditures were large in the Carter and Reagan campaigns, other spending of interest occurred. The major candidates commanded not only the $29.4 million in public funding but also the supplementary spending by the national party committees, and through the DNC and RNC, the outlays of state party committees. According to the FEC and national party figures, actual spending was as follows:

|  | Reagan | Carter |
|---|---|---|
| Federal grant | $29,188,887.50 | $29,352,767.98 |
| RNC/DNC | 4,523,789.27 | 4,000,000.00 |
|  | $33,712,676.77 | $33,352,767.98 |

It is extremely difficult for the candidates to spend to the penny the complete federal grant ($29,440,000) and the permissible party amount ($4,638,000), a total of $34,077,000. Careful planning is necessary, contingency money is retained for any last-minute problems, and FEC audits may require repayments for nonqualified expenditures or for other reasons: Carter's campaign repaid $87,323.02 and Reagan's $252,112.50. Even though the repayments were made, the campaign organizations benefited from the use of the money during the campaign.

Expenditures for private polling were similar in the Reagan and Carter campaigns. The Reagan-Bush Committee paid $1,038,300 for polls, mainly to the prime contractor, Decision/Making/Information, with about $300,000 of that going to Market Opinion Research and several other firms. Richard Wirthlin, president of DMI, was deputy campaign manager for strategy, and some additional $300,000 was paid to DMI for strategy and modeling. In all, eight national surveys were done, including some piggybacked with other candidates at other levels; 21 states were monitored throughout; 17 required two to four surveys each; and 11 states were tracked closely in the final three weeks.

The Carter campaign allocated $1 million for polling by Patrick H. Caddell's Cambridge Survey Research, Inc., but several hundred thousand dollars have been in dispute with the Carter committee and the DNC, and final resolution has not been achieved at this writing.

Carter-Mondale expenditures were closely controlled and tracked by computer, according to cost centers broken down by function and by national committee or state committee designation. Separate accountings were made for federal funds, exempt funds, and compliance funds. The DNC kept a separate account for its spending.

By agreement with the FEC, compliance accounts were governed by a formula holding costs to about 6 percent of campaign expenses but allowing for state-by-state adjustments when necessary. Compliance includes wind-down expenses and costs relating to the FEC audit, as well as legal, accounting, and bookkeeping costs. Litigation, as in the Reagan audit suit, is in the compliance category, but defense in case of enforcement actions is beyond any ceiling. Funds for compliance are privately raised, and both Reagan and Carter raised $1.6 million for this purpose. If there is any surplus in the Carter compliance account, funds can be transferred to the DNC to help pay off remaining debts or make repayments required by the FEC.

In the Carter campaign, the big ticket items, apart from the media, were

| | |
|---|---|
| Payroll | $    955,755 |
| Consultants | 1,191,299 |
| Contracted services | 1,985,124 |
| Telephone | 1,826,916 |
| Travel | 2,089,725 |

The combination of payroll, consultants, and contracted services brings staff and related costs to be the second largest item, after media, and more costly than travel, which ranks third, with telephone ranking fourth.

### THE ANDERSON CAMPAIGN

Independent candidate John Anderson campaigned at a severe disadvantage. While his major-party opponents received government subsidies to carry on their campaigns, Anderson was forced to raise money from private sources under the federal law's $1000 individual contribution limit. An innovative FEC decision in September 1980 recognized Anderson's National Unity Campaign as the functional equivalent of a minor party; this provided the candidate with some measure of relief because it meant Anderson could qualify for retroactive public funds if he won at least 5 percent of the vote. Banks approached for loans against the hoped-for federal funds as collateral, however, found Anderson's prospects too risky, and the candidate was forced mainly to seek small loans from thousands of previous contributors. The need to pay off campaign debts and loans put pressure on Anderson to qualify for public money, dictating his strategy until election day.

In all, Anderson raised $12.1 million in contributions and loans, most of which came in response to expensive direct mail appeals. A surplus of $713,000 was transferred from his Republican nomination campaign. The $4,242,304 he received in federal funds allowed him to erase all but about $500,000 of his debts. Some $14.4 million was spent in the campaign. Just as Anderson had to rely on private sources of funds while his major-party opponents received federal grants, his major spending was different from that of his adversaries. For example, in addition to $3 million in direct mail costs, including payments to vendors for design, printing, postage, and related costs, the campaign spent $400,000 for other fund raising, consisting of events and newspaper ads. The campaign expended $2 million in organizing signature petition drives and legal assistance in getting on state ballots, and another $320,000 in legal fees, excluding ballot-access costs.

Fund-raising difficulties and legal and ballot-access problems did not leave much money to mount a television campaign. In all, Anderson spent about $2.3 million on media including about $140,000 on media advertising production costs. Candidate travel cost $2 million and $1.7 million was spent on personnel.

In addition, during the campaign Anderson received wide exposure in his single debate with Ronald Reagan. Because debates attract huge audiences, they give candidates more exposure than available money can possibly buy, and at no direct cost to the candidates. The decision by the League of Women Voters not to invite Anderson to participate in the later debate between Carter and Reagan undoubtedly hurt Anderson's campaign.

The FEC audit recommended that $639,950 be repaid for federal funds received for which the committee was not entitled; the largest part was for loans subsequently converted into donations by the lenders. Another portion of the funds constituted interest earned on federal funds invested until they were spent for campaign purposes. The National Unity Campaign challenged the audit findings.[37]

Since independent candidate John Anderson did not organize a political party to support his candidacy, he did not benefit from such party involvement. He tried to get the FEC and the courts to permit private contributions of up to $20,000 to his NUC, that amount being the contribution limit that applied to political parties, but this effort failed.

## The Campaigns in Retrospect

The 1980 presidential campaigns were notable for the dissatisfaction that they aroused over the laws that regulate campaign financing. Three significant studies illustrate this point.

In a joint letter dated April 30, 1981, the counsel for nine 1980 presidential campaigns and attorneys for the Republican and Democratic National Committees petitioned the FEC to postpone for 30 days the publication of presidential campaign audits while correcting what they perceived as serious problems in the prenomination campaign audit process.[38] Accusing the commission of being insensitive "to the realities of the Presidential campaign process and the First Amendment expression which is the heart of every political campaign," the Campaign Counsel Group, as it called itself, registered five complaints about the audit process: (1) retroactive rule making regarding questions arising out of campaigns; (2) lack of standard auditing procedures; (3) denial of access to information bearing on audit issues; (4) lack of an FEC hearing; and (5) excessive length of the process.

This remarkable agreement among campaign representatives brought a negative response from the FEC, which defended the commission's procedures while pointing to a bookkeeping manual published by the commission as a guide for those to be audited.[39] The commission's response omitted reference to two 1979 studies of its audit policies and procedures that were commissioned by the agency.[40] Both reviewed the audit processes in depth, and both made significant recommendations for change. The FEC then revised its audit policies but, presumably, not to the satisfaction of most of the 1980 presidential campaigns.

Presidential finance officers were no happier than the counsels. In 1981 some 20 finance officers from the 1976 and 1980 presidential campaigns proposed amendments to the FECA's contribution and spending limit provisions. Based on a conference convened in December 1980 by the Citizens' Research Foundation and on responses to a subsequent mailed questionnaire, the finance officers proposed to raise the individual contribution limit of $1000 and repeal the current $25,000 calendar year limit on aggregate contributions made by an individual; to eliminate the prohibition on private contributions to the campaign committees of presidential candidates in the general election period because it imposes a barrier to citizen participation and encourages potentially harmful independent expenditures on behalf of presidential candidates; to retain existing provisions for matching funds in the presidential prenomination period; to replace the current method of indexing the expenditure limit according to increases in the Consumer Price Index by a method that would better reflect increases in those items that relate specifically to campaign costs; to eliminate state-by-state expenditure limits, but continue to require of candidates full and timely disclosure of expenditures on a state-by-state basis; and to remove from federal regulations concerning independent expenditures any presumptions of coordination between candidates and their campaign committees and those making the independent expenditures, by shifting the burden of proof to the Federal Election Commission.[41]

The third major study was that of the Campaign Finance Study Group of the Institute of Politics at Harvard University, which was commissioned by the Committee on Rules and Administration of the U.S. Senate to examine the effects of campaign finance laws on the conduct of presidential campaigns. Its main recommendation was to increase the amounts of money available from both public funding and individual contributions. Otherwise, they said, "less accountable" funds, such as independent expenditures, would help finance candidates. A further finding was that if existing laws and regulations were too stringent, many campaign decisions would have to be made on the basis of financial considerations rather than political need. The research report is very comprehensive and is too detailed to bear summary here;[42] many of the recommendations are described in other contexts and under other auspices elsewhere in this chapter.

Although much of the criticism of the laws regulating the conduct of presidential campaigns and the presidential selection process in general is valid, several points can be made in favor of the present system. The structure of public financing and regulation did not discourage important potential candidates from running; in fact, some who otherwise might not have chosen to do so were probably encouraged by the system in existence in 1980. In 1976 the public matching funds provided qualified but little-known outsiders the opportunity to compete effectively in the primary campaigns. Lacking access to traditional sources of large Democratic contributions, Jimmy Carter, without public funding, probably would have lost out early in the primary season to candidates, such as Senator Henry M. Jackson, who enjoyed such access. But the combination of contribution limits, which lowered the advantage large contributors could provide, and matching funds, which enhanced the value of small contributions, had an equalizing effect. Public funding allowed Carter, a Washington outsider and a regional candidate, to break into the field and establish his candidacy.[43]

In 1980 the public money similarly helped candidates such as George Bush and John Anderson, who were not well known nationally and did not have ready access to large amounts of private money, to stay the course of primaries and caucuses until the choice of nominees was clear. Thus it is fair to say that the Federal Election Campaign Act opened up the electoral process to some candidates who otherwise might not have had staying power in prenomination contests.

RECOMMENDATIONS

Two presidential elections have taken place since the basic federal election campaign laws were enacted. The discontent occasioned by some aspects of the law, notably the low level of contribution and spending limits, should be addressed. Based on the 1980 experience, a number of recommendations are worth considering:

1. The individual contribution limit should be raised from $1000 to $5000, and the aggregate individual contribution limit of $25,000 to all federal campaigns annually should be repealed. This change might help shorten campaigns because the candidates would no longer be required to start as early to raise sufficient money to mount a serious campaign. It also would make independent expenditures in behalf of candidates less attractive or necessary because it would widen the avenue of direct financial participation in the presidential campaigns.

2. Private contributions to presidential general election campaigns should be allowed. This change would open up a significant avenue for personal involvement in campaigns and would serve to decrease independent expenditures, which, however well intentioned, may be harmful to the candidate in whose behalf they are made because candidates cannot control them. This sytem could follow the principle of floors without ceilings, that is, a public funding grant without expenditure limits. A flat grant could be made to the nominated candidates, perhaps $20-$25 million each, and candidates could spend as much beyond that amount as they could raise. A flat grant in the same or lesser amounts also could be made to significant independent or minor-party candidates, such as John Anderson.

3. Currently, expenditure limits are indexed according to the Consumer Price Index. The CPI, however, does not take account of the fact that many of the costs of campaigning have escalated more rapidly than the costs on which the CPI is constructed. Nor, in regard to the prenomination period, does the

current indexing procedure recognize that the number of primaries has increased significantly, that candidates find it necessary to start their campaigns earlier than ever and to participate in a variety of costly exercises, such as straw polls. For example, though the rise in the cost of living for the period from 1976 to 1980 was 35 percent, the costs of many things campaigns have to buy increased by even greater percentages. Charges for a minute of prime-time television network advertising nearly doubled in some areas; the costs of producing television commercials increased as much as 100 percent. The cost of direct mail appeals is up by as much as 50 percent. The cost for a 96-seat chartered jet on a four-day trip to nine eastern cities increased from $37,500 in 1976 to $91,200 in 1980.

4. The status of "draft nominees" should be clarified. Following a Carter campaign complaint, the FEC subpoenaed records dealing with multiple contributions of $5000 made to "draft Kennedy" committees, possibly in violation of the contribution limits. A challenge to prevent implementation of the subpoena process led to consolidation of several suits, a court decision refusing to uphold the subpoenas, the joining in appeal by Democratic party committees, and a further appeal for a U.S. Supreme Court review (which was refused). The courts held that the FECA applied to candidates but contributions to draft committees designed to work for a candidate who is not yet running are outside the jurisdiction of the law and the FEC. The FEC has requested Congress to legislate to assert FEC authority over draft committees. In view of the larger contribution limit ($5000) and the possibility of multiple contributions, the Congress should act to redefine draft committee status; money spent in behalf of a person who later becomes a candidate, as Senator Kennedy did in 1979-80, gives unfair advantage over declared candidates.

5. The overall expenditure limit in presidential prenomination campaigns should be raised significantly or repealed to permit elimination of the 20 percent exemption for fund-raising expenses and abolition of the legal, accounting, and compliance exemptions. This action would simplify accounting and bookkeeping for the campaigns because, at present, separate books need to be kept and allocations need to be made to comply with the law; thus lawyers and accountants are hired to help campaigns negotiate the maze of complex restrictions. A simpler but larger limit, or no limit, would ease the regulatory burdens on campaigns substantially and would tend to reduce costs.

6. State-by-state expenditure limits in the prenomination period, as well as the overall expenditure limits in general election periods, should be eliminated. This change would allow campaigns to operate more flexibly and spontaneously and would encourage the grass-roots campaigning discouraged by current limits, which demand centralized budgetary control. It also would tend to discourage independent expenditures.

7. Limitations placed on the amounts national, state, and local party committees are allowed to spend on their presidential ticket should be eliminated. The limits to be repealed are of two kinds: overall limits on spending by the

national party committees, and segmental limits on state and local party committees, which permit them to spend unlimited amounts only for voluntary grass-roots activities. Instead, national party committees should be allowed to spend unlimited amounts on the nominated ticket for President and Vice-President,[44] and state and local party committees should be allowed to spend unlimited amounts for media, direct mail, and other forms of communication, as well as for organization or grass-roots activity.[45]

The campaign reform laws of the 1970s, by creating matching funds, made direct contributions to individual candidates more attractive; also, by making presidential candidates' campaigns self-contained for purposes of public financing, they have weakened the link between candidates and political parties and made it more difficult for parties to serve as intermediate structures between policy makers and the many organized groups that now seek to make their voices heard. This unintended consequence of election reform would be redressed if limits on what political parties can do for candidates on their tickets were repealed. The tendency would be toward more joint activity by candidates and parties. Parties are permanent committees that can provide, in an era of high campaign costs, economies of size by pooling polling, computer, and other campaign services for use by presidential and other candidates on the ticket, thus saving individual candidates significant funds.

Critics of the current contribution and expenditure limits see in the rise of independent expenditures a growing desire on the part of interested citizens and groups to participate financially in the election process, and these suggested changes would be a step in that direction. Even though the 1979 amendments increased the ability of state and local party committees to participate in presidential campaigns in behalf of the party's ticket, the parties are still too restricted. The role of the parties should be strengthened in order to overcome the growing trend toward personal politics and the lack of cohesiveness in government that personalization fosters.

The tightly drawn system of expenditure limitations did not work well in 1980. The significant use of independent expenditures, although focused on only a few candidates, pointed up the many openings for disbursement for or against a candidate in the pluralistic American system derived from the number of exceptions that have been made to the law's limitations.[46] As described earlier in comments relating to table 1.4, the concept of campaign limits in which the candidate's organization controls the spending is unrealistic in an environment in which unlimited but coordinated activities by interest groups and state and local party committees are legally sanctioned, while unlimited independent expenditures are allowed by court decisions.

The fiction that in the general election period each major-party candidate would spend only $29.4 million supplemented by $4.6 million spent by the national party committee was apparent to the most casual observer. Spending for Reagan of $64.3 million and for Carter of $53.9 million can be documented and still not include additional advantages for one or the other in media, issue, or incumbency spending. In Reagan's case, the noncandidate spending almost equaled the combined public funds and national party supplement fully controlled by the candidate. The conclusion follows that if limitations are not effective, then they are illusory and breed disrespect for the law; if they are effective, then they tend to inhibit free expression. A false impression of limits serves no purpose and creates compliance problems and costs for the candidates.

Rethinking reform thus leads to the ideal concept of floors without ceilings: a system that would provide candidates with partial public funding but no expenditure limits. Caps can be placed on the amounts of public funds disbursed to qualified candidates, but caps should be high enough to ensure that candidates get at least threshold exposure to the electorate. With full disclosure, the overall, segmental, and state-by-state spending limits could all be repealed safely. The desired result should be to create conditions that would make candidates more accountable for activities undertaken in their behalf, by permitting the campaign organization to spend more effectively and efficiently and diminishing the need or opportunities for groups that the candidate cannot legally control. Repealing all limits on contributions by individuals and committees to the parties, and removing all limits on party activity in support of nominated candidates, would be another beneficial step that would help bring the nominated candidates and their parties closer together.

On the positive side, the FECA in 1980 continued to provide high levels of disclosure and encourage new elements of fiscal accountability in political campaigns. Rates of compliance remain high, and the ability to dissect the workings of political campaigns, based on the flow of information provided by law, is more evident than ever.

Whatever revisions of law are undertaken, the values of enabling citizens to do more, of strengthening ties between the parties and the candidates topping their tickets, and of lightening the compliance burdens on the candidate, represent goals worthy of a revitalized presidential selection process synchronized with an effective political finance law.

## Notes

1. "Washington Focus," *Campaign Practices Reports,* May 11, 1981, 1. The $80 million estimate left over for the 1984 presidential elections includes repayments to the fund required by Federal Election Commission, as of March 1982.
2. *FEC Reports on Financial Activity, 1979-1980, Final Report, Presidential Pre-Nomination Campaigns* (Washington, D.C.: Federal Election Commission, October 1981).
3. In 1980, larger amounts of public funds actually were available to many candidates during the campaigns, but following audits after the election, they were required by the FEC to pay back certain amounts; accordingly, those candidates had more money available for use during the crucial campaigns.
4. Christopher Buchanan, "Candidates Must Adjust to Spending Lid," *Congressional Quarterly Weekly Report,* May 10, 1980, 1244.

5. "Candidates Spend Their Budgets Away," *Business Week,* March 17, 1980, 27.
6. Reports of the Audit Division on the Reagan for President Committee, February 3, 1981; Carter/Mondale Presidential Committee Inc., January 21, 1981; Kennedy for President Committee, September 28, 1981.
7. Maxwell Glen, "Free Spenders—The 'Other' Campaign for Reagan Chooses Its Targets," *National Journal,* September 13, 1980, 1513.
8. Ibid.
9. Douglas E. Kneeland, "Connally to Forego U.S. Campaign Funds," *New York Times,* December 12, 1979.
10. Robert G. Kaiser, "Reselling of Carter: A Living Room Pitch for the President," *Washington Post,* March 18, 1980.
11. Richard Bergholz, "Reagan and GOP Losers Band Together to Pay Off Campaign Debts—For 'Unity,' " *Los Angeles Times,* March 29, 1980.
12. Ibid.
13. Ibid.
14. "GOP Gets Its Candidates to Join in Unique TV Fund-Raiser," *Campaign Practices Reports,* July 7, 1980, 6.
15. "Baker Pays Off Campaign Debt of $1.3 Million," *Los Angeles Times,* July 16, 1980.
16. "Connally Plan to Sell Art Works Is Limited to $1,000 by FEC," *Campaign Practices Reports,* May 26, 1980, 708.
17. "Connally Artists Return to Drawing Boards," *Political Finance/Lobby Reporter,* May 28, 1980.
18. See Michael J. Malbin, "How Many Go to the Polls Could Settle the Election," *National Journal,* November 1, 1980, 1840. See also Curtis Wilkie, "A $400,000 Tab for Last Carter Polls," *Boston Globe,* November 21, 1980, for a report on post-election DNC fund raising to cover campaign debts.
19. Malbin, "How Many Go to the Polls," 1841.
20. Ibid., 1840.
21. Michael J. Malbin, "What Should Be Done About Independent Campaign Expenditures?" *Regulation,* January/February 1982, 41-46.
22. Michael J. Malbin, "Neither a Mountain nor a Molehill," *Regulation,* May/June 1979, 43.
23. *FEC Index of Communication Costs,* Federal Election Commission, September 1981.
24. *Buckley* v. *Valeo,* 424 U.S. 1 (1976).
25. "Independent Expenditures Suddenly Become Hottest Item in Campaign Financing," *Campaign Practices Reports,* July 7, 1980, 8.
26. Amounts updated, but see Richard E. Cohen, "Democrats Take a Leaf from GOP Book with Early Campaign Financing Start," *National Journal,* May 23, 1981, 920.
27. David M. Ifshin and Roger E. Warin, "Litigating the 1980 Presidential Election," *American University Law Review* 31 (1982): 485-550.
28. Ibid.
29. *FEC Index of Independent Expenditures,* Federal Election Commission, November 1981.
30. For data and listings of independent expenditures by individuals and committees, see ibid. and "FEC Study Shows Independent Expenditures Top $16 Million," Federal Election Commission Press Release, November 19, 1981.
31. See Ed Magnuson, "Taking Those Spot Shots," *Time,* September 29, 1980, 18ff.
32. See Jack Nelson, "Carter Accepts Dare, Wins Applause as He Campaigns in High

Jobless Areas," *Los Angeles Times,* October 2, 1980; and Richard E. Meyer, "Anderson's Attacks on Carter Grow More Bitter," *Los Angeles Times,* October 2, 1980.

33. See Richard Wirthlin, Vincent Breglio, and Richard Beal, "Campaign Chronicle," *Public Opinion* 4, no. 1 (February/March 1981): 43-49.

34. See, for example, ibid., 49.

35. "Anderson, Reagan Join in Demand for Equal Time," *Los Angeles Times,* September 20, 1980.

36. See Wirthlin et al., "Campaign Chronicle," 49.

37. "FEC Asks John Anderson to Refund $645,000," *Washington Post,* October 21, 1981. The amount does not conform to an update, "Public Financing 1980 Presidential Election," Federal Election Commission release compilation, March 1982.

38. Edward L. Weidenfeld, Timothy G. Smith, et al., letter from the Campaign Counsel Group to John McGarry, chairman of the Federal Election Commission, April 30, 1981; see also "Campaign Lawyers Join in Asking FEC to Remedy Audit Problems," *Campaign Practices Reports,* May 11, 1981, 2; and "FEC Auditors Called Insensitive, Arbitrary by Campaign Lawyers," *Political Finance/ Lobby Reporter,* May 13, 1981, 120.

39. John W. McGarry, Frank P. Reiche, et al., letter to the Campaign Counsel Group, May 14, 1981; see also "FEC Defends Audit Process; Takes Criticisms 'Under Advisement,'" *Campaign Practices Reports,* May 25, 1981, 4; and "FEC Offers No Apology for Presidential Audits," *Political Finance/Lobby Reporter,* May 20, 1981, 127.

40. Federal Election Commission, "Review of the Political Campaign Auditing Process by Arthur Andersen & Co.," September 1979. Mimeo. Also, Federal Election Commission, untitled study of the Federal Election Commission's audit process by Accountants for the Public Interest, September 1979. Mimeo.

41. Herbert E. Alexander and Brian A. Haggerty, *The Federal Election Campaign Act: After a Decade of Political Reform* (Los Angeles: Citizens' Research Foundation, 1981), "Presidential Finance Officers' Statement," appendix B, 131-35.

42. *Financing Presidential Campaigns: An Examination of the Ongoing Effects of the Federal Election Campaign Laws upon the Conduct of Presidential Campaigns.* Research report by the Campaign Finance Study Group to the Committee on Rules and Administration of the U.S. Senate (Cambridge, Mass.: Institute of Politics, John F. Kennedy School of Government, Harvard University, January 1982).

43. Herbert E. Alexander, *Financing the 1976 Election* (Washington, D.C.: Congressional Quarterly Press, 1979), 5-6.

44. Statement by Richard Richards, chairman of the Republican National Committee, Before the Senate Committee on Rules and Administration, November 20, 1981, 1-6. Mimeo.

45. See Malbin, "What Should Be Done."

46. See summary of remarks of John G. Murphy, in Alexander and Haggerty, *Federal Election Campaign Act,* 52-53.

GARY C. JACOBSON

# 2. Money in the 1980 and 1982 Congressional Elections

The 1980 and 1982 elections were extraordinary, though in different ways. The signal event of 1980 was not the election of Ronald Reagan; Republicans have, after all, won five of the last eight presidential elections. It was the Republican takeover of the Senate. Republicans picked up 12 seats there, winning a solid majority for the first time since 1952. They also gained 33 House seats, producing a conservative, if not Republican, majority in that chamber. The result was a sharp change in the focus and direction of American national politics.

In 1982 a deep recession, with record postwar unemployment, turned the political tide against the Republican party, and some seats won in 1980 were lost. But the overall outcome—no change in the Senate, Republicans losing a net 26 House seats—was far more favorable to Republicans than national conditions would, on historical evidence, have warranted.[1]

The first two elections of the 1980s also marked the fifth and sixth consecutive elections for which usable data on campaign finances have been gathered and published. Although some important theoretical issues remain unresolved, studies of data from the previous four elections have taught us a great deal about how money works in congressional elections.[2] In general, findings about the patterns of campaign contributions or the effects of campaign spending have been remarkably consistent across election years. But it has also become clear that campaign finance practices undergo continual modification, reflecting the boundless ingenuity of people who deal with political money. Against the background of knowledge culled from earlier election years, this chapter examines the role of campaign money in the electoral events of 1980 and 1982, the continuing evolution of campaign finance practices, and the implications of both for the future politics of congressional elections.

I begin with a discussion of 1980 and 1982 congressional campaign finance at its most general level: the average amount of money raised by House and Senate candidates and the share provided by each major source. At this level of analysis, the pattern is one of strong continuity with previous election years. More detailed examination turns up some notable changes in the source of campaign funds, particularly regarding political action committees (PACs). I consider these changes, and a few political implications, in the second section.

The most striking departures in the financing of the 1980 and 1982 elections are not captured by an analysis of contributions given directly to candidates. They lie, rather, in the unprecedented amounts of money spent by political parties (particularly the Republican) and in the sharp increase in money spent by groups independent of any campaign. I analyze these developments in the third and fourth sections.

In the fifth section I explore the pattern of strategic behavior revealed by the flow of money in these congressional campaigns and estimate the effects of campaign spending on the outcomes. Based on this analysis and on the theoretical understanding of congressional election processes derived from previous work, I assess, in the final section, the role of campaign money in the Repub-

TABLE 2.1.

SOURCES OF CAMPAIGN CONTRIBUTIONS TO MAJOR-PARTY
HOUSE AND SENATE GENERAL ELECTION CANDIDATES, 1974-82

|  | 1974 | 1976 | 1978 | 1980 | 1982 |
|---|---|---|---|---|---|
| **House Elections** | | | | | |
| Average | | | | | |
| Contribution | $61,084 | $79,421 | $111,232 | $148,268 | $222,620 |
| Percentage from: | | | | | |
| Individuals | 73 | 59 | 61 | 67[a] | 63[a] |
| Parties[b] | 4 | 8 | 5 | 4 | 6 |
| PACs | 17 | 23 | 25 | 29 | 31 |
| Candidates[c] | 6 | 9 | 9 | — | — |
| | | | | | |
| **Senate Elections** | | | | | |
| Average | | | | | |
| Contribution | $455,515 | $624,094 | $951,390 | $1,079,346 | $1,771,167 |
| Percentage from: | | | | | |
| Individuals | 76 | 69 | 76 | 78[a] | 81[a] |
| Parties[b] | 6 | 4 | 2 | 2 | 1 |
| PACs | 11 | 15 | 14 | 21 | 18 |
| Candidates[c] | 1 | 12 | 8 | — | — |
| Source not known | 6 | — | — | — | — |

SOURCES: Compiled from the following sources. For 1974, Common Cause, *1974 Congressional Campaign Finances*, vol. 1 (Washington, D.C., 1976). For 1976, Federal Election Commission, *Disclosure Series No. 9* (House of Representatives Campaigns), September 1977; and *Disclosure Series No. 6* (Senatorial Campaigns), April 1977. For 1978, Federal Election Commission, *Reports on Financial Activity, 1977-78, Interim Report No. 5* (U.S. Senate and House Campaigns). For 1980, Federal Election Commission, *Reports on Financial Activity, 1979-80, Final Report* (U.S. House and Senate Campaigns). For 1982, Federal Election Commission, *Reports on Financial Activity, 1981-82, Interim Report No. 3* (U.S. House and Senate Campaigns).

a. Includes candidates' contributions to their own campaigns, loans, transfers, and other items.
b. Does not include party expenditures in behalf of candidates.
c. Includes candidates' loans unrepaid at time of filing.

lican victories of 1980 and damage control of 1982. From this perspective, I argue that recent innovations in congressional campaign finance have produced noteworthy changes in congressional election politics.

## Campaign Contributions

Viewed generally, the contributions to congressional candidates in 1980 and 1982 follow closely the patterns and trends evident from earlier election years. Table 2.1 on page 39 lists the average amount contributed to House and Senate candidates since 1974 (the first election completely covered by the present system of disclosure) and the percentage contributed by each major source. Table 2.2 indicates the percentage change in total contributions and contributions from each source between election years and over the entire period. At this level of analysis, contributions to House and Senate candidates in 1980 and 1982 clearly continue trends of the recent past. To be specific:

1. The amount of money available to congressional candidates has grown steadily since 1974. In 1980 the average House candidate raised more than $148,000, the average Senate candidate more than $1,079,000. By 1982 the House average had surpassed $222,000, the Senate average, $1,771,000. Three-quarters of the growth since 1974 has been purely nominal, to be sure, a consequence of inflation. Still, the inflation-adjusted growth in campaign contribu-

TABLE 2.2.
PERCENTAGE CHANGE IN CONGRESSIONAL CAMPAIGN CONTRIBUTIONS, 1974-82
(IN CONSTANT DOLLARS)

|  | 1974-76 | 1976-78 | 1978-80 | 1980-82 | 1974-82 |
|---|---|---|---|---|---|
| Contributions to House Campaigns | | | | | |
| Individuals and candidates | − 3 | 26 | 1 | 19 | 47 |
| Political parties | 126 | − 24 | − 15 | 90 | 176 |
| PACs | 53 | 32 | 23 | 35 | 235 |
| TOTAL | 13 | 22 | 6 | 27 | 84 |
| Contributions to Senate Campaigns | | | | | |
| Individuals and candidates | 6 | 34 | 0 | 44 | 109 |
| Political parties | − 22 | 100 | − 78 | − 8 | − 68 |
| PACs | 65 | 15 | 45 | 19 | 220 |
| TOTAL | 19 | 32 | − 10 | 38 | 96 |

SOURCES: See table 2.1. Adjustment for inflation is based on the Consumer Price Index in the Bureau of Labor Statistics, *Monthly Labor Review* and *Handbook of Labor Statistics,* annual.

tions to House and Senate candidates has generally been significant, with a particularly large jump between 1980 and 1982. Between 1974 and 1980 the increase from one election year to the next averaged about 14 percent. At best this probably kept up with the cost of campaigning; the costs of television time and other advertising media greatly outstripped inflation during the 1970s.[3] But the increase from 1980 to 1982 was more than twice the earlier average and certainly outdid any increase in campaign costs.

Constant-dollar contributions to Senate candidates were actually lower in 1980 than they were in 1978. But this is not a very informative figure because the data are from different sets of states. Campaign contributions vary from state to state in complicated ways. They increase with the population of the state, but at a decreasing rate; the larger the state, the more money raised and spent in total, but the less raised and spent per voter. A more meaningful comparison is with 1974, when the same seats were up for election; contributions to Senate candidates were 42 percent higher in 1980 than in 1974. Similarly, real contributions were 65 percent greater in 1982 than in 1976.

2. Private individuals continue to be the most important source of campaign funds. Their share has remained rather constant over these elections. Individuals (including candidates) generally supply about two-thirds of the money raised by House candidates, more than three-quarters of that raised by Senate candidates.

3. Donations from nonparty political action committees have grown steadily both in real dollars and as a proportion of all contributions to House campaigns and, with the exception of the 1982 proportion, to Senate campaigns as well. In 1980 House candidates received 29 percent of their funds from PACs; Senate candidates, 21 percent. In 1982 the respective figures were 31 percent and 18 percent. PAC contributions to House and Senate candidates increased by an average of 36 percent from one election to the next over the entire period. PACs are by no means the dominant element in congressional campaign finance, but their relative importance has clearly grown.

4. The share of direct campaign contributions provided by political parties reached a low point in 1980, rebounding somewhat, in House elections, in 1982. But these are deceptive figures. The national parties, particularly the Republican, were actually much more active in these campaigns than ever before. But most of their assistance did not take the form of direct contributions to candidates. The full range of national party intervention in the 1980 and 1982 campaigns is discussed later.

Considered at this level of aggregation, then, 1980 and 1982 congressional campaign finances were not very unusual; the pattern of contributions basically continued familiar trends. Within these larger patterns, however, politically important changes have been taking place. And beyond that, 1980 and 1982 saw the development of innovations in campaign finance activity that do not show up in data of this kind. Both of these phenomena reward a closer examination.

## Political Action Committees

Political action committees have never been without their critics—the most obviously "interested" donations to candidates come from PACs—and they continue to be the most controversial source of campaign money.[4] One reason the controversy is not likely to fade has already been noted: the absolute and proportionate increase in PAC contributions to congressional candidates. But there is more to it than this. If PACs were merely gradually increasing their proportion of total contributions, alarm would be greatly muted. The controversy arises from striking changes in the amounts contributed by different kinds of PACs. Table 2.3 tells part of the story.

Contributions from corporate PACs have increased sharply since 1974; in 1980 and 1982 they constituted the single largest source of PAC funds. Gifts from trade, membership, and health PACs have grown almost as much and have become the second largest source of PAC money. Despite a substantial increase

TABLE 2.3.
PAC CONTRIBUTIONS TO CONGRESSIONAL CANDIDATES, 1974-82
(IN MILLIONS)

| | 1974 | 1976 | 1978 | 1980 | 1982 |
|---|---|---|---|---|---|
| Type of PAC Contribtution | | | | | |
| Labor | $6.3 | $8.2 | $10.3 | $13.2 | $20.2 |
| | (50)[a] | (36) | (29) | (24) | (24) |
| Corporate | 2.5 | 7.1 | 9.8 | 19.2 | 27.4 |
| | (20) | (31) | (28) | (35) | (33) |
| Trade/membership/ | 2.3 | 4.5 | 11.5 | 15.9 | 21.7 |
| health | (18) | (20) | (33) | (29) | (26) |
| Other | 1.4 | 2.8 | 3.5 | 6.9 | 13.9 |
| | (11) | (12) | (10) | (12) | (17) |
| TOTAL | 12.5 | 22.6 | 35.1 | 55.2 | 83.1 |
| Adjusted for inflation | | | | | |
| (1980 = 1.00) | 20.9 | 32.7 | 44.3 | 55.2 | 70.4 |

| | Percentage Change (adjusted for inflation) | | | | |
|---|---|---|---|---|---|
| | 1974-76 | 1976-78 | 1978-80 | 1980-82 | 1974-82 |
| Type of PAC Contribution | | | | | |
| Labor | 13 | 7 | 2 | 30 | 62 |
| Corporate | 146 | 17 | 55 | 20 | 450 |
| Trade/membership/ | | | | | |
| health | 169 | 117 | 12 | 16 | 381 |
| Other | 73 | 6 | 56 | 70 | 502 |
| TOTAL | 57 | 32 | 25 | 28 | 235 |

SOURCES: For 1976, Common Cause, *1976 Federal Campaign Finances: Interest Group and Political Party Contributions to Congressional Candidates* (Washington, D.C., 1978). For other years, see table 2.1.

    *a.* Percentage of all PAC contributions; numbers may not sum to 100 because of rounding.

in 1982, labor PAC contributions have grown comparatively slowly over these years, and labor's share of PAC contributions has dropped from one-half to less than one-quarter.

Clearly, organized labor's relative importance as a source of campaign money has waned. Labor's clout in Washington has also eroded noticeably over the last decade (labor's inability to get a solidly Democratic Congress to pass the common situs picketing bill or the labor reform package are well-known illustrations of labor's weakness), and it is hardly surprising that labor leaders and their allies in Congress have assumed a connection between the two phenomena. The threat would not seem so great if it were merely that business-oriented PACs were using their growing pool of resources to support Republicans. But a substantial share of this money goes to Democrats. Although the data indicate that corporate PACs have been shifting their resources to Republicans, particularly nonincumbents, in the last three elections, Democrats have continued to receive a significant share of corporate PAC money.

The proportion of money contributed to Democrats by labor, by corporate, and by trade, membership, and health PACs in elections from 1974 through 1982 is presented in table 2.4. Labor consistently gives almost all its money to Democrats. Corporate PACs, while favoring Republicans, continue to give

TABLE 2.4.
PERCENT OF PAC CONTRIBUTIONS GIVEN TO
DEMOCRATIC CONGRESSIONAL CANDIDATES, 1974-82

|  | 1974 | 1976 | 1978 | 1980 | 1982 |
|---|---|---|---|---|---|
| Type of PAC Contribution |  |  |  |  |  |
| Labor | 93 | 97 | 94 | 93 | 95 |
| Corporate | 39 | 43 | 34 | 36 | 34 |
| Trade/membership/health | 28 | 38 | 42 | 43 | 43 |
| Other | 50 | 46 | 23 | 30 | 53 |
| TOTAL | 68 | 66 | 54 | 52 | 54 |

SOURCES: See table 2.3.

more than a third of their money to Democrats. And the share Democrats receive from trade, membership, and health PACs has increased noticeably. The Democratic share of gifts from groups in the "other" category fell off in 1978 and 1980 but rebounded in 1982. This category includes both ideological and issue groups. PACs on the conservative side of the spectrum were much more prominently involved in 1980; liberal groups — organized around issues like the nuclear freeze, women's rights, and the environment — entered the lists in 1982, restoring the partisan balance. The two parties now divide the PAC largess about equally; Republicans have overcome the Democrats' earlier advantage because corporate PACs, which favor Republicans, have increased their contributions steeply.

One net consequence of these developments is that labor's financial importance to Democratic congressional candidates has declined sharply relative to that of corporate and other PACs. This is clear from table 2.5. More than

TABLE 2.5.
AVERAGE CAMPAIGN CONTRIBUTIONS BY LABOR PACs AND CORPORATE, TRADE,
AND PROFESSIONAL PACs TO DEMOCRATIC HOUSE CANDIDATES, 1972-82

|  | 1972 | 1974 | 1976 | 1978 | 1980 | 1982 |
|---|---|---|---|---|---|---|
| Labor PAC |  |  |  |  |  |  |
| Contributions | $6,429 | $9,494 | $11,820 | $14,820 | $19,690 | $33,566 |
| Percentage of all |  |  |  |  |  |  |
| PAC contributions | 66 | 69 | 53 | 48 | 43 | 43 |
| Percentage of total |  |  |  |  |  |  |
| contributions | 12 | 15 | 14 | 13 | 14 | 16 |
|  |  |  |  |  |  |  |
| Corporate, Trade, |  |  |  |  |  |  |
| and Professional |  |  |  |  |  |  |
| PAC Contributions | $2,083 | $2,776 | $8,485 | $13,999 | $21,704 | $32,294 |
| Percentage of all |  |  |  |  |  |  |
| PAC contributions | 21 | 20 | 38 | 45 | 48 | 41 |
| Percentage of total |  |  |  |  |  |  |
| contributions | 4 | 4 | 10 | 12 | 15 | 15 |

NOTE: Data from 1978, 1980, and 1982 include all major-party candidates; data from 1972-76 include only candidates with major-party opposition.

SOURCES: See table 2.3.

two-thirds of the PAC money received by Democrats in 1972 and 1974 came from labor groups; by the early 1980s that figure had fallen to 43 percent. Over the same period, contributions from corporate, trade, and professional PACs grew rapidly, more than doubling as a proportion of total PAC contributions. In 1980 they supplied more money to Democrats than did labor PACs; labor regained a slight lead in 1982.

One need not assume that campaign contributions buy the souls of congressmen to find these figures significant. A very large proportion of the money that business-oriented PACs give to Democratic candidates goes to incumbents; the figure for 1982 is about 88 percent; in 1980 it was closer to 90 percent. This means that congressional Democrats are financially independent of organized labor and are thus free to vote contrary to its wishes if changing popular moods make it seem prudent or necessary. If they offend labor, other sources of funds are ready to be tapped. The shift to the right in national politics after the 1980 election was not simply a consequence of more Republicans in Congress (or the Republican in the White House). It depended as well on a large number of Democratic votes, particularly in the House. Democrats did not, for the most part, vigorously resist the conservative tide; the electoral costs of doing so appeared to be high, the costs of not doing so, negligible. And one reason was clearly the current system of congressional campaign finance. Of course, once the declining economy raised issues and opportunities that reawakened congressional Democrats and organized labor to each other's virtues, Democrats had little trouble moving in the other direction.

A broader implication of this argument is that it is possible to have policy realignments without having partisan realignments. Republicans did not have to become the majority party for traditional Republican concerns—a balanced budget, lower taxes, less regulation, more defense spending, lower spending on social welfare—to dominate the political agenda of the 97th Congress. Democrats are perfectly capable of pursuing these objectives if they find political profit in doing so. They need not suffer any financial or organizational costs from offending the remaining liberal/labor wing of the party because they can get resources elsewhere. Neither do corporations and other business-oriented groups need to elect Republicans to have friends in Congress. They can influence policy just as well by helping to elect and reelect cooperative Democrats.

Similarly, changing political and economic conditions later in Reagan's first term could produce successful bipartisan challenges to the administration's tax program and budget proposals. Republicans are no less sensitive than Democrats to the moods of their constituents and are equally free to respond to them without fearing serious financial repercussions.

None of this is surprising in a system of electoral politics in which candidates operate primarily as individual political entrepreneurs and parties are unimportant (if not irrelevant). And this is clearly the kind of system the United States has had in recent years.[5] But nothing is permanent in politics; signs of a major party revival were plainly evident in 1980 and 1982.

## Party Money

Less than a decade ago, party assistance to congressional candidates could be measured almost completely by adding up the amount given directly to the candidates. If this were still the case, the data in table 2.1 would mean that parties are financially irrelevant to congressional campaigns. But it is not; direct contributions form only a small part of the help, financial and otherwise, parties provided to their congressional candidates in 1980 and 1982. A dramatic increase in national-level party activity, especially among Republicans, is the most striking recent development in congressional campaign finance.

National Republican party organizations—the party's National Committee and Senatorial and Congressional Campaign Committees—have become important forces in congressional election politics for two basic reasons: (1) They have raised enormous amounts of money, and (2) they have found ways to spend lavishly for their candidates while remaining within the framework of law established by the Federal Election Campaign Act and its amendments.

The Republicans have become remarkably successful in raising money by making a virtue out of what was once a necessity. After the Watergate revelations, it was impossible for the party to solicit money as it had in the past; people who had given large gifts in 1972 had reason to regret it and could not be expected to do so again; large contributions had become thoroughly suspect in any case. Party officials decided to concentrate on soliciting small donations from a large number of individuals through the mails. They used the first gifts that trickled in to solicit more, gradually enlarging their list of willing donors and weeding out unproductive names. The system has generated ever-increasing amounts of money with each passing year. The three major national Republican committees raised $121 million in 1980 and $190 million in 1982; more than three-quarters of this money came in small amounts through the mail. Their Democratic counterparts, still depending on large donations from individuals and interest groups, raised only $19 million and $28 million, respectively, in 1980 and 1982.

All this money would not have done Republican congressional candidates much good if it had been used only for direct contributions to their campaigns. The FECA limits direct party contributions to a maximum of $5000 per candidate per election for House candidates; parties are treated in this respect as if they were no different from PACs. This means that any party committee can give, at most, $10,000 to a candidate in an election year ($15,000 if there is a runoff primary). Both the national committees and the national congressional campaign committees of each party can contribute this amount, so direct national party contributions can amount to $20,000 in House elections—roughly 10 percent of what it now typically takes to run a minimally competitive campaign. State party organizations may also contribute $10,000.

But the FECA also allows parties to make *coordinated* expenditures on behalf of congressional candidates. Coordinated expenditures can be made for almost any campaign activity. The only condition is that the party have some control over how the money is spent. National parties typically foot the bill for conducting polls, producing campaign ads, and buying media time—major expenses in areas where technical expertise is essential. Unlike contribution limits, coordinated spending limits are adjusted for changes in the cost of living; for 1980, the limit for House campaigns was $14,720; for 1982, it was $18,440. National parties can actually spend twice this limit by working with state parties (see below); so, for example, in 1980, national party committees could put as much as $59,440 into a House race (twice $14,720 plus $20,000 plus the state party's $10,000); the same figure for 1982 was $66,880. This is a considerable sum of money, but still only about 25 percent of what it is likely to cost to run a competitive campaign.

Parties can spend much more on Senate contests. Direct party contributions are limited to a total of $17,500 per candidate from all national party committees. But the ceilings on coordinated expenditures are much higher and were effectively doubled by Republicans through a clever legal ploy. The 1980 limit on coordinated expenditures in Senate races was two cents times the voting-age population of the state, adjusted for inflation since 1974, or $29,440, whichever was greater. Fourteen states had $29,440 ceilings; California, the most populous state, had a coordinated spending limit of $485,024. Two years later, population growth and inflation had raised the limit in California to $665,874; the minimum was $36,880.

State parties are allowed to spend an identical amount on behalf of Senate candidates and may give $10,000 directly to their campaigns; but few of them have the money to do it. Republican leaders adopted an interpretation of the law that allows national committees to pick up a state party's share if the state party agrees to let the national party act as its agent. They entered into agency agreements with 33 of the 34 states with Senate elections, leaving out only Indiana, where local Republicans did not need the help. Republican national party committees could thus spend as much as $997,548 on a Senate candidate (twice $485,024, plus $17,500, plus the state party's direct contribution of $10,000 in California); the lowest limit was $86,380 overall. Democrats challenged the legality of this scheme but were unable to stop it for 1980 and eventually lost their case before the Supreme Court.[6] By 1982, national party committees could spend as much as $1,399,248 (California) on a statewide campaign; the lowest limit was $101,260.

National Republican party committees were thus in a position to inject impressive sums of money into Senate campaigns. The Senate candidates for whom more than $200,000 was spent in 1980 and 1982 are listed in table 2.6. Some idea of the national party's importance in these contests is suggested by the fact that in about three-quarters of them, the national party spent more on the candidate than the candidate received from all PACs combined. Note that only one Democratic candidate made the list.

TABLE 2.6.
SENATE CANDIDATES FOR WHOM NATIONAL PARTY COMMITTEES SPENT
MORE THAN $200,000 IN 1980 AND 1982

| Candidate | State | Amount Spent by Party |
|---|---|---|
| **1980** | | |
| Republicans | | |
| *Alphonse D'Amato | New York | $754,497 |
| Paul Gann | California | 521,741 |
| *Arlen Specter | Pennsylvania | 508,701 |
| David O'Neal | Illinois | 461,103 |
| *Paula Hawkins | Florida | 382,825 |
| *John East | North Carolina | 231,816 |
| *Dan Quayle | Indiana | 215,227 |
| *Slade Gorton | Washington | 214,459 |
| *Mack Mattingly | Georgia | 208,085 |

TABLE 2.6 (Continued)

| Candidate | State | Amount Spent by Party |
|---|---|---|
| **1982** | | |
| Republicans | | |
| *Pete Wilson | California | $1,311,272 |
| James Collins | Texas | 763,817 |
| *John Heinz | Pennsylvania | 648,690 |
| Van Poole | Florida | 573,038 |
| Philip Ruppe | Michigan | 451,748 |
| Millicent Fenwick | New Jersey | 402,871 |
| Florence Sullivan | New York | 332,440 |
| Raymond Shamie | Massachusetts | 318,863 |
| *Paul Trible | Virginia | 295,334 |
| *Richard Lugar | Indiana | 287,145 |
| *John Danforth | Missouri | 265,608 |
| Robin Beard | Tennessee | 246,063 |
| Lawrence Hogan | Maryland | 229,944 |
| Douglas Jewett | Washington | 223,465 |
| *David Durenberger | Minnesota | 217,517 |
| Scott McCallum | Wisconsin | 207,161 |
| | | |
| Democrat | | |
| Richard Davis | Virginia | $237,570 |

SOURCES: See table 2.1.
    * Denotes winner.

A more general picture of party participation in financing recent congressional elections is presented in table 2.7. Republicans get much more from their party, directly and indirectly, than Democrats do. As a consequence, the party supplies them with a much higher proportion of the money that pays for their campaigning. Both parties increased their spending on congressional candidates between 1978 and 1982, Republicans much more than Democrats, and both parties more for Senate than for House candidates. Republicans spent more because they had more to spend; greater spending for Senate candidates was a consequence of both structural (the FECA regulations discussed earlier) and strategic (see below) considerations.

The national party committees, again most notably the Republican, now do a great deal more than merely give money to candidates or spend it on their campaigns. They work hard to recruit good candidates and have set up an elaborate program to train those they find in the techniques of organizing successful campaigns. Good candidates are crucial to winning congressional campaigns under present-day electoral conditions.[7] In the past, experienced politicians, people who held elective office, usually made the strongest candidates; candidate schools run by the national parties teach the skills that political experi-

TABLE 2.7.
AVERAGE PARTY CONTRIBUTIONS AND SPENDING,
CONGRESSIONAL ELECTIONS, 1978-82

| | | Democrats | Republicans |
|---|---|---|---|
| **House** | | | |
| 1978 | Direct contributions | $2,963 | $9,430 |
| | Spending for candidate | 171 | 3,378 |
| | Total | $3,134 | $12,808 |
| | Percent of total[a] | 2.7 | 11.1 |
| 1980 | Direct contributions | $2,386 | $8,681 |
| | Spending for candidate | 596 | 5,418 |
| | Total | $2,982 | $14,149 |
| | Percent of total | 2.1 | 8.8 |
| 1982 | Direct contributions | $2,410 | $11,717 |
| | Spending for candidate | 1,584 | 12,131 |
| | Total | $3,994 | $23,848 |
| | Percent of total | 1.8 | 10.3 |
| **Senate** | | | |
| 1978 | Direct contributions | $12,613 | $21,309 |
| | Spending for candidate | 6,195 | 82,542 |
| | Total | $18,808 | $103,851 |
| | Percent of total | 2.5 | 9.0 |
| 1980 | Direct contributions | $13,728 | $18,805 |
| | Spending for candidate | 32,370 | 150,966 |
| | Total | $46,097 | $169,772 |
| | Percent of total | 3.9 | 14.8 |
| 1982 | Direct contributions | $17,556 | $18,189 |
| | Spending for candidate | 68,509 | 264,114 |
| | Total | $80,065 | $282,303 |
| | Percent of total | 4.4 | 15.6 |

SOURCES: See table 2.1.
   *a.* Percent of total contributions plus spending for the candidate.

ence normally provides and so strengthens otherwise attractive but inexperienced candidates. Finally, the national party committees have also taken to letting cooperative PAC officials know where they think money will be most helpful, guiding contribution strategies and thereby expanding the party's financial role in yet another direction.

In 1980 the Republicans also ran a $9 million nationwide television advertising campaign designed to blame the nation's problems on the Democrats in Congress as well as the Democrat in the White House. (See David Adamany's chapter in this volume.) It is impossible to say whether the ads made any difference; it has been suggested that at the least they raised Republican morale, giving a psychological lift to challengers waging uphill fights against entrenched Democratic incumbents.[8] In any case it represented something uncommon in recent years: a national campaign for the whole party ticket with a common theme and focus.

It is clear, then, that something new and important has been added to congressional campaign finance. It used to be sufficient to analyze just the money raised and spent in individual campaigns to make sense of the role of money in elections. Not so any longer. With the 1980 election, national party activity beyond putting money into individual campaigns became too extensive to ignore.

National party involvement was even more extensive in the 1982 elections. The three major national Republican committees raised more than $190 million during the 1982 election cycle, a constant-dollar increase of 32 percent over 1980. Their Democratic counterparts raised $28 million (18 percent more than in 1980), losing ground despite a serious effort to close the gap. With such ample resources, Republicans were able to provide the maximum allowable assistance (nearly $67,000) to the campaigns of every Republican House candidate with any plausible chance of winning and to be at least as generous to its Senate candidates as it had been in 1980. National Republican party committees ended up spending $18.6 million (in direct donations and coordinated expenditures) on congressional candidates in 1982.

The party was also able to finance an $11 million national advertising campaign aimed at persuading voters to "stay the course." The wisdom of reminding voters that the election could be viewed as a referendum on the administration's progress may be questionable, but in general the party made shrewd use of its money. The Republicans' strategic deployment of centrally controlled campaign resources was crucial in keeping their 1982 losses far below what should otherwise have been expected, or so I argue in the conclusion to this chapter.

The Democratic party had much less to offer its candidates. Its House and Senate campaign committees spent $3.3 million on individual campaigns, one-sixth of what Republican committees spent. As in the past, Democratic candidates had to fend for themselves. Challengers in particular were ignored. Late in the campaign, Paul Offner, a Democratic House challenger from Wisconsin, remarked that "they tell me I'm the party's third-highest priority challenger this year, but if you add up all the money I've gotten from the national committee, from the congressional campaign committee, from the state party, it comes to $1000."[9]

It is tempting to predict that more extensive national party participation in congressional elections will inevitably increase party cohesion in Congress.

Members grateful for past assistance or fearful that it will not be forthcoming in the future should be more amenable to persuasion by party leaders in or out of Congress. Certainly the Republicans were extraordinarily unified in the first session of the 97th Congress, supporting most of President Reagan's proposals with virtual unanimity. "The Republicans have been marching in lockstep," said House Budget Committee Chairman James Jones, "and the key to that is finance."[10] But I suspect that the party's electoral work ultimately had little to do with it; euphoria over the election, ideological cohesion, and the perception that Reagan and his policies were popular with a large majority of their constituents were much more important factors.

Later legislative struggles, such as that over the tax increase, found Republicans less unified, and administration officials used explicit threats to withhold campaign assistance to try to bring recalcitrant members around. They were by no means always successful. For it is clear that, at present, Republican members of Congress are not really dependent on the party for financial support, and they know it. As incumbents, they are in a position to raise adequate funds from individuals and PACs. Moreover, Republican leaders are not about to risk losing congressional seats by withholding support and thus deliberately weakening their incumbents. It is an old dilemma faced by party leaders, and their traditional resolution has been to remind members that their first job is to get reelected; there is no reason to believe that this has changed. If greater party unity among Republicans turns out to be more than a temporary phenomenon, it will be a consequence of factors other than the financial resources controlled by the party.

## Independent Expenditures

The expanded role of national party organizations is not the only important development in congressional campaign finance that does not show up in the data on money raised and spent by candidates; another is the sharp increase in the amount of money spent by individuals and groups independent of official campaigns. Congress tried to limit such expenditures (to $1000 yearly in behalf of a candidate) as part of the FECA of 1974, but the Supreme Court ruled, in *Buckley* v. *Valeo*, that the limit interfered with freedom of speech and was therefore unconstitutional under the First Amendment.[11] At present there is no ceiling on how much any individual or group can spend to support or attack a candidate as long as the campaign activity is not coordinated in any way with an official campaign. This means, in effect, that any person or group that wants to spend any amount of money to influence voters can find a legal way to do so. It is the most important reason that further attempts to limit the flow of money into electoral politics seem doomed to failure.

At first, little use was made of the opportunity provided by the *Buckley* decision. Independent expenditures barely surpassed $300,000 for the 1977-78 election cycle. But $2.4 million was spent independently for and against 1980 congressional candidates, and the total reached $5.7 million for the 1981-82 cycle. This represents a hefty increase, although it still amounts to less than 2 percent of all the money spent in congressional campaigns. It would hardly have been noticed had it been spread evenly among candidates. But it was not; most of it was concentrated in a few races, and most of it was spent attacking candidates rather than supporting them.

TABLE 2.8.
INDEPENDENT EXPENDITURES IN 1979-80 AND 1981-82,
CONGRESSIONAL CAMPAIGNS

| Campaign | For Candidate | Against Candidate |
|---|---|---|
| 1979-80 | | |
| Senate | | |
| Democrats | $127,381 | $1,282,613 |
| Republicans | 261,678 | 12,430 |
| Total | 389,059 | 1,295,043 |
| House | | |
| Democrats | 190,615 | 38,023 |
| Republicans | 410,478 | 45,132 |
| Total | 601,093 | 83,155 |
| 1981-82 | | |
| Senate | | |
| Democrats | $142,512 | $3,119,593 |
| Republicans | 291,325 | 493,326 |
| Total | 433,837 | 3,612,919 |
| House | | |
| Democrats | 229,477 | 825,524 |
| Republicans | 492,170 | 97,089 |
| Total | 722,187 | 922,613 |

NOTE: Some of the money reported during any election cycle may reflect bills paid from the previous election cycle.

SOURCE: For 1979-80, "FEC Study Shows Independent Expenditures Top $16 Million" (FEC press release, November 29, 1981). For 1981-82, "Independent Spending Increases" (FEC press release, March 22, 1983).

Figures on independent campaign spending in 1980 and 1982 Senate and House elections are in table 2.8. The largest share of the money by far was spent attacking incumbent Senate Democrats. Almost 80 percent of independent expenditures in Senate campaigns went for negative campaigning. The reverse was true of House elections in 1980, when much more was spent for candidates than against them. In 1982, negative spending against Democratic candidates for the House increased substantially.

TABLE 2.9.
INDEPENDENT EXPENDITURES, CANDIDATES MOST AFFECTED,
1979-80 AND 1981-82

| Candidate | For | Against | Total |
|---|---|---|---|
| **1979-80** | | | |
| Senate | | | |
| Frank Church (D-Idaho) | $1,945 | $339,018 | $340,963 |
| John C. Culver (D-Iowa) | 59,584 | 186,613 | 246,197 |
| George McGovern (D-S.Dak.) | 3,553 | 222,044 | 225,597 |
| Alan Cranston (D-Calif.) | 2,285 | 192,039 | 194,324 |
| Birch Bayh (D-Ind.) | 1,027 | 180,723 | 181,750 |
| Thomas F. Eagleton (D-Mo.) | 22,910 | 101,794 | 124,704 |
| House | | | |
| Robert W. Edgar (D-Pa.) | 39,182 | 30 | 39,212 |
| Jack M. Fields (R-Tex.) | 38,376 | 0 | 38,376 |
| Carey Peck (D-Calif.) | 37,734 | 0 | 37,734 |
| Harold S. Sawyer (R-Mich.) | 14,219 | 13,912 | 28,131 |
| Harold Volkmer (D-Mo.) | 26,917 | 0 | 26,917 |
| Robert F. Drinan (D-Mass.) | 0 | 23,147 | 23,147 |
| W.J. "Billy" Tauzin (D-La.) | 22,535 | 0 | 22,535 |
| **1981-82** | | | |
| Senate | | | |
| Edward Kennedy (D-Mass.) | $1,350 | $1,078,434 | $1,079,784 |
| Paul Sarbanes (D-Md.) | 30,351 | 697,763 | 728,114 |
| Robert Byrd (D-W.Va.) | 10,034 | 270,168 | 280,202 |
| John Melcher (D-Mont.) | 40,968 | 228,011 | 268,979 |
| Lloyd Bentsen (D-Tex.) | 0 | 225,119 | 225,119 |
| Lowell Weicker (R-Conn.) | 21,248 | 200,508 | 221,756 |
| Howard Cannon (D-Nev.) | 0 | 192,801 | 192,801 |
| Edmund Brown (D-Calif.) | 9,482 | 165,176 | 174,658 |
| Orrin Hatch (R-Utah) | 22,081 | 85,964 | 108,045 |
| Harrison Schmitt (R-N.M.) | 5,682 | 79,767 | 85,449 |
| House | | | |
| Thomas P. O'Neill (D-Mass.) | 0 | 301,055 | 301,055 |
| Jim Wright (D-Tex.) | 0 | 217,115 | 217,115 |
| Jim Jones (D-Okla.) | 13,266 | 127,029 | 140,295 |
| Dan Rostenkowski (D-Ill.) | 0 | 57,507 | 57,507 |
| Robert W. Edgar (D-Pa.) | 24,762 | 8,943 | 33,705 |
| Jim Dunn (R-Mich.) | 24,013 | 8,692 | 32,705 |
| Bill Chappell (D-Fla.) | 30,332 | 0 | 30,332 |
| John Kasich (R-Ohio) | 27,294 | 0 | 27,294 |
| Jim Coyne (R.Pa.) | 25,019 | 1,681 | 26,700 |
| Edward Weber (R-Ohio) | 17,442 | 8,692 | 26,134 |

NOTE: Some of the money reported during any election cycle may reflect bills paid from the previous election cycle.

SOURCE: See table 2.8.

Most of the money spent in 1980 attacking Senate candidates went for campaigns to defeat six liberal Democratic incumbents. The independent spending figures for these campaigns are included in table 2.9 on page 53. The numbers for the campaigns in Idaho and South Dakota are particularly striking; they represent impressive amounts of money in states with such small populations. Of the heavily targeted incumbents that year, only two, Cranston and Eagleton, survived. The largest share of this money—$1.2 million—was spent by the National Conservative Political Action Committee (NCPAC). NCPAC began its negative campaigning more than a year before the election, long before it was known who the Republican candidate would be. Its purpose was to undermine the support of the incumbent for whomever turned out to be the challenger.

NCPAC's tactics generated controversy on a number of grounds. Not surprisingly, its targets challenged the fairness and accuracy of the negative advertisements. But even Republicans whose cause NCPAC was supposed to be helping were less than grateful. James Abdnor, who defeated George McGovern, not only refused to credit NCPAC for his success but filed a complaint with the FEC accusing NCPAC of using his name without permission. An aide to Steven Symms, who defeated Frank Church in Idaho, even claimed that the NCPAC campaign hurt his candidate, making "erroneous charges" that gave Church a campaign issue.[12] Nor was the Republican Senatorial Campaign Committee pleased at the attention NCPAC's campaign took away from its own extensive work in these campaigns. On the other hand, Senator McGovern's administrative assistant said that the senator's "favorability rating" dropped 20 points during NCPAC's preprimary campaign.[13]

NCPAC's chairman, Terry Dolan, did nothing to quiet criticism when he said in a interview after the election that "a group like ours could lie through its teeth and the candidate it helps stays clean,"[14] precisely what the critics of independent political campaigns claim will happen. They argue that people running independent campaigns cannot be held accountable by voters for what they do; therefore, nothing compels them to be responsible. Since independent spending cannot be curbed directly, proposals have been made to counteract its effects by providing assistance of some kind to candidates under attack. Common Cause has recommended that candidates assaulted by an independent campaign on radio or television be given an equal amount of time, free, to respond. This would also presumably discourage broadcasters from selling time to independent groups. Others, including Herbert Alexander, have argued that the ceiling on individual campaign contributions to candidates, which has remained at $1000 despite a rate of inflation that has halved its real value, has forced contributors to channel some of their money through independent groups; the solution is therefore to raise the limit on individual contributions.[15] None of these proposals has yet been seriously considered by Congress.

Independent groups were certainly not daunted by criticism; they were openly delighted with the attention they got in 1980. A few days after the election, NCPAC announced its preliminary list of targets for 1982: Senators Kennedy, Sarbanes, Metzenbaum, Riegle, Jackson, Moynihan, and even a Republican, Weicker. (As the data in table 2.9 indicate, only Kennedy, Sarbanes, and Weicker ended up facing well-funded independent attacks.) All these senators are still in office; only one (Senator Cannon of Nevada) of the nine incumbents who made NCPAC's final 1982 hit list was defeated, and he had more serious problems. There is considerable evidence that NCPAC's tactics actually backfired in 1982 as targeted candidates used the specter of NCPAC to raise money and rally support.[16]

Independent spending is still too recent and limited a phenomenon to have altered congressional campaign finance in any fundamental way. It looks rather less like the wave of the future after 1982 than it did after 1980 (one reason being that TV and radio stations have begun refusing to sell time to independent PACs). It appears from table 2.9 that it was used in 1982 mainly to harass Democratic leaders (Kennedy, Minority Leader Byrd, Speaker O'Neill, Majority Leader Wright, Budget Committee Chairman Jones, Ways and Means Committee Chairman Rostenkowski) with no serious expectation of defeating them. Still, it is something to keep an eye on. For now, three things are clear: Almost no one among candidates, parties, or campaign professionals likes independent spending; there is not much they can do about it; and they are likely to see a lot more of it.

## Campaign Finance Strategies

The movement of money through congressional campaigns is the aggregate consequence of strategic decisions made by candidates, party and PAC officials, and other political activists. The flow of campaign money in 1980 and 1982 conforms to both the broader patterns typical of any election year and the more specific patterns expected when national political conditions favor one party over the other. To begin, the evidence of the previous four elections is that incumbents spend more than challengers and that candidates for open seats usually outspend both. The 1980 and 1982 elections were no exception, as tables

TABLE 2.10.
AVERAGE CAMPAIGN EXPENDITURES BY HOUSE CANDIDATES, 1972-82,
BY PARTY AND INCUMBENCY STATUS
(IN THOUSANDS)

| Year and Party | Incumbents | Challengers | Open Seats |
|---|---|---|---|
| 1972 | | | |
| Democrats | $49 | $30 | $100 |
| Republicans | 52 | 32 | 91 |
| 1974 | | | |
| Democrats | 46 | 59 | 103 |
| Republicans | 81 | 21 | 80 |

TABLE 2.10. *(Continued)*

| Year and Party | Incumbents | Challengers | Open Seats |
|---|---|---|---|
| 1976 | | | |
| Democrats | $79 | $45 | $144 |
| Republicans | 90 | 55 | 98 |
| 1978 | | | |
| Democrats | 111 | 71 | 213 |
| Republicans | 139 | 73 | 192 |
| 1980 | | | |
| Democrats | 166 | 69 | 189 |
| Republicans | 191 | 111 | 204 |
| 1982 | | | |
| Democrats | 246 | 127 | 266 |
| Republicans | 286 | 129 | 324 |

NOTE: Data for 1972-80 include candidates with major-party opposition only; data for 1982 include all major-party general election candidates.

SOURCES: For 1972, Common Cause, *1972 Congressional Campaign Finance,* 10 vols. (Washington, D.C., 1974). For other years, see table 2.1.

2.10 and 2.11 indicate. House incumbents of both parties typically spent more than their opponents, and House candidates for open seats spent more than their fellow partisans in either category. Senate incumbents also outspent their opponents, as usual, in both elections. Although comparisons among Senate races in different sets of states are likely to be misleading, Senate campaigns for open seats appear to have been generously funded as well in 1980; they certainly were so in 1982.

TABLE 2.11.
AVERAGE CAMPAIGN EXPENDITURES BY SENATE CANDIDATES, 1972-82,
BY PARTY AND INCUMBENCY STATUS
(IN THOUSANDS)

| Year and Party | Incumbents | Challengers | Open Seats |
|---|---|---|---|
| 1972 | | | |
| Democrats | $381 | $206 | $481 |
| Republicans | 560 | 312 | 460 |
| 1974 | | | |
| Democrats | 562 | 390 | 532 |
| Republicans | 600 | 284 | 273 |
| 1976 | | | |
| Democrats | 556 | 645 | 636 |
| Republicans | 880 | 349 | 878 |
| 1978 | | | |
| Democrats | 594 | 830 | 809 |
| Republicans | 2,065 | 552 | 812 |

TABLE 2.11. *(Continued)*

| Year and Party | Incumbents | Challengers | Open Seats |
|---|---|---|---|
| 1980 | | | |
| Democrats | $1,381 | $530 | $1,153 |
| Republicans | 1,133 | 939 | 1,018 |
| 1982 | | | |
| Democrats | 1,607 | 1,524 | 4,332 |
| Republicans | 2,140 | 980 | 4,526 |

NOTE: Includes candidates with major-party opposition only.
SOURCES: See table 2.10.

The reason for this consistent pattern is by now well known. More money flows into campaigns that have a better chance of success. Hopeless candidacies do not attract much money from anyone; contributors pursuing influence or access naturally ignore them, and even people who contribute for the sake of an issue or cause prefer to put their money into campaigns that are close enough for money to matter. Normally, a large proportion of challenges are perceived as hopeless. As a consequence, most challengers are severely underfinanced.[17]

Incumbents can raise whatever they think they need. They are very likely to win, and even when they lose, it is almost always in a close contest. Incumbents readily attract money from contributors for whom a donation (whether or not it is needed for the campaign) is an investment in future access, and other potential supporters — parties, ideological and issue constituencies — are anxious to help incumbents when a serious challenge arises. Incumbent spending is therefore largely reactive; the stronger the challenge (operationally, the more the challenger raises and spends), the more the incumbent raises and spends. This was true for 1980 and 1982 as it has been for all the other elections for which data are available. A simple linear regression equation for 1980 House elections estimates an incumbent's spending as $107,027 plus .73 times the challenger's spending ($R^2 = .39$; regression equations are explained below). This coefficient does not change as additional relevant variables (e.g., party, party strength in the district, or whether the incumbent ran in a primary election) are taken into account.

Data are not yet available in the appropriate form from the FEC to perform the same analysis for 1982, but the figures in table 2.10 and a variety of anecdotal sources suggest that many incumbents of both parties were, for different reasons, raising funds preemptively that year in anticipation of formidable challenges that sometimes did not materialize. Republicans sensibly feared the consequences of the deep recession and Reagan's low approval ratings. But Democratic fund raising often appeared wildly *overreactive*. Even the most secure Democrats had evidently been stunned by the licking their party took in 1980 and were worried about all that money Republican committees and conservative PACs were raising to use against them. Indeed, safe incumbents absorbed so much of the campaign money available to Democrats that many otherwise attractive Democratic challengers were underfunded and unable to take full advantage of national conditions.

Candidates for open seats tend to raise and spend the most money because when neither candidate enjoys the benefits of incumbency, both parties normally field strong candidates, and the election is usually close. Contributors are attracted to these campaigns by the quality of the candidates and the expectation of a real contest. The same tends to be true of Senate elections, even those involving incumbents. Incumbent senators are, for a variety of reasons (not the least being that a higher proportion of them lose elections[18]), more often perceived to be vulnerable. Senate challengers are much more likely than House challengers to be well-known public figures. A Senate election also has a greater political impact because the Senate is a much smaller body than the House; each senator is worth, as it were, 4.35 representatives. All these things attract campaign contributions.[19]

Tables 2.10 and 2.11 reveal another pattern that should be expected on theoretical grounds. Samuel Kernell and I have argued that national political conditions have a predictable effect on the strategies of the elites who finance congressional elections. When national conditions—the state of the economy, the popular standing of the President, national scandals, or foreign policy disasters—seem to favor one party decisively, its leaders and financial supporters are encouraged to invest in challenges to incumbents of the other party. The improved election odds attract better challengers and supply them with more money than usual. People associated with the party in trouble figure the odds against defeating incumbents to be even longer than normal, and so they finance few challenges. They put their money into campaigns of congenial incumbents, more of whom than usual face formidable challengers.[20]

The financial consequence of such strategic behavior is best illustrated by the 1974 elections. Observe the figures for 1974 in table 2.10. Republicans, expecting disaster because of Watergate and recession, ignored their House challengers and concentrated on saving incumbents. Democrats did the opposite, producing the only instance on record in which a party's challengers outspent its incumbents. These expectations about the 1974 elections were fulfilled, but in no small part because of the strategic behavior they produced.[21]

Partisan financial differences in the 1980 House races generally look as they should for a year in which electoral forces are expected to favor Republicans (though not so decisively as they favored Democrats in 1974). Republican challengers were especially well funded; their Democratic counterparts were slighted. The average Democratic incumbent spent 2.4 times as much as the average Democratic challenger, the largest such ratio by far in the time series. The only anomalous note is that Republican incumbents spent so much money in a year when few were seriously challenged. Two possible explanations come to mind; they are not mutually exclusive. One is that political forces working in the 1980 elections look much more decisive in retrospect than they did in prospect; Carter's popularity fluctuated widely during the year preceding the election, to mention only one source of uncertainty.[22] Uncertainty may have recommended a more cautious defensive stance to Republican incumbents. The other explanation is that so much money was available to Republican candidates that there was plenty to go around for incumbents, plausible challengers, and candidates for open seats alike.

By all the usual measures, 1982 promised to be a very good year for Democrats, rather like 1974.[23] But the partisan pattern of contributions reflects this only partially. Republican money—and the shrewd and well-financed work of national Republican committees—is the reason. Republican contribution strategies were clearly defensive, as expected; in real terms, the average Republican challenger actually had less to spend in 1982 than in 1980; the average Republican incumbent, in contrast, spent about 27 percent more in 1982 than in 1980. Republicans had enough money to provide generously for candidates for open seats, so it is clear that they deliberately wrote off most of their challengers.

Among Democrats, money was not distributed as we would expect in a very good Democratic year. To be sure, challengers were better funded than they had been in 1980; but they had no more to spend than Republican challengers; compare this to 1974 or, parties reversed, to 1980. Democratic incumbents, on the other hand, raised and spent substantially more in 1982 than they had in the bad Democratic year of 1980. Many spent much more lavishly than could be justified by the opposition they faced. As suggested earlier, the main reason seems to be that Republican wealth and organizational resources, along with the shock of 1980, had them running scared. By the time it became clear that economic conditions should produce an extraordinarily good Democratic year, it was too late to take full advantage of it by redirecting money into campaigns of plausible challengers.[24]

As always, Senate comparisons are tricky, but the figures in table 2.11 suggest that Republican strategies in 1980 were even more aggressive, Democratic strategies more defensive, in Senate than in House elections. Certainly the pattern of contributions from parties and PACs supports this conclusion. The data in table 2.12 show that Republican party money was concentrated in Senate campaigns of challengers and candidates for open seats. Democratic party money, however, was much scarcer in these contests, and the largest amount of help went to the Senate incumbents. In House elections, both parties were most generous to candidates for open seats; Republicans typically favored challengers over incumbents; Democrats did the opposite, although these differences are small.

The pattern of contributions from PACs is somewhat different but supports the same conclusion. More was given to incumbents of both parties in House and Senate elections, reflecting the strong bias many of these groups have toward investing in incumbents. But PACs gave relatively more to Republican challengers and Democratic incumbents, relatively less to Republican incumbents and Democratic challengers, in both types of elections in 1980. The differences are again greatest for the Senate contests.

TABLE 2.12.
AVERAGE CAMPAIGN CONTRIBUTIONS BY PARTIES AND PACs IN 1980 AND 1982
CONGRESSIONAL ELECTIONS, BY PARTY AND INCUMBENCY STATUS

| | Parties[a] | | PACs | |
|---|---|---|---|---|
| | Democrats | Republicans | Democrats | Republicans |
| **1980** | | | | |
| Senate Elections | | | | |
| Incumbents | $48,389 | $ 80,254 | $310,429 | $287,502 |
| Challengers | 46,581 | 172,978 | 62,956 | 220,521 |
| Open Seats | 36,317 | 279,705 | 150,848 | 254,084 |
| House Elections | | | | |
| Incumbents | 2,887 | 10,940 | 63,412 | 59,167 |
| Challengers | 2,402 | 13,663 | 13,584 | 24,379 |
| Open Seats | 5,929 | 29,999 | 42,718 | 67,051 |
| **1982** | | | | |
| Senate Elections | | | | |
| Incumbents | $74,520 | $230,720 | $413,141 | $579,293 |
| Challengers | 83,030 | 262,939 | 187,434 | 140,647 |
| Open Seats | 170,302 | 693,075 | 281,955 | 613,799 |
| House Elections | | | | |
| Incumbents | 3,008 | 25,250 | 101,864 | 104,471 |
| Challengers | 4,882 | 18,840 | 36,364 | 23,977 |
| Open Seats | 5,324 | 42,935 | 74,986 | 73,684 |

SOURCES: See table 2.1.
    a. Includes coordinated party spending for candidates.

Table 2.11 reveals a pattern of spending in 1982 Senate elections typical of a year favoring Democrats. Table 2.12 shows that both parties favored challengers slightly that year. Democrats were relatively more generous, Republicans relatively less generous, to Senate challengers than they had been in 1980, which is as expected. The same is true of PACs. And the same is true of both parties and PACs in the 1982 House elections. Again evident in 1982 is the PACs' preference for giving money to incumbents and candidates for open seats. National tides may affect this tendency marginally, but not enough to upset the dominant pattern.

Campaign contributions and expenditures reflect the strategic decisions of congressional election activists—candidates, their contributors, and active supporters. Their strategic behavior is of more than passing interest because strategic decisions have a major effect on congressional election results. Individual decisions about running or contributing generate the collective pattern of candidacies across districts. The pattern reflects expectations about how national conditions will affect voters in the fall election. A favored party fields stronger, better-funded challengers; the other party fields weaker challengers and uses its resources to defend incumbents. Voters respond to the choices offered in their individual districts; the aggregate result is that the party expected to be favored by national conditions indeed does well; a strong element of self-fulfilling prophecy is at work. The effect of national events and conditions on congressional voters is mediated through the strategic decisions of campaign activists. Samuel Kernell and I have presented the full argument for this view elsewhere,[25] so I need not repeat it here. One reason that contribution decisions matter is of immediate interest, however.

Campaign expenditures have a direct impact on the vote, but not all campaign spending is equally effective. Challengers gain much more from a given amount of spending than do incumbents. This is clear from analyses of every election since 1972 and was apparent in 1980 as well (data to repeat the analysis for 1982 are not yet available in the appropriate form). It means that the defensive strategy of shoring up incumbents is less effective, in terms of its effect on the share of the vote candidates receive, than the offensive strategy of financing strong challengers.

Regression estimates of the effects of campaign spending in the 1980 congressional elections are found in tables 2.13 and 2.14. The equations are specified as they were in my previous work on campaign spending effects, and a fuller justification of the forms adopted can be found there.[26] A regression equation measures the amount of change expected, on average, in a dependent variable (in these equations, the percentage share of the vote a candidate receives) from a given amount of change in an independent variable (e.g., the amount of money spent by the challenger), controlling for the effects of the other independent variables. The amount of change is indicated by the regression coefficient for each independent variable. The standard error of the regression coefficient measures its statistical significance; conventionally, a regression coefficient that is at least twice as large as its standard error is considered statistically significant (i.e., not merely a result of chance). The standardized regression coefficient gives a comparative measure of the strength of the effects of the different indepedent variables by reducing them to a common metric. The multiple correlation coefficient squared (the $R^2$) indicates the proportion of the variance in the dependent variable that is explained, statistically, by all independent variables acting together.

The first equation in table 2.13 estimates the challenger's percentage of the two-party vote as a function of the challenger's spending, the incumbent's spending, whether the challenger is a Democrat (a dummy variable that takes the value of 1 for Democratic challengers, 0 for Republican challengers), and the strength of the challenger's party in the district (estimated as the percentage of the two-party vote won by the challenger's party's candidate in the pre-

TABLE 2.13.
EFFECTS OF CAMPAIGN SPENDING IN HOUSE ELECTIONS, 1980

| | Regression Coefficient | Standard Error | Standardized Regression Coefficient |
|---|---|---|---|
| **Incumbents and Challengers** | | | |
| Dependent Variable: | | | |
| Challenger's Vote | | | |
| Independent Variables | | | |
| Intercept | 19.3 | | |
| Challenger's spending | .35 | .04 | .47 |
| Incumbent's spending | − .04 | .03 | − .06 |
| Challenger is Democrat | − 4.2 | 1.00 | − .18 |
| Challenger's party's | | | |
| district vote in 1978 | .41 | .05 | .35 |
| $R^2 = .49, N = 302.$ | | | |
| **Open Seats** | | | |
| Dependent Variable: | | | |
| Democrat's Vote | | | |
| Independent Variables | | | |
| Intercept | 29.5 | | |
| Democrat's spending | − .10 | .13 | − .09 |
| Republican's spending | − .31 | .13 | − .29 |
| Democratic candidate's | | | |
| district vote in 1978 | .57 | .12 | .59 |
| $R^2 = .56, N = 40.$ | | | |

NOTE: Campaign spending is in tens of thousands of dollars.
SOURCES: Campaign spending, see table 2.1. 1978 vote: "Complete, Official 1978 Election Returns," *Congressional Quarterly Weekly Report* 20 (March 31, 1979): 576-82. 1980 vote: "State Returns for President, Governor, Congress," *Congressional Quarterly Weekly Report* 22 (April 25, 1981): 717-25.

vious election). Clearly, the amount spent by the challenger has the largest impact on the vote in these elections. The regression coefficient on the challenger's spending indicates that a challenger's vote increases by 3.5 percentage points for every $100,000 he spends. This is a smaller coefficient than has been found previously (even considering inflation). The reason seems to be the larger number of extreme cases (challengers spending more than $500,000) in 1980. If these cases are ignored, the regression coefficient is .65, virtually identical to those found in earlier years once inflation is taken into account.[27]

As in every election since data have become available, the amount spent by the incumbent has a much smaller effect on the outcome; its regression coefficient is much less than twice its standard error and so does not reach the conventional level required for statistical significance. The simple correlation (not controlling for the effects of the other variables) between incumbent spending and the challenger's vote is actually positive, as it has been in the four previous elections; the more incumbents spent in 1980, the worse they did in the election. But again, this is only because incumbents spend reactively, mobilizing more resources when strongly challenged. The vigor of the challenge has a much greater effect on the outcome than does the vigor of the response.[28]

The first equation in table 2.13 also indicates that, other things equal, Republican challengers received 4.2 percent more of the vote than did Democratic challengers; the only larger party trend coefficient in the last five election years favored the Democrats in 1974 (by almost ten percentage points). And as in previous years, the control variable measuring the challenger's party strength had a substantial and statistically significant effect on the vote.

The second equation in table 2.13 analyzes the relationship between campaign spending and the vote in contests for open seats. The Republican candidate's level of campaign spending has a significant impact on the vote (Republicans typically gained 3.1 percentage points for every $100,000 they spent), while that of the Democrat does not and shows the wrong sign. These results are again in line with those from previous elections. In every election year since 1972 the coefficient for the Republican's spending has been larger than that for the Democrat's spending, and in only two of the five election years does the latter reach conventional levels of statistical significance (the former always does).[29] By the evidence of these contests, Republicans consistently get more out of their campaign expenditures than do Democrats in House elections. The only explanation that has occurred to me is that this is a consequence of their party's minority status among voters in almost every district. Campaign spending is evidently most effective for candidates who are at a disadvantage for any reason—because they face incumbents or because they must overcome an unfavorable partisan balance.

Table 2.14 on page 64 presents the regression evidence from the 1980 Senate elections. The first equation estimates the effects of campaign spending in Senate elections between incumbents and challengers. Because of the complex variations in campaign spending associated with state population differences, the spending variables are entered as the natural logarithm of expenditures per voting-age individual in the state. As in House elections and in the previous four election years, spending by Senate challengers has a large, statistically significant effect on the vote. Its regression coefficient indicates that the challenger's vote would be expected to increase by about 5.2 percentage points every time expenditures per voting-age person doubled. The incumbent's spending has a much smaller, statistically insignificant, impact on the vote. Other things equal, a Republican challenger's vote was six percentage points higher than that of a Democratic challenger in 1980.

Coordinated spending by party committees and independent spending by other groups were also prominent features of many Senate campaigns. It is, of course, impossible to determine precisely what difference, if any, this additional money made. But the second equation in table 2.14 supports (very mod-

TABLE 2.14.
EFFECTS OF CAMPAIGN SPENDING IN SENATE ELECTIONS, 1980

| | Regression Coefficient | Standard Error | Standardized Regression Coefficient |
|---|---|---|---|
| EQUATION 1 | | | |
| Dependent Variable: Challenger's Vote | | | |
| Independent Variables | | | |
| Intercept | 51.8 | | |
| Challenger's spending | 5.2 | 1.3 | .81 |
| Incumbent's spending | -1.7 | 2.1 | -.15 |
| Challenger is Democrat | -6.0 | 3.5 | -.25 |
| $R^2 = .60, N = 24.$ | | | |
| EQUATION 2 | | | |
| Dependent Variable: Challenger's Vote | | | |
| Independent Variables | | | |
| Intercept | 50.0 | | |
| Spending for challenger[a] | 5.3 | 1.2 | .82 |
| Spending for incumbent[a] | -1.6 | 2.2 | -.15 |
| Challenger is Democrat | -5.8 | 3.5 | -.24 |
| $R^2 = .62, N = 24.$ | | | |

NOTE: Spending is measured as the natural log of the candidate's campaign expenditures in dollars per voting-age person in the state.

SOURCES: See table 2.13.

a. Includes spending reported by candidate, coordinated spending for candidate by party committees, and independent expenditures for the candidate and against the opponent.

estly) the notion that it may help challengers. This equation repeats the analysis with each expenditure variable augmented by (1) the amount spent by party groups on behalf of the candidate, (2) the amount spent independently for the candidate, and (3) the amount spent independently against the candidate's opponent. None of the estimated regression coefficients differs significantly from its equivalent in the first equation, but the coefficient on the challenger's spending is larger in the second equation, even though, with the total spending increased, the coefficient would be expected to decrease (on the assumption of diminishing returns to scale).

There were only nine open Senate seats in 1980, so not much can be concluded from regression analysis of these contests. I tested several specifications, with rather mixed results. The most interesting equation suggested that spending by Democratic Senate candidates for open seats had a much larger effect on the vote than did spending by their Republican opponents if the presidential vote is taken into account. Without this control, neither of the campaign spending coefficients is statistically significant, although their signs are in the expected direction. It might be inviting to speculate about coattail effects and the disadvantages these Democrats faced because they were on the ticket with Carter (increasing the importance of their own campaign spending), but there is simply not enough evidence to support any strong conclusions about this small class of contests.

## Conclusions and Speculations

Taken together, the evidence from these two election years and the knowledge of campaign spending effects in congressional elections acquired since 1972 suggest that money played a central role in the Republican victories of 1980 and avoidance of disaster in 1982. To a large extent, the 1980 and 1982 elections confirm what we already know about contemporary congressional campaigns. Consider the following points:

1. Campaign spending has a significant effect on the outcomes of congressional elections. In contests between incumbents and challengers, the challenger's level of spending is most consequential. This means that, in aggregate, the better funded a party's challengers, the better the party does in the election. Republican challengers were unusually well funded in 1980, and so Republicans did unusually well. In 1982, Democratic challengers were not as well funded as political conditions seemed to warrant, so Democrats did not do as well as they might have in what should have been a very good year for them.

2. The shift of congressional voters to Republicans in 1980 and to Democrats in 1982 was by no means uniform across states and districts; it varied enormously from one state or district to the next. Of the Democratic House incumbents, 41 percent improved on their 1978 vote in 1980; 26 percent of their Republican counterparts received a lower share of the vote in 1980 than in 1978. The standard deviation of the partisan vote change between 1978 and 1980 among House districts was more than nine percentage points. Preliminary analysis of vote shifts between 1980 and 1982 reveals a similar pattern; the Republican House vote shifted as much as 25 percentage points in either direction, for example. How well any particular Republican did in 1980 was closely connected to campaign funding. One illustration of this is found in table 2.15 on page 66. The table lists the percentage of winning Republican challengers according to two variables: whether the seat was marginal (the Democrat won it in 1978 with less than 60 percent of the vote) and whether the challenger spent more than $100,000 on the campaign. The strength of the challenger's candidacy—measured by his or her campaign expenditures—is plainly the crucial variable. One-third of the challengers who spent more than $100,000 were successful; only three of the others defeated incumbents, two of whom were involved in Abscam. Marginal incumbents naturally attracted more serious challengers, but well-funded challengers actually had a higher success rate in the nonmarginal districts. No Republican challenger who spent less than $100,000 was able to take a marginal seat from a Democrat in 1980.

3. Strong individual candidates and campaigns are, under present electoral conditions, essential components of victory no matter what national forces

TABLE 2.15.
WINNING REPUBLICAN CHALLENGERS, 1980 HOUSE ELECTIONS (IN PERCENT)

|  | Democratic Incumbent | | |
|  | Marginal | Nonmarginal | Total |
| --- | --- | --- | --- |
| Republican Challenger | | | |
| Strong challenge | 29 | 48 | 37 |
|  | (38)a | (27) | (65) |
| Weak challenge | 0 | 3 | 2 |
|  | (27) | (117) | (144) |
| TOTAL | 17 | 11 | 13 |

NOTE: Marginal seats are those in which the Democratic incumbent won less than 60 percent of
the two-party vote in 1978. Strong challenges are those in which the challenger spent
at least $100,000. Table includes data from contested elections only.
SOURCE: Gary C. Jacobson, *The Politics of Congressional Elections* (Boston: Little, Brown, 1983),
table 6.11.
a. Number of cases from which percentages were computed.

are operating. The Republicans fielded a larger proportion of politically experienced challengers in 1980 than in any election since 1972.[30] National Republican committees also invested a great deal of money and effort in recruiting attractive House candidates and teaching them the techniques of successful
campaigning.

This does not mean that high inflation, the failures of the Carter administration, or enthusiasm for the Republican presidential nominee were unimportant, or that unemployment and social security played no role in 1982. Quite
the opposite. But the crucial effect of these national forces was on the strategic
decisions of candidates and people who finance campaigns. These decisions
created an aggregate of relatively strong Republican challenges and relatively
weak Democratic challenges in 1980; in 1982, to a lesser degree (for reasons
explained below), the opposite was true. Voters, responding to the choices offered between pairs of candidates across constituencies, moved, in the aggregate,
to the Republican column in 1980 and to the Democratic column in 1982. Strategic choices strongly reinforced the direct effects these forces were expected
to have on individual voting decisions. At least in recent years, this has been
the normal mechanism by which short-term national forces are translated into
election results. The system is driven by potential candidates and potential sup-
pliers of campaign resources making individually rational strategic decisions
about when to run or when to support a candidate.

But while the 1980 elections largely conformed to this scenario, the 1982
elections raised the possibility that the growth of national party involvement
in congressional election politics has begun to alter this pattern. The organizational strength of national-level party committees need not vary with short-
term changes in political fortunes. Direct mail fund raising seems capable of
providing a relatively steady, predictable income, allowing the organizational

work of recruiting, training, and financing candidates to continue regardless of fluctuations in the political environment. Centrally controlled campaign resources can also be deployed more efficiently as the course of the various campaigns becomes clearer. National parties may thus be able to work counter-cyclically, fostering strong candidacies and shoring up threatened incumbents, even in bad years, thereby dampening the effects of contrary political tides.

Although all the necessary evidence to prove the case is not yet in, it appears that this is precisely what happened in 1982. Had the election followed the usual pattern of postwar midterm elections, economic conditions and the public's assessment of Reagan's performance as President should have cost the Republicans more than double the 26 House seats they actually lost.[31] Republicans were able to limit their losses in several ways. Campaigns of threatened incumbents were lavishly financed. Even though the marginal returns on spending by incumbents are relatively small, they are still positive; $500,000 may increase the vote by only two percentage points — as the coefficient for 1980 incumbents suggests — but that may be decisive in a close election; incumbents who lose almost always are defeated in a close race.

Republicans also succeeded in recruiting a much stronger set of challengers than political conditions normally would have produced (heavy recruiting was done in 1981 when political conditions were much more favorable than they later became). Although only one was successful, many had to be taken seriously by Democratic incumbents, who therefore soaked up more of the money available to Democrats than would otherwise have been felt necessary in a "good" Democratic year. Many of the strong Democratic challengers who were attracted, as expected, by the favorable political conditions evidently suffered from a serious shortage of funds and so were unable to take full advantage of Republican problems. An unusually large proportion of campaign contributions went to incumbents of both parties in 1982 (see table 2.10); this made sense for Republicans, but Democrats did not use their resources as efficiently as they have in the past (see the data for 1974).

Republican committees on the national level were also able to direct substantial amounts of money into the tightest campaigns during the last few weeks before the election. Representative Tony Coelho, chairman of the Democratic Congressional Campaign Committee, claimed that this money saved the Republicans at least ten seats; Republican officials were of the same opinion.[32] Republicans not only benefited by having extraordinarily abundant funds but also by having the organizational capacity to use them with unprecedented efficiency.

This analysis, assuming it remains tenable once complete data for the 1982 election are available, holds a crucial lesson for students and practitioners of electoral politics: A centralized party organization with access to plenty of money and the skill to use it intelligently becomes an important independent electoral force, capable of sharply limiting the damage inflicted by strongly contrary national forces. Recognition of this will alter the strategic environment of congressional politics, with consequences that are certain to be fascinating.

## Notes

1. See Gary C. Jacobson and Samuel Kernell, *Strategy and Choice in Congressional Elections,* 2nd ed. (New Haven: Yale University Press, 1983), epilogue.
2. See Gary C. Jacobson, *Money in Congressional Elections* (New Haven: Yale University Press, 1980); see also W.P. Welch, "Money and Votes: A Simultaneous Equation Model," *Public Choice* 36 (1981): 209-34.
3. Institute of Politics, John F. Kennedy School of Government, *An Analysis of the Impact of the Federal Election Campaign Act, 1972-78.* Prepared for the Committee on House Administration of the U.S. House of Representatives (Washington, D.C.: Government Printing Office, 1979), 8.
4. See Michael J. Malbin, ed., *Parties, Interest Groups, and Campaign Finance Laws* (Washington, D.C.: American Enterprise Institute, 1980).
5. See Gary C. Jacobson, *The Politics of Congressional Elections* (Boston: Little, Brown, 1983).
6. *FEC v. Republican Senatorial Campaign Committee,* 80-939; and *Republican Senatorial Committee v. Democratic Senatorial Campaign Committee,* 80-1102 (slip opinion).
7. The full argument is in Jacobson and Kernell, *Strategy and Choice.*
8. Charles W. Hucker, "Battle of Attrition for GOP Comeback Bid," *Congressional Quarterly Weekly Report* 38 (February 23, 1980): 437.
9. Dennis Farney and Brooks Jackson, "Buying Seats: GOP Channels Money into Those Campaigns That Need It Most," *Wall Street Journal,* October 19, 1982, 22.
10. Dennis Farney, Leonard M. Apcar, and Rich Jaroslavsky, "Playing Hardball: How Reaganites Push Reluctant Republicans to Back Tax-Rise Bill," *Wall Street Journal,* September 18, 1982, 14.
11. *Buckley v. Valeo,* 424 U.S.1, 96 S.Ct. 612, 46 L.Ed. 2nd 659 (1976).
12. *Dollar Politics,* 3rd ed. (Washington, D.C.: Congressional Quarterly, 1982), 86.
13. Ibid., 87.
14. Ibid., 88; originally quoted in the *Washington Post,* August 10, 1980.
15. Ibid., 85-86.
16. Rhodes Cook, "Senate Elections: A Dull Affair Compared to 1980's Upheaval," *Congressional Quarterly Weekly Report* 40 (November 6, 1982): 2792.
17. Jacobson, *Money,* chaps. 3 and 4.
18. In the last six elections, 1972-82, Senate incumbents won 78 percent and House incumbents 94 percent of the general election contests they entered.
19. Jacobson, *Politics of Congressional Elections,* chap. 4.
20. Jacobson and Kernell, *Strategy and Choice,* chap. 4.
21. Ibid.
22. Ibid., 79.
23. Ibid., epilogue.
24. Ibid.
25. Ibid., passim.
26. Jacobson, *Money,* 38-41.
27. Ibid., 235.
28. These conclusions are also supported by estimates of a simultaneous equation model that takes the possibility of reciprocal causation—(expected) votes producing

money, as well as money producing votes—into account. The estimated model can be found in Jacobson, *Money,* 136-45.

29. Ibid., 47 and 235.
30. Jacobson and Kernell, *Strategy and Choice,* 78.
31. Ibid., epilogue.
32. Adam Clymer, "Campaign Funds Called a Key to Outcome of House Races," *New York Times,* November 5, 1982, 10.

David Adamany

# 3. Political Parties in the 1980s

American political parties are in decline. So say scholars and political analysts repeatedly and with conviction.[1] Voters are reluctant to characterize themselves as strongly committed Democrats or Republicans, and a larger and larger number portray themselves as independents.[2] Party organizations are so weakened that they cannot deliver political resources or votes. In Congress, the pattern of party-line voting remains weak.[3] The spread of primaries and the public financing of campaigns have deprived party activists of important roles in nominating candidates and providing them crucial resources.[4] The Democratic party's own reform rules before 1982 caused officeholders and party leaders to be largely excluded from the national convention, further dividing the centers of activity and influence that traditionally have comprised the party structure.

This gloomy chorus has recently been interrupted by voices of modest dissent.[5] The "theory of party decline," these commentators argue, overlooks important countervailing tendencies. There is evidence of new party vitality in fund raising, especially by the Republicans. National party committees, again on the Republican side, are providing a vast array of services as well as healthy campaign contributions to local, state, and federal candidates. There is greater professionalism in parties—partly to meet the complexity of campaign finance laws, but also to provide the expertise required by new campaign technologies.

The need to comply with rigid restrictions on presidential campaign fund raising and spending has forced the centralization of campaigns and parties.[6] But this centralization has been heightened by fund-raising and campaign technologies whose expense and complexity have encouraged their application at the national level first. The Democratic national party's assertion of authority over the process of selecting national convention delegates has also nationalized politics.[7] If traditional parties are in decline, these commentators say, there is a new kind of party that, if not as capable of delivering votes and policies, is nonetheless influential and well adapted to the modern conditions of American society.

The 1980 election is only a single point on a continuum in party decline, conversion, or revival, depending on one's interpretation. For analysis, it is likely to be an important event in a longer series of events.[8] Ronald Reagan won the Presidency, and the Republicans captured the Senate for the first time in

26 years. The Democratic majority in the House of Representatives was reduced from 84 to 51. Republican national party organizations had been developing financial and organizational strength under the impressive leadership of National Chairman Bill Brock, Senate Campaign Committee Chairman John Heinz of Pennsylvania, and National Congressional Committee Chairman Guy Vander Jagt of Michigan. The Democratic National Committee was, following tradition, an arm of the White House; and the campaign committees on Capitol Hill worked in the shadow of Democratic incumbency. The evolution of political action committees, emerging as institutional rivals to parties, was well under way in the new incarnation mandated by the Federal Election Campaign Act.

In short, 1980 was a year of important political events. Not the least of these was the first full appearance of the national Republican party in its modern form. In retrospect, 1980 was also a point of departure. The activities of parties in the 1982 congressional elections appear, in hindsight, to be direct extensions and expansions of party roles in 1980. From these two elections, this chapter sets itself two tasks: (1) It surveys the conditions and activities of parties as the United States embarked on the 1980s; and (2) it asks whether there is continued vitality in American political parties or whether the task remaining to analysts is merely to pronounce their eulogy and ponder the causes of their demise.

## The Parties at Law

American political parties are unknown to the text of the Constitution and were not mentioned by federal statute until the enactment of political finance reforms in the early 1970s.[9] In the states, by contrast, regulations of political parties are embedded in constitutions and in a complex fabric of legislation.[10] These laws prescribe the rules under which parties may nominate candidates and often set the structure and operating procedures of party organizations. These same laws also grant political parties privileges and benefits, especially placing candidates on ballots with few, if any, qualification requirements.

In the modern period, there has been an acceleration of the number of legal benefits to political parties. In eight of the 12 states that provide public subsidies for politics, some or all of the public payments go to political parties, which have often used them for organization-building activities as well as candidate support.[11] The Federal Election Campaign Act (FECA) provides a subsidy to national parties to support the national nominating conventions. In 1980, the inflation-adjusted subsidy was $4.7 million. In 1978, Congress authorized preferential third-class mailing rates for national and state political party committees and for congressional committees of the two major parties.

Beyond subsidies, the FECA has extended other preferences to political parties. They may receive contributions of up to $20,000 from individuals and $15,000 from multicandidate committees. These are the highest contribution limits in the law, and they contrast favorably with the limit of $5000 that can be contributed to nonparty committees.

Parties are also advantaged in the amounts they can contribute to candidates. In Senate campaigns, national party committees can contribute up to $17,500, which is not subject to inflationary adjustment. Vastly more important, national party committees may make coordinated expenditures in Senate races in the amount of $20,000 or two cents per voting-age person in the state, adjusted for inflation since 1974. In 1982, permissible coordinated expenditures were $685,874 in California, the nation's largest state, and $36,880 in the nation's smallest jurisdiction. In states with only a single member in the House of Representatives, the limit in House campaigns is the same as for the U.S. Senate, generally $36,880. In other states, the limit is $10,000 adjusted for inflation. In 1982 this amount was $18,440. Coordinated expenditures in an equal amount can be made by state party committees in both Senate and House races. In 1980 the Republican party developed an arrangement in which the national party organizations were designated as "agents" of the state parties for the purpose of making these coordinated expenditures. Challenged by the Federal Election Commission and the Democratic Senatorial Campaign Committee, this unique arrangement, which greatly strengthens the hand of national party committees, was approved by the Supreme Court.[12]

In addition, state and local party committees are allowed to make unlimited expenditures for three kinds of activities. First, there is no limit on their spending for the preparation, display, mailing, or other distribution of sample ballots or slate cards. Second, state and local party committees may make unlimited outlays for registration and get-out-the-vote drives on behalf of presidential and vice-presidential candidates. It has been suggested that parties would be greatly strengthened if this authorization were extended to congressional candidates as well.[13] Third, the 1979 amendments to the FECA permit state and local party committees to make unlimited expenditures for grass-roots campaign activity including pins, bumper stickers, handbills, brochures, posters, party tabloids, and yard signs. No money may be spent on mass media advertising under any of these three exemptions for state and local party spending.

On the whole, these authorizations for party contributions and expenditures are favorable to political parties. By contrast, individuals are limited to contributions of $1000 to a candidate in each election. Multicandidate committees are limited to contributions of $5000 in each election. On the other hand, there is total exemption for expenditures by all groups to engage in "nonpartisan" registration and get-out-the-vote drives. This does not quite put other organizations on an equal footing with parties, since these "nonpartisan" efforts cannot urge voters to support particular candidates or party tickets.

Judicial decisions have weakened party advantages to some extent. The Supreme Court has held that the First Amendment protects the right of individuals or groups to make unlimited "independent expenditures"—that is, expenditures not conducted in conjunction with a candidate.[14] Nonparty groups can therefore engage in spending for media advertising or campaign activities to support or oppose candidates. This advantage is only partly offset by the unlimited authorization of parties to engage in grass-roots activity and by the opportunity to coordinate party expenditures with the candidates they are intended to assist. Parties have taken one additional step to offset these independent expenditures; they have engaged in "institutional advertising" that promotes the party as a whole, advances the party position on issues, or assails the opposition's record or program.

The FECA's provisions for public financing of presidential nomination and general election campaigns have sparked widely differing views about their effects on political parties. In short, the Presidential Election Campaign Fund Act makes each presidential candidate of a major party eligible for advance funding support of $20 million, adjusted for inflation, while smaller parties become eligible for proportional postelection funds if they gain 5 percent of the vote, and receive proportional preelection funds in the next election. The 1980 grants to major-party candidates were $29.4 million, while John Anderson qualified for postelection funds. During nomination campaigns, qualified candidates receive matching grants for individual contributions up to $250. Candidates become qualified by raising $5000 in each of 20 states in individual contributions of $250 or less.

The FECA provides that the public grant in the general election is also an expenditure limit and that total contributions and expenditures in publicly financed nomination campaigns should not exceed $10 million, which adjusted for inflation was $14.7 million in 1980. These expenditure limits have been sustained by the Supreme Court as conditions for receiving public grants.[15]

In the general election, national party committees can make coordinated expenditures to support their presidential candidate up to two cents per voting-age person, which in 1980 allowed party outlays of $4.6 million. Additional spending is allowed to pay for costs of complying with campaign finance laws and for political fund raising, in an amount up to 20 percent of the expenditure limit.

The expenditure limits have been criticized as too low to meet real campaign costs.[16] Consequently, scarce funds are hoarded for media campaigning, candidate travel, national staff, and similar centralized campaign activities. Party activity is discouraged because there is little money to support materials and organization at the grass-roots level. This complaint has partly been ameliorated by the 1979 amendments, authorizing state and local parties to engage in virtually unlimited grass-roots campaigning. And under a special provision of the law, unlimited transfers of funds between party committees are permitted so that national party organizations can supply money, beyond their coordinated expenditures, to support grass-roots campaigning.[17]

A similar complaint asserts that the limit on coordinated expenditures is too low.[18] And a further objection is that public subsidies reduce the dependence of candidates on party leaders and thus separate party organizations from their nominees.[19] The opportunities for direct "institutional" expenditures and for unlimited grass-roots campaign outlays tend to mitigate these complaints also. A further concern is that the ban on private contributions to presidential candidates in the general election deters citizen participation and harms parties by preventing party identifiers from supporting the party's most visible candidate and symbol. A counterargument, however, is that the prohibition of individual contributions promotes the success of party-based fund raising, which does not face the competition of presidential solicitations because of the FECA ban.[20]

There is no doubt that presidential campaigns have become much more centralized in order to control the flow of scarce funds and comply with the complex expenditure, contribution, and disclosure requirements of the law.[21] Part of this centralization is due to advances in modern technology that make it possible—and perhaps desirable—to conduct a campaign relying largely on media advertising, polls, computer analysis, computer-directed mailings, and a professional staff skilled in the use of these devices.[22] To the extent that the vote-delivering ability of parties has declined, centralized campaigns, employing modern technology, become necessary. Overall, the law provides major opportunities for political parties to continue to participate in publicly funded presidential campaigns—through coordinated expenditures, grass-roots activity, and party-oriented advertising—and to raise money for these purposes.

The extension of campaign finance laws to parties presents an odd juxtaposition to other trends in the legal regulation of parties. The statutes written by Congress single parties out for preferred treatment and thus encourage them. But in constitutional litigation the Supreme Court has authorized the application of campaign finance laws to parties to the same extent as to candidates, nonparty groups, and individuals. Hence, parties are constitutionally subject to legislatively mandated disclosure rules, contribution limits, ceilings on coordinated expenditures, and—where conditioned on public financing—expenditure limits.

Constitutional doctrine making parties subject to these sweeping regulations contrasts sharply with the judiciary's tendency in other cases to free the parties from legislative regulation. Relying on First Amendment associational rights, the courts have held that national party conventions may prescribe and enforce rules for delegate selection, even in the face of contrary state laws and judicial rules,[23] and that a state may not supersede a party rule limiting primary ballot access to candidates receiving a minimum percentage of delegate votes in the state party convention.[24] The Supreme Court has also sustained party rules for selecting public officials, to replace deceased or resigned officials of the same party, against the challenge that the party's procedures excluded nonmembers from the selection of those officials.[25] And judges have allowed the parties very wide latitude under the equal protection clause to apportion state convention delegations and party committee seats in order to represent various party constituencies, even at the expense of the one-man, one-vote standard.[26] Hence, while the courts have sanctioned sweeping legislative regulation of party financing activities, they have increasingly limited legislative restrictions on internal party governance and on party nominating procedures.

## Party Resources in 1980

American politics have changed dramatically from an earlier time when political parties were the dominant organizational force in elections. Traditional incentives for party activity—patronage; voluntary welfare; the sociability of the clubhouse; or affiliation of the party with religious, ethnic, or racial groups—have declined with merit systems, government welfare programs, and the amelioration of traditional divisions in society. The direct primary and the "reform" of party caucuses and conventions have weakened the benefits of participation in party affairs.

Modern technology—polling, telephone appeals, mass-mailing techniques, electronic media advertising—has not only made many traditional party methods obsolete but has given rise to a new professional class of technicians who provide the services, for a fee, that parties formerly supplied. Even in the mobilization of political workers, modern technology holds sway. Candidate personality and highly salient issues are more important than party label or allegiance in seeking workers; and today's activists are as likely to gather in small clusters in private homes to be reached by closed-circuit TV as to be rallied in public squares or brought to headquarters and clubhouses. A more mobile, educated, attentive, and independent electorate relies less on party labels to make assessments of issues and candidates.

The most important resource in this modern environment is money. It buys the technicians and technology that are the most efficient means to reach contributors, workers, and voters. On the eve of the 1980 election, Frank Sorauf observed that "political parties have historically dealt largely in nonfinancial resources and have never successfully made the transition to the cash economy of the new campaign politics."[27] Political action committees, on the other hand, are virtually the children of the campaign finance laws that gave them legal standing. And it has been widely believed that PACs will supply the resources, especially money, that are appropriate to modern politics.

The story of political parties in 1980 was a tale of one party that has been successfully making the transition to "the cash economy of the new . . . politics" and of its rival that has not. The surge of party activity described in this chapter depends, by and large, on the prior success of the parties in raising campaign funds. The disparity between Republican and Democratic party campaign activities and organization efforts is largely a reflection of the disparity in their finances.

In gross terms, the Republican national party raised $130.3 million in 1979-80; their Democratic counterparts mustered about $23 million.[28] Federally registered Republican state and local party committees had net receipts (i.e., receipts excluding transfers among party committees) of $33.8 million, while Democratic state and local organizations raised a net amount of $9.1 million. Spending by state and local party committees for campaign materials, registration, get-out-the-vote drives, and other grass-roots activities has been estimated at $15 million for the GOP and $4 million for the Democrats.[29] The vast Republican lead in campaign funds is both the product of superior fund-raising techniques and the key to its superior party organizational efforts and campaign activities.

The centerpiece of Republican National Committee (RNC) fund raising is a mass-mail and small-contributor solicitation program that accounted for about 70 percent of the committee's 1980 net receipts of $76.2 million. In 1977 the RNC claimed about 350,000 contributors. The roster had been building gradually since the Goldwater campaign in 1964 brought the first outpouring of small contributions through the mail. In 1980 the RNC had expanded its giver base to 1.2 million, about 20 percent above its goal. Average gifts had risen from about $26 to about $29.[30] The escalation of mass-mail fund raising was aided by the special postal subsidy provided the parties by Congress late in 1978.[31]

The Republicans' success at mass fund raising has not diminished their efforts to obtain large contributions, although the definition of large contributions has changed dramatically since 1972 when the Republican presidential campaign received gifts of $50,000 or more from 153 individuals.[32] The Eagles Program, which seeks $10,000 gifts, increased from 198 persons in 1975 to 865 in 1980.[33] A "Victory '80" program, soliciting gifts of $500, $1000, or $2500, raised more than $1 million. A convention gala and a network of 19 fundraising dinners in early September 1980 raised more than $4 million, which was shared with state and local party committees. Political action committees were systematically solicited for the PAC 40 Club, which sponsored monthly breakfasts with Republican congressional leaders for those giving $5000 annually. These events and large-giver solicitations raised about $13.8 million, 30 percent of the RNC's gross receipts in 1980.

Both the National Republican Congressional Committee (NRCC) and the National Republican Senatorial Committee (NRSC) began building independent financial bases in 1976 and 1977. The NRCC, with receipts of $28.6 million in 1979-80, relied very heavily on direct mail: about 90 percent of its funds came from a contributor base of about 300,000 whose gifts averaged $23.[34] The NRCC's Republican Congressional Leadership Council has about 400 members who contribute $2500 and receive special briefings from the GOP congressional leadership.

The NRSC had never given more than $400,000 to candidates prior to 1977. In 1980 its net receipts were $23.3 million. Between $13 and $14 million was raised by direct mail from 350,000 contributors. The remainder came from large-giver units such as the 4000-member Business Advisory Board, whose members contribute between $250 and $750, and the Senate Republican Trust, a group of about 200 corporate executives who contribute $10,000 annually. The RNC, NRSC, and NRCC raised a small amount of money—perhaps only $800,000—from PACs. This was part of a deliberate strategy to channel available PAC funds directly to candidates rather than put party committees in competition for PAC dollars.

The NRSC mass-mail fund-raising costs were approximately 50 percent of its total 1980 receipts. The start-up costs of mass-mail fund raising lie in the development and testing of lists, the preparation of computer files and software, the purchase or lease of computer hardware, and the hiring of professionals to get the operation under way. These costs are likely to decline as rising receipts permit economies of scale and start-up costs are amortized over an extended time period. Fund-raising costs at the RNC, for example, have fallen steadily, dropping to about 19 percent of receipts in 1980.

Democratic fund raising in 1980 was as chaotic as Republican financing was effective. The Democrats were still paying off the $9.3 million debt incurred in 1968 when the party, in an attempt to promote unity, absorbed not only the debts of Hubert Humphrey's presidential campaign but also the deficits amassed by Eugene McCarthy and Robert Kennedy, his opponents for the nomination. Democratic National Committee (DNC) Chairman Robert Strauss had reduced the party's debt to about $2.5 million when he left office in 1976. Much of this was accomplished by negotiating payment at a reduced rate. In addition, the Democrats held four telethons between 1972 and 1975, raising $23 million in small gifts averaging $15 and establishing a fund-raising list of small donors, half of whom had not contributed to any campaign in 1972.[35]

When the campaign finance laws made it illegal to borrow large sums, the deficit-ridden Democrats could not obtain start-up money for additional telethons or the solicitation and development of their small contributor list. Moreover, the party debt began to rise again in 1976 and 1977. The party's 1978 midterm convention, mandated by the Democrats' charter adopted in 1974, cost about $800,000 and further deepened the DNC's financial plight. Late in 1977, John White became party chairman, and he set his highest goal as ending the decade-long pull of the debt on the party's activities. "Not having money is bad enough," he explained, "but being in debt is a cancer that eats at the insides of the party."

DNC budgets were cut each year, from a level of $7 million in 1976 to $4 million in 1979. Without the funds to develop a mass-mail fund-raising program, the Democrats continued to solicit large givers and hold traditional fund-raising events. Competition between President Carter and Senator Edward Kennedy through most of 1980 made it difficult even to sponsor the usual round of dinners, cocktail affairs, and entertainments to raise party funds. In 1979-80 the DNC's net receipts were about $15.1 million, slightly more than its goal of $14 million. About $8 million was raised from events and moderate-to-large gifts; about $2.5 million was obtained by direct mail; and about $3 million came from the party's Finance Council, composed of people who give $5000 or raise $10,000. The party ended the 1980 election with about $1 million in debts and about $600,000 in its accounts. Its small-giver list was only 25,000 names.

The Democratic Congressional Campaign Committee(DCCC) raised about $2 million in 1979-80 and the Democratic Senatorial Campaign Committee (DSCC) mustered about $1.7 million. Both solicited PACs. The Democratic House and Senate Council is a separate fund-raising committee that transfers its receipts to the two congressional committees. It annually sponsors a major congressional dinner and maintains an organization of givers of $1500 or more annually, who receive special newsletters, congressional briefings, and other amenities. The DSCC made a modest mail solicitation to a few thousand persons, and the DCCC apparently made no mass-based appeals. Neither committee had a broad funding base in 1980 to match the activities of its GOP rival.

## National Republican Party Activities in 1980

The three principal national Republican party organizations had developed sufficient funding bases in 1980 to support broad and continuous campaign activities. The RNC and NRCC emphasized traditional activities: recruitment of candidates, training of party workers and candidates, mobilizing voters and party workers, contributing campaign funds, supplying research and issue information to GOP office seekers, and providing such services to candidates as polling and technical media assistance. The NRSC gave greater emphasis to financing candidates' campaigns. As recently as 1976, the Senate committee was virtually a shadow organization. Its rapid resurgence in 1979 and 1980 did not allow much time to develop the broad array of campaign committee services offered by other GOP committees. To assure that its substantial financial support for Senate candidates was used effectively, the committee assigned a "consultant" to each senatorial campaign, with the dual assignments of auditing fund expenditures and offering political advice when called upon.

Despite these differences in emphasis, the overall picture of Republican national party activity was impressive. It signaled a remarkable party revival following the neglect of the party during the Nixon Presidency and party demoralization following Watergate. Former Senator Bill Brock, who became party chairman of the RNC in 1977, was the primary architect of this revival.[36] He not only realized the potential of a national political party in the modern era but built the financial capacity and established the structure to convert this potential into reality. Brock's vision of the national Republican party built upon the pioneering view of Ray Bliss, the Ohio Republican chairman who became national party chairman following the Republican debacle in 1964: National party committees could be direct political action groups rather than holding companies of other party units. Brock's approach established a pace-setting model for other party committees; and the RNC has made efforts to give financial, technical, and planning assistance to other Republican party groups.

In 1978, the RNC began its program of financial assistance to local and state candidates, expanded its direct-mail fund raising, and initiated many of its technical assistance programs. These efforts were conducted on a comparatively small scale. By 1979, however, it became apparent that the Republicans had the will and capacity to continue and greatly expand these activities. The RNC and its congressional counterparts were plainly not a party in decline. The variety, scope, and intensity of Republican party activities in 1980 reached the highest level attained by either national party in the post-World War II era.

## ORGANIZATION

The Republican National Committee entered the 1980 campaign with a headquarters operation employing 350 persons to provide the varied services and carry out the array of projects that had been planned well in advance. The NRSC started the 1979-80 election cycle with about 20 employees, and on election day boasted 70 people, including student interns. Substantial numbers of headquarters people in all three committees were exclusively occupied with routine tasks associated with mass-mail fund raising, accounting, financial reporting, and so forth. But these personnel reflect the success and scope of the Republican party's financial operation, which undergirds all its activites. In addition to headquarters personnel, the Republicans operated a network of field offices and sponsored field directors — as many as 14 at one point — who worked with local, state, and congressional candidates as well as with party organizations. The NRSC "consultants"—who were generally not full-time personnel but savvy private practitioners, Republican party staff people, or experienced politicians who traveled on behalf of the NRSC — increased the GOP national party presence in states and localities.

## CANDIDATE RECRUITMENT

The Republicans engaged in direct and indirect candidate recruitment activities. Relatively few candidates for the House or Senate were actually sought out by party leaders and urged to run in the traditional party organization model. The chairman of the NRCC did announce in August 1980 that the Republicans had "made a conscious decision to recruit outstanding candidates to confront Democratic 'leaders' and committee chairmen. Even if they are not all defeated, the survivors will be frightened enough so that they will become more conservative once they return."[37] In addition, beginning in 1978, the Republicans identified a shifting list of seats, perhaps 70 or 80, where they thought prospects were good. As attractive potential Republican candidates emerged or Democratic incumbents seemed to be in trouble, some of these districts were firmly identified for special assistance, including encouraging strong Republican candidates to make the race. On balance, direct recruiting of candidates by the national party was "disappointing," according to one GOP senior staff member.

The broader Republican approach was to create a political environment that made strong challenges to incumbent Democrats possible. Recent scholarly studies have shown that effective campaigns by challengers turn heavily on their ability to garner political resources, such as money and workers.[38] Resource-contributing elites, in turn, support challengers whose prospects are good. But the decisions of strong candidates to enter the race are often conditioned on the availability of political resources. The calculations of both candidates and contributors are affected by the political environment—including voters' party affiliations, presidential popularity, national economic conditions, and the perceived personal weaknesses or failings of specific incumbents. The Republican strategy after 1976 was to enlarge the list of potential Republican candidates, to supply the resources that would encourage those candidates to run, and to create a political climate encouraging to Republican candidates and resource-contributing elites.

The Republicans began in 1976 "to restock the primary recruitment pools for congressional candidates" by emphasizing state legislative elections. In 1978, they gained over 300 state legislative seats, and in 1980 they added another 220 seats.[39] In addition to electing individual state legislators, who became potential candidates for higher office, the Republicans attempted to strengthen their position in the redistricting of House seats that would follow the 1980 census. In 1980 they gained control of five state legislative houses in addition to the 11 chambers that had shifted to the Republicans in 1978.

Republican recruitment efforts did not turn solely on electing candidates to local and state legislative offices. The availability of substantial financial resources, staff support from field directors, campaign training for candidates and managers, and technical assistance in developing polls and media materials also encouraged strong Republican candidates to come forward. Although the effectiveness of party organizational efforts to shape public opinion is unclear, the national Republican party engaged in sweeping media and public relations activities designed to improve the GOP image and exploit public concerns about the Democratic President and Congress. Even if these efforts had only modest effects on public opinion, they may have created a climate that persuaded able Republican candidates to seek office because they believed their party's prospects looked bright.

TRAINING

The Republican National Committee's Local Elections Division reported conducting more than 96 seminars to train 5000 local candidates and their staffs in basic political operations. One Republican party staff member reported that these 1980 training activities were only the culmination of a long-range effort; between 1976 and 1980, more than 10,000 Republicans attended seminars sponsored by the Local Elections Division. An additional 800 campaign managers and senior staff members for both local and state campaigns attended 16 regional campaign management workshops that emphasized specific campaign techniques. A special Campaign Management College was conducted for 150 senior staff people or campaign managers in House and Senate campaigns;

this program focused on sophisticated technologies and fund-raising activites as well as more conventional campaign methods.

## SUPPORT SERVICES

The Republican national party also provided certain technical services in districts where candidates could use them effectively. Polling was a particularly useful service, and one report credits the RNC with conducting 210 polls to assist selected candidates.[40] By 1980 the RNC had built a survey research staff that assisted local candidates to conduct professional-quality polls at low cost. The RNC developed survey instruments, trained volunteer interviewers, supervised interviewing, coded and analyzed data, and made recommendations. Candidates paid as little as $250 for this package, with other costs borne by the RNC and many of the ordinary costs of polling eliminated by the use of volunteer interviewers. When polls were completed, field directors would sit down with candidates and their staffs to review the poll results and assist in designing a campaign strategy that took those results into account.

Media spots were produced for congressional candidates by the RNC and NRCC working together. Staff professionals could write scripts, shoot film, edit materials, or produce finished spots, depending on candidate preferences and needs. About 70 congressional campaigns received such assistance. But RNC media services were not available in state and local races.

Political analysis and targeting was a third technical capability developed by the Republican national party. It developed a data bank of voting patterns and demographic characteristics throughout the country. Party units and candidates were advised to use this information for targeting voter registration efforts, get-out-the-vote drives, and candidate recruitment activities.

## FINANCIAL CONTRIBUTIONS

The prosperity of the national Republican party permitted it to undertake the most extensive program of direct financial support to party candidates in modern history. Continuing the pattern developed in 1978—when the RNC contributed $530,000 to GOP gubernatorial candidates and spent $1.7 million to aid the party's state legislative contenders[41]—the Republican national party in 1980 contributed generously in state as well as federal office campaigns. The RNC gave the Reagan-Bush campaign more than $4.6 million, the maximum permitted by the Federal Election Campaign Act. It also acknowledged contributions of $6.2 million in direct cash and in-kind support to candidates for the Senate, House, governorships, and state legislative seats.[42]

Federal Election Commission reports show that in 1980 Republican Senate candidates in the general election made expenditures of $35 million and were the beneficiaries of another $5.4 million in coordinated party expenditures.[43] Party contributions of $677,000 together with the party coordinated expenditures of $5.4 million brought total party support to $6.1 million, or 15.1 percent of total candidate and party expenditures of $40.4 million. Republican

House candidates who ran in the general election spent a total of $58.6 million and were supported by party spending of $2.2 million, for total outlays of $60.8 million. Of this amount, 9.4 percent, or $5.7 million — $3.5 million in contributions and $2.2 million in coordinated expenditures — represented direct party financial assistance.

## VOTER PERSUASION

In addition to contributions and expenditures in support of specific candidates, the national Republican party undertook a broad-gauge advertising campaign intended to improve public attitudes toward the Republican party and focus criticism on the Democrats. A nationwide television campaign featured six different spots attacking Democratic "failures" in the areas of inflation, unemployment, energy, national security, and government spending. The spots concluded with the slogan "Vote Republican. For a Change." The most discussed advertisement featured a look-alike for House Speaker Tip O'Neill, thus focusing negative commentary on the Democrats through a particular personality. The campaign was originally intended to run only prior to the Republican National Convention, during the period when the party had not yet nominated its presidential candidate.

After a full flight of spots in 50 major media markets in February, April, and June, the Republicans decided to continue the advertising program during the fall campaign. An unanticipated flow of funds into GOP committees and opinion surveys showing high voter recall of the spots were crucial factors in the decision. The final wave of spots, aired during the last 16 days of the campaign, ran at the same frequency as did spot advertisements for Democratic and Republican presidential contenders. Republican leaders claimed that their media blitz "gave us two nationwide election campaigns while the Democrats were operating only one."[44]

The initiative for the "Vote Republican. For a Change" campaign came from RNC Chairman Bill Brock. During visits to Great Britain, he has been impressed by the interelection "institutional advertising" campaigns waged by the Tories. Building upon a modest 1978 NRCC institutional advertising campaign, the NRCC and RNC sponsored an extensive GOP advertising campaign during the winter and spring of 1980. When surveys in late spring showed high voter recall of the GOP ads, the NRSC signed on as a co-sponsor. The total cost of this institutional advertising program was $9.4 million, with the RNC providing approximately $6 million of that amount. In addition, the national committee sponsored party advertising in ethnic and religious newspapers and publications across the country.

Beyond its advertising campaign, the national Republican party waged an extensive public relations program to reach voters with the party's message. Special efforts were made to provide information about President Carter's alleged record of broken promises and about the Republican position on the SALT II treaty. Information was regularly provided to local party leaders and candidates about Democratic leaders' current statements on the issues, voting records of Democratic incumbents, and new survey data that showed Republican strength or portrayed trends in public opinion on various policy issues. A series of ten platform hearings was intended to develop visibility for Republicans on issues, and several hundred prominent Republicans served on policy advisory groups that issued statements and papers outlining party approaches on national issues.

## Voter Mobilization

Canvassing, registration, and getting out the vote are traditional party activities closely identified with local party organizations. The extent of national party involvement in these activities in 1980 is therefore surprising. The RNC and the Reagan-Bush campaign jointly conducted a voter registration, identification, and get-out-the-vote program called Commitment '80.[45] Eventually between 800,000 and 1,000,000 people were involved in some grass-roots activity; 100,000 volunteers hosted parties in their homes to get the massive voter drive under way; and 85,000 volunteers participated in training and leadership meetings to give direction to these efforts. Republican party sources estimate that 700,000 Republican voters were registered as a direct result of these efforts; but there is no estimate of how many Republican voters were identified and gotten to the polls.

Indeed, one commentator has skeptically said that "whether those [800,000] volunteers later went out into the neighborhoods is questionable."[46] She does not attribute this to financial or organizational failure but to changes in American society that have made old-style party organizations obsolete.

Most believe the kinds of grass-roots activities called for in the [Commitment '80] program were no longer functional and no amount of money or planning could alter that fact. . . . Explanations reflect the changed nature of American society from the days when such activities were more common: people no longer welcome strangers at the door, nor are they eager to knock on strange doors; in a great many households all adults are employed outside the house and when they are at home, they are less eager to have interruptions than they might have in the past. . . . Changes in communication technology . . . have eliminated the need for door-to-door activities: direct mail and paid media enable the party—or any other group —to communicate directly and fully with voters in a far more sophisticated and complete manner than volunteer message carriers, however well-trained and articulate.[47]

This skepticism is somewhat blunted by the very large commitment made by both national parties in 1980 to grass-roots campaigning by state and local party units. Republican state and local party committees apparently spent about $15 million for campaign materials, registration, get-out-the-vote drives, and other grass-roots activities permitted under the 1979 FECA amendments. Some of this money was garnered from fund-raising affairs jointly sponsored by the national and state parties, while other funds were directly transferred from the

RNC to state and local party committees. Substantial financial support for these grass-roots activities was also channeled to state parties by national GOP leaders who urged large contributors to direct their late gifts to committees that could make expenditures under the 1979 amendments. Democratic state and local committees apparently spent about $4 million on grass-roots efforts. Most of these funds were raised locally to assist the national party ticket.

## GROUP MOBILIZATION

Parties have traditionally sought the support of interest groups and organizations. Ethnic, religious, and racial groups have been traditional targets of Republican activity, but in 1980 such efforts were apparently not given high priority. The GOP's repudiation of its long-standing position in favor of the Equal Rights Amendment diminished its effectiveness in making special appeals to women, an area where it had been especially active. Women were recruited for visible places in the national convention, and campaign tours of six key states in a five-day period by prominent Republican women and celebrities were conducted.

The wooing of political action committees became an art in 1980, and the Republicans organized these efforts with special care. The main thrust of their efforts was to raise money, but the Republicans understood the other kinds of support that PACs might give. The staff of the NRSC arranged meetings of leading PAC directors in major cities to offer advice about the prospects of Republican candidates. Using polls and other information, the Senate committee representatives attempted to assist PAC directors to funnel money to likely winners. They also steered PACs away from GOP candidates who did not need funds or whose prospects seemed slim. This controversial strategy was intended to build credibility with PAC directors who were under pressure from their organizations and corporations to allocate money wisely—to races that could be won and candidates friendly to the organizations' concerns. The explosion of new PACs, particularly those affiliated with corporations, meant that many of their directors or officers had little experience in politics and were forced to rely on others for advice in making contributions. The NRSC operation capitalized on this inexperience. By the end of the campaign, one staff member spent almost full time responding to requests from PACs for information about various races in which money might be contributed.

Both the NRCC and the NRSC arranged cocktail parties, breakfasts, and other events to introduce nonincumbent candidates to PAC directors in Washington. And both committees, as well as the RNC, supplied speakers for meetings sponsored by political action committees, especially trade association and corporate PACs. There is little evidence that Republican party organizations encouraged PACs to engage in direct political action, such as independent expenditures to reach the public on behalf of GOP candidates or endorsements, registration drives, and get-out-the-vote programs directed at employees or stockholders. Beginning in 1978, however, the Republicans did provide special training opportunities for young business and professional men and women interested but inexperienced in politics. More than 600 people attended five regional training meetings sponsored by this Concord Group in 1980; several hundred had participated in similar meetings in 1978 and 1979. Although not directly aimed at business or professional organizations, the Concord Group has the important secondary effect of assuring that well-trained and committed young Republicans will be strategically placed in the business and professional communities.

COORDINATION

Political parties encompass many centers of influence, activity, and power. In 1980, the national Republican party made an impressive effort to coordinate these centers. Beginning in November 1979, RNC Chairman Bill Brock brought together representatives of the candidates for the GOP presidential nomination to begin postconvention planning. Whether the group actually did much planning is disputed, but its regular meetings slowed the centrifugal forces in the party, especially among candidate staffs, which, in their zeal, are often "more royalist than the king." These regular meetings also provided some cover for party committees to continue their activities without complaints from presidential candidates. After Ronald Reagan was nominated, coordination between the RNC and the presidential campaign—initially uneven because of hostility toward Brock by some Reagan loyalists—developed well, with Drew Lewis, one of Reagan's leading operatives in the East, becoming deputy chairman of the RNC.

Collaboration among party committees was even more impressive. Representatives of the three national-level committees met regularly to discuss fund allocations and expenditures for candidates. They jointly sponsored the institutional advertising campaign, training sessions, and other activities. The campaign finance laws permit coordinated expenditures for candidates and other kinds of collaboration, and this was an impetus for party committees to meet regularly. The "agency agreements" between national and state party committees were dramatic examples of successful cooperation.

The RNC's fund-raising success also played a role. A senior staff member put it bluntly: "The RNC was sending money out to the Senate Committee, the Congressional Committee, state and local parties. So coordination was required. Dollars were being targeted to key races. And coordination was forced on us by a desire not to waste money." But money was not the sole basis for extensive collaboration, as the presidential planning group and jointly sponsored activities attest. The National Committee was plainly a catalyst for some concerted efforts by diverse centers within the Republican party.

## National Democratic Party Activities in 1980

Compared to the efforts of the national Republican party, the Democrats appeared as the proverbial 98-pound weakling. The foremost reason was the finan-ial anemia that had sapped the party since 1968. But other reasons were also important. Democratic party committees suffered from Democratic incumbency. Although President Carter had begun his term of office with a commitment to building up the Democratic National Committee, he soon followed the prac-tice of other Presidents by massing his political operations in the White House staff and in his reelection committee.

A well-placed Democratic party staff member described the 1980 role of the DNC "as a surrogate for the Carter-Mondale Committee"; he argued that the best talent was siphoned off to the White House and the presidential cam-paign committee so that "the DNC was a place to put the C-team. . . ." An-other waved off the Democratic National Committee in 1980 as "a joke." He characterized the Carter-Mondale Committee and the DNC as "interchange-able" and argued that "in 1980 the DNC existed solely to assist the President." To support these judgments, he pointed out that the DNC had "ripped off" the party by funding polls by presidential pollster Pat Caddell, but the informa-tion developed from these polls, although circulated to congressional candi-dates, was essentially useful only to President Carter. And the DNC strategy of litigating to keep John Anderson off the ballot would, if successful, have harmed Democratic congressional, state, and local candidates who might be favored by moderate-to-liberal voters drawn to the polls by the Anderson-Lucey ticket.

A different impact of presidential incumbency was the diversion of nation-al party committee efforts to assist the President's renomination. President Car-ter began the nomination campaign running behind Senator Kennedy in the polls; even after he outdistanced Kennedy in primaries and caucuses, the sena-tor continued a long, debilitating race on the issues that lasted until the plat-form was adopted. The nomination contest was also especially distracting be-cause differences on issues were heightened by deep divisions in style, by strong polarizing symbols, and by the emotional hold that the Kennedy family con-tinued to exert on the liberal wing of the Democratic party. The DNC and its chairman scarcely maintained even the fiction of neutrality. "The long, bit-ter nomination campaign left the DNC unprepared in the general election to take advantage of the resources which are usually available—such as prepar-ing state parties to help in the presidential campaign, targeting key precincts, establishing federal accounts to allow spending for federal candidates," accord-ing to a former DNC staff member.

Congressional incumbency, combined with the party's long-standing con-gressional majority, also diminished the role of national Democratic party com-mittees.[48] Incumbents had direct access to fund sources and support groups, and they used this access to seek resources for themselves. Without the sup-port of the party's incumbents—indeed, in competition with them—Democratic party committees found it difficult to raise funds. A congressional staff source argued that "money was not a problem for Democratic incumbents," but "it was the main problem for Democratic challengers." The Democratic party committees could not provide them funds; PACs mainly focused on Democratic incumbents or, to a smaller extent, on Democratic candidates for seats where no incumbent sought reelection.

The staff resources of incumbents also weakened the need for party activity. The public relations and field services provided for Republicans by their party were conducted for Democrats by the staffs of the large Democratic majority in Congress, whose members saw little need to obtain such services through party committees. In this respect, they differed from Republican incumbents, who wanted desperately to become a majority, and from the Democrats of 1981-82, who feared the Republicans might succeed. The attitude of the Democratic incumbents of 1980 worked to the disadvantage of the Democratic challengers.

The staffs of incumbent Democrats not only made party activity seem less necessary but also tended to hinder party activity by making parochial demands on party committees and bitterly criticizing the modest activities undertaken by the Democratic party. The Democratic national chairman observed that "the Democratic party is overloaded with [congressional] staff people who have only a view about their congressman or their district. These people continually complained during the campaign. The National Committee can't sacrifice the national campaign to save a particular congressman."

Incumbency may also have made Democrats careless or overconfident, inviting neglect of party committees and the potential role they might play. From the outset of the 1980 campaign, no one, including the Republican leadership, claimed that the Democratic majorities in Congress would be displaced. The announced Republican goal was to reduce those majorities and then to win control in 1982. A DCCC staff member said "the Democratic congressmen were not prepared for a full court press by the Republicans. Many had not kept up their campaign organizations." In the Senate, "Democratic incumbents last faced the voters in 1974. 1972 scared them, so they started early. But they won so big in '74—because of Watergate and Nixon—that they let down and weren't prepared in 1980." In the House, "the defensive task was immense. Committee leaders in Congress were under assault, and they couldn't believe it. The DCCC had to 'babysit' many of the incumbents because they weren't prepared for the idea of a tough campaign."

The leadership of the Democratic national party may also have had an approach to politics that did not emphasize the kinds of activities the Republicans engaged in. Democratic National Chairman John R. White acknowledged the importance of money—or, in the Democratic case, the lack of it—in waging a campaign. But he disagreed with "the political scientists' conception of politics" as an "organizational type activity."

> Politics is an emotional experience, not a logical one. It's like being in love. You know when you're in love but not why. It's a reflection of a deeper motivation.

A campaign, he argued, cannot be broken down into polls, organization, and all its component parts, even though each of these is useful. Instead,

> when one party gets a tide going, it sweeps everything else up on the beach. The secret is to catch the wave. Timing is the most important thing in politics. Everything else is just a tool to get a wave going or to catch the wave.

Since these "political waves" are largely emotional and cannot be easily predicted or launched, the most important role of parties is to "absorb new movements" and bring people into the party. The Democrats followed this strategy during the Carter administration.

> That is why the Democrats continue to be the majority party. The Democrats spent money for ERA and to develop women's issues. The women's equality issue is the new issue which brings people, men and women, into the Democratic party. This is like civil rights was in the 1950s. The party needs to be continually reborn by bringing new people in.

There is probably great wisdom in this approach. There is only modest evidence showing that organizational activities win modern elections. Moreover, some evidence suggests that both women voters and women activists have responded to the Democrats' favorable posture toward them.[49] Nonetheless, if the party committee leadership begins with this approach, very little party organizational activity is likely to develop, and whatever marginal or modest advantages are generally gained from organizational effort will not be accrued.

The efforts of the national Democratic party must be assessed in this context of financial weakness, incumbency, and attitudes that minimized the role of party organization. In addition, it is difficult to ascertain just what the Democratic party did do in 1980. On the one hand, Leslie Francis, executive director of the DNC, has circulated a report to the National Committee that pointed to much wider efforts than the press or party adherents have generally acknowledged.[50] On the other hand, an influential party staff member has said that "the Francis Report is an outrageous lie." Others confirmed this less stridently and more charitably by pointing to a large number of DNC initiatives that faltered for the reasons mentioned previously.

## ORGANIZATION

The DNC staff in 1980 numbered about 80, many of them occupied with routine operations rather than direct political action. The Senate's DSCC had a staff of only four or five; and the House's DCCC staff was about nine. These tiny congressional committee complements must, however, be seen in the perspective of the substantial staff resources of the Democratic congressional incumbents and also of the small but high-quality staff services provided by the Democratic Study Group, an organization of liberal House Democrats.

The Democrats tried twice following the 1976 election to develop a field network. In 1977 ten "field desks" were established at the DNC to maintain contact with state and local party organizations and with the candidate organizations sustained by incumbent Democratic officeholders. These field desks were scrapped in early 1978. In late 1978, a somewhat smaller field operation was launched; this included operatives actually working in states and localities. But by late spring 1979 this effort was also closed down. Budget stringency was the apparent reason for the short life of these organizational efforts. The Francis Report details a further field operation, which assigned a small number of experienced party professionals to 17 marginal states in the summer of 1980; these field representatives worked on a volunteer basis with state parties to develop campaign and fund-raising plans.

## RECRUITMENT AND TRAINING

There was, at best, only modest recruitment and training activity by the national Democratic party in 1980. With an incumbent President and substantial majorities in both houses of Congress, recruitment of candidates for federal office would have been a lower priority than for Republicans in any case. In addition, the Democrats' budgetary stringency, their preoccupation with protecting incumbents who found themselves subject to the GOP's "full court press," the apparent unpopularity of President Carter and his policies, and the disruption of party activities during the long prenomination struggle left the Democrats with few resources and little energy to recruit candidates for Republican or open seats in Congress. And the Democrats never had any plan for national party involvement in, or encouragement of, local candidate recruitment. A staff member for the Carter-Mondale Committee acknowledged the Democratic recruitment problem:

> Democratic candidates [for Congress] were emerging later than Republican candidates. They had less time to get organized and to get early [campaign] mistakes behind them. The Republican recruitment money and field organization gave them a big lead in fielding strong candidates.

Democratic training efforts were also modest. The DNC and DCCC jointly ran a few training sessions in Texas, Indiana, and Washington, D.C. The Francis Report calculates that representatives of about 100 campaigns participated. This was less training activity than the Democrats had sponsored in 1977-78. The 1980 sessions were, in addition, "not very sophisticated when compared to Republican training of their candidates," according to a Democratic staffer. Another made the harsher judgment that the training sessions were largely "trade fairs" where political consultants hawked their services. He also characterized the sessions as "too conceptual" and not "nuts and bolts oriented."

The Women's Division at the DNC apparently sponsored two or three schools in 1979 and 1980, aimed at women candidates and party workers. The DNC also circulated ten "how-to-do-it" campaign manuals, which the Francis Report says "have been universally praised." Otherwise, there was no national party thrust to build expertise at the local, congressional district, or state level.

## SUPPORT SERVICES

As in other areas, the Democrats lagged in providing support services to their candidates. The strongest efforts were to provide issue information and roll-call analyses. A special focus was in facing attacks by the New Right. Several committee staff members reported spending a great deal of time advising candidates on techniques of responding to New Right accusations on social issues and foreign policy. Simply supplying "correct information" about Democratic positions constituted much of this assistance, but tactics for deflecting or responding to attacks were also a major concern. In a few cases Democratic staff members reported distributing financial disclosure information about Republican incumbents. The DCCC, DSCC, and DSG all made issue information available to Democratic candidates.

The Francis Report makes special mention of the DNC Radio Office's efforts to train some congressional candidates in the development and dissemination of radio "actualities" intended for use by newscasters. The production of these radio comments was provided as an "in-kind" contribution by the DNC, although there is little evidence of widespread use of this service. A DNC staffer who traveled with the Carter campaign taped daily comments, sometimes featuring Democratic state or congressional candidates; these tapes about national issues and the presidential campaign were phoned to radio stations in targeted states from a phone bank at the national headquarters. Otherwise there was no assistance to Democratic candidates in preparing electronic media materials. All national Democratic committees did make some effort to match candidates up with consultants who could effectively assist in media production.

Finally, the Francis Report mentions a major new targeting effort by the DNC. Vote histories were developed on 75,000 precincts in 20 states, compared with information on only 44,000 precincts in 23 states developed in 1976. The report warns that "the tremendous amount of highly valuable work done in 1980 not be lost, as was the case after 1976." Even if the 1980 effort is the first step toward a comprehensive voting information system, the Democrats are far behind the Republicans, whose information base not only covers virtually the whole nation but also includes demographic and other useful information beyond voting in districts.

## FINANCIAL ASSISTANCE

The Democratic National Committee was unable to raise enough money to spend the full $4.6 million allowed by law to support its presidential ticket; it spent about $4 million.[51] Financial assistance to congressional candidates was also slim. National party committees contributed $480,000 to Democratic general election candidates for the U.S. Senate and made coordinated expenditures of an additional $1.1 million. These efforts were only 3.9 percent ($1.6 million) of total direct and coordinated expenditures of $41 million for the campaigns of Democratic general election candidates.

Party committees provided even less assistance to Democratic candidates for the House of Representatives, reflecting the extent to which the Democrats ran an "incumbent preservation" campaign in which officeholders used their influence to raise money for their reelection bids. Party committee contributions were $1 million, and coordinated outlays were $300,000. This $1.3 million in party efforts was only 2.3 percent of the $57.5 million in direct spending and coordinated outlays for Democratic general election candidates for the House of Representatives. Moreover, some of the coordinated expenditures for Democratic candidates were the costs of national committee polls, which were generally regarded as having little real use to congressional candidates.

## VOTER PERSUASION AND MOBILIZATION

The Democrats had neither the money nor the organization to wage party-oriented paid media campaigns in 1980. Except for its attempt to place taped comments with radio newscasters, the DNC's voter persuasion efforts were limited to the secondary benefits accruing to Democrats from the issue information and other assistance given to candidates and used by them in campaigning.

One of the most controversial claims of the Francis Report relates to the DNC's voter mobilization activities. Using polls and targeting analysis, the DNC claims to have registered about 1.1 million new Democratic voters in 15 states at a cost of $750,000 and to have made telephone contact with 5 million voters in 22 states at a cost of about $600,000. About 1.5 million of these calls were to get out the vote; the remainder urged support for the Democratic ticket and sought volunteer workers. The Francis Report claims that a master file was developed identifying 42 million individuals in 200 counties in 22 states as potential Democratic voters. These efforts would certainly constitute one of the most aggressive recent voter mobilization campaigns carried out by the Democrats, apart from the vast efforts mounted by labor unions, although some party leaders consider the claims exaggerated.

## GROUP MOBILIZATION

The Democrats have historically been a coalition party relying heavily on group mobilization. In 1980 the DNC maintained staff liaison personnel for contact with blacks and Hispanics. Union leaders have generally declined to estimate their efforts to persuade, register, and get out union voters. But the general impression among party staff members is that labor efforts in 1980 were below those in some previous years. Labor's doubts about President Carter, including the defection of some of the most politically militant union leadership to Senator Kennedy during the nomination campaign, and the drift of union members to conservative views and Ronald Reagan were advanced as explanations for this slowed pace of labor's efforts.

A somewhat different view portrays union expenditures and efforts in behalf of Democrats as remaining roughly constant from 1976 to 1980. In 1976, organized labor is estimated to have spent $11 million on voter registration and get-out-the-vote efforts as well as political advocacy, most in a fashion carefully "coordinated to benefit the Carter-Mondale ticket."[52] In 1980, union expenditures reached $15 million. About $1.5 million was spent by the Teamsters and other unions supporting Ronald Reagan. The remainder, including some $1.3 million in pro-Carter communication by unions to their members, was spent for labor political activities that "supported Carter, however reluctantly."[53] At best, then, labor activity in behalf of the Democratic ticket almost kept up with inflation from 1976 to 1980.

Like the Republicans, Democrats reached out to PACs for funds and support. Staff members reported occasionally speaking to business and trade association PACs (they were mainly greeted by hostile audiences) and making arrangements for candidates to meet PAC representatives who might contribute to their campaigns. For the most part, contact with PACs was directly handled by Democratic officeholders, since their incumbency gave them access that party committees did not have.

The Democratic advantage in support from PACs continued to decline in 1980.[54] A Democratic staff member put the facts squarely and graphically in comparing the 1980 efforts of the two parties to mobilize PAC support.

> Democratic party organizations went after PACs for their own treasuries. The Republican party went to PACs on behalf of a list of Republican challengers, and they got money for them. The important thing about PAC giving is not the incumbents, but what they give to challengers. Republicans persuaded business PACs to give money to Republican challengers. The Democrats haven't seen PACs as anything except sources of money. Business PACs are doing training, and people they train are manning phone banks for the Republicans. Workshops are being run to train young executives. The Democrats did not reach out to this group in 1980. PACs are bringing a broad base of white-collar workers into politics. The Republicans have gotten their message through to these people through PAC newsletters and by getting speakers before meetings called by PACs in the business world.

If these observations are correct, then 1980 marked a turning point in group mobilization. Democrats continued to work on their traditional coalition, but Republicans apparently appealed effectively both to an increasingly important cluster of organized groups and to individual Republicans for money, workers, and votes.

### COORDINATION

The DNC in 1980 was really a "surrogate" for the Carter-Mondale campaign, one staff member explained. Coordination between the presidential campaign and the national committee therefore was close; indeed, they were one and the same. There was also some coordination between the DCCC and DSCC, primarily because they were housed in the same building. One staff member reported that they exchanged issue information, strategies for dealing with the New Right, assignments related to Democratic party litigation under campaign finance laws, and intelligence received from various state and district contacts. There was almost no cooperation between the presidential campaign, including the DNC, and the congressional party committees or candidates. Since there was no sharing of services, the need for collaboration that was compelling in the GOP was not important among the Democrats.

A congressional party staff member went farther by asserting that the DNC was so closely tied to the presidential campaign that it "had no desire to co-ordinate with any other institution in the Democratic party. Period!" Another was more charitable, spreading the responsibility for Democratic disarray to the party's incumbents, especially senators, who "knew the President was un-popular and wanted to keep their distance." This was confirmed by the more critical Democratic staffer, who acknowledged "there was little or no coordina-tion because everyone [congressional incumbents] was running on their own."

Coordination was made especially difficult in 1980 by the long prenomina-tion campaign and DNC Chairman John White's active campaigning on behalf of the President. Many in the party did not want to become involved in joint efforts under White's leadership because they wanted to avoid the appearance of supporting the President against Senator Kennedy. Certainly White's role as an advocate made it impossible for him to bring the Kennedy and Carter forces together in the way that Bill Brock held regular prenomination planning meetings of representatives of the GOP candidates.

So incumbency and factionalism played major roles in the party's splin-tered efforts in 1980, but the absence of party resources and services made co-ordination appear less important than in the Republican party. Conversely, with-out resources and services, the Democratic party leadership had little leverage to bring the various committees and candidates together into even a loosely knit campaign effort.

## State and Local Political Parties in 1980

State and local parties continued in 1980 to operate largely out of sight; there is little systematic data on their activities. One survey suggests the condition of party organizations on the eve of the presidential contest. About 90 percent of a sample of state party organizations reported that a permanent state head-quarters was maintained in the capital city or a major city, and 11 percent had branch offices. Similarly, 90 percent of state committees had either a full-time state chairman or executive director, a substantial change from the early 1980s when only 63 percent had full-time executives. In addition, while 37 percent of state parties had fewer than five staff members, one-fourth had ten or more. State party budgets averaged $340,000, but the variation was enormous with the smallest having $14,000 and the largest $2.5 million.[55]

More than two-thirds of the state party organizations claimed to operate ongoing electoral mobilization programs involving voter identification, voter registration, or get-out-the-vote efforts. About 55 percent of the state parties engage in at least occasional polling activity. Most parties also offer training sessions for workers or candidates. Large majorities make at least modest contributions to candidates and are involved in candidate recruitment, especially of state legislative candidates; but there has been a decline in both activities over the last two decades.[56] Party activity is strongest among Republicans in all sections of the country, but the largest recent increases in state party activity have occurred among southern Republicans, followed by southern Democrats. The emergence of party competition in the South has apparently spurred organization activity.[57]

A survey of local committees (county, town, or district committees, as appropriate) suggests that Democrats had no organization in only 73 of the 3662 jurisdictions, and a Republican presence was missing in only 209. But in general the party organization presence at the local level was skeletal. In only 8 percent of the districts whose party officers provided information did they report any full-time or part-time staff support. Only 13 percent of the local party organizations maintained year-round headquarters, and only 26 percent had budgets. But 75 percent of the parties met at least quarterly, and 41 percent met nine times or more each year (apparently monthly, except in the summer).[58]

Despite the thinness of the continuing party apparatus, local parties reported a moderate level of campaign activity. In candidate recruitment, about 60 percent reported involvement in seeking congressional candidates, 73 percent in encouraging county office aspirants, and 75 percent in seeking state legislative candidates. Other widespread activities were distributing literature (78 percent), organizing meetings or events (66 percent), conducting telephone campaigns (62 percent), distributing posters or signs (60 percent), and buying advertising (62 percent). In all, local parties were asked about 14 different activities, and the majority reported engaging in at least eight services to candidates.[59]

There is no reason to doubt that in 1980 state and local parties continued the activities they had been engaged in for the previous two decades. In addition, the national party committees themselves were involved in considerable local party activity through the GOP's "Commitment '80" and the DNC's registration and get-out-the-vote drives. Beyond these specific programs sponsored by national party committees, it is difficult to know how much continuing local party activity was focused on campaigns for federal offices.

Some local party activities—such as making contributions to the presidential campaign—are prohibited by law. The elaborate reporting requirements of the FECA may also discourage parties from directly supporting federal office candidates. Nonetheless, a preliminary survey of FEC reports shows that 68 state Democratic party committees in 45 states registered for federal election activity; 71 Republican committees registered in 50 states. Thirty-seven Democratic congressional district party committees registered in 12 states, and 27 counterpart Republican committees registered in 13 states.

Considering the vast number of local jurisdictions (almost 4000) in which local parties might organize, only a handful—124 Democratic committees in

26 states, 186 Republican committees in 27 states — actually registered to spend money in federal election campaigns. In all, FEC-registered Democratic state and local committees reported net receipts of $9.1 million and expenditures of $8.9 million. Their Republican counterparts maintained the long financial lead evident at the national level by raising $33.8 million and spending $34.6 million.

These figures do not portray the full scope of local party activity. The FECA amendments of 1979 exempted party committees from registering or reporting expenditures if they received or made only small contributions (under $1000) and did not spend more than $5000 on such activities as publishing and circulating slate cards or sample ballots, preparing and distributing campaign materials (except mass media advertising), and registering voters or getting out the vote. State and local Republican expenditures for federal office campaigns were roughly $15 million, while Democratic outlays were about $4 million for such purposes.[60] Republican national committee staff members apparently directed contributions from individuals and PACs to local and state party committees to finance their extensive grass-roots activities.

## 1982: Toward an Era of Party Strength?

On November 4, 1980, Ronald Reagan captured the Presidency by a comfortable margin; his party scored a stunning upset by gaining control of the Senate; and the GOP captured 33 additional seats in the House, leaving the Democrats with an edge of 243 seats to 192 and only nominal control. These events challenged both national party organizations. For the Republicans, the question was whether the national party committees would continue their broad-gauge program of party renewal or whether they would become creatures of the White House. For the Democrats, the issue was whether deep internal divisions within the party and the loss of the Presidency would retard efforts to create a party structure that would compete effectively under modern conditions.

The newly selected party leadership in both parties had a strong organizational perspective. On January 17, 1981, Richard Richards, Ronald Reagan's campaign director in the western states, was elected chairman of the Republican National Committee. Described as a "nut-and-bolts and grass-roots politician," Richards's announced strategy was to maintain the comprehensive organizational program already in place and build on it.[61]

A month later, on February 27, the Democratic National Committee named Charles Manatt as party chairman.[62] Manatt had served two terms as Democratic party chairman in California, where he had emphasized fund-raising and party-building activities. He set out to balance a new emphasis on policy development by the party, embodied in a new national policy council, with a determined effort to launch mass-mail fund raising to build a secure financial base for the Democrats. He also pledged to remain neutral in the 1984 contest for the Democratic presidential nomination. During his canvass for the chairmanship, he met with congressional leaders and party officials throughout the nation. He would later endorse changes in party rules that would give party leaders a prominent role in the party's midterm conference and that would assure the seating of 561 members of Congress, state and local elected officials, and party leaders as uncommitted delegates at the national Democratic convention.[63] One report greeted these developments with the headline: "Regulars Reassert Control in Democratic Party."[64] This might overstate the results, but the new national party leadership was plainly committed to rebuilding the party structure.

These efforts in the Democratic National Committee were matched by party-oriented developments in the House of Representatives. Representative Tony Coelho of California was elected chairman of the Democratic Congressional Campaign Committee. Like Manatt, Coelho placed an emphasis on fund raising by party committees. "My people still think of Congressional politics as separate races," he observed. "They don't understand the national dimensions of Congressional campaigns."[65] The "national dimensions" included renewed efforts by the DCCC to provide services to congressional candidates as well as build a stable funding base.

Under strong organization-minded leadership, both parties gained greater financial strength in the period between Ronald Reagan's election and the 1982 congressional polling. The Republican national party committees raised $191.0 million in 1981-82, compared to $130.4 million during 1979-80.[66] Federally reported state and local party receipts were $23.9 million, compared to $33.8 million in 1980. Republicans accelerated their small-giver appeals in 1981 and 1982. National Republican committees reportedly contacted more than 40 million households with their fund appeals, and by 1981 they had an active contributor list variously estimated between 1.7 million and more than 2.0 million.[67]

Democratic dollar gains were not as impressive. In the 1981-82 campaign season, their national party committees raised $31.4 million. This was a modest improvement over their 1979-80 receipts of $23 million. Federally reported state and local party committees reported receipts of $7.6 million, a decline from the $9.1 million they raised in 1980. More impressive was the Democrats' final liquidation of the heavy national party debt that had burdened them since 1968. The DNC and DCCC also made commitments to invest modestly in mail appeals and reinvest the revenues to expand their contributor base. They reportedly raised $2.7 million from mass-mail appeals and reinvested $2.1 million in further appeals.[68] One commentator has assessed 1982 as a year in which "the Democrats demonstrated the self-discipline necessary to develop a successful direct mail program by reinvesting the proceeds of early 'prospecting' mailings into additional solicitations"; and the party's list of contributors consequently increased from 25,000 in 1981 to more than 220,000 in 1982.[69]

The continuing financial vitality of the Republican party allowed it to increase its assistance to party candidates. In 1981-82, Republican party committees contributed $600,000 to general election Senate candidates and made $8.7 million in coordinated expenditures on their behalf.[70] This $9.3 million easily exceeded the $5.4 million the party committed to its Senate candidates during the 1980 campaign season. It represented about 14.9 percent of $62.5 million in total candidate disbursements, only a slight decrease from 1980. Republican general election candidates for the House of Representatives received $4.6 million in party contributions and benefited from another $5.3 million in coordinated expenditures. This $9.9 million was greater than the $5.7 million provided by the GOP to its candidates in 1980; it represented 10.7 percent of the $92.7 million in total GOP House campaign expenditures, a slight improvement from the 9.4 percent provided by the party two years earlier.

Democratic party committees continued to lag well behind the Republicans in candidate support, but they did offer greater help than in 1980. In 1981-82, Democratic Senate candidates in the general election had received about $600,000 in party contributions and $2.3 million in coordinated expenditures. This $2.9 million was 4.6 percent of candidate expenditures of $62.5 million, and it easily outran the $1.6 million (3.9 percent of total expenditures) that the party had provided its 1980 candidates. The Democratic party role in House campaigns was still smaller. Party contributions were $1 million and coordinated expenditures were $689,000, so party assistance constituted only 1.9 percent of reported outlays of $89 million. This was a smaller percent than the 2.1 percent ($1.3 million) that party committees had supplied to House candidates in 1980.

Republican affluence also allowed the party to engage in substantial inter-election activities to give it a strategic advantage at the beginning of the 1982 campaign. The national party committees spent approximately $1 million to provide research and legal assistance to state parties and GOP state officials to assist them to achieve congressional and state legislative apportionments favorable to the GOP. In states where the Republicans dominated state government, such as Indiana, district lines were drawn to their advantage. In other states, especially California and in the South, however, the Democrats managed to devise apportionment schemes favorable to their candidates, despite Republican expenditures for litigation and occasionally for referendum petitions.[71] Indeed, after suggesting that Republicans might gain as many as 12 House seats because of reapportionment, party leaders finally conceded that the party was likely only to "break dead even" when all states had concluded their redistricting activities.[72]

The Republicans also extended their 1980 program of party-oriented, "institutional" advertising to the 1981-82 interelection period. In July 1981 Republicans launched a $500,000 radio and television campaign attacking House Speaker Tip O'Neill and the Democratic tax plan, alleging that it was "no tax cut at all" and promoting President Reagan's alternative.[73] In late September the three national Republican committees launched the $2.3 million first wave of a national advertising campaign touting the theme "Republicans. Leadership that works. For a change." Plainly carrying forward the 1980 theme of "Vote Republican. For a Change." This GOP advertising began at a time when polls showed a slight decline in voter support for the Republicans and Republican congressional candidates.[74] Without funds to pay for a counterattack, the national Democratic party committees filed complaints with the Federal Communications Commission, unsuccessfully seeking time to reply under the fairness doctrine.[75]

In addition to their advertising campaign, the Republican National Committee used its substantial financial resources to wage a grass-roots campaign to mobilize support for President Reagan's tax and budget packages.[76] Organized groups and individual supporters were asked to communicate their support for the President's program to members of Congress. These efforts were largely aimed at Democratic congressmen and therefore had the double effect of putting pressure on them during the legislative session and softening them up for attack during the 1982 campaign.

Both parties made efforts to assist their legislative cause and their incumbents by obtaining free media coverage. The Republican Senate Conference, the tax-supported party organization within the Senate, began providing editorial comments, press releases, issue "updates," and radio actualities to media outlets around the nation. The conference staff also assisted Republican senators by staging press conferences, producing media spots, and writing or editing press releases.[77] House Democrats operated a telephone "boiler room" and mounted a modest mail campaign to develop pressure on their members and on a handful of Republicans to support the House leadership's tax plan. The DCCC sought free publicity with an aggressive news release campaign criticizing Republican congressmen for cuts in social security benefits and student loan programs. But there is little evidence—except complaints by Republican party leaders—that these broadsides gained wide circulation or had much effect.[78] What is notable about these efforts is the national party organizations' acceleration of interelection activity, elaborate and well funded in the Republican case and improvised by the weakly financed Democrats.

Another area of expanded party activity was congressional recruitment. The Republicans began early to identify and encourage strong candidates for the House. Many candidates committed themselves during the late fall of 1981, when the President had successfully pressed his legislative program through Congress and his popularity was high. The prospects of substantial party funding and ample support services were also important factors in attracting strong Republican challengers, however. The fielding of strong candidates helped the Republicans overcome the disadvantage that would ordinarily have befallen them when the economy and the President's popularity deteriorated in the winter and early spring of 1982. Under such conditions, it is the Democrats who should have attracted strong candidates, while able Republican contenders normally would have avoided candidacy because of their calculation that both voters and resource-providing elites would be difficult to woo.

Scholars emphasize the bearing of resource availability and election prospects on the ability of parties to recruit strong candidates. Candidate recruitment, in turn, has a major impact on election outcomes. The 1982 election was described as a special case.

> At present it appears that both parties will be fielding strong challengers in 1982 but for very different reasons. Strong Democratic challengers have been attracted in the usual way: by their belief that serious economic problems and Reagan's declining popularity made it a good year to go after Republican incumbents. Republican challengers have emerged *despite* unfavorable national conditions through the work and money of national-level party committees.[79]

As a result, 1982 was not expected to be as good a year for Democrats as would ordinarily be predicted, because of strong Republican candidate recruitment.[80] This prediction was at least partly affirmed when Republicans lost only 26 seats in the House rather than the roughly 45 seats predicted from the nation's deteriorated economic condition.[81] Hence, "although Democrats achieved moderate advances in 1982, it can be argued that they should have done much better—and the explanation for their relative lack of success is clearly tied to the abundance of Republican money and campaign services."[82]

The Republicans expanded their institutional advertising in 1982, and the Democrats launched a modest campaign of their own. The Republicans spent about $15 million to praise the President, urge voters to "stay the course," and claim credit for cost-of-living increases in social security checks.[83] One Republican advertisement that blamed the nation's economic woes on past Democratic leadership, using look-alike actors representing President Carter and Speaker O'Neill, was quickly withdrawn because of adverse reaction by the press, the public, and congressional leaders.[84]

The Democrats were able to spend only about $1 million for party-oriented advertising in 1982.[85] In one spot announcement a Republican elephant rampaged through a china shop, trampling social programs such as social security. In another, a Baltimore factory worker featured in Republican ads in 1980 recanted his support for the GOP and reported that many of his fellow workers had become unemployed because of the Reagan program. The Democrats were forced to limit their advertising to secondary media markets—such as Sacramento and Flint—in order to gain the widest possible exposure with their limited budget.[86] Nonetheless, the acceleration of Republican institutional advertising and the initiation of Democratic party-oriented media campaigning signal a significant change in the role of national party organizations during campaigns.

Republicans continued to offer strong training programs for their candidates in 1982. In addition, regional party staff members assisted GOP candidates in organizing and conducting campaigns. The Republicans also expanded their polling and media services. They used sophisticated tracking polls in which 150 to 200 persons were sampled on successive days, with the earliest group dropped from a total cumulative sample of about 500 as each new group was polled. These polls showed trends in public opinion and allowed candidates to make continuing adjustments in campaign strategy.[87]

Republican media assistance to candidates in 1982 included the development of campaign commercials and the purchase of media time, which saved candidates considerable sums. One commentary reports that the RNC aided 92 GOP candidates with the production of 180 television advertisements and other media services. This was a dramatic increase from the eight candidates assisted in 1978 and about 50 helped in 1980.[88] Republican party organizations also provided their candidates with extensive research materials on issues and with precinct analysis and targeting data for use in organizing canvasses, registration efforts, and get-out-the-vote drives.

The Democratic program was much smaller. Issues material was prepared and circulated. Labor unions apparently helped Democratic candidates with some polling and precinct targeting, although neither unions nor party committees made these efforts on a scale comparable to Republican programs.

The two parties found themselves going in opposite directions in their assistance to local candidates and parties. The Democratic National Committee hired a well-known political consultant to strengthen Democratic party organizations in 18 states. Voter registration, identification, and turnout were especially emphasized.[89] Democrats were not able to maintain a field staff, and indeed they were forced to reduce staff and expenses in mid-campaign.[90] But they were able to send volunteer consultants and troubleshooters, largely experienced Democratic politicians, into some states and districts to give advice and encouragement to candidates.[91] The DNC's political affairs division worked with state party officials in 16 states to develop a local campaign apparatus to assist candidates for state as well as national offices. Phone and mail lists, data bases, and local political consulting services were developed wherever possible.[92] Democrats also spent between $500,000 and $1 million to assist gubernatorial candidates.

Republicans, who had contributed substantially to state legislative and gubernatorial candidates in the two preceding elections, dropped their contributions from $2.9 million in 1980 to $600,000 in 1982. Another $500,000 was distributed by GOPAC, a Republican political action committee organized specifically to raise money for state campaigns.[93] The Republicans did, however, strengthen their field efforts and training programs for local party workers. In early 1983, the new Republican national chairman, Frank Fahrenkopf, proposed an extensive program to build state and local party strength. His plan would grade state and county parties on their existing effectiveness and their strategic importance in 1984 races; the RNC would then provide the most important and promising party units with staff assistance and financial aid to build up their organizational, campaign, and fund-raising capabilities.[94]

Both parties in 1982 continued the trend toward strong national organization staffs. The RNC was reported to have a staff of 350, the NRCC 84, and the NRSC 40. Democratic staffs were much smaller, but they increased from 1980. This was partly due to Democratic efforts to develop mass-mail fund raising and other activities requiring professional staff and technicians. The DNC staff was 103, the DCCC 32, and the DSCC six. The necessity for extensive national party bureaucracy may be one of the hallmarks of modern politics, which is marked by complex campaign finance regulations and by sophisticated technologies for information gathering, campaigning, fund raising, and political organizing.[95]

## Parties and PACs

While the evidence of party revival is impressive, the importance of parties in the 1980s is still in doubt. Michael Malbin has aptly observed that "for the most part, the [FECA] has neither helped nor hurt the parties; it has simply stayed out of their way."[96] This assessment may be somewhat pessimistic, considering the special contribution and expenditure limits and the public subsidies extended to parties in the FECA and in many state laws. These direct applications of campaign finance laws to parties may actually assist them. But the secondary effects of other provisions of law may hurt parties substantially. F. Christopher Arterton has observed:

> . . . the most detrimental aspects of the [FECA] for political parties come about through the advantages open to institutional competitors. For example, over the past five elections, congressional candidates have become increasingly dependent upon funds channeled through political action committees. . . . At the governing stage, they are real competitors to parties for influence upon the behavior of public officials.[97]

Political action committees in the aggregate now exceed political parties in the amounts of money contributed to candidates and the amounts expended on direct efforts to influence voter choices among candidates. The strength of political action committees is not entirely rooted in law, however. The "nonconnected" committees—mainly ideological and issue-oriented groups unconnected with economic institutions—raise most of their funds through mass-mail appeals. And they devote most of their campaign expenditures to mass media advertising and mass-mail appeals urging voters to support or oppose specific candidates. Their fund-raising and advocacy activities are possible because of modern technology; their authorization for these activities is not found in the FECA but in the Supreme Court's decisions extending First Amendment protection to independent expenditures.

Corporate political committees have grown most rapidly in money and numbers. And it is among them that some authors find the greatest potential for further growth.[98] The FECA's authorization for corporations and unions to establish PACs, to use treasury funds for administration and solicitation, to contribute to candidates through PACs, and to spend treasury funds to engage in candidate advocacy among members, stockholders, and employees has principally spawned these fierce competitors to parties. In addition, PACs created with treasury money can use the contributions they obtain to engage in unlimited independent expenditures urging the public at large to support or oppose candidates. This is the lesson of the Supreme Court's rulings protecting independent expenditures.

The total number of PACs registered with the FEC rose from 608 in 1974 to 3371 at the end of 1982. In 1976, total PAC receipts were $54.4 million. By 1982, PACs boasted receipts of $199.2 million. They have virtually achieved parity with the national political parties, whose 1982 receipts were $222.5 million. (State and local party receipts reported to the FEC were an additional $31.5 million.)

In making contibutions, PACs have already outdistanced political parties. In 1980, PACs contributed $60.2 million to candidates, and they made independent expenditures of another $14.2 million to support or oppose candidates. Party committees, by contrast, made only $6.2 million in contributions and spent $17.4 million in coordinated expenditures in behalf of candidates. Hence, PACs outdistanced parties by more than three to one in candidate advocacy or opposition. This margin was somewhat reduced by party institutional advertising, which in 1980 was about $15 million—virtually all of it on the Republican side.

In 1982, PAC contributions and independent expenditures totaled $92.6 million, compared to party contributions and coordinated expenditures of $24.9 million, a disparity of 3.7 to 1. The parties spent an additional $16 million or more on institutional advertising in 1982. They were also able to offer campaign services, staff support, and other forms of assistance in both 1980 and 1982; but these were unlikely to tip the balance of candidate support from PACs to parties.

PACs and interest groups also compete with parties in traditional campaign activities. "Nonpartisan" registration and get-out-the-vote drives are excluded from the FECA's various limitations and regulations. It is not difficult for unions or corporations to determine which members, employees, or stockholders are most likely to vote for candidates generally favorable toward the institution's position and to target them for voter mobilization efforts.

In addition, the law permits membership organizations, including unions and corporations, to communicate to members, stockholders, or administrative personnel about issues and candidates. Such communications can be made from treasury funds, and they allow the PACs' institutional sponsors to perform the same voter persuasion efforts undertaken by parties.

Independent expenditures by PACs to reach the general public compete with party advertising for candidates as well as party institutional advertising. In 1982, independent expenditures to influence congressional races were $5.7 million, a 143 percent increase from the $2.3 million spent for that purpose in 1980.

Labor's voter mobilization and persuasion activities were greater in 1982 than at any time since 1976, according to one observer.[99] More than 3 million members of union households were registered to vote; an estimated 150,000 labor volunteers and several thousand staff members canvassed union neighborhoods and conducted registration and get-out-the-vote drives. Mass-mail appeals were added to the long-standing union technique of using phone banks to contact union members. The AFL-CIO's Committee on Political Education supported these efforts with a computerized data bank containing information on most of the 15 million affiliated union members. There is little evidence of direct corporate appeals to stockholders or employees on behalf of specific candidates; but companies may expand these efforts as they become more familiar with the law. A trade association, the Realtors' PAC, could serve as an example for business campaigning. In 1982 it made telephone calls and direct mail appeals in behalf of its endorsed candidates.[100].

The parties have attempted to direct PAC contributions and activities. The RNC and NRSC assigned staff members full-time in 1980 to work with PACs. These staffers met with PACs in Washington and at specially called meetings in major cities across the country, urging them to funnel contributions to Republican candidates, especially challengers with strong prospects of winning. In 1982 the Republicans expanded their outreach to PACs, and the Democrats assigned staff members to similar efforts.

But parties have strong competitors for the privilege of guiding PAC money and activities. The liberal National Committee for an Effective Congress and the conservative Committee for the Survival of a Free Congress provide lists of favored candidates in races judged to be closely contested. Most influential are efforts of the Business-Industry Political Action Committee (BIPAC), which has been providing lists of business-oriented candidates in competitive races since the mid-1960s. BIPAC holds periodic meetings for PAC staff members in Washington and other cities to brief them on key races. In 1982, the Chamber of Commerce attempted to influence and direct PAC resources by conducting a closed-circuit, satellite-transmitted program for 250 PAC managers in seven cities to urge their support for 100 business-oriented candidates. Moreover, as PAC managers themselves become more sophisticated about politics, develop independent sources of information, and gain confidence in their own judgment, they will increasingly make political decisions without the need for party or interest group guidance.

One of the nation's leading students of political parties has suggested that PACs might align themselves more or less with political parties with which they largely share program commitments and philosophic outlook.[101] Liberal and labor PACs would be expected to be loosely affiliated with the Democrats; conservative, business, and trade association PACs would cooperate with the Republicans. While this pattern has already emerged for liberal, labor, conservative, and some business PACs, most trade associations, professional groups, and corporate PACs have followed a more independent strategy. They have focused heavily on incumbents, in part because of their need for access in government.

The corporate PACs have been characterized as "risk averters"; yet in 1980 there was evidence that they made a dramatic last-minute effort to contribute to strong Republican challengers rather than continue to support Democratic incumbents.[102] In 1982, Republican incumbents received a substantially larger share of total corporate PAC contributions, while Democratic incumbents received a slightly smaller share of those contributions.[103] Corporate PAC support for Republican challengers declined sharply. A former Republican party staff member said after the 1982 election:

> The flirtation by PACs [in 1980] with high-risk politics quickly reversed itself this year for two reasons. PACs looked at the candidates and concluded by last June that this would not be a year to sacrifice their position with certain incumbents and, second, that the Democrats had very creative lobbying efforts among the PACs.[104]

On balance, PACs have emerged as major competitors of political parties. They raise almost as much money, and they give much greater financial support to candidates. They have the legal right to engage in unlimited independent expenditures; and the law allows them to use treasury funds for advocacy and voter mobilization among their members, stockholders, and employees. They are not yet aligned along party lines, and the parties' efforts to direct and channel PAC resources are increasingly duplicated, thus diluted by others.

## Into the Future

When party exertions ended on November 2, 1982, the voters gave the Democrats a victory at the polls. In the House of Representatives, the Democrats held 264 seats to 166 for the Republicans, a net Democratic gain of 26 seats. The Democrats also captured seven additional governorships, increasing their hold on state executive offices from 27 to 34. After a six-year decline in state legislative strength, the Democrats increased their seats by 33 in the nation's upper houses and 129 in the lower chambers. This small shift was sufficient, however, for the Democrats to retake four of the five chambers captured in 1980 by the GOP, while the Republicans were able to capture two new chambers. The Democrats increased the number of legislatures in which they controlled both houses from 28 to 34, while the GOP's dominance of legislatures declined from 15 to 11. On the other hand, the Republicans fought the Democrats to a standstill in the U.S. Senate, where they retained a 54 to 46 margin. And some observers credited the Republicans with a strong showing in House races, where their loss of 26 seats fell short of the 40 to 45 seat loss that might have been predicted from national economic conditions. This Republican resistance to national trends was credited to party financial resources and organizational efforts.[105]

MONEY

Money thus emerges as the first and most essential element in political party activity and effectiveness in the 1980s. The Republican's financial bumper crop, well beyond the party's estimates, allowed the recruitment and subsidization of candidates, a broad range of field activities, an effective headquarters operation, an impressive mass media campaign, and, of course, the raising of still more money. The Democratic party, in debt, drifted and bailed during most of 1980. The campaign waged by the Democrats was, at bottom, fueled by the advantages of incumbency and supported by the efforts of allied groups such as unions and racial or ethnic minorities.

In 1982, Democratic fund raising improved somewhat, and the first signs of a mass-mail funding base became visible. Incumbency and national economic conditions, together with greater Democratic alertness in meeting Republican attacks, allowed Democrats to make modest electoral gains. But the underlying organizational basis for continuing competitiveness was not yet in place.

Since the first tide of small Republican contributions through the mail, during the Goldwater campaign of 1964, GOP fund raising has been based on strongly worded appeals attacking the Democrats. As the opposition party, the Republicans have been able — except during the Watergate period — to select their messages and targets with care. Can party fund raising, long based on inflammatory and negative messages, continue to be successful during periods of incumbency? The answer seems a resounding yes. The national Republican committees raised $191 million in the 1981-82 cycle. Both their small-contributor base and their large-contributor contingent increased substantially. However, with only 14.2 percent of their funds coming from individual gifts of $500 or more and another 0.6 percent from PACs, the Republicans are still raising the vast majority of their money in small gifts.

Democratic financial prospects are much more uncertain.[106] Contributing to politics is disproportionately an activity of the well educated, higher-income groups, and those who engage in other political activities as well. These groups are primarily Republican. Even contributors to the Democratic telethons of the early 1970s were drawn from these groups, leading the authors of a major study of telethon givers to suggest that the failure of the Democrats' fourth telethon may have reflected the exhaustion of a narrow base.[107]

A further complication for the Democrats is the ideological division within the party. Givers to the Democratic telethons were more liberal than other Democratic contributors in 1972 and much more liberal than the Democratic electorate.[108] DNC finance director Peter Kelley explained that 1980 Democratic mass-mail fund raising had lagged because the party was appealing to "moderate Democrats, who do not carry the same level of commitment to political causes as conservatives or liberals."[109]

Democrats draw the support of a vast majority of the nation's liberal activists, but the party is so diverse that it includes important groups of moderates and conservatives as well. It would therefore risk alienating important constituencies if it pitched its financial appeals to one ideological group within the party coalition.

> [For the Democrats] . . . emulating the Republicans may be difficult. When the GOP began to coordinate technology and grass-roots politics in the late 1960s, the party was generally agreed on a conservative philosophy. Their agreement on basic tenets enabled the development of a successful direct-mail fund-raising effort.[110]

A senior staff member at the DNC has forcefully argued, however, that the purported difficulties facing the Democrats are largely chimerical. They mistakenly assume that large demographic and political patterns control mass-based financial support, which is in fact a relatively small-scale activity. The Republican giver list of 1.2 million people in 1980 was, he pointed out, less than 1 percent of the voting-age population, about 1.5 percent of those who voted, and just under 3 percent of those who voted for Ronald Reagan. In the spring of 1982 the *New York Times*/CBS poll showed that 52 percent of respondents still identified themselves as Democrats, while only 36 percent announced for the Republicans.[111]

If only 1.5 percent of these 88 million Democratic identifiers were to contribute, the argument goes, the party's funding base would exceed the 1.2 million givers claimed by the Republicans in 1980. And certainly that small percentage of Democratic identifiers has the financial ability and political interest to contribute, if they are reached with appealing messages. This argument seems somewhat more plausible with the Democrats' successful development of a giver roster exceeding 200,000 in 1982. Attacks on right-wing Republican leaders and Reagan programs proved popular among potential Democratic donors. Whether the Democrats can build a stable and substantial financial base to pay for the expensive technologies and expertise necessary for political action in the modern era remains untested, however.

The Democrats did increase the proportion of their money coming from small givers between 1980 and 1982. In 1980 national Democratic committees received 40.5 percent of their funds in individual contributions of $500 or more and another 7.5 percent from PACs. In 1982 the corresponding percentages were 19.7 percent from large individual contributions and 8.9 percent from PACs. The 28.6 percent total is a marked decrease from the 48.0 percent of 1980, although still well above the Republicans' 14.8 percent for 1982. In both percentage and absolute terms, therefore, the Democrats have a long way to go.

CENTRALIZATION
A second important direction of American parties as they move beyond the 1980 election is their "centralization" or "nationalization."[112] American parties were largely national entities during the earliest years of the Republic, when members of congressional caucuses not only nominated presidential candidates but gave leadership to state and local parties. That period ended decisively in

1828. From the Jacksonian era to the early 1970s, parties were largely "confederations"—to use Leon Epstein's persuasive formulation;[113] state and local organizations commanded the major resources of politics—patronage, nominations for public office, public services, and the local activists necessary to mobilize the vote. Recent developments have strengthened the national party organizations, while the vitality of local and state committees has become uncertain.

It has been argued that presidential politics has become centralized because public financing puts large sums of money into the hands of the candidate's national organization and requires it to monitor and audit the uses of that money to achieve the disclosures required by law.[114] State-by-state expenditure limits during the nomination contest and the total spending limits in both the nomination and general election battles also concentrate authority centrally. That trend may now be weakened, however, by the 1979 amendments, which allow local parties unlimited spending and important reporting exemptions for grass-roots activity.

Perhaps as important as this legal centralization is the emergence of "presidential parties" consisting of activists in each political party who continue from one presidential campaign to the next. They are largely ideological in orientation, and they provide a nationwide support base for candidates that tends to displace the local and state leaders who formerly dominated the nomination process.[115] At least some of these activists assume party offices, thus bringing a national orientation to local and state party structures as well as to the conduct of presidential nomination and election campaigns.

Nationalization is also occurring as a consequence of national Republican party fund raising, services, and technical skills. In recent years the RNC has attempted to persuade state parties to develop plans for party expansion and for campaigns. State and local party leaders and candidates are influenced by the national Republican party because of the valuable—indeed, increasingly indispensable—money, services, and know-how the RNC provides to local and state as well as federal candidates.

John Bibby, observing the "RNC's demonstration of the party nationalizing capacity of national committees, when armed with significant campaign resources,"[116] quotes a Republican state chairman as saying, "I figure that I should go along with the National Committee as much as possible because I want as much of their money as I can get."[117] Leon Epstein has aptly compared this mode of nationalization within the Republican party to the nationalization of government services promoted by the grant-in-aid device.[118]

A further element in the centralization of parties is the development of "party law" by the national parties. The Democratic Charter is virtually a nationwide party constitution. Courts have upheld Republican rules apportioning national convention delegates and Democratic regulations prescribing delegate selection processes. In 1982 the Democrats amended their rules to regulate the timing of presidential primaries; and their decision automatically to seat 561 state and local party and government officials presses their assertion of control over delegate selection farther than before. The First Amendment right of association may still be interpreted to allow state as well as national parties extensive control over the manner in which they conduct internal party business and name their candidates. In any case, the authority of national parties has been greatly strengthened by Democratic party actions and the judicial decisions which approved them.

## PROFESSIONALIZATION

A third trend in party affairs is professionalization in politics. Indeed, perhaps this should be referred to as "re-professionalization," since the ward and district leaders of an earlier time were plainly professionals, who not only earned a livelihood from politics but also masterfully employed the techniques of their time to persuade, register, and mobilize voters. The modern trend toward professionalization is especially pronounced in the Republican party. It employs a large staff whose functions are clearly differentiated so that expertise and continuity of operation characterize party activities. Although there is some movement of staff among committees and between various staff roles, there is considerable stability in the Republican staff, which is made possible largely because the party has sufficient resources to hire capable people, pay them well, and assure them a satisfying working environment. The remarkable stability of the professional Republican party bureaucracy was apparent after the 1980 election when only a handful of party organization staff people, mainly at senior levels, left party committees to take positions in the Reagan administration.

A crucial element in the professionalization of the GOP is the relative insulation of party staffs from internal party politics and, more important, from the ideological activists who dominate presidential campaigns.[119] There is an anomaly here: Those who contribute the money to support the Republican party apparatus, largely in response to ideological appeals, have no direct voice in selecting party leaders or making decisions about party organization or activities. At most, they can withdraw their financial support if they become discontented. But they are so numerous that they are unlikely to do this in concert, except in response to some event like Watergate. As a consequence, the Republican party is able to maintain a professional bureaucracy that directs vast resources and activities precisely because the skilled professionals who know how to conduct modern political operations are largely insulated from local and state party organization influence and, indeed, even from those who provide the resources for the national party committees.

The Democratic party, by contrast, has not yet developed a professional, insulated party bureaucracy. Pay has been low, and most Democratic staff members have moved to White House or congressional staff positions as opportunities have presented themselves. Others have gone into the consulting business — a reflection of the incumbency orientation and coalition nature of the Democratic party. One Democratic staff member pointed out that the intense pressure on the Democratic committees to raise funds and the overload imposed on small staffs to provide a wide array of political services quickly produce "burn-out" at the DNC. Finally, of course, the Democratic party's reform rules have often put ideological and presidential activists very much in charge of the national party committees, with the consequence that staffs have tended to be deeply embroiled in the party's internal rifts and to change with each new party chairman and each new presidential nominee.

It remains to be seen whether the Manatt regime as DNC chairman, paralleled by Representative Coelho's leadership at the DCCC, marks the beginning of a more bureaucratic structure within the Democratic national party organizations. Both Manatt and Coelho have organizational perspectives. Both are committed to expanding the Democratic funding base, and both understand that continuity in professional staff and extensive financial investment are essential to accomplish that. In 1982 the staffs at the DNC and the DCCC were somewhat larger than previously, although not yet so large as to suggest extensive specialization of functions or bureaucratization.

## PARTIES AND OFFICEHOLDERS

The most important question about the future of American party organizations is whether they are developing new strength in their relations with party officeholders. For advocates of party government, the central purpose of political parties is to propose policies, mobilize support to elect candidates who support those policies, and assure that officeholders bearing the party label enact and administer those policies.

Other theorists view parties as having a less central role in policy making, but most would agree that parties should have some coherence on issues, that they should mobilize electoral support and thus partly insulate officeholders from pressures from narrower interest groups, and that they should be vehicles for the negotiations and compromises necessary to make policy. Indeed, they welcome the diversity of groups and blocs within each major party. This diversity forces negotiation over issues and promotes a moderate brand of politics. The coalitional character of parties has made them, in the words of one of their admirers, "the unwitting but forceful suppressors of the 'civil-war potential' we carry always in the bowels of our diverse nation."[120]

It should be clear that American parties, at least in the modern era, have never had the ideological coherence or organizational strength to endorse and then enact policies.

> . . . parties in America fall well short of the ideal of democracy or even of the reality of parties in many other countries. They are especially ineffectual in the task of formulating policies and transforming them into governmental programs, and thus they get only low marks for their performance of the great, overriding function of channeling and disciplining the struggle for power.[121]

This assessment was written in 1960, before the occurrence of two major developments that have further weakened parties in governance. First, modern campaign technology now allows candidates to reach voters directly, using mass media, computer-generated mailings, telephone banks, polls, and paid professional staff to perform the canvassing and get-out-the-vote functions once performed by party workers. The principal requirement for modern campaigning is ample financing.

Second, the emergence of PACs has greatly changed the character of politics and government. They provide much of the money needed by candidates to wage modern campaigns and also wage such campaigns themselves, through independent expenditures for media advertising, advocacy among members and stockholders, and registration and get-out-the-vote drives. And they participate directly in the governing process, bypassing party brokers in both the party organization structure and in the Congress. Indeed, they are increasingly bold in pressing candidates, as a condition for receiving campaign support, to respond to very specific questionnaires about their stances on policy issues. They have thus achieved a degree of commitment to their programs that parties have never been able to obtain for their own platforms. PAC influence in the policy process may have become so pervasive in 1982 that restless members of Congress will seek another round of "reform" legislation aimed at curbing PAC influence. [122]

During the opening session of the 97th Congress there were remarkable signs of Republican unity, with party members in both houses voting almost unanimously for the President's budget and tax plans. But proposed cuts in social security benefits as well as a proposed second round of budget cuts in social services broke the unity of the Republicans in 1982.[123] There is no evidence that the strong GOP party organization was able to influence defecting Republicans to support the party leadership.

The Democrats have also been divided, but their divisions are along expected, traditional lines. The House Democrats who abandoned the party leadership to support the Reagan tax plan were mainly conservatives, generally from the South, who had balked at party policies in the past. At the same time, there was impressive unity among moderate and liberal Democrats, who supported the party leadership despite the absence of party organization strength.

When the 98th Congress convened, the Democrats showed a rare degree of organizational discipline. The party leadership had been placed firmly in charge of the Steering and Policy Committee and the Rules Committee by the reforms of the 1970s. They proceeded to oust Representative Phil Gramm from the House Budget Committee because of his open collaboration with the White House and the Republicans in shaping and passing President Reagan's budget and tax program in the prior session. Representative G. V. Montgomery, who had also sided with the Republicans, was given only a 16 to 11 vote in the Steering and Policy Committee to retain his chairmanship of the Veterans' Affairs Committee. He was finally approved by the caucus only after "repenting" his position and making clear that he "got the message" to support the party leadership whenever possible. [124] In a bold move, the House leadership brought its own budget proposal to the floor early in the new session—indeed, early on the very evening that President Reagan would make a nationwide television appeal for *his* program—and passed it virtually without Republican votes.

There is other evidence of renewed party coherence. Roll-call voting along party lines, after dropping dramatically from the 1890s to the 1920s, has actually remained reasonably constant across the six intervening decades and has not shown particularly great erosion in recent years. Ideological voting is strong in Congress and tends to fall along party lines.[125] Voters are also now more ideologically consistent in their views, and they tend more than previously to vote for candidates who share their views. Party activists have tended also to be ideological or program oriented in outlook, and that pattern is confirmed by contemporary evidence.[126]

One commentator has argued that "politicians and voters have been rearranging themselves on either side of the progressive-conservative line of cleavage that was defined so sharply in the 1930s, so that the diversity within each party is lessening year by year."[127] He does not, however, credit the party organizations with a role in the newly revived party cohesion. Indeed, he concludes that "fortuitously, events over which the two parties themselves have no control now bring the promise that the two major parties may shortly be—if they are not already—more ideologically united than they have been for more than a hundred years."[128]

Has the revitalized Republican party been a force to influence the conduct of its officeholders by its disposition of resources in campaigns? It might be supposed that the party would attempt to recruit candidates whose views were consistent with the President's or that it would deploy its financial resources and services specially to assist party loyalists. Indeed, the RNC did enter a few primaries in 1980 and 1982. But in the end, the party organization's campaign "decision making was not based upon the policy positions of the candidates; as in the grand old days, estimates of electability dominated the party choice. According to the RNC's counsel, "neither ideology nor issues entered into decisions of which candidates should receive the maximum support."[129]

Once in office, members of Congress may be largely invulnerable to party pressure based on past or prospective allocations of party campaign resources. There was some suggestion early in the 97th Congress that party leaders and the White House were attempting to influence the behavior of Republican members of Congress by directly or indirectly suggesting that campaign funds might be withheld if they did not support the President's program.[130] But there is certainly no evidence that such tactics were widespread or that they were successful. As James Sundquist has observed, even the regular use of such tactics is unlikely:

> . . . once a new member takes his seat, whether money proves to be an instrument of continuing discipline will depend on the willingness of party leaders to withhold funds in future campaigns from members who defy the leadership. If past

experience is a guide, it can be assumed that such penalties would be imposed only on the rarest of occasions, and the Republicans therefore, despite their greater resources, will encounter much the same degree of difficulty the Democrats have always faced in molding a cohesive majority party out of an assemblage of individualists.[131]

It would be difficult under any but the most extreme circumstances for a party to refuse resources to a party incumbent, despite his independence on many policy issues. A congressman of the opposition party, elected because the party had withdrawn support from the incumbent, would certainly not be more congenial on policy. And his vote would be assured to help the opposition party organize the chamber, dominate committee action, and support the opposition leadership on procedural and rules votes.

It is unclear, in any case, how much effect the withdrawal of party campaign resources would have on an incumbent. Even with its newly developed financial muscle, the Republican national parties account for only between 10 and 16 percent of the contributions and coordinated expenditures in behalf of their congressional candidates who run in the general election. Assuming some targeting of these funds, they still are not so large a share of campaign resources as to allow the party to exercise much influence over officeholders. The party's role is generally larger in the campaigns of challengers than of incumbents because officeholders have other sources of support. Once elected, these challengers too can look elsewhere for campaign funds. The relatively small role of party committees is illustrated by the 1980 funding patterns in Congress: PACs contributed twice as much as parties to general election candidates for both houses, with incumbents faring especially well and thus less beholden to parties for support. In grass-roots support, like financial support, PACs are competitors with parties, thus reducing the reliance of officeholders on the party apparatus. Labor unions engage in canvassing, registration, and get-out-the-vote drives. They mail campaign endorsements to members and distribute slate cards. They also hold conventions to endorse candidates and adopt comprehensive programs touching virtually all public issues. A labor spokesman has argued that "there are really four political 'parties' operating today, only partly within the confines of the two older parties: business and the New Right on one side, and labor and the Liberal Left on the other."[132]

A former business PAC staff person has described political action committees as the "precincts of the '80s." She has argued:

> The demise of the neighborhood as the center of social or economic activity . . . has signaled the demise of neighborhood or precinct politics. Today, we are not influenced by neighborhood leaders, but rather by particular occupational or socioeconomic group leaders. Consequently our politics are no longer neighborhood based, but directed toward particular occupational or socioeconomic groups. . . . PACs have clearly substituted socioeconomic or occupational groups for geographic or neighborhood associations. Now the ABC Corporation PAC is a socioeconomic precinct along with Precinct 42, a geographic precinct.[133]

Party leaders seem acutely aware that the fulfillment of party objectives requires close connection between party committees, on the one hand, and candidates and officeholders, on the other. The Democrats have adopted delegate selection rules that will automatically seat a large number of party and elected officials in the national convention. In addition, Charles Manatt, the new DNC chairman, made appearances before Democratic members of Congress and the party's governors as part of his campaign for that post. Since taking office he has worked closely with Democratic congressional leaders and governors.

On the Republican side, former RNC chairman (1981-83) Richard Richards was openly critical of ideological PACs, warning that their inflammatory attacks on some Democrats caused sympathy for their targets and brought public criticism onto regular Republicans, with whom the public identifies these attacks. The pressing of single issues by ideological PACs, who are "not reponsible to anyone," may also jeopardize the total Republican program in Congress, Richards argued. Finally, he complained that ideological PACs overstated their roles in electing President Reagan and Republican members of Congress and consequently made exaggerated policy claims on them—especially to oppose abortion, school busing, and homosexual rights and to take hard-line approaches to left-leaning foreign regimes. Whether these party counterattacks on PACs will be successful, considering the emerging parity of PACs in political resources and activities, is one of the major imponderables in assessing the influence party organizations will have on party candidates and officeholders in the 1980s.

Perhaps the question should be turned on its head. There has recently been great emphasis on "executive centered" party coalitions and "candidate centered" politics.[134] It is said either that party officeholders now dominate parties or that incumbents reach out directly to party voters, making party organizations "the odd man out."[135] In either case, the influence of party organizations on candidates and officeholders, and therefore on policy making, would be negligible. The Democratic National Committee was plainly a catspaw of the Carter White House. This was not true of presidential campaign activists: a considerable number of them supported Senator Kennedy for the nomination, and they insisted on pressing their case on the national convention floor. Both the DCCC and DSCC are arms of congressional incumbents. But contrary to conventional wisdom, they have not devoted their efforts exclusively to aiding sitting congressional Democrats.[136]

The RNC is a more interesting case. It has developed financial independence from the party officeholders, and it has worked closely both with nonincumbent candidates and with party leaders at the local and state as well as national levels. When it became apparent, before the 1980 national convention, that Ronald Reagan would be the Republican nominee, some of his closest allies called for the removal of RNC Chairman Bill Brock and a "housecleaning" of the party staff. Reagan received more than 100 calls and letters from important party leaders and officeholders in support of Brock.[137] And he did retain Brock during the campaign.

Both White House and RNC staff members made clear in interviews, however, that Reagan could have displaced the RNC leadership and staff if he had insisted on it. The selection of Richard Richards as RNC chairman after the election confirmed the ultimate authority of the President over the RNC as, is traditional. And when White House political operatives became disenchanted with Richards—partly because of his outspokenness about conservative PACs— they first supplanted his authority at the RNC, then forced him into retirement and replaced him with the former Nevada GOP chairman, Frank Fahrenkopf. [138]

Both Republican congressional committees are dominated by the party's officeholders. But both also showed independence—and had sufficient resources —to commit funds, staff, and services to nonincumbents, thus taking the broad view that the party's interests were in electing a congressional majority rather than the narrow view that every resource and effort must be bent solely to aid Republican incumbents. Despite the independence of the GOP congressional committees, there is still a measure of presidential influence evident in their operations. Senator Bob Packwood, under whose leadership the NRSC built up its finances from $2 million to $49 million, was ousted as chairman and replaced by Senator Richard Lugar, largely because of Packwood's criticisms of President Reagan for ignoring the needs of women and minorities. [139]

On balance, the Republican party has effectively adapted to the "cash economy" of modern politics; has developed a professional staff able to provide the expertise, technology, and services essential to politics in the modern age; and has gained some insulation from ideological activists and contributors. But it has not developed substantial influence over policy making by Republican officeholders. Indeed, influence tends to run the other way, with officeholders in a position to sway the course of party affairs if necessary. But the national Republican party's effectiveness in building party organization and aiding candidates does have a substantial secondary influence on policy: By electing Republican candidates, who are mainly conservative, the RNC and its financial and activist supporters promote the conservative approach to government to which they are committed.

The Democrats have not yet become effective in raising the money, providing the services, or establishing the professional staff required in modern politics. In 1982 there were tentative efforts at the DNC and DCCC to modernize national party structures and operations following the Republican model. The liberal presidential campaign activists have had considerable effect on the candidate selection process, and they have nationalized the party by formal rule making. But a Democratic President may still dominate the party organization if he wishes. The exclusion of Democratic officeholders from the national convention and from the midterm conference hurt the party organization even more than it hurt Democratic elected officials, causing the party leadership to court their renewed participation in the 1980s. The national Democratic party, like its Republican counterpart, has developed virtually no direct influence over national policy making. Whether the Democrats have the constituency or the leadership to follow the Republican lead in financing and building a modern, service-providing national party organization in the 1980s is still problematic.

## Notes

1. The literature is momentous. Among the well-argued pieces are William J. Crotty and Gary C. Jacobson, *American Parties in Decline* (Boston: Little, Brown, 1980); Jeane J. Kirkpatrick, *Dismantling the Parties* (Washington, D.C.: American Enterprise Institute, 1978); Austin Ranney, "Political Parties: Reform and Decline," in *The New American Political System*, ed. Anthony King (Washington, D.C.: American Enterprise Institute, 1979), 213-48; and Edward C. Banfield, "Party 'Reform' in Retrospect," in *Political Parties in the Eighties*, ed. Robert Goldwin (Washington, D.C.: American Enterprise Institute, 1980), 20-33.
2. Norman Nie, Sidney Verba, and John Petrocik, *The Changing American Voter* (Cambridge, Mass.: Harvard University Press, 1976), chap. 4.
3. Julius Turner, *Party and Constituency: Pressures on Congress*, rev. ed. by Edward Schneier (Baltimore: Johns Hopkins University Press, 1970), 15-39.
4. Ranney, "Political Parties," 231-45; Frank Sorauf, *Party Politics in America*, 4th ed. (Boston: Little, Brown, 1980), chap. 9.
5. See, for example, Cornelius P. Cotter and John F. Bibby, "Institutional Development of Parties and the Thesis of Party Decline," *Political Science Quarterly* 95 (Spring 1980): 1-27; Gerald M. Pomper, ed., *Party Renewal in America* (New York: Praeger, 1980); and Xandra Kayden, "The Nationalizing of the Party System" in *Parties, Interest Groups, and Campaign Finance Laws*, ed. Michael J. Malbin (Washington, D.C.: American Enterprise Institute, 1980), 257-82. A cautiously optimistic report on the growing strength of state party organizations is Robert Huckshorn, *Party Leadership in the States* (Amherst: University of Massachusetts Press, 1976). See also James L. Gibson, Cornelius P. Cotter, John F. Bibby, and Robert J. Huckshorn, "Assessing Institutional Party Strength" (paper presented at the 1981 annual meeting of the Midwest Political Science Association).
6. Robert Keefe, "Presidential Campaign Strategy Under the Law," in Malbin, *Parties, Interest Groups*, 233-37; and Richard B. Cheney, "The Law's Impact on Presidential and Congressional Election Campaigns," in ibid., 239-40, 247.
7. Robert Huckshorn and John Bibby, "State Parties in an Era of Political Change," in *The Future of American Political Parties*, ed. Joel Fleishman (Englewood Cliffs, N.J.: Prentice-Hall, 1982), 80-82.
8. For a detailed review of the 1980 presidential election, see *The American Elections of 1980*, ed. Austin Ranney (Washington, D.C.: American Enterprise Institute, 1981).
9. Federal Election Campaign Act of 1971, P.L. 92-225, 86 Stat. 3 (1972); Revenue Act of 1971, P.L. 92-178, 85 Stat. 51, as amended 87 Stat. 138 (1972); Federal Election Campaign Act Amendments of 1974, P.L. 93-443, 88 Stat. 1263 (1974); Federal Election Campaign Act Amendments of 1976, P.L. 94-283, 90 Stat. 475 (1976); and Federal Election Campaign Act Amendments of 1979, P.L. 96-187, 93 Stat. 1339 (1979). The Supreme Court has said that "partisan politics bears the imprimatur only of tradition, not the Constitution." *Elrod* v. *Burns*, 427 U.S. 347, 369 n22 (1976).

10. Joseph Starr, "The Legal Status of American Political Parties, 1," *American Political Science Review* 34 (June 1940): 439-55; "The Legal Status of American Political Parties, 11," *American Political Science Review* 34 (September 1940): 685-701; and Robert Huckshorn, John Bibby, Cornelius Cotter, and James Gibson, "State Law and Party Rule on Party Organization: Implications for Institutionalization" (unpublished paper, 1982).

11. Ruth Jones, "State Public Financing and the State Parties," in Malbin, *Parties, Interest Groups,* 283-303; and Ruth Jones, "Patterns of Campaign Finance in the Public Funding States" (paper presented to the 1982 annual meeting of the Midwest Political Science Association).

12. *Federal Election Commission v. Democratic Senatorial Campaign Committee,* 454 U.S. 27 (1981).

13. Michael J. Malbin, "What Should Be Done about Independent Campaign Expenditures?" *Regulation* 6 (January/February 1982): 46.

14. *Buckley v. Valeo,* 424 U.S. 1, 14-23, 64-69 (1976).

15. *Federal Election Commission v. Republican National Committee,* 487 F.Supp. 280 (1980), *aff'd,* 100 S.Ct. 1639 (1980). For a critical comment on the result, see Marlene Nicholson, "Political Campaign Expenditure Limitations as Unconstitutional Conditions," *Hastings Constitutional Law Quarterly* 10, no. 3 (Spring 1983).

16. Herbert E. Alexander, *Financing the 1976 Election* (Washington, D.C.: Congressional Quarterly, 1979), 6.

17. 2 U.S.C. s. 441a(a)(3)(1976).

18. David Adamany, "Letters," *Regulation* 6 (May/June 1982): 3.

19. Ranney, "Political Parties," 242.

20. Recommendations to allow small private contributions to presidential candidates are advanced in Note, "Independent Political Committees and the Federal Election Laws," *University of Pennsylvania Law Review* 129 (1981): 988-99; Adamany, "Letters," 2. The argument that such contributions would weaken parties is fashioned by Malbin, "Independent Campaign Expenditures," 45.

21. See references in note 6.

22. Robert Agranoff, "The New Style of Campaigning: The Decline of Party and the Rise of Candidate-Centered Technology," in *The New Style in Election Campaigns,* ed. Robert Agranoff (Boston: Holbrook, 1976), 23-42.

23. *Democratic Party v. Wisconsin* 450 U.S. 107 (1981); *Cousins v. Wigoda* 419 U.S. 477 (1975).

24. *Opinion of the Justices* 385 Mass. 1201, 434 N.E. 2d 960 (1982).

25. *Rivera-Rodriguez v. Popular Democratic Party,* 50 U.S.L.W. 4599 (S.Ct. 1982).

26. *Ripon Society v. National Republican Party,* 525 F.2d 548 (D.C. Cir. 1975), *rev'd,* 525 F.2d 567 (D.C. Cir. 1975) (en banc), *cert. denied,* 425 U.S. 933 (1976).

27. Frank Sorauf, "Political Parties and Political Action Committees: Two Life Cycles," *Arizona Law Review* 22 (1980) 451.

28. Unless otherwise noted, all expenditures and contribution figures in the chapter are drawn from Federal Election Commission reports or press releases. These sources are cited separately only when specific financial figures are used. Political party receipts and expenditures for 1979-80 are reported in "FEC Releases Final Figures on 1979-80 Major Political Party Activity" (Federal Election Commission press release, February 21, 1981; corrected release). These receipts omit public grants awarded to the parties to pay for their national convention costs.

29. Herbert E. Alexander, "Making Sense About Dollars in the 1980 Presidential Campaigns," chap. 1 in this volume.

30. Timothy Clark, "The RNC Prospers, the DNC Struggles as They Face the 1980 Elections," *National Journal* 12 (September 27, 1980): 1618. See also Republican National Committee, *1981 Chairman's Report* (Washington, 1981), 12-13, 22-23, 31-32.

31. Clark, "RNC Prospers," 1618.

32. Large-contributor activity before enactment of the FECA is reported in Herbert E. Alexander, *Financing the 1972 Election* (Lexington, Mass.: Lexington Books, 1976), 370-99.

33. Reports of large gifts to the Republican National Committee in 1980 are found in *1981 Chairman's Report,* 32-33.

34. Richard Cohen, "Democrats Take a Leaf from GOP Book with Early Campaign Financing Start," *National Journal* 13 (May 23, 1981): 923.

35. John W. Ellwood and Robert J. Spitzer, "The Democratic National Telethons: Their Strengths and Failures," *Journal of Politics* 41 (August 1979): 328-64; and Alexander, *Financing the 1976 Election,* 396.

36. Brock's activities as chairman of the Republican National Committee have gained wide attention. See, for example, Michael J. Malbin, "The Republican Revival," *Fortune,* August 25, 1980, 85-88; Morton Kondracke, "The G.O.P. Gets Its Act Together," *New York Times Magazine,* July 13, 1980, 18-47; and Edward Walsh, "Bill Brock: Architect of Republican Revival," *Washington Post,* November 20, 1980, A21-A24.

37. Thomas E. Mann and Norman J. Ornstein, "The Republican Surge in Congress," in Ranney, *American Elections of 1980,* 284.

38. Thomas E. Mann and Raymond E. Wolfinger, "Candidates and Parties in Congressional Elections," *American Political Science Review* 74 (September 1980): 617-33; Gary C. Jacobson, *Money in Congressional Elections* (New Haven: Yale University Press, 1980); and Gary C. Jacobson and Samuel Kernell, *Strategy and Choice in Congressional Elections* (New Haven: Yale University Press, 1981).

39. Mann and Ornstein, "Republican Surge," 264-66; *1981 Chairman's Report,* 21.

40. Huckshorn and Bibby, "State Parties," 82.

41. John Bibby, "Political Parties and Federalism: The Republican National Committee Involvement in Gubernatorial and Legislative Elections," *Publius* 9 (Winter 1979): 231.

42. *1981 Chairman's Report,* 12.

43. "FEC Releases Final Statistics on 1979-80 Congressional Races" (Federal Election Commission press release, March 7, 1982; corrected release).

44. *1981 Chairman's Report,* 12.

45. Ibid., 24-25.

46. Xandra Kayden, "Parties and the 1980 Presidential Election," in *Financing Presidential Campaigns: An Examination of the Ongoing Effects of the Federal Election Campaign Laws upon the Conduct of Presidential Campaigns* (Cambridge, Mass.: Institute of Politics/John F. Kennedy School of Government, Harvard University, 1982), 6.12.

47. Ibid., 6.13.

48. F. Christopher Arterton, "Political Money and Party Strength," in Fleishman, *Future of American Political Parties,* 110.

49. Dom Bonafede, "Women's Movement Broadens the Scope of Its Role in American Politics," *National Journal 14* (December 11, 1982): 2108-11.
50. Leslie Francis, *The Democratic National Committee and the 1980 Elections* (Washington, D.C.: Democratic National Committee, 1981).
51. Alexander, "Making Sense About Dollars," 21.
52. Ibid., 22.
53. Ibid.
54. "FEC Releases Final PAC Report for 1979-80 Election Cycle" (Federal Election Commission news release, January 21, 1982). For details, see Gary Jacobson, "Money in the 1980 and 1982 Congressional Elections," chap. 2 in this volume.
55. Gibson et al., "Assessing Institutional Party Strength," 18-20.
56. Ibid., 24-27.
57. Cornelius Cotter, James Gibson, John Bibby, and Robert Huckshorn, "State Party Organizations and the Thesis of Party Decline" (paper presented at the 1980 annual meeting of the American Political Science Association), p. 8 and figures 1-3.
58. Gibson et al., "Assessing Institutional Party Strength," 38.
59. Ibid., 37-40.
60. Alexander, "Making Sense About Dollars," 21.
61. "Party's Organizational Man," *New York Times,* January 18, 1981, 18; Adam Clymer, "New G.O.P. Chairman Criticizes Party's Right Wing," *New York Times,* January 18, 1981, 18.
62. Alan Murray, "Campaign Blitz Makes Manatt DNC Chairman," *Congressional Quarterly Weekly Report 39* (February 28, 1981): 394.
63. Rhodes Cook, "Democrats' Rules Weaken Representation," *Congressional Quarterly Weekly Report 40* (April 3, 1982): 749-51; Susan Smith, "Power Shifts South for '84 Democratic Meet," *Congressional Quarterly Weekly Report 41* (February 12, 1983): 351-52.
64. Rhodes Cook, "Regulars Reassert Control in Democratic Party," *Congressional Quarterly Weekly Report 39* (September 26, 1981): 1857.
65. Steven Roberts, "Parties Stamped with National Role," *New York Times,* May 4, 1982, A28.
66. "FEC Reports Republicans Outspent Democrats By More Than 5-to-1 in '82 Elections" (Federal Election Commission press release, April 26, 1983).
67. Kayden, "Parties and the 1980 Presidential Election," 6.11; and Larry Sabato, "Parties, PACs, and Independent Groups," in *The American Elections of 1982,* ed. Thomas Mann and Norman Ornstein (Washington, D.C.: American Enterprise Institute, 1983), 75.
68. Rhodes Cook, "Democrats Develop Tactics: Laying Groundwork for 1984," *Congressional Quarterly Weekly Report 40* (July 3, 1982): 1595.
69. Sabato, "Parties, PACs, and Independent Groups," 83.
70. "FEC Releases Data on 1981-82 Congressional Spending" (Federal Election Commission press release, May 23, 1983).
71. Christopher Buchanan, "GOP Takes Advantage of Redistricting," *Congressional Quarterly Weekly Report 39* (August 29, 1981): 1588; and Edward Walsh, "GOP Plays Chess with Indiana Hill Democrats," *Washington Post,* May 11, 1981, A4.
72. Fred Barnes, "GOP Aide Pessimistic on Redistricting Gains," *Baltimore Sun,* February 3, 1982, A1; Robert Gurwitt, "Redistricting Bitter Disappointment to GOP," *Congressional Quarterly Weekly Report 40* (November 6, 1962): 2787-88.

73. Robert Timberg, "GOP TV Ad Portrays O'Neill as the Grinch Who Stole the Tax Cut," *Baltimore Sun,* July 24, 1981, A1.

74. Paul Taylor, "GOP Launches Ad Blitz 13 Months Before Vote, Aims to Deflect Griping," *Washington Post,* September 29, 1981, A7.

75. "GOP T.V. Campaign Evokes Complaint," *New York Times,* October 21, 1981, A7.

76. Arterton, "Political Money and Party Strength," 130-31.

77. Irwin Arieff, "Senate Republicans Using Incumbency to Advantage in Snappy Media Operation," *Congressional Quarterly Weekly Report* 39 (June 6, 1981): 993-95.

78. Martin Tolchin, "G.O.P. Cries 'Foul' on News Release," *New York Times,* October 19, 1981, A18.

79. Gary Jacobson and Samuel Kernell, "Strategy and Choice in the 1982 Congressional Elections," *PS* 15 (Summer 1982): 429.

80. Ibid., 429-30.

81. Sabato, "Parties, PACs, and Independent Groups," 80.

82. Ibid.

83. Ibid., 78.

84. Adam Clymer, "G.O.P. Ads Feature Carter and O'Neill Lookalikes," *New York Times,* May 18, 1982, A16; and Howell Raines, "A Preview of Democrats' New Commercials," *New York Times,* September 22, 1983, A24.

85. Sabato, "Parties, PACs, and Independent Groups," 85.

86. David Broder, "Dixie the Elephant Is Smashing in Democratic Ad Debut," *Washington Post,* September 15, 1982, A18.

87. Sabato, "Parties, PACs, and Independent Goups," 76.

88. Ibid., 77.

89. Ibid., 84.

90. Bill Peterson, "Cash Short Democrats Cutting Back Staff, Travel," *Washington Post,* July 23, 1982, A2.

91. Stevens, "Parties Stamped with National Role."

92. Bob Gurwitt and Tom Watson, "Democrats Recoup State Legislative Losses," *Congressional Quarterly Weekly Report* 40 (November 13, 1982): 2849.

93. Ibid.

94. "GOP Acts to Better State, County Units," *Washington Post,* March 29, 1983, A5.

95. Martin Schram, "GOP Meets Reality—on the Button," *Washington Post,* May 16, 1982, A1.

96. Malbin, "Independent Campaign Expenditures," 45.

97. Arterton, "Political Money and Party Strength," 118.

98. Edwin M. Epstein, "PACs and the Modern Political Process" (paper delivered at the Conference on the Impact of the Modern Corporation, 1982); and Epstein, "Business and Labor." Federal Election Commission reports detail the growth in the number of PACs and in their financial activity: "FEC Releases Final PAC Report for 1979-80 Election Cycle" (Federal Election Commission press release, February 21, 1982); "PACs Increase in Number" (Federal Election Commission press release, January 14, 1983); and "1981-82 PAC Giving Up 51%" (Federal Election Commission press release, April 29, 1983).

99. Sabato, "Parties, PACs, and Independent Groups," 88-89. On labor's political role generally, see Bill Keller, "Organized Labor's Vital Signs Show Waning Political Clout; But Numbers Don't Tell All," *Congressional Quarterly Weekly Report* 40 (August 28, 1982): 2111-18; and "Once a Washington Power, Labor Now Plays

Catch-up in Lobbying and Politics," *Congressional Quarterly Weekly Report* 40 (September 4, 1982): 2189-95.

100. Sabato, "Parties, PACs, and Independent Groups," 96.

101. Sorauf, "Political Parties and Political Action Committees," 463.

102. Epstein, "PACs and the Modern Political Process."

103. Cohen, "Giving Till It Hurts," 2145.

104. Ibid.

105. Richard Cohen, "1982 Post Mortem," *National Journal* 15 (April 2, 1983): 712.

106. David Adamany, "Commentary," in Malbin, *Parties, Interest Groups,* 317-18.

107. Ellwood and Spitzer, "Democratic National Telethons," 861-62.

108. Ibid., 852-58.

109. Clark, "RNC Prospers," 1619.

110. Rhodes Cook, "Chorus of Democratic Voices Urges New Policies, Methods," *Congressional Quarterly Weekly Report* 39 (January 17, 1981): 137.

111. "With an Eye on Elections," *New York Times,* April 25, 1982, 4E.

112. A perceptive treatment of this subject is Leon D. Epstein, "Party Confederations and Political Nationalization," *Publius* 12 (Fall 1982): 67-102. See also Bibby, "Political Parties and Federalism"; and Charles H. Longley, "National Party Renewal," in Pomper, *Party Renewal in America,* 69-86.

113. Epstein, "Party Confederations," 1-3.

114. Kayden, "The Nationalizing of the Party System," 262, 264-65; Keefe, "Presidential Campaign Strategy"; and Cheney, "The Law's Impact."

115. John Kessel, *Presidential Campaign Politics: Coalition Strategies and Citizen Response* (Homewood, Ill.: Dorsey, 1980), 32-65.

116. Bibby, "Political Parties and Federalism," 234.

117. Ibid., 236.

118. Epstein, "Party Confederations," 26-27.

119. Ibid., 28-30.

120. Clinton Rossiter, *Parties and Politics in America* (Ithaca, N.Y.: Cornell University Press, 1960), 59.

121. Ibid., 51.

122. Paul Taylor, "Efforts to Revise Campaign Laws Aim at PACs," *Washington Post,* February 28, 1983: A1; and Jeremy Gaunt, "Campaign Financing Faces Senate Scrutiny," *Congressional Quarterly Weekly Report* 41 (January 22, 1983): 170.

123. Andy Plattner, "Congress in 1982: Stirrings of Independence," *Congressional Quarterly Weekly Report* 40 (December 31, 1982): 3143; and, "Presidential Support Study Shows Reagan Rating Fell Ten Percentage Points in 1982" *Congressional Quarterly Weekly Report* 41 (January 15, 1983): 94-97.

124. Andy Plattner, "House Panel Seats Assigned; Democrats Tighten Control," *Congressional Quarterly Weekly Report* 41 (January 8, 1983): 4-6.

125. William Shaffer, "Party and Ideology in the House of Representatives," *Western Political Quarterly* 35 (March 1982): 92-106.

126. Herbert McClosky, Paul Hoffman, and Rosemary O'Hara, "Issue Conflict and Consensus among Party Leaders and Followers," *American Political Science Review* 54 (June 1960): 406-27; Thomas A. Flinn and Frederick Wirt, "Local Party Leaders: Groups of Like Minded Men," *Midwest Journal of Political Science* 9 (February 1965): 77-98; David Nexon, "Asymmetry in the Political System: Occasional Activists in the Republican and Democratic Parties: 1956-64," *American Political Science*

*Review* 65 (September 1971): 716-30; and Nie, Verba, and Petrocik, *Changing American Voter,* 200-209.

127. James Sundquist, "Party Decay and the Capacity to Govern," in Fleishman, *Future of American Political Parties,* 58.

128. Ibid., 57.

129. Arterton, "Political Money and Party Strength," 129.

130. Rowland Evans and Robert Novak, "Nixon Style Noted in Tax Bill Fight," *Detroit News,* August 16, 1982, 11A.

131. Sundquist, "Party Decay," 52.

132. David Jessup, "Can Political Influence Be Democratized? A Labor Perspective," in Malbin, *Parties, Interest Groups,* 53.

133. Lee Ann Elliott, "Political Action Committees — Precincts of the '80s," *Arizona Law Review* 22 (1980): 540-41.

134. Judson James, *American Political Parties* (New York: Pegasus, 1969), 163-70; and Sorauf, *Party Politics in America,* 350-58.

135. Sorauf, *Party Politics in America,* 358.

136. Arterton, "Political Money and Party Strength," 112-15.

137. Malbin, "Republican Revival," 88.

138. Bill Peterson, "White House Tightens Its Control Over GOP," *Washington Post,* December 11, 1981, A6; "GOP Staff Changes Leave Richards Weakened," *Baltimore Sun,* December 23, 1981, A5; and "GOP's Richards to Quit," *Congressional Quarterly Weekly Report* 40 (October 9, 1982): 2657.

139. "Packwood Ousted as Campaign Head," *Congressional Quarterly Weekly Report* 40 (December 4, 1982): 2973.

THEODORE J. EISMEIER AND PHILIP H. POLLOCK III

# 4. Political Action Committees: Varieties of Organization and Strategy

It would be difficult to name a recent electoral trend that has attracted more critical attention, or stirred more popular debate, than the remarkable rise of a new form of political organization: the political action committee (PAC). In 1980, 2155 PACs gave $55 million to House and Senate campaigns. In 1982, political committees continued to grow, both in numbers—2655 were active in federal elections—and in financial strength—$83.6 million in direct contributions to congressional candidates. (For more details, see the appendix in this volume, tables A.14-A.15.) PACs have begun to rearrange the channels through which money flows into politics, and they may, it has been argued, signal a change in patterns of legislative access and influence.

These developments have spawned a burgeoning literature on several fronts. There has been, for example, a heightened attention to the legal context of PAC formation and regulation.[1] And the unforeseen growth in the number of corporate committees has sparked a polemical debate between the advocates and detractors of the PAC "phenomenon." Indeed, the growth of this organized mode of fund raising and spending raises some important issues. The rise of PACs, it has been argued, portends the centralization or "nationalization" of campaign finance—a development that will lead to the detachment of congressmen from their electoral constituencies.[2] Moreover, the incumbent-oriented behavior of these organizations has been said to bode ill for the fortunes of challengers, who are already at a distinct electoral disadvantage.[3] More broadly, the way political action committees spend their money has been seen to imply serious problems for representative government because, as Sorauf observes, "all evidence suggests that PACs are chiefly motivated to give money by a strategy of maximizing legislative access and influence."[4] These related concerns are vividly summarized in Adamany's troubling characterization:

> Even when PACs do not focus mainly on obtaining direct economic benefits, they create a problem for representative government. Because money is transferable, PACs nationalize funding sources. They collect ample treasuries in small individual gifts from many locales, centralize those funds in the hands of institutional officers, and make large contributions in strategically important races anywhere in the country. The real and effective financial constituency in these circumstances

is the PAC and its leadership, not the small givers to campaign warchests. The candidate knows the programs and objectives of the PAC, and it is to the PAC officers that preferred access is given. These nationally centralized institutions thus compete with local constituents, including those who supply political resources, for the attention of public officials. . . .

While important constitutional values involving speech and association and the civic virtue of greater individual participation may be promoted by the growth of PACs, it is difficult to be sanguine about their adverse effects on political competition and accountability, on economic, ideological, and partisan balances, and on the policy-making process. More than a minor threat to democratic politics has accompanied whatever happy consequences have flowed from the emergence of PACs.[5]

All these things—the nationalization of resources, the purchase of access and influence, the distortion of partisan balance and electoral competition—comprise an orthodoxy of sorts for serious students of political action committees. What evidence can be brought to bear on the accuracy of this characterization?

That political action committees prefer to influence congressmen and not only congressional elections is a point of agreement among many knowledgeable observers. That PACs actually succeed in their legislative purposes is a point to which scholarly analysis is only beginning to speak. A few correlational studies have connected PAC spending with congressional behavior,[6] but they cannot help us to untangle cause and effect: Do congressmen change their behavior in response to (or in anticipation of) PAC largess, or do PACs alter their contribution patterns in response to (or in anticipation of) the voting behavior of congressmen? Simple correlations tend to confuse these two different effects. Studies that account for the simultaneity of votes and money have begun to appear in the literature;[7] and they provide more convincing evidence. These studies support this substantive conclusion: Compared to the other influences on congressional voting—ideology, party, constituency interests—the effect of PAC spending is small. PAC strategies, it appears, are remarkably unsophisticated. Instead of targeting their resources for maximum legislative effect (e.g., giving to a member of Congress uncommitted on the PAC's favored bill), political action committees tend to reward the past behavior of congressmen positively predisposed toward the interest group's legislation to begin with. This is the crudest and least effective of all "exchange" strategies:

> . . . money was used to reward a legislator for his past voting without regard to whether he truly did the group a favor or whether his future behavior was likely to be influenced by a contribution. These results are not consistent with the concept of a "rational" contributor.[8]

Political action committees prefer to support candidates who are more likely to win; and incumbents' seniority and committee assignments can be important, if not decisive, in choosing whom to support. But beyond these blunt access-seeking maneuvers, PACs do not seem to be living up to their nefarious, vote buying reputations.

In fact, PAC behavior is considerably richer and more varied than even the above tendencies would suggest. In perusing the Federal Election Commission's records, one is struck more by the variation in PAC spending allocations than by the monotony of these patterns. Why do some PACs spend all or most of their money on nonincumbents? Are these the well-financed organizations that can afford such risks or the underfunded PACs with little to lose? What lies behind a strategic option based on independent expenditures? Is this tactic the exclusive preserve of the much-publicized ideological PACs, or do larger organizational forces explain its use? The aggregate data, too, suggest these questions. After all, by focusing on the general tendency of political action committees to support incumbents, it is easy to miss these interesting and substantial departures: In 1979-80 almost 20 percent of all PACs spent over half their congressional budgets on challengers, and more than 40 percent allocated less than half their budgets to incumbents.[9]

To be sure, some political committees do fit the characterization with which we began. They are well-heeled, highly centralized, Washington-based access seekers; and they probably are influential in the policy-making process. But many—indeed most—PACs are less formidable organizations. They have small budgets, few staff, and chronic problems of fund raising, communication, and organizational maintenance. The typical PAC, too, is headquartered outside Washington and thus is not so privy to the day-to-day machinations of the policy "insiders." More generally, when one looks past the most visible manifestations of PAC behavior, one sees an "almost exotic diversity" in size, structure, and strategy.[10]

Political action committees may be most profitably studied as organizations that vary systematically on the basis of several intragroup dimensions. Here we suggest that four organizational variables, in particular, have important effects on strategy. First, PACs that maintain a Washington office behave very differently from their non-Washington counterparts. Second, as PACs grow in financial size, they begin to alter their spending patterns in interesting and, we think, counterintuitive ways. Third, all else being equal, PACs with "parent" organizations may differ predictably from PACs with no organizational sponsor and so may PACs with different types of parents. Finally, the strategies PACs adopt will depend on both their objective interests and organizational ideologies.

These attributes of political action committees reflect meaningful organizational differences: the degree of centralization, the potential for risk taking, and the presence (or absence) of a formalized constituency to whom the PAC is accountable. Furthermore, we are convinced that these internal differences provide explanations for the ways PACs spend their money as important as, or more important than, the simple knowledge of what bills they favor or what legislative purposes they seek. PACs are not, as it turns out, influence-maximizing actors guided by questionable ethics and armed with limitless dollars and perfect information. They are political organizations whose behavior turns on a variety of decision rules and whose spending strategies are shaped by the internal structures they have and the financial resources they control.

## Questions Worth Asking

### THE WASHINGTON OFFICE

We start with whether what PACs do depends on where they sit. There are good reasons to expect Washington-based PACs to behave differently from other committees. One pole of this difference is widely remarked: Washington representatives normally enjoy a good measure of strategic independence; and they tend to become pragmatic, incumbent oriented, and narrowly concerned with legislative access. Three prominent features of "nationalized" PACs help account for this.

First, the presence of a Washington office indicates an important disjunction between the organizational and decision-making aspects of the PAC. National trade and labor PACs, for example, rarely conduct their own fund-raising, "membership" drives. They prefer to leave this task to the organization's state and local committees. Funds are then channeled to national offices that are usually (at least for trade and membership PACs) obliged by contract to redistribute a certain percentage to the state and local affiliates. The remainder, however, may be allocated by Washington representatives relatively independently of local pressure.

Second, the Washington PAC's staff often works in close proximity to the parent organization's Washington lobbyists, frequently in the same suite of offices. (PAC staffers typically refer to these lobbyists, with no discernible sense of irony, as the group's "political people.") The lobbyists' resources—the contacts they maintain, the information they command—doubtless are useful and influential for PAC decision makers, and vice versa.

Third, Washington PAC representatives are likely to depend on other members of the Washington community for information, if not strategic counsel. Certain well-established Washington PACs, such as the Business-Industry Political Action Committee (BIPAC), are generally recognized by other PAC directors as important sources of information about congressional campaigns. BIPAC publishes a regular newsletter, and it even conducts seminars and workshops for neophyte organizers. Indeed, the dominant role of some committees is that of "go-between" for congressmen and the leaders of Washington-based PACs. For example, Americans for Constitutional Action (ACA), in addition to compiling and disseminating its well-known rankings of incumbents, sponsors fund-raising dinners that bring conservative congressmen together with checkbook-wielding PAC officials. (The ACA's *own* congressional campaign budget, oddly enough, is small and inconsequential.)

The Washington PAC, in short, is structurally remote from its donors and is liable to become immersed in a network of "coalition partners" who share some legislative purpose.[11] This may explain why a recent study of 71 corporate committees finds that Washington representatives have strongly incumbent-oriented spending strategies.[12]

The presence of a Washington headquarters — and the remoteness and centralization that may go with it — is treated as a "given" by the scholarly orthodoxy on political action committees. But the Washington PAC is the exception to the rule, encountered only now and then as one studies the data.[13] Indeed, there is some reason to believe that the increase in the number of committees, especially the growth of corporate PACs, may be associated with a decentralization of PAC resources. The registration files of the FEC contain the names of many state-level PACs that contribute to congressional candidates but whose main interests are in state and local contests. Also, state laws regulating solicitation and financial disclosure may differ from federal regulations. This, according to Budde,[14] has encouraged many corporations to establish state PACs, not as fund-raising conduits that channel money to the national organization (the "parent/child" model), but as separate fund-raising and decision-making entities (the "independent adult" model). Furthermore, as Sorauf points out, in many corporate PACs there is a "natural tension between the 'inside Washington' pragmatism of the lobbyists, their desire to maintain access and open doors, and the purer ideological impulses of management at the home office."[15] This tension often is decisive. For many PAC experts, the salience of local pressure "is the chief explanation for allocation decisions that appear to fall short of the canons of rational political [i.e., legislative] strategy."[16]

Thus we expect that the presence or absence of a national headquarters is a very important organizational variable affecting the spending allocations of political action committees. Indeed, for labor unions, corporations, and trade associations it is not inaccurate to speak of "two worlds" of PAC behavior: the insiders' world of legislative pragmatism in the Washington community; and the less centralized world of the home office and local affiliate in which donor preferences as well as ideological predispositions may be of more importance. For nonconnected PACs, on the other hand, a Washington location may signal less a difference in tactics than an effort to give the PAC's views a national showcase.

## The Parent Organization

In addition to location, the parentage, if any, of PACs may influence strategies of action. The FEC recognizes six kinds of political action committees. These are based on characteristics of the committee's sponsor, not on organizational properties of the PAC.[17] Even so, these categories are routinely treated by scholars as surrogates for differences in policy preferences and legislative goals. We think it is more useful to view the FEC's categories as reflecting both policy-related differences and differences in internal structure. Most important, the internal lives of the five kinds of PACs with parent organizations differ markedly from the internal workings of PACs with no organizational sponsor. The decision makers for nonconnected PACs have no responsibility—not even nominal responsibility—to any cohesive group of donors who share a profession or workplace. Thus the leaders are free to pursue ideological, challenger-oriented strategies, or to spend independently of any candidate organization. This "entrepreneurial" style of fund raising and spending contrasts sharply with the more "participatory" organizational model of connected PACs.[18] Connected committees tend more than nonconnected PACs to support incumbents, and they spend in a way that suggests the influence of donors on allocative decisions.

There are, of course, well-established partisan differences between business and labor PACs. Unlike some recent analysts, however, we do not assume that other aggregate strategic differences are the results only of differences in "doctrinal disposition." Rather, we think such strategies ought to be considered as possible products both of policy differences and organizational differences.

BUDGET SIZE

The most obvious and in many ways most theoretically interesting variable affecting PAC behavior is size. Here we find somewhat divergent views in the PAC literature and the apposite literature in organization theory. To the extent that size is closely related to professionalization—and that is certainly true for the non-Washington PACs, the smaller of which are typically run not by political professionals but by part-time executive labor—we might expect the larger PACs to follow most closely the "insider" strategy of dispensing goodwill money among incumbents. On the other hand, such professionals may also be better connected to national party and PAC networks, from which they might learn about electable challengers from, say, the slick material on "Opportunity Races" supplied by the Republican National Committee. Armed with this information about such electoral prizes and perhaps trying to curry party favor, large, professionalized PACs might in some instances be more likely to support challengers.

Moreover, if departures from a pure incumbency strategy can be regarded as "innovations," theory and evidence about organizational behavior suggest that such departures might be most likely to take place among large, resource-rich PACs.[19] Thus, small PACs may have only enough resources to accomplish very basic objectives, and for those with legislative purposes, that might require, first, the funding of key incumbents. As PACs grow larger they might, of course, increase the size of such gifts, but at some point they might also begin to spread their largess to less important incumbents and eventually to challengers. For example, Realtors PAC, the biggest giver in 1980, gave to hundreds of incumbents, but also to 105 challengers and 60 open-seat races. For these reasons, we would expect that regardless of the impact of professionalization, risk taking in the form of supporting nonincumbents would actually be most prevalent in the larger PACs.

INTEREST AND IDEOLOGY

A final point tends to get lost in the stereotypical view of PAC strategy: Observed diversity in PAC strategies reflects very different interests and ideologies. Although there is a tendency in much of the literature simply to assume a substantial homogeneity of interests and tactics at least within PAC types, even the narrowest economic analysis would suggest otherwise. Clearly, firms in different kinds of industries have different things to win or lose from government, and those differences may affect a broad range of strategic behavior. Thus one might, for example, want to look for possible differences between "accommodationist" PACs, which seek to preserve and incrementally expand government benefits by supporting incumbents of the party of government, and "adversarial" PACs, which seek either redress or perhaps retribution for some perceived government wrong.

Although accommodationist PACs, it seems, would be the most common by far, ideology could in some instances incline PACs toward a more adversarial position. Not all PACs even have a coherent ideology, but some do. That at least is what our reading of Margolis's recent work on the theory of collective action leads us to expect:

> Even in organizations that to an outsider look like associations to advance narrow self-interested concerns there will be a substantial effort to develop an ideology explaining how the goals the group seeks are actually in the interest of society at large, or consistent with and even required by some higher ethical authority. . . .[20]

Of course, ideology need not always get in the way of practical strategic choices. Yet for PACs that have relatively diffuse legislative goals or whose parent organizations have more effective ways of achieving those goals, ideology may have an autonomous effect.

It is beyond our present purpose to consider the issue of ideology in detail. What we do hope to show is that for reasons either of interest or ideology, PACs representing different kinds of industries do in fact adopt different strategies.

## PAC Portraits

In order to match these ideas against data, we examined the behavior of 1349 nonparty political action committees in the 1980 election. These constitute all the PACs that were active in 1979-80 and made total contributions to federal candidates of at least $5000 in the period January 1, 1977, through December 31, 1980. Together these PACs accounted for almost all nonparty PAC spending in 1980, since most of the excluded PACs are organizations in name only that spent nothing or virtually nothing. Our information on the PACs in question, compiled in *The PAC Directory*,[21] includes all the most frequently cited FEC data—total contributions, contributions to incumbents, and so forth. But it also includes other information—the number of candidates supported, the average contribution, the Standard Industrial Classifications of corporate PACs, and more—which provides a much richer data base for the organizational inquiry in which we are now engaged.[22]

We begin with some obvious questions. How big are the budgets of PACs? To how many candidates do they contribute, and how large are their contributions? How do they vary in their distribution of largess to incumbents versus challengers and Democrats versus Republicans? As we suggested earlier, what emerges from a closer look even at the summary data about PACs is a more complex picture than the usual stereotypes. In the first place, there is the great range of size and activity. Table 4.1 shows the percentage distributions of PACs according to budget size, number of donees, and average contributions. The most striking feature of the data is the modesty of PAC operations, particularly when we remember that hundreds of the smallest PACs are excluded here.

TABLE 4.1.
OVERVIEW OF MAJOR PACs: DOLLARS AND DONEES
(IN PERCENT)

| | Nonconnected N = 113 | Trade N = 328 | Labor N = 140 | Corporate N = 786 | All N = 1349 |
|---|---|---|---|---|---|
| Total direct contributions to candidates | | | | | |
| 0-$9,999 | 40 | 41 | 31 | 36 | 37 |
| $10,000-24,999 | 22 | 25 | 24 | 30 | 28 |
| $25,000-49,999 | 14 | 13 | 14 | 18 | 16 |
| $50,000-99,999 | 11 | 11 | 10 | 12 | 11 |
| $100,000-199,999 | 9 | 5 | 7 | 3 | 5 |
| $200,000-299,999 | 3 | 2 | 3 | .5 | 1 |
| $300,000 and over | 2 | 4 | 11 | 0 | 2 |
| Total number of donees | | | | | |
| 0-12 | 30 | 27 | 41 | 21 | 26 |
| 13-25 | 21 | 17 | 11 | 22 | 20 |
| 26-50 | 26 | 23 | 9 | 24 | 22 |
| 51-75 | 7 | 9 | 7 | 13 | 11 |
| 76-100 | 4 | 5 | 4 | 8 | 7 |
| 101 and over | 5 | 19 | 27 | 12 | 15 |
| Average contribution per donee | | | | | |
| 0-$499 | 20 | 46 | 21 | 46 | 42 |
| $500-$999 | 28 | 27 | 36 | 42 | 36 |
| $1,000-$1,499 | 25 | 11 | 16 | 8 | 11 |
| $1,500-$1,999 | 10 | 5 | 14 | 3 | 5 |
| $2,000 and over | 17 | 11 | 13 | 1 | 6 |

PACs making total direct contributions of $10,000 or less comprise 37 percent of the total, while those with budgets of more than $300,000 account for only 2 percent of all PACs. Most of the PAC giants have homes either in trade/membership organizations or labor unions, but even here the percentage of such PACs is quite small.

A similar pattern is found in the number of candidates supported. More than a quarter of the PACs gave to a dozen or fewer candidates and almost half gave to no more than 25. To be sure, there are many PACs, particularly among trade organizations and labor unions, with widespread, "national" candidate connections, but the more usual case is limited and probably "local" giving. Corporate PACs, it will be noted, contributed to a relatively greater number of candidates than might be expected given their typically modest budgets, but of course their average contributions tended to be quite small. If Sorauf is right—and we think he is—the fact that almost 90 percent of corporate PACs gave contributions that averaged less than $1000 per candidate may indicate a tendency to accommodate diverse donor preferences.[23]

This pattern of tokenism is less prevalent among other kinds of PACs. Perhaps because they are most interested in influencing or appearing to influence election outcomes, or perhaps because there are fewer candidates who meet their standards of purity, nonconnected PACs tend to give larger contributions to smaller numbers of people. And although a large share of labor PACs and an even larger share of trade PACs make relatively small average contributions, both also have among them a significant percentage of large givers.

TABLE 4.2.
CONTRIBUTION PATTERNS OF MAJOR PACs: PERCENT OF PACs ALLOCATING SPECIFIED
PROPORTIONS OF THEIR BUDGETS TO DEMOCRATS, INCUMBENTS, AND WINNERS

|  | Nonconnected | Trade | Labor | Corporate | All |
|---|---|---|---|---|---|
| Percentage of total contributions to Democrats |  |  |  |  |  |
| 0-19 | 50 | 16 | 1 | 29 | 25 |
| 20-39 | 4 | 19 | 0 | 25 | 20 |
| 40-59 | 6 | 21 | 1 | 26 | 20 |
| 60-79 | 12 | 30 | 5 | 15 | 18 |
| 80-100 | 27 | 14 | 93 | 5 | 18 |
| Percentage of total contributions to incumbents |  |  |  |  |  |
| 0-19 | 44 | 9 | 7 | 8 | 11 |
| 20-39 | 9 | 6 | 8 | 19 | 14 |
| 40-59 | 12 | 13 | 14 | 24 | 19 |
| 60-79 | 14 | 26 | 36 | 29 | 28 |
| 80-100 | 21 | 47 | 36 | 20 | 28 |

TABLE 4.2. *(Continued)*

|  | Nonconnected | Trade | Labor | Corporate | All |
|---|---|---|---|---|---|
| Percentage of total direct contributions to winners |  |  |  |  |  |
| 0-19 | 10 | 3 | 11 | 1 | 3 |
| 20-39 | 10 | 5 | 20 | 6 | 7 |
| 40-59 | 34 | 17 | 36 | 18 | 21 |
| 60-79 | 34 | 48 | 25 | 61 | 52 |
| 80-100 | 13 | 28 | 8 | 15 | 17 |

In table 4.2 we see the percentage distributions of PAC giving to different kinds of candidates. The data show significant variation in contribution patterns, beginning with party preferences. Nonconnected PACs, not surprisingly, either tend to be predominantly Republican in their giving or predominantly Democratic. Corporate and trade PACs tend to be more bipartisan, with a corporate tilt toward Republicans counterbalanced by the slightly Democratic tilt on the part of trade association PACs and the nearly total Democratic allegiance of labor PACs.

The overall tendency for PAC money to go primarily to incumbents is a familiar fact, but once again important variation across and within PAC types needs to be emphasized. Compared to the others, nonconnected PACs were the most likely to support challengers or open-seat candidates, while trade association PACs devoted large shares of their budgets to incumbents and winners. More corporate PACs than labor PACs were inclined to stray from an incumbency strategy, which may be explained by the possibility that, in 1980, wise Democratic money was spent defensively and wise Republican money offensively.[24] Indeed, the figures on support for winners indicate that corporate PACs' contributions to nonincumbents seem to have been well chosen.

A different perspective on PACs is presented in table 4.3 on page 132, where we show the average contributions to different kinds of candidates by different types of PACs as well as the average number of such contributions. Given the enormous differences in size and behavior within PAC types, caution should be exercised in inferring from averages a picture of a "typical" PAC. But the data give at least some idea of scale. Again, we see how corporate PACs tend to spread themselves thin, making small contributions to a fairly large number of all kinds of candidates. The largest average contributions come from nonconnected and labor PACs, with trade PACs averaging a large number of somewhat smaller gifts.

The variation among political action committees and the relatively small size of their contributions suggest that the simple and widely accepted model of buyers in an access bidding war fits the realities of PAC behavior only in procrustean fashion. We turn now to what we regard as simple but organizationally richer models of that behavior.

TABLE 4.3.
OVERVIEW OF MAJOR PACs: AVERAGE CONTRIBUTIONS

| | Nonconnected | Trade | Labor | Corporate | All |
|---|---|---|---|---|---|
| Average contribution per incumbent | $1175 | $790 | $1292 | $517 | $745 |
| (Average number of contributions) | (10) | (47) | (55) | (31) | (36) |
| Average contribution per challenger | 1647 | 1241 | 1436 | 759 | 1025 |
| | (13) | (10) | (12) | (12) | (11) |
| Average contribution per open-seat candidate | 1623 | 1170 | 1617 | 612 | 963 |
| | (5) | (6) | (7) | (5) | (6) |
| Average contribution per Senate candidate | 2213 | 1287 | 2482 | 893 | 1243 |
| | (7) | (12) | (12) | (11) | (11) |
| Average contribution per House candidate | 1226 | 795 | 1130 | 464 | 702 |
| | (21) | (50) | (61) | (35) | (40) |
| Average contribution per Democrat | 1416 | 823 | 1380 | 566 | 891 |
| | (8) | (31) | (67) | (17) | (25) |
| Average contribution per Republican | 1499 | 950 | 996 | 595 | 736 |
| | (20) | (32) | (7) | (30) | (27) |

## Budget Size and Contribution Behavior

All PACs make three primary contribution decisions: to how many candidates to contribute, to which candidates to contribute, and how much to contribute to each. In order to explore how patterns of choice in these matters may change from small to large PACs we estimated several simple models for each kind of PAC. What the models allow us to do is to estimate the elasticity of certain interesting PAC behavior with respect to budget size—using a specific example, to estimate the relationship between a percentage change in budget size and a percentage change in the amount of money spent on challengers.[25] Included as well in each analysis is a variable to determine the effect of the presence of a Washington office.

### NONCONNECTED PACs

Table 4.4 reports the results of the analysis for the nonconnected PACs in the sample. First, we see the effects of budget size on the number and size of contributions. The coefficients for the budget variable indicate that a 1 percent increase in budget size is associated with a .59 percent increase in the total number of donees and a .35 percent increase in average contributions.[26] That is to say, both the number of contributions and the size of contributions grow, though less than proportionally, as the size of nonconnected PACs increases.

TABLE 4.4.
RELATIONSHIP BETWEEN BUDGET SIZE AND CONTRIBUTION BEHAVIOR:
NONCONNECTED PACs

| Percentage Increase in: | For Each 1% Increase in Total Budget | Additional Increase If PAC Has a Washington Office | Amount of Variance Explained ($R^2$) |
|---|---|---|---|
| Number of donees | .59 | .08 | .71 |
| | (.03)[a] | (.05) | |
| Average contributions | .35 | − .08 | .40 |
| | (.04) | (.06) | |
| Number of contributions of $5000 or more | .48 | .04 | .54 |
| | (.04) | (.06) | |
| Number of challenger donees | .66 | − .01 | .58 |
| | (.05) | (.07) | |
| Total dollar amount of contributions to challengers | 1.53 | − .15 | .46 |
| | (.16) | (.21) | |
| Number of open-seat donees | .57 | .04 | .62 |
| | (.04) | (.06) | |
| Total dollar amount of contributions to open-seat candidates | 1.79 | − .08 | .45 |
| | (.19) | (.25) | |
| Total dollar amount of Senate contributions | 1.56 | − .10 | .42 |
| | (.18) | (.23) | |

*a*. Standard errors are in parentheses.

This is also true for the number of large contributions of $5000 or more. More interesting is the evidence about contributions to challengers and open-seat candidates. As we see, the *number* of challenger and open-seat contributions increases at about the same rate as it does for all donees, but the *amount of money* contributed to those races increases quite rapidly as budgets increase. The fact that a 1 percent increase in budget is associated with a 1.53 percent increase in challenger spending and a 1.79 percent increase in open-seat spending indicates that at least for nonconnected PACs, increased resources tend to translate into even larger budget shares devoted to nonincumbents.

If a Washington location makes a great deal of difference, its effect on nonconnected PACs is muted. The presence of a Washington base does tend to shift upward the relationship between the size of the budget and the number of donees and to shift downward the relationship between budget size and contributions to nonincumbents. But in all cases the magnitude of the coefficients is small relative to their standard errors. Evidently, the Washington circles in which some nonconnected PACs travel do not alter too much their basic proclivities.

## Trade and Labor PACs

On this score the comparison between nonconnected PACs and trade PACs is stark. Here too, as table 4.5 shows, the effect of a Washington location on challenger and open-seat spending is in the expected direction, but small. There is, however, a very pronounced Washington effect on the number and size of contributions. For the Washington trade PACs, the relationship between budget size and number of donees is shifted dramatically upward, which, of course, means the relationship between budget size and average size of contribution is shifted downward. There may be both supply-side and demand-side explanations for this phenomenon. On the supply side, if the goal of Washington trade organizations is to maximize access opportunities, that may be best achieved by giving relatively small gifts to large numbers of candidates. On the demand side, Washington PACs personally face more claimants. One trade PAC manager we spoke with in Washington, for example, complained about the 350 invitations to campaign dinners and receptions she received in 1982. Thus in many instances token gifts may be given defensively or as concessions to persistence.

As in the nonconnected PACs, however, increases in budget size in trade PACs produce more than proportional increases in spending on challengers and

TABLE 4.5.
RELATIONSHIP BETWEEN BUDGET SIZE AND CONTRIBUTION BEHAVIOR:
TRADE PACs

| Percentage Increase in: | For Each 1% Increase in Total Budget | Additional Increase If PAC Has a Washington Office | Amount of Variance Explained ($R^2$) |
|---|---|---|---|
| Number of donees | .67 (.03)[a] | .29 (.03) | .73 |
| Average contributions | .29 (.03) | −.31 (.03) | .32 |
| Number of contributions of $5000 or more | .47 (.03) | −.08 (.03) | .53 |
| Number of challenger donees | .58 (.03) | .05 (.04) | .52 |
| Total dollar amount of contributions to challengers | 1.45 (.10) | −.01 (.12) | .39 |
| Number of open-seat donees | .58 (.03) | .05 (.03) | .56 |
| Total dollar amount of contributions to open seats | 1.66 (.12) | −.07 (.15) | .38 |
| Total dollar amount of Senate contributions | 1.28 (.09) | .38 (.11) | .44 |

a. Standard errors are in parentheses.

open seats. An increase of 1 percent of trade PAC budgets is associated with about a 1.5 percent increase in spending for both challengers and open seats. As was true for the nonconnected PACs, spending on Senate races also increases more than proportionally as budget size increases. Indeed, the pattern, as shown in table 4.6, is much the same for labor PACs—increases in budget size produce disproportionate increases in spending on challengers, open seats, and Senate races. And like the trade PACs, labor PACs in Washington tend to give smaller contributions to a larger number of donees than would be expected by their size alone.

TABLE 4.6.
RELATIONSHIP BETWEEN BUDGET SIZE AND CONTRIBUTION BEHAVIOR:
LABOR PACs

| Percentage Increase in: | For Each 1% Increase in Total Budget | Additional Increase If PAC Has a Washington Office | Amount of Variance Explained ($R^2$) |
|---|---|---|---|
| Number of donees | .68<br>(.04)[a] | .31<br>(.05) | .84 |
| Average contributions | .28<br>(.04) | −.33<br>(.06) | .29 |
| Number of contributions of $5000 or more | .65<br>(.04) | −.18<br>(.06) | .71 |
| Number of challenger donees | .58<br>(.04) | .14<br>(.06) | .75 |
| Total dollar amount of contributions to challengers | 1.42<br>(.14) | −.15<br>(.21) | .50 |
| Number of open-seat donees | .56<br>(.03) | .14<br>(.05) | .76 |
| Total dollar amount of contributions to open seats | 1.56<br>(.16) | .18<br>(.24) | .51 |
| Total dollar amount of Senate contributions | 1.50<br>(.14) | .20<br>(.21) | .57 |

*a*. Standard errors are in parentheses.

## CORPORATE PACs

The analysis of corporate PACs, we see in table 4.7 on page 136, turns up interesting patterns of similarity and difference with the other PAC types. Again, increases in size are associated with disproportionate increases in riskier spending, and a Washington location elevates the number of donations and decreases the likelihood that they will go to nonincumbents.

But note the relationships between percentage increase in budget size and percentage increases in number of donees and average contributions. As we

TABLE 4.7.
RELATIONSHIP BETWEEN BUDGET SIZE AND CONTRIBUTION BEHAVIOR:
CORPORATE PACs

| Percentage Increase in: | For Each 1% Increase in Total Budget | Additional Increase If PAC Has a Washington Office | Amount of Variance Explained ($R^2$) |
|---|---|---|---|
| Number of donees | .81 (.02)[a] | .10 (.04) | .76 |
| Average contributions | .16 (.02) | −.11 (.04) | .10 |
| Number of contributions of $5000 or more | .24 (.02) | −.08 (.04) | .24 |
| Number of challenger donees | .66 (.02) | −.15 (.06) | .50 |
| Total dollar amount of contributions to challengers | 1.30 (.06) | −.31 (.15) | .35 |
| Number of open-seat donees | .63 (.02) | −.07 (.05) | .48 |
| Total dollar amount of contributions to open seats | 1.67 (.09) | −.30 (.19) | .33 |
| Total dollar amount of Senate contributions | 1.22 (.04) | −.01 (.09) | .58 |

a. Standard errors are in parentheses.

move from smaller to larger corporate PACs, the number of donees increases rapidly as compared to other PACs, meaning that the average contribution increases slowly. So also does the number of large contributions. Taken together with the data presented earlier, this evidence suggests that the idea of corporate PACs as ultrarational influence maximizers is easily overstated. Indeed, for many the notion of political United Way campaigns may be more on the mark.

## Interindustry Differences in Contribution Behavior

Previous work has identified significant variation in ideology and tactics among corporate PACs,[27] variation that, we argued earlier, might be related to industry differences. Although we are still in the process of developing a more fully specified model of these differences, we report here some interesting initial results. What we have done is to see whether on two important dimensions of contribution behavior—percent of total budget contributed to Republicans and percent of total budget contributed to incumbents—there are detectable interindustry differences. Specifically, we tested for differences in such behavior among some of the more prominent of the many industries PACs represent while controlling for the presence of a Washington office.[28] Some PACs, it should be noted, represent parent corporations with more than one Standard Industrial Classification. In such cases, our simple model assumes that the net effect of being in several industry types can be estimated by summing the specific industry effects.

TABLE 4.8.
INTERINDUSTRY DIFFERENCES IN CONTRIBUTION BEHAVIOR

| Independent Variables | Dependent Variables | | | |
|---|---|---|---|---|
| | Percent of Budget to Republicans | | Percent of Budget to Incumbents | |
| Banking | − .10 | (.03)[a] | .04 | (.03) |
| Transportation | − .13 | (.03) | .14 | (.03) |
| Tobacco | − .28 | (.13) | .19 | (.14) |
| Communication | − .07 | (.04) | .11 | (.04) |
| Utilities | − .09 | (.03) | .06 | (.03) |
| Oil and gas | .05 | (.025) | − .08 | (.03) |
| Construction | .08 | (.04) | − .09 | (.04) |
| Chemicals, rubber, plastics | .07 | (.02) | − .02 | (.02) |
| Paper and allied products | .08 | (.04) | − .05 | (.04) |
| Machinery | .08 | (.02) | − .10 | (.03) |
| Washington office | − .13 | (.04) | .13 | (.05) |
| $R^2$ | .15 | | .12 | |

a. Standard errors are in parentheses.

The results of the analysis are presented in table 4.8. Across all industries, the effects of the industry types form a striking pattern. For the banking, transportation, tobacco, communication, and utilities industries there is a consistent downward effect on Republican giving and a consistent upward effect on incumbent giving. For the oil and gas, construction, chemical and rubber, paper, and machinery industries the effect is the opposite. In almost all cases, the coefficients are large compared to their standard errors. The presence of a Washington base has the expected significant effects — an average 13 percent less contributed to Republicans and 13 percent more contributed to incumbents.

Our assessment of these intriguing differences is as yet tentative, but we are tempted to argue that accommodationist and adversarial tactics are in part related to perceived industry-government relations. Most of the industries with accommodationist effects — more Democratic giving and more incumbent giving — are targets, perhaps beneficiaries, of old-style "economic regulation." Most of the industries with adversarial effects — more Republican giving and more nonincumbent giving — are targets, perhaps perceived victims, of new-style "social regulation" and other economic policies. Thus, we are led to think that the analysis of corporate PAC behavior might profitably draw on ideas about the perceived impact of government policies.[29]

## Implications

Our primary considerations have been empirical rather than normative, but a few words should be said about the implications of the organizational perspective taken here for appraisals of the PAC phenomenon and for proposals to change yet again the laws governing campaign finance. There has been a regrettable tendency for judgments and reform to run well ahead of our knowledge about PACs, and only now are the facts beginning to catch up with conjecture. We conclude with some thoughts about how our work bears on several important issues.

First, the nationalization issue: Certainly there are many large PACs that centralize and rationalize small individual contributions, a worrisome development perhaps. But the data show a good deal of surviving localism in campaign finance. The typical PAC is a modest operation and, we suspect, a locally oriented one. Corporate PACs rewarding members who serve the district, trade and labor PACs acting as auxiliaries of local party organizations, locally based purposive PACs rewarding or punishing local incumbents on the basis of one or another litmus test—these are as important a part of the PAC story as the more notorious nationalized operations. Indeed, for better or worse, much of what is going on at the local level may not be too different from the pre-PAC era.

Second, the influence issue: One should never discount the prospects for venality in American politics, but as Alexander Hamilton reminds us in *Federalist No. 76,* "the supposition of universal venality in human nature is little less an error in political reasoning than the supposition of universal rectitude." Combined with other evidence about the diversity of sources in the typical campaign war chest[30] and the limited purchase PAC dollars seem to get,[31] our data about choices concerning the size and number of contributions raise serious questions about the alleged legislative intent and effectiveness of much PAC money.

Finally, the competition issue: Whether PACs help or hinder challengers is a complex empirical issue, conclusions about which depend on whether one looks at PAC giving in all races or, more realistically, at races in which challengers have a serious chance of winning.[32] We would add these points to the argument.

First, given the accumulating evidence that money makes much more difference for challengers than incumbents,[33] the total amount of money going to challengers is probably a more relevant statistic than the more commonly cited ratio of challenger to incumbent giving. Second, our analysis would suggest that if there is continued growth not only in the number of PACs but also in the budgets of existing PACs, the dollar volume of challenger contributions may increase substantially in the years ahead. Thus, to the extent that simple competitiveness and not partisan flow is their paramount concern, critics may be happy to find more, not less, turnover in a future PAC era. Third, all this will be affected by changes in the law now under consideration. Limits on candidate receipts of PAC money, like the $70,000 limit included in the 1979 Obey-Railsback bill, would in all likelihood disadvantage challengers. Although they might have less salutary effects, lower limits on PAC contributions, like the $3000 per candidate per election limit in that same bill, could possibly advantage challengers by forcing PACs more quickly to spread out their budgets to more candidates.

The foregoing arguments cast some doubt on a few of the most publicized fears about PACs, but they hardly make us panglossian about the PAC phenomenon. Even if some of their effects were actually benign, troublesome questions about PACs would remain. There are, to begin with, a host of questions about how, if at all, the internal governance structures of PACs fit with traditional ideas of democratic theory. Then, of course, there is the issue of PACs' effects on coalition building in an already atomized polity. These matters go to the heart of the PAC issue, and discussion of them will profit from a richer understanding of the internal and external behavior of this new breed of political organization.

## Notes

A preliminary version of this chapter was presented at the 1983 annual meeting of the Midwest Political Science Association. For his valuable advice we wish to thank Daniel J. Richards.

1. Herbert E. Alexander, "The Impact of the Federal Election Campaign Act on the 1976 Presidential Campaign: The Complexities of Compliance," *Emory Law Review* 29 (Spring 1980): 315-37.
2. This was one of the concerns in the report prepared by the Institute of Politics, John F. Kennedy School of Government for the Committee on House Administration in 1979, *An Analysis of the Impact of the Federal Election Campaign Act, 1972-78.*
3. Edwin M. Epstein, "The PAC Phenomenon—An Overview Introduction," *Arizona Law Review* 22, no. 2 (1980): 355-72.
4. Frank J. Sorauf, "Accountability in Political Action Committees: Who's in Charge?" (paper delivered at the 1982 annual meeting of the American Political Science Association).
5. David Adamany, "PACs and the Democratic Financing of Politics," *Arizona Law Review* 22, no. 2 (1980): 596-97.
6. See, for example, Benjamin Ginsberg, *The Consequences of Consent: Elections, Citizen Control and Popular Acquiescence* (Reading, Mass.: Addison-Wesley, 1982), 220-33; and Jonathan I. Silberman and Gary C. Durden, "Determining Legislative Preferences on the Minimum Wage: An Economic Approach," *Journal of Political Economy* 84 (April 1976): 317-29.
7. Henry W. Chappell, "Campaign Contributions and Congressional Voting: A Simultaneous Probit-Tobit Model," *Review of Economics and Statistics* 64 (February 1982): 77-83; and James B. Kau, Donald Keenan, and Paul H. Rubin, "A General Equilibrium Model of Congressional Voting," *Quarterly Journal of Economics* 97, no. 2 (May 1982): 271-93.

8. W.P. Welch, "Campaign Contributions and Legislative Voting: Milk Money and Dairy Price Supports," *Western Political Quarterly* 35, no. 4 (December 1982): 478-95.

9. Of the 2785 PACs registered with the Federal Election Commission during 1979-80, 471 (16.9%) spent over half of their congressional budgets on challengers; 1217 (43.7%) spent 50 percent or less on incumbents. See Federal Election Commission, *Reports on Financial Activity, 1979-80.*

10. Sorauf, "Accountability in Political Action Committees," 4-5.

11. Frank J. Sorauf, "Political Parties and Political Action Committees: Two Life Cycles," *Arizona Law Review* 22, no. 2 (1980): 455.

12. Edward Handler and John R. Mulkern, *Business in Politics: Campaign Strategies of Corporate Political Action Committees* (Lexington, Mass.: Heath, 1982), 26-27.

13. FEC records showed only 379 Washington PACs in 1979-80. This represented 13.6% of all registered committees.

14. Bernadette A. Budde, "The Practical Role of Corporate PACs in the Political Process," *Arizona Law Review* 22, no. 2 (1980): 564-65.

15. Sorauf, "Accountability in Political Action Committees," 8.

16. Ibid., 18.

17. In 1979-80 there were 1251 corporate PACs (44.9%), 331 labor (11.9%), 635 trade (22.8%), 471 "nonconnected" PACs (16.9%), 61 corporations without stock (2.2%), and 36 cooperatives (1.3%).

18. Sorauf, "Accountability in Political Action Committees," 21-22.

19. Lawrence B. Mohr, "Determinants of Innovation in Organizations," *American Political Science Review* 63 (March 1969): 111-26.

20. Howard Margolis, *Selfishness, Altruism, and Rationality* (Cambridge, England: Cambridge University Press, 1982), 100.

21. Marvin Weinberger and David U. Greevy, *The PAC Directory* (Cambridge, Mass.: Ballinger, 1982).

22. We draw your attention to one feature of the data—presidential and congressional giving are combined. Thus, contributions to Jimmy Carter are counted as incumbent giving, while contributions to his Democratic rivals and to aspirants for the Republican nomination are counted as challenger giving. Presidential giving accounted for only about 2% of PAC giving in our sample. Let us also note that in the analysis that follows, corporations without stock are combined with other corporations and cooperatives are combined with trade/membership organizations.

23. Sorauf, "Accountability in Political Action Committees," 9.

24. Gary C. Jacobson, "Money in the 1980 and 1982 Congressional Elections," chap. 2 in this volume.

25. The technique used to estimate such elasticities is to transform the independent variable—budget size—and the various dependent variables into logarithms. Thus in tables 4.4 to 4.7, the coefficients tell us the effect of a 1% increase in budget size on the percentage increase in number of donees, average contributions, number of contributions of $5000 or more, etc. Although the specific numerical effect of the presence of a Washington office will depend on budget size, the signs of these coefficients tell us whether the relationship between percentage increases in budget size and percentage increases in the dependent variables is shifted upward or downward. See Eric A. Hanushek and John E. Jackson, *Statistical Methods for Social Scientists* (New York: Academic Press, 1977); and Edward R. Tufte, *Data Analysis for Politics and Policy* (Englewood Cliffs, N.J.: Prentice-Hall, 1974).

26. The relationship between budget size and average contribution is implied by the relationship between size and number of donees.
27. Handler and Mulkern, *Business in Politics.*
28. In some instances, we have combined similar industrial codes.
29. For suggestive ideas, see Handler and Mulkern, *Business in Politics;* and James Q. Wilson, "The Politics of Regulation," in *Social Responsibility and the Business Predicament,* ed. James D. McKie (Washington, D.C.: Brookings Institution, 1975).
30. Michael J. Malbin, "Campaign Financing and the 'Special Interests,' " *The Public Interest,* December 1979, 21-42.
31. Chappell, "Campaign Contributions and Congressional Voting."
32. Compare, for example, Malbin, "Campaign Financing and the 'Special Interests,' " and Fred Wertheimer, "The PAC Phenomenon in American Politics," *Arizona Law Review* 22, no. 2 (1980): 603-26.
33. Gary C. Jacobson, *Money in Congressional Elections* (New Haven: Yale University Press, 1980).

# 5. Assessing Ideological PACs: From Outrage to Understanding

The emergence of ideological political action committees (PACs) has flavored campaigns and elections in the 1980s. Conservative multi-issue and single-issue PACs joined the Moral Majority and President Reagan in claiming credit for the defeat of liberal congressional candidates in 1980. Energized by these losses, liberal multi-issue and single-issue PACs fought back in 1982 and declared that subsequent losses by conservatives represented a rout of the New Right and its PACs.[1]

In addition to their electoral activities, conservative PACs have been blamed for fostering pernicious "negative independent expenditures" in recent elections, thereby "distorting democracy." Critics argue that such PACs operate irresponsibly without accountability to supporters, candidates, or voters.[2] Whatever the truth of such assertions, the pervasive perception is clearly that ideological PACs are important forces in congressional elections.

What are ideological PACs? How do they compare to more conventional business, labor, and trade association PACs? What do they do to influence elections? What do we need to consider in order to assess their impact in the 1980 and 1982 elections or predict how they may affect American politics in the future?

## Ideological PACs: An Overview

Exactly what *is* an ideological PAC? Although the term is commonly used, it is difficult to define in a way that both makes analytical sense and reflects the positions of actual PACs. In common usage, the term refers to PACs that favor policies or philosophies usually identified as liberal (progressive) or conservative in contemporary American politics.[3] Ideological PACs are not only those favoring multiple issues encompassing a general philosophy but also those focusing on a narrow issue area (e.g., abortion, national defense, or gun control) where opposing positions are commonly identified as liberal or conservative.

In theory, ideological PACs are radically different from corporate or labor PACs because of their motivations. The electoral objectives of liberal and conservative multi- and single-issue PACs are not principally intended *selectively* and *materially* to benefit the PAC or its members generally.[4] They are not seeking a specific special interest such as a tax loophole, government contract, or pro-union legislation that will benefit their members financially. Instead, they seek to further "selfless" causes (often described as "the public interest"): defeating communism, promoting civil liberties, prohibiting abortions, preserving free enterprise, or protecting the environment.

There were over 400 ideological PACs registered with the Federal Election Commission during the 1982 election cycle, of which one-quarter were sponsored by related membership organizations or corporations without stock. The rest were "independent" PACs—falling into the category of nonconnected PACs, according to the Federal Election Commission (FEC).[5] Of these PACs, about 130 were identifiably liberal in focus, whereas over twice as many favored conservative views.

How do ideological PACs differ from business, labor, or trade association PACs? We can get a sense of PAC growth and patterns of contributing from Federal Election Commission aggregate reports that categorize PACs as corporate, labor, trade/membership/health associations, corporations without stock, or nonconnected. Most major ideological PACs are listed in the nonconnected category. Unfortunately, notable exceptions are filed under corporations without stock (e.g., Handgun Control Inc. PAC) or the trade/membership/health association category (e.g., Gun Owners of America Campaign Committee or, in 1980, the National Abortion Rights Action League Political Action Committee). On the other hand, the nonconnected category also includes several PACs established to further the interests of specific politicians,[6] and other entries such as the Dallas Energy Political Action Committee (the third largest nonconnected PAC in contributions to federal candidates in 1982). Nonetheless, most nonconnected PACs have an ideological bent, and most of the leading liberal and conservative PACs fall into this category.

In the past eight years, the number of business, labor, and trade association PACs has multiplied from 608 at the end of 1974 to 2475 at the end of 1982. Although the ideological (nonconnected) category of PACs originated in 1977, their ranks expanded from 110 in 1977 to 746 in 1982.[7] The rates at which different kinds of PACs have grown show that ideological PACs are the most prolific, increasing by an average of 47 percent per year, or about 260 new PACs each election cycle. Over the past four election cycles, corporate PACs have grown at the slower average annual rate of 21 percent, but their ranks still increase by about 370 PACs per congressional election. Over the same period, trade, membership, and health association PACs grew slightly, increasing by 8 percent annually on average, or 86 PACs per election cycle. In contrast, labor PACs have grown by only 12 percent per year, adding an average 66 PACs to their ranks each election, compared to the 456 for corporations and associations combined.

Not only are ideological PACs outstripping all other PACs in their rate of growth, but during the 1980 and 1982 elections they also raised more money than any other category of PACs. The superior financial resources of ideological PACs does not necessarily mean they exercise more power in campaigns, however. Frequently their independent status forces them to spend more on overhead and fund-raising costs and less on contributions to candidates. Table 5.1 shows that ideological PACs spent less than one-quarter of the funds they raised in the 1982 election on political expenditures—either direct contributions to candidates or independent expenditures (made to support or oppose specific candidates but without any coordination with candidates or their committees). Liberal and conservative PACs spent less on campaigns than did corporate, trade, or labor PACs in 1982. Furthermore, ideological PACs ended both the 1980 and 1982 election cycles further in debt than the other PACs.

The reason ideological PACs tend to spend less on campaigns at the same time they incur greater debts than corporate, trade, or labor PACs is tied to their independent status. Committees in the other three categories are affiliated with a parent organization and thus are permitted to have their fund-raising and overhead costs paid by the PAC's sponsoring organization.[8] Nonconnected PACs must raise funds to cover all their expenses, including the cost of fund raising. Direct-mail fund raising, perhaps the most popular tactic used by ideological PACs, usually requires spending at least 50 cents to raise a dollar.[9] Thus, it is not surprising that nonconnected PACs spend less than half their receipts on political expenditures. As for the remainder of their expenditures on administrative and other costs, the proportion is comparable to that spent by sponsored PACs (corporate, labor, and trade) on nonpolitical expenditures.

Finally, the large debts carried by several ideological PACs are also the consequence of their reliance on direct mail fund raising. The consulting firms that conduct the bulk of ideological fund raising (run by Richard Viguerie on the right and Roger Craver on the left) often extend substantial credit to their clients in the anticipation of conducting additional mailings to eliminate these debts. Debts mount near the end of campaigns when, in order to increase the funds available for contributions to candidates, ideological PACs engage in "deficit financing." They can then use the need to retire their postelection debt in fervent appeals to contributors during the nonelection year when the political enthusiasm of contributors might otherwise wane.

In short, examination of table 5.1 suggests that nonconnected ideological PACs may have less impact in elections than sponsored PACs because they must spend so much on fund raising. The distinction is important to assess the relative influence of corporate, labor, trade, and ideological PACs. In addition, since about one-quarter of the ideological PACs are sponsored (even though most are not), the different financial constraints faced by nonconnected and affiliated PACs also affect the financial status of individual ideological PACs.

There is, in fact, an important tradeoff for independent ideological PACs versus their sponsored counterparts. Sections 114.5 and 114.7 of 11 Code of Federal Regulations—Federal Elections require that PACs affiliated with parent corporations must limit their solicitations to the established membership rolls.

TABLE 5.1.

FINANCIAL STATUS OF POLITICAL ACTION COMMITTEES, 1980 AND 1982

| PAC Type | Election | Adjusted Receipts[a] (in millions) | Contributions to Candidates (in millions) | Independent Expenditures | Total Political Expenditures (in millions) | Debts Owed |
|---|---|---|---|---|---|---|
| Corporate | 1982 | $47.1 | $29.4 | $20,058 | $29.4 | $346,299 |
| | 1980 | 33.9 | 21.6 | 20,190 | 21.6 | 274,997 |
| Labor | 1982 | 37.5 | 20.9 | 10,947 | 20.8 | 251,349 |
| | 1980 | 25.7 | 14.2 | 87,174 | 14.3 | 20,502 |
| Trade/member- | 1982 | 43.4 | 22.9 | 787,507 | 23.7 | 385,598 |
| ship/health | 1980 | 33.9 | 17.0 | 968,812 | 18.0 | 393,319 |
| Nonconnected | 1982 | 64.7 | 11.0 | 4,863,575 | 15.9 | 4,206,209 |
| (ideological) | 1980 | 40.1 | 5.2 | 13,096,484 | 18.3 | 1,612,068 |

SOURCES: 1980 data from "FEC Releases Final PAC Report for 1979-80 Election Cycle" (FEC press release, February 21, 1982). 1982 data from "FEC Publishes Final 1981-82 PAC Study" (FEC press release, November 29, 1983).

a. Adjusted receipts exclude monies transferred among affiliated committees.

For a PAC that wishes to solicit more widely, this restriction may offset the financial advantage of having the parent group provide its fund-raising and administrative expenditures. Several sponsored PACs attempt to circumvent this limitation by combining PAC solicitations with membership drives. Others have simply adopted a loose definition of membership that includes anyone who contributes to their cause or expresses interest in their objectives. The Supreme Court ruled against such a vague conception of membership in a case concerning the National Right to Work Committee's PAC. The Court argued that to consider as a member "anyone who has responded to one of the corporation's essentially mass mailings would, we think, open the door to all but unlimited corporate solicitation and thereby render meaningless the statutory limitation to 'members.' "[10]

Presumably, given the National Right to Work Committee decision, in order for individuals to be solicited as members of affiliated PACs in the future they will have to exhibit "some relatively enduring and independently significant financial or organizational attachment."[11] Sponsored ideological PACs unwilling to accept the burden of somehow incorporating members into the operations of the PAC may choose to sever their parental ties and join the ranks of nonconnected PACs. Indeed, the day after the ruling against it, the National Right to Work Committee filed registrations to create three antilabor, independent PACs, "identical in every respect except their names."[12] Thus, in addition to the normal proliferation of nonconnected PACs, there may be a shift from the ranks of corporations without stock PACs or the membership association PACs to nonconnected PACs as sponsored ideological PACs respond to the 1982 Court ruling.

Apart from the differences in the financial status of corporate, labor, trade, and ideological PACs, are ideological PACs unique in other significant ways? Figures 5.1 and 5.2 indicate important differences in the contribution patterns of ideological PACs in 1980 and 1982 compared to the more traditional types of PACs. For example, in 1980 when every other category of PAC gave more to incumbents than to challengers, ideological PACs aggressively favored challengers or open-seat candidates.

Some analysts suggest that nonconnected PACs prefer challengers because PACs that are independent of business or labor lobbying organizations are more willing to risk alienating incumbent congressmen.[13] This is fallacious, for no PAC purposely alienates those whose help it is bound to need. Presumably all PACs are concerned directly with influencing elections because they hope indirectly to influence public policy either by lobbying or simply by assuring that their interests are represented. The key is whether the PACs believe enough legislators are listening to them. In 1978 and 1980 the conservative PACs that supported challengers did so because they sought to maximize their representation in Congress by electing members more sympathetic to their views. In 1982, both liberal *and* conservative PACs attempted to elect new members and protect incumbents who supported their views. If in the process they risked alien-

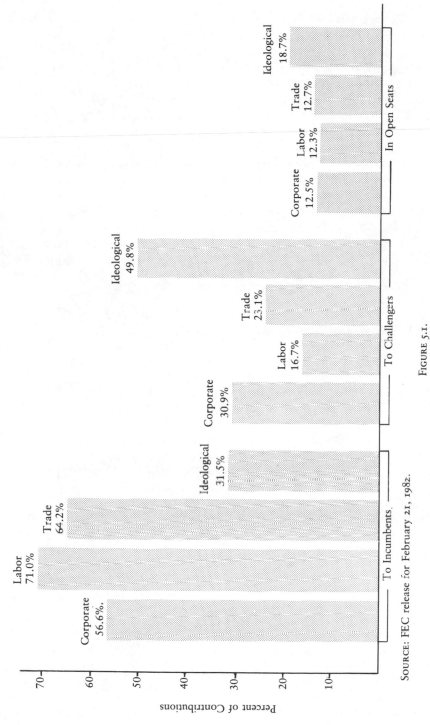

SOURCE: FEC release for February 21, 1982.

FIGURE 5.1.

1980 CONTRIBUTION PATTERNS OF POLITICAL ACTION COMMITTEES

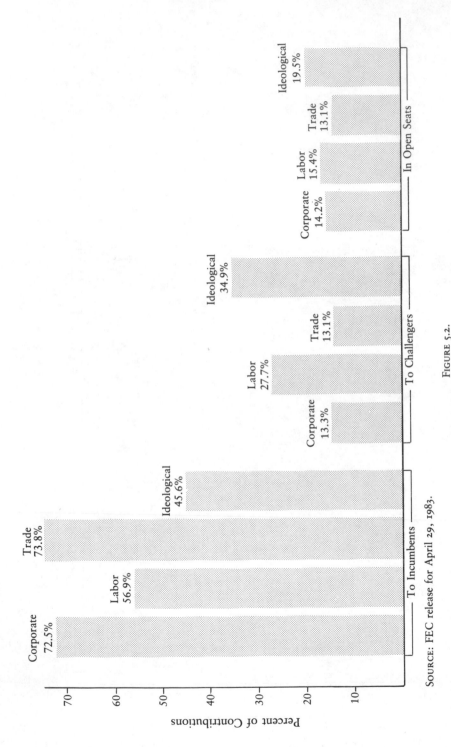

SOURCE: FEC release for April 29, 1983.

FIGURE 5.2.

1982 CONTRIBUTION PATTERNS OF POLITICAL ACTION COMMITTEES

ating incumbents, it was because they sought to replace these incumbents, who were opposed to their views anyway.

The data in figures 5.1 and 5.2 support the previous interpretation of the contribution patterns in 1980 and 1982. In 1980, conservative PACs (largely responsible for ideological PAC expenditures) adopted an offensive strategy, seeking to oust vulnerable liberal incumbents. In 1982, conservatives had to protect many of the incumbents they helped elect in 1980 in addition to supporting challengers to liberal incumbents. One must also remember that liberal PACs were more active in 1982 than in 1980, especially since several of the larger progressive contributors emerged in reaction to the 1980 defeats of liberals. These liberal PACs both sought to defend favorite incumbents from conservative attacks and to target vulnerable conservative incumbents. Thus the 1982 contributions by ideological PACs reflect the tension between the offensive and defensive strategies of liberal and conservative PACs as both seek to maximize their cohort in Congress. Despite the shift to favoring more incumbents in 1982, ideological PACs still exhibited a greater propensity to support challengers than any other category of PACs.

## Independent Expenditures

The final difference between ideological and other PACs is that ideological PACs are far more willing to conduct independent expenditure campaigns, as is evident in table 5.1. The Federal Election Commission defines an independent expenditure as

> . . . [A]n expenditure by a person expressly advocating the election or defeat of a clearly identified candidate which is made without cooperation or consultation with any candidate, or any authorized agency of such candidate, and which is not made in concert with, or at the request or suggestion of, any such candidate.[14]

The Federal Election Campaign Act of 1974 sought to restrict independent expenditures to $1000 per candidate. This provision was struck down as an unconstitutional abridgment of free speech by the Supreme Court in *Buckley* v. *Valeo*.[15] Thus, by the 1978 elections, the independent expenditure loophole was firmly established. Certain ideological PACs have exploited it eagerly ever since.

The common perception is that only independent ideological PACs make independent expenditures. In fact, only half of the PACs making independent expenditures in 1980 were nonconnected PACs, but they made 93 percent of all independent expenditures in that election, including $1.8 million in negative expenditures (against specific candidates).[16] In the 1980 election, more than $16 million were made in independent expenditures, $13.7 million of which were spent in the presidential race.

Absent a presidential election in 1982, $5.8 million was spent on independent expenditures in congressional races. Nonetheless, this figure represents a substantial increase from the $2.3 million spent in congressional races in 1980 and $317,000 spent in 1978. Moreover, although about 70 PACs engaged in independent expenditures in 1982 (fewer than the 105 active in 1980), approximately 40 nonconnected (ideological) PACs spent 90 percent of the total amount and about 95 percent of the $4.6 million spent in negative independent expenditures. [17]

Why are independent expenditures more popular among independent (ideological) PACs than the more traditional PACs? Independent expenditures are strategically well suited to the efforts of nonconnected PACs. These groups tend to be nationally based, with a wide constituency formed through their mail solicitations. They often have a head start in grass-roots organizing and the use of mass media, since these tactics are usually components of efforts to build and fund ideological PACs. Strategically, ideological PACs may believe that negative expenditures enable them to be the "bad guys" who undermine targeted opponents, while their candidate remains untainted by the mudslinging. [18] Finally, ideological PACs may perceive that even the largest permissible contribution to a candidate may not make him as responsive to their interests as will an independent expenditure campaign—or the threat of one—to fire up his constituents. [19]

Independent expenditures by PACs are widely criticized for their pernicious impact on American politics. Ironically, when *Buckley* struck down restrictions on independent expenditures, the Court asserted:

> We find that the governmental interest in preventing corruption and the appearance of corruption is inadequate to justify [the] . . . ceiling on independent expenditures. [20]
>
> [T]he independent advocacy restricted by the provision does not presently appear to pose dangers of real or apparent corruption comparable to those identified with large campaign contributions. [21]

Contrary to these optimistic claims, opponents of independent expenditures level numerous charges:

1. Independent expenditures undermine the efforts of campaign finance laws to reduce the influence of large contributors in elections. [22]
2. The tactic of independent expenditures tends to preclude any accountability of the spending committee to its contributors, to the candidates they support or oppose, or to the voters they seek to influence. [23]
3. In many instances, expenditures are made with enough shared information to call their "independence" into question. [24]
4. The tendency of independent expenditures to favor negative approaches lowers the quality of political debate and increases the disillusionment of voters. [25]

Although many of these charges confuse the actions of independent (nonconnected) PACs with those of PACs that make independent expenditures, they clearly indicate dissatisfaction with the benign view toward independent expenditures expressed in *Buckley*. Since ideological PACs have been most active in using independent expenditures, efforts to curb the use of this tactic will doubtless have a chilling effect on the activities of ideological PACs in the future.

## Influencing Elections: A Closer Look at Ten Ideological PACs

In the aggregate, ideological PACs are unique in several significant ways: their motivations, their rate of growth, their focus on challengers, the amount of resources spent on overhead, and their propensity to use the volatile tactic of independent expenditures. To understand how liberal and conservative PACs seek to influence elections, however, one must turn from aggregate data to specific cases. Though there is great diversity in the way ideological PACs are organized, the way decisions are made, and the resources at their disposal, examination of a selected group of PACs will generate some conclusions about the strategies and tactics ideological PACs use to influence elections. The ten PACs selected for study are among the foremost multi-issue and single-issue liberal and conservative PACs in American politics today. They include two liberal and two conservative general-issue groups and three pairs of single-issue groups. Table 5.2 on page 152 introduces the selected PACs and the acronyms commonly used to refer to them.

The National Conservative Political Action Committee (NCPAC) has been one of the top two PACs since 1978, according to FEC records on PAC receipts and expenditures. (Jesse Helms's National Congressional Club is the other.) NCPAC raised over $7.6 million in 1980, spending $3.3 million on independent expenditures but only $237,806 on contributions to candidates. In 1981-82, NCPAC raised over $10 million. Begun by Roger Stone, Charles Black, and Terry Dolan in 1975, NCPAC has grown from "three people and a mimeograph machine"[26] to a staff of over 50. Perhaps best known for its independent expenditures to help defeat four liberal senators in 1980,[27] NCPAC is also heavily involved in making direct contributions to candidates, training candidates and their staff, and providing consultant services. Plans for the future include grassroots mobilizing efforts complete with the formation of local chapters.

Like NCPAC, the Committee for the Survival of a Free Congress (CSFC) is a conservative, multi-issue committee. Formed in 1974 by key New Right strategist Paul Weyrich (with the help of fund-raiser Richard Viguerie), CSFC led the way for conservatives to become aggressively involved in elections. The CSFC developed a network of field workers to gather political information and recruit candidates. It also ran the first conservative campaign training schools and led other New Right PACs to target their resources to challenge liberal incumbents. Even in 1982, a year when many conservative PACs were retrenching to protect vulnerable incumbents, CSFC still contributed 88 percent of its funds to challengers, with a 40 percent success record over all (down slightly from 47 percent in 1980).

TABLE 5.2.
SELECTED IDEOLOGICAL POLITICAL ACTION COMMITTEES

| Acronym | Political Action Committee | FEC Category in 1982 | Description |
|---|---|---|---|
| ADA/PAC | Americans for Democratic Action/PAC | Nonconnected | Liberal, multi-issue |
| ASC/PAC | American Security Council/PAC | Corporation[a] | Conservative, pro-defense |
| CLW | Council for a Livable World | Nonconnected | Liberal, anti-nuclear arms |
| CSFC | Committee for the Survival of a Free Congress | Nonconnected | Conservative, multi-issue |
| GOACC | Gun Owners of America Campaign Committee | Trade/membership/health | Conservative, pro-gun |
| HCI/PAC | Handgun Control, Inc./PAC | Corporation without stock | Liberal, anti-handguns |
| LAPAC | Life Amendment PAC | Nonconnected | Conservative, pro-life |
| NARAL-PAC | National Abortion Rights Action League—PAC | Nonconnected[b] | Liberal, pro-choice |
| NCEC | National Committee for an Effective Congress | Nonconnected | Liberal, multi-issue |
| NCPAC | National Conservative PAC | Nonconnected | Conservative, multi-issue |

a. Nonconnected in 1980.
b. Trade/membership/health in 1980.

Weyrich insists that he patterned the CSFC after the leading liberal group, the National Committee for an Effective Congress (NCEC), which has been active since Maurice Rosenblatt founded it in 1948 with the support of noteworthy individuals such as Eleanor Roosevelt. NCEC remains the top liberal PAC in receipts, ranking fourth among ideological PACs and sixth among all PACs in 1982. Originally, NCEC provided substantial sums to individual candidates and sponsored fund-raising events for them. Since 1976, however, it has focused less on raising funds for candidates and more on providing campaign services such as polling, research, targeting studies, and media consultation. NCEC retains consultants and donates their services as in-kind contributions that cost much less than the consultants would charge the individual candidates. NCEC is also developing a program to recruit entertainment celebrities to assist targeted congressional campaigns. But NCEC is most noted within the liberal PAC community as a primary source of information on the merits and status of campaigns and candidates.

Only one other multi-issue (nonlabor) liberal PAC existed prior to the 1980 election: ADA/PAC, itself a fledgling group of modest means. Although Americans for Democratic Action has been active in lobbying and educational activities since 1947, its PAC was not begun until 1978, when it formed at the urging of an important member of ADA's board of directors. ADA/PAC did not become active in campaigns until the 1980 election cycle, raising nearly $50,000 and contributing over $46,000 to candidates. Because of limited financial and staff resources, ADA/PAC provides few campaign services other than checks to candidates.

In addition to these multi-issue PACs, three pairs of single-issue PACs, representing liberal or conservative stances on abortion, gun control, and nuclear arms proliferation — all important issues in the policy agenda of the New Right — were examined. The PACs chosen for each issue were the leading PACs on each side, according to FEC figures on receipts in 1980.

In 1977, Life Amendment Political Action Committee (LAPAC) was founded by its present director, Paul Brown, to mobilize prolife supporters to become active in elections. Brown discerned a need for a national organization to train and organize people for involvement at the local level, while targeting prolife funds into key marginal races. To enable prolife supporters to serve as valuable volunteers in local campaigns, LAPAC holds grass-roots training seminars based on a packet of campaigning materials they designed. To promote the visibility and salience of the prolife cause, Brown also places heavy emphasis on attracting media attention. Thus, in 1982 LAPAC concentrated on a campaign to defeat Senator Edward Kennedy based on a comic book portraying him as the black sheep of the family.

Since 1969, almost a decade before LAPAC was formed, the National Abortion Rights Action League (NARAL) has been using national lobbying and local affiliate groups to promote its prochoice objectives. In 1980, however, it decided that providing information and lobbying against antiabortion legislation were not enough to protect its interests, especially if prolife forces ever succeeded in passing an antiabortion amendment. NARAL-PAC was begun in affiliation with NARAL to protect incumbents on antiabortion "hit lists" in 1980. The PAC altered its tactics significantly for 1982, stressing grass-roots organizing in congressional races and directing its financial and grass-roots support to prochoice leaders in Congress or prochoice challengers in marginal races. It also trained its local affiliates in seven states to campaign for legislative candidates who will be able to block the ratification of an antiabortion amendment at the state level.

Turning to the issue of gun control, Gun Owners of America Campaign Committee (GOACC) is the representative conservative PAC. At the instigation of Richard Viguerie, GOACC was founded by California State Senator H.L. Richardson in 1975. A related PAC for California state electoral activities was formed at the same time. GOACC raised over $1.4 million in 1980, but spent only $183,480 on contributions to candidates and $119,871 on independent expenditures. In 1982, according to Executive Director Bill Saracino, most of the staff's efforts focused on California politics, with GOACC restricted to making direct cash contributions to federal candidates to further their campaigns. The California committee also works to educate gun owners to get involved in local races. The task of Gun Owners has not been easy, for its constituency is traditionally apolitical, even though its commitment to the right to bear arms is unwavering.

To counter the activities of GOACC and the National Rifle Association, Handgun Control Inc. Political Action Committee (HCI/PAC) was founded in 1979. Formally affiliated with the lobbying organization, Handgun Control Inc., the PAC initially attempted to use anti-incumbent tactics and grass-roots mobilization efforts to influence the 1980 elections. It raised $171,589, contributed $6300, and spent $43,055 in independent expenditures in 1980—trivial amounts compared to GOACC. Given limited financial and staff resources in 1982 as well, the PAC settled for simply writing checks to sympathetic candidates, especially rewarding every supporter of the Kennedy-Rodino Handgun Crime Control Act with at least a token gift.

Concentrating on an issue more tied to foreign policy are two organizations that have been involved for decades in lobbying, research, and education, and in electoral activities to promote their policy preferences on national defense matters. The American Security Council was founded in 1955 by retired officers of the U.S. armed services to promote national security. The ASC Political Action Committee (ASC/PAC) was not set up until 1980, when over $100,000 was contributed to 104 candidates. The PAC mainly held fund-raising events for incumbents on ASC's Coalition for Peace through Strength.

On the other side, the Council for a Livable World (CLW) was formed in 1962 by physicist Leo Szilard, out of his concern about the prospect of a nuclear holocaust. From its inception, CLW conducted research and educational activities, lobbied, and was involved in elections by soliciting funds for senatorial candidates opposed to nuclear proliferation. Its tactics, little changed in 21 years, are still very effective: CLW asks members to write checks directly to specific candidates but send them via the CLW. In this way, CLW can raise more money for candidates than it can contribute directly. For example, in 1980 the CLW gave only $32,584 in cash and in-kind contributions to candidates, whereas their supporters contributed $256,653 directly to CLW-endorsed candidates including $46,271 to Senator John Culver.

The CLW has always dealt only with senators because it believes the Senate has the most control over issues of national defense. In 1982, however, the Nuclear Freeze Resolution and other political developments prompted the CLW to form PeacePAC to contribute to House candidates. After less than six months in existence, PeacePAC was able to contribute a total of $58,248 and transmit another $15,045 to House candidates.

The financial statuses of each of these ideological PACs differ widely, as seen in table 5.3 on page 156. Contrary to the post-1980 election claims that conservatives were far ahead of liberal PACs, the evidence from these ten PACs is mixed. The conservative PACs selected raised over $11.4 million in 1980 and $13.8 million in 1982, compared to the liberals $2.7 million and $4.2 million, respectively. NCPAC is largely responsible for skewing the figures, however, for there is no clear pattern of conservative superiority in either 1980 or 1982 when PACs are considered in pairs: NCEC v. CSFC, ADA/PAC v. NCPAC, NARAL-PAC v. LAPAC, HCI/PAC v. GOACC, and CLW v. ASC/PAC. In fact, in many instances the liberal PACs spent more on political activities than their conservative counterparts, even though the conservative PACs raised considerably more money. Even where conservative PACs had greater total political expenditures, liberals gave more in direct contributions, whereas conservatives engaged more in independent expenditures.

The independent expenditure campaigns of the PACs listed in table 5.3 tend to focus on presidential elections or on negative campaigns. In 1980, GOACC spent $114,213 in support of candidate Ronald Reagan and NCPAC spent $1,872,730 for Reagan and $364,410 against other presidential candidates. Even in 1982, NCPAC spent $75,904 to support President Reagan's programs. As for negative campaigning, all of HCI/PAC's 1980 expenditures funded attacks on congressional candidates rather than endorsements for their opponents. Negativism prevailed in 1982 as well, for LAPAC spent $219,055 against congressional candidates and NCPAC spent $3,039,490 attacking candidates for Congress compared to $61,820 in positive expenditures.[28]

Even if independent expenditures are counted among the political expenditures of PACs, the liberal PACs still spend less of their total resources on overhead and fund-raising costs than do these conservative PACs. Not only do the conservatives tend to channel a smaller proportion of their receipts into political expenditures, they also tend to carry substantial debts. (I discussed such "deficit financing" when explaining the differences between ideological PACs and business or labor PACs. Among the ideological PACs, however, conserva-

## TABLE 5.3.
### Financial Status of Selected Ideological Political Action Committees, 1980 and 1982

| PAC[a] | Election | Adjusted Receipts[b] | Contributions to Candidates | Indendent Expenditures[c] | Total Political Expenditures | Debts Owed |
|---|---|---|---|---|---|---|
| NCEC | 1982 | $2,434,356 | $408,929 | none | $408,929 | $65,183 |
|  | 1980 | 1,570,788 | 424,008 | none | 424,008 | 36,771 |
| CSFC | 1982 | 2,339,401 | 156,123 | none | 156,123 | 271,706 |
|  | 1980 | 1,623,750 | 132,588 | none | 132,588 | 138,259 |
| ADA/PAC | 1982 | 88,283 | 76,950 | none | 76,950 | none |
|  | 1980 | 49,380 | 46,750 | none | 46,750 | none |
| NCPAC | 1982 | 10,000,931 | 264,357 | $3,177,214 | 3,441,571 | 970,702 |
|  | 1980 | 7,648,540 | 237,806 | 3,307,962 | 3,545,768 | 176,593 |
| NARAL-PAC | 1982 | 611,490 | 296,863 | none | 296,863 | none |
|  | 1980 | 413,891 | 201,032 | 2,934 | 203,966 | none |
| LAPAC | 1982 | 414,093 | 1,500 | 255,510 | 257,010 | 17,215 |
|  | 1980 | 625,748 | 20,121 | 65,536 | 85,657 | 90,904 |
| HCI/PAC | 1982 | 200,718 | 108,925 | 286 | 109,211 | none |
|  | 1980 | 170,589 | 6,300 | 43,055 | 49,355 | 1,698 |
| GOACC | 1982 | 932,329 | 73,600 | 15,540 | 89,140 | 90,830 |
|  | 1980 | 1,414,951 | 183,480 | 119,891 | 303,371 | 178,321 |
| CLW | 1982 | 839,534 | 51,103 | [460,606[d]] | 51,103 + | none |
|  | 1980 | 452,756 | 32,584 | [256,663[d]] | 32,584 + | none |
| ASC/PAC | 1982 | 115,581 | 120,882 | none | 120,882 | none[e] |
|  | 1980 | 157,365 | 101,280 | none | 101,280 | none |

Note: Table 5.3 continued at foot of p. 157.

tive PACs far exceed liberal PACs in their propensity to tolerate large debts.) Two final conclusions can be drawn from table 5.3: The financial power of these larger ideological PACs is increasing, and in many cases the sums involved are considerable.

Receipt and expenditure figures alone are not adequate for understanding the impact ideological PACs may have in congressional elections. The strategies and tactics used to enhance the impact of PAC expenditures should also be examined. Four strategies of influence are used by ideological PACs, providing general political goals for their diverse campaign activities. These strategies are the basic approaches by which all PACs seek to gain power through affecting electoral outcomes. Various tactics are used (1) to influence the quality of the candidates running, (2) to improve the quality of the campaigns they run, (3) to alter the issue environment of the campaign, and (4) to increase the turnout of voters supporting the candidates the PACs favor. Table 5.4 on page 158 indicates which strategies and tactics were used by each of ten PACs in 1982. Rather than give the details on each of the PAC's use of each tactic, key examples will be described to illustrate how various tactics further the strategies of influence.

## Influencing the Quality of the Candidate

Although influenced by national trends, congressional elections remain local contests between candidates.[29] Thus the character of candidates, their expertise in campaigning and in office, their level of name recognition, and the image they project to the electorate affect the outcome of individual races. PACs can influence the quality of candidates by recruitment, training programs, and provision of consultant services.

The CSFC has always placed great emphasis on recruiting conservative candidates in districts targeted as ones that look promising for conservative

TABLE 5.3 *(continued)*

SOURCES: 1980 figures are from the Federal Election Commission, *Reports on Financial Activity, 1979-1980* (Party and Non-Party Political Committees), vol. 4, Final Report, January 1982. 1982 figures are from the Federal Election Commission, *Reports on Financial Activity, 1981-1982, Final Report* (Party and Non-Party Political Committees), vols. 3 and 4, October 1983.

a. Conservative PACs are underlined.

b. Adjusted receipts exclude monies transferred among affiliated committees.

c. Independent expenditure figures are taken from the FEC *Index of Independent Expenditures 1979-1980,* November 1981, and the FEC *Index of Independent Expenditures 1981-1982,* September 1983.

d. Figures in brackets show what CLW raised *for* candidates in addition to what it gave in contributions. The figures, from CLW records, indicate the importance of CLW's fundraising activities on behalf of candidates.

e. Because ASC/PAC began 1982 with $25,000 cash on hand, it could spend more than it raised in 1982-82 without showing a debt.

TABLE 5.4.
IDEOLOGICAL PACS: APPROACHES TO INFLUENCING ELECTIONS IN 1982

| Strategy | Tactic | Conservatives | | | | | | Liberals | | | |
|---|---|---|---|---|---|---|---|---|---|---|---|
| | | NCPAC | CSFC | ASC/PAC | GOACC | LAPAC | NCEC | ADA/PAC | CLW or Peace PAC | HCI/PAC | NARAL |
| Influence quality of candidate | Candidate training and recruitment (training schools or seminars) | * | * | — | — | — | — | — | — | — | — |
| | Consultation and services (polls, media production, organizing) | * | * | * | — | — | * | — | * | — | * |
| | Training and placement of staff (schools for paid staff and volunteers) | * | * | — | — | — | — | * | — | — | * |
| Influence quality of campaign | Fund-raising assistance (direct mailings, events with other PACs) | * | — | * | — | — | * | — | * | * | * |
| | Direct contributions | * | * | * | * | * | * | — | * | — | * |
| | Independent expenditures (broadcasting, grass-roots mobilizing) | * | — | — | * | * | — | — | * | — | — |
| Influence campaign issue environment | Report cards or candidate rating ("hit lists") | * | * | * | — | * | * | — | * | * | — |
| | Endorsements | * | * | * | * | * | * | — | * | * | * |
| Influence voter mobilization | Voter registration | — | — | — | * | — | — | — | — | — | — |
| | Canvassing | — | — | — | * | — | — | — | — | — | * |
| | Volunteer recruitment | * | * | — | * | * | — | — | — | — | * |

NOTE: * signifies that a committee engaged in the activity indicated. — signifies that it did not.

victories. A 1981 brochure proposed that CSFC recruiting efforts continue from February of 1981 through April of 1982, with $110,000 budgeted to cover the candidate targeting and recruitment program. Among the candidates CSFC claims to have helped recruit over the years are Senators Charles Grassley, Jeremiah Denton, Gordon Humphrey, Dan Quayle, and Jim Abdnor.[30] Nonetheless, the best recruitment efforts by PACs can go astray. Weyrich estimated that there were 20 additional congressional districts in 1980 where a conservative candidacy should have been viable but where no strong candidate could be found to oppose a potentially vulnerable liberal.[31] And in 1982, CSFC's recruitment and training efforts were stymied by the uncertainty of redistricting, making it difficult to persuade good conservative candidates to run.[32]

Once candidates are recruited, they and their staff need to be trained in the art of campaigning. Toward this end, NCPAC has developed an extensive network of training programs. Over 200 people attended NCPAC's first "training seminar" in 1976. The seminar featured a campaign management school plus concurrent sessions on finance management, public relations, and advertising.[33] By 1982 the program split into three separate schools: one each for candidates, finance directors, and campaign managers. The candidate schools feature three days of close interaction among ten or 12 carefully selected students and "experts" on virtually all aspects of campaigning: polling, scheduling, advertising, recruiting volunteers, soliciting support from PACs, and dealing with the media.[34] About 45 candidates attended the four schools NCPAC sponsored in 1982.

The campaign management and campaign finance schools held in connection with NCPAC in 1980 and 1982 were actually sponsored by the National Conservative Foundation (NCF)—NCPAC's unofficially affiliated research and educational arm. Each three-day-long school had around 30 students, about half of whom were already affiliated with conservative campaigns. In 1981-82, 337 students attended the 11 management schools NCF hosted, for a total cost of over $160,000. Speakers covered many of the same topics as the candidate schools, but from the perspective of the manager. The six campaign finance schools NCF sponsored in 1981-82 trained 147 students in many aspects of fund raising, for a total cost of $58,000.[35] Thus, in terms of the number of students trained and the resources committed to conducting the schools, NCPAC's and NCF's efforts are substantial.

## Influencing the Quality of the Campaign

Once candidates are recruited and trained, ideological PACs often serve as clearinghouses for consultant services. They may advise candidates on whom to use for polling, media, or fund raising; they may contract to have these provided as in-kind contributions, or they may provide them themselves. Ideological PACs give in-kind services to exert greater control over how their resources are used by campaigns and to maximize the value of their contributions.

The National Committee for an Effective Congress provides a more extensive range of campaign services than any other ideological PAC. Since 1974, NCEC has retained consultants to assist candidates with campaign organization, volunteer recruitment, media relations, canvassing and get-out-the-vote activities, polling, and advertising, at the equivalent of bulk rates. In 1982, NCEC funded 30 polls, ten direct mail fund-raising or persuasion programs, 50 research projects, and 35 on-site visits by consultants, for a total cost of $153,000. The PAC estimates these services would have cost the campaigns over three times as much if purchased individually.

Foremost of all NCEC's campaign services are its detailed targeting reports. NCEC's in-house computers analyze past election data from each state or district and provide precinct-level information on previous voting patterns to guide candidates in their campaigns. Candidates receive reports tailored to their needs to plan media programs, target persuadable voters, concentrate get-out-the-vote drives, or direct other campaign activities. In 1982, NCEC provided 102 Senate and House campaigns with precinct targeting studies. In addition, the AFL-CIO's Committee on Political Education (COPE) contracted to receive copies of these studies to guide the voter registration and voter turnout efforts of its labor unions.[36]

Perhaps NCEC's most intriguing campaign service in 1982 came from celebrities recruited through its new Citizens in Politics program. Designed to be a clearinghouse matching politically progressive entertainers with congressional candidates who could benefit from their support, Citizens in Politics channeled celebrities into 19 campaigns. For example, Michael Farrell, better known as "B.J. Honeycutt," helped Barney Frank with three fund raisers in Boston, then appeared with Robert Edgar in Philadelphia, concluding with a campaign visit on behalf of Peter Kostmayer, also in Pennsylvania—all in a single weekend. The celebrity visits were designed to convince fans of the entertainers that they should become supporters of the candidates.

Of all the in-kind services ideological PACs may provide to candidates, fund-raising assistance is the most universally appreciated. By hosting fund-raising events attended by other PACs and by mailing solicitations to their supporters on behalf of candidates, PACs may multiply the amount of money they are responsible for providing to a candidate tenfold or more. For several liberal and conservative PACs, fund-raising assistance is the principal in-kind service provided to candidates, meriting consideration as a tactic separate from the provision of consulting and services.

The two national defense-related PACs—American Security Council PAC and the Council for a Livable World—concentrate on raising funds for candidates they endorse. In 1981 alone, members of ASC's Washington staff served on 47 steering committees for fund raisers for congressmen.[37] "Steering Committee" breakfasts, arranged for candidates to solicit interested PAC representatives, cost ASC/PAC only about $200 each to conduct, but usually raised between $30,000 and $100,000 for the candidate, according to Richard Sellers.[38]

Whereas ASC works to direct the flow of PAC money to candidates committed to defense, the CLW works to funnel individual contributions to candidates opposed to nuclear arms. Each CLW endorsement letter usually makes a pitch for two senatorial candidates in addition to requesting support for the organization. Contributors are asked to make out a check to the candidate they prefer. If there is no preference, supporters are requested to fund specific candidates or the CLW, depending on the letter with which their last name begins. Checks are then "bundled" in the CLW's office and delivered to candidates in a lump sum. The tactic enables the council to contribute more than the $5000 per candidate per election permitted by the Federal Election Campaign Act restrictions. In fact, CLW raised over $460,000 for 19 senatorial candidates in 1982, 15 of whom received more than $10,000, five of whom received over $40,000 each. In 1980, whereas the CLW gave only $32,584 in direct or in-kind contributions to candidates, its solicitations raised a total of $256,663 for 12 candidates.[39]

The importance of fund-raising assistance as a tactic for influencing the quality of campaigns is too often ignored. Yet, the previous cases show that PACs of seemingly modest means may make far greater contributions to campaigns than FEC figures indicate. Although such PACs may not always eagerly disclose how much money they raised for candidates they supported, undoubtedly the candidates are kept informed.

## Influencing the Campaign Issue Environment

Use of independent expenditures, already discussed at length, is a tactic that can influence directly the quality of specific campaigns or indirectly affect the issue environment of the campaigns. Frequently, both effects occur, although perhaps in ways unintended. For example, early NCPAC ads against Senator Sarbanes (D-Md.) in 1982 were designed to focus campaign debate on whether "Paul Sarbanes is too liberal for Maryland." By weakening Sarbanes's standing in polls, NCPAC sought to increase the viability of an opposing conservative candidate. Successful weakening of Sarbanes could have boosted the early fund-raising and campaign organizing efforts of an opponent. Indeed, NCPAC hoped it would help persuade Congresswoman Marjorie Holt to bid for the seat. Thus, the implicit NCPAC strategy was to influence the quality of the campaign by framing the issue environment—possibly even influencing the quality of the candidate.

Unfortunately for NCPAC, the strategy backfired in virtually every respect. Sarbanes made NCPAC's interference, not his liberalism, the central issue. The NCPAC attack energized his campaign rhetoric and fund raising. Sarbanes raised $12,000 at a single anti-NCPAC event in September 1982.[40] Liberal PACs made Sarbanes a *cause célèbre*. Finally, although NCPAC polls indicate their ads helped polarize the electorate, Larry Hogan failed to use this to his advantage. Vic Gresham, NCPAC political director, complained, "We created negatives and then the negatives would go away. Hogan just never got the money to take advantage of the negatives we generated."[41]

Another major independent expenditure campaign was waged in 1982 against Senator Kennedy by Life Amendment Political Action Committee. The LAPAC campaign demonstrates how independent expenditures can be used to accomplish multiple objectives, including public relations and fund raising. *Every Family Has One,* a comic book portraying Teddy Kennedy as the black sheep of the Kennedy family, was the focus of LAPAC's efforts. Over 200,000 copies were distributed throughout Massachusetts, including one to every household in Speaker Tip O'Neill's district.[42] The total fell short of the 1 to 2 million copies LAPAC hoped to distribute under the auspices of Citizens Organized to Replace Kennedy (CORK), the title LAPAC gave to its "special project" of 1982.

Most of LAPAC's involvement in the 1982 election centered on the CORK program. The fact that Kennedy won (albeit with a much lower margin than in 1976) failed to convince Paul Brown that the program flopped. "We accomplished our objectives," he claimed.[43] CORK wanted to "expose Kennedy's record" and make him attentive to the views of the prolife movement. But the comic book also generated media attention for LAPAC, including a column by Jack Anderson and a mention in the *Washington Post.* And CORK solicitations raised over $200,000 from 25,000 supporters. In addition, CORK sent out over 8000 copies of the comic book after requests from individuals willing to pay $1.50 for it. Since it cost CORK about 20 cents each for production and mailing, the orders alone raised over $10,000 unsolicited.[44] Thus, even though LAPAC's independent expenditure project may not have altered the electoral outcome, Brown is convinced it paid substantial dividends.

## Mobilizing Voters

Whereas many of the tactics discussed above are ways PACs influence elections by altering technical aspects of the campaigns, efforts to mobilize voters rely on the most basic campaign resource — people — to generate the ultimate campaign objective — votes. Since at least the beginning of COPE in 1944, business and labor interests have encouraged citizens to exercise their civic duty to vote. Several ideological PACs have refined grass-roots organizing programs to make strategic manipulation of voter turnout a fundamental strategy of electoral influence. Especially when midterm election turnout averages less than 40 percent of the number of eligible voters, PACs can have a critical influence if they register supporters to vote and make sure that a larger than normal proportion of their supporters turns out to vote.

Ideological PACs may be involved in tactics of voter mobilization independently or in coordination with campaign organizations. For example, the League of Conservation Voters concentrated on independent canvassing and voter registration drives in 1982, but the efforts were targeted to further the campaigns of favored candidates. On the other hand, GOACC lacked the resources for canvassing, but it concentrated on getting supporters to register to vote by providing forms in the mail or at local sporting goods shops. Furthermore, GOACC encouraged hunters to vote by absentee ballot, since the November elections fall in the heart of prime hunting seasons.[45] None of these efforts was tied to support for specific candidates.

Instead of independent registration, canvassing, or get-out-the-vote drives, some PACs recruit and train volunteers to assist selected candidates in their campaigns. For example, LAPAC estimated that in 1982 over 500 prolife supporters were trained to assist campaigns at seminars based on the PAC's Priority Volunteer Module Program.[46] On the other side, one of the most extensive volunteer training and recruitment efforts in 1982 was launched by LAPAC's opponent, NARAL. The important difference in the focus of the two efforts was that NARAL targeted volunteers to assist state legislative candidates in seven states. The 10,000 volunteers activated in these races tried to help NARAL garner enough representation in these state legislatures to block ratification of an antiabortion amendment to the Constitution if one is proposed. The mobilization of so many volunteers in 1982 also increases the potential for mobilizing more experienced volunteers in federal races in 1984, if desired. "That depends on how the targeted congressional races match up with our grass-roots strength and on how our leadership feels about the effectiveness of such activities," explained NARAL-PAC Director Marie Bass. "At either the state or federal level, I think our organizational model and volunteer training is more sophisticated than that of any other group on our side of the issue."[47]

## Tactical Standbys: Cash Contributions, Endorsements, and Hit Lists

Three other tactics listed in table 5.4 — direct contributions, endorsements, and report cards or hit lists — hardly require special consideration as they are the fundamental activities ideological PACs use to influence elections. Although the reasons for using these tactics are obvious, how decisions are made about whom to support or oppose deserves discussion because there is great variation. Approaches range from systematic to chaotic. NARAL-PAC ranked candidates in four categories for support in 1982, stipulating the maximum contribution to be given. HCI/PAC and CSFC used detailed questionnaires to decide whether candidates merited support. ADA/PAC, NCEC, and NCPAC relied heavily on interviews with candidates and evidence from polls. Several PACs, such as ADA/PAC and CLW, required final decisions to be approved by their boards of directors. Others, such as NCPAC, frequently decided ad hoc. Finally, although most ideological PACs insist they prefer to focus on marginal races where their support may make or break the election, all admit that intervening factors may force them to support some "sure things" and other "lost causes." Members of the board of directors may demand that their friends receive token support. Endorsements by local affiliates may trap the national organization into supporting their choices. And PACs may feel obligated to reward incumbents who have faithfully supported their causes.[48]

Not only do PACs vary on how decisions are made, they differ on the timing of contributions or endorsements and on the ways of using ratings or hit lists. Early contributions are designed to influence primary outcomes and assure the early viability of campaigns. Contributions near the end of the campaign may help candidates at their time of greatest desperation. These may also evade disclosure on FEC preelection reports, preventing opponents from publicizing support from groups of which some constituents may disapprove. (The Human Rights Campaign Fund, a PAC for homosexuals, gives late contributions for this reason.) Similarly, endorsements may be public or private (by mail) depending on the PAC's willingness to risk mobilizing its opposition.

Finally, consider some of the reasoning behind candidate ratings, report cards, or hit lists. Ratings or report cards that provide detailed information on congressional roll-call votes or candidate positions are excellent ways to enhance the knowledge voters have about candidates. They also justify PAC decisions about whom to support or oppose. In addition, when sent to supporters, ratings may guide individuals' decisions to provide financial or volunteer assistance. Publicized in the mass media, report cards attract attention to the PAC and its efforts, perhaps helping to raise funds from new supporters. Hit lists are especially popular for such public relations purposes. In 1982, PeacePAC issued its "Doomsday Dozen"; LAPAC cited its "Deadly Dozen"; CSFC sent contributors its list of ten defeatable liberals, and NCEC countered by providing pictures of at least 18 congressmen who needed help and 16 congressmen the PAC intended to defeat.

In short, the tactics used by ideological PACs to influence elections may range from mere endorsements and cash contributions to precinct organizations and campaign services as effective as those of the actual campaigns. Each ideological PAC has its areas of expertise, emphasizing some tactics over others. Even among PACs engaged in the same sort of activities, the extent and effectiveness may vary greatly depending upon the expertise of the PAC and the resources at its disposal. When evaluating the impact of individual ideological PACs in the elections of the '80s, the many differences in the tactics used must be taken into consideration.

## Cautions on Evaluating Ideological PACs

Evaluating the extent to which specific ideological PACs or liberal or conservative PACs in general had an impact on the 1980 and 1982 elections is beyond the scope of this study.[49] Instead, the above descriptions suggest that evaluating the impact of ideological PACs may be more complicated than evaluating corporate, labor, or trade association PACs. Ideological PACs differ from traditional PACs in their rate of growth, the proportion of their funds spent on overhead, their contribution patterns, their propensity to make independent expenditures, and their use of many other tactics to influence elections. Aggregate figures on PAC receipts and expenditures belie the tremendous diversity among ideological PACs in the scope and range of their activities. Similar contribution figures may conceal the fact that different tactics may have widely different impacts in campaigns. Unfortunately, whereas financial data on PACs is readily available from the FEC, the information necessary to assess the effectiveness of the many tactics of the many different ideological PACs is difficult to obtain. Thus, at the least, political analysts ought to temper their claims about the influence of ideological PACs with a more complete understanding of how these PACs attempt to influence electoral outcomes.

In addition to considering the diverse tactics used by ideological PACs, one should remember that any influence they have is most likely to be exerted at the margin—in close electoral contests. Despite the occasional exaggerated claims about how NCPAC or prolife PACs or Nuclear Freeze activists have "determined" the outcome of certain elections, most leaders of ideological PACs privately admit that their aim is to help at the margin. They believe that a critical campaign contribution or the mobilization of 2 to 8 percent of the voters in a district can be enough to provide the margin of victory. Combined with the baseline vote of party supporters and the other clusters of supporters mobilized to vote, the additional 2 to 8 percent can make a significant difference.

The difference between the outcomes of close races in 1982 versus 1980 indicates that the marginal impact of contributions by ideological PACs (or any other electoral force) depends upon other macro- and micro-political factors. Macro-political factors include the state of the economy and attitudes toward the President. Conservatives benefited from both in 1980 and were hindered in 1982. Micro-political factors include local variations such as redistricting decisions or whether promising candidates can be recruited. In 1982, some conservative leaders claimed their aggressive support of challengers was undermined by uncertainty over district lines and difficulty recruiting conservative candidates.[50]

In short, any analysis of ideological PAC influence in elections must recognize that no single PAC or cluster of PACs "makes or breaks" individual elections independent of contributing factors. Terry Dolan himself acknowledged that NCPAC alone cannot determine the outcome of an election. In a letter to supporters explaining NCPAC's losses in 1982 he admits, "Our experience in Maryland and West Virginia simply demonstrates that NCPAC cannot defeat Democratic Senators in strongly Democratic states without the help of other factors."[51] And if conservative or liberal PACs cannot control individual elections, they are even less deserving of credit for nationwide "mandates."

When considering what impact ideological PACs may have in future elections, the elections of 1980 and 1982 indicate that doomsayers should be cautious. Despite short-term tactical, technological, and resource advantages by one side over the other, the principle that "mobilization begets coutermobilization" holds true for ideological PACs, suggesting a balance in the long term. New Right PACs emerged in the 1970s by following the example of liberal PACs such as NCEC or CLW and labor's COPE. By 1980 student appeared to have surpassed teacher. But by 1982 new liberal PACs and revitalized old PACs fought back with many of the conservatives' tactics. Looking to the 1984 elections, neither side has a clear advantage.

Perhaps the most interesting and important questions about the past and future influence of ideological PACs are the ones that are the hardest to answer. They do not concern whether liberals or conservatives are ahead, or the relative importance of ideological PACs compared to corporate or labor PACs and the national parties. Instead, they focus on matters that are basic to the welfare of democratic government.

Some critics charge that the distortion, negativism, and stridency common in ideological advertisements and appeals adversely affect both congressional representatives and those they seek to represent. David S. Broder claims that the proliferation of negative campaigns "leads to gutless government, where the art of survival means avoiding any controversial stands that an opponent could use in a future 'attack' ad."[52] Former Senator Thomas McIntyre (D-N.H.) argues that the uncompromising intensity with which members of the New Right and others pursue certain issues creates a "balkanized political milieu" where "the purposeful course of government is disrupted by distraction."[53] These charges, and others like them, suggest that policy formation in Congress is being perverted or precluded because legislators are wary of "ideological bullies." At the same time, other critics imply that voters are being infected in various ways by the insidious influence of PACs. Peter Fenn, director of the new Center for Responsive Politics, suggests that declines in voter turnout and citizen confidence in government are tied to disgust with the growing influence of PACs and ideological interests.[54] Judge J. Skelly Wright of the U.S. Court of Appeals for the District of Columbia implies that the disruptive activities of independent PACs have discouraged "civic spirit, hope, and participation." The consequence, he argues, is "that disillusionment breeds alienation; that alienation breeds apathy; [and] that apathy menaces the democratic idea."[55] As early as 1978, Maurice Rosenblatt of the Committee for the Study of the American Electorate warned that the nation "may be losing the votes of the broadly concerned citizen, leaving the field to those motivated by narrow, parochial, and emotional interests."[56]

If these doomsayers are correct, radical campaign finance reform surgery may be necessary to excise these insidious ideological PACs. Clearly, the questions the critics raise are important to ponder. On the other hand, confidence in American politics can also be severely undermined by irresponsible, uninformed, and uncritical assertions that the democratic sky is falling. Most of the charges leveled against PACs in general and ideological PACs in particular lack both a clear articulation of the democratic values supposedly being subverted and systematic evidence that such subversion is occurring. Instead, what evidence exists indicates that the activities of ideological PACs and their related organizations may simply represent "politics as usual." For example, after a systematic study of the political tactics in the battle over abortion in America, Gilbert Y. Steiner concludes:

> Techniques used by the respective sides are not substantially different from those used by numerous other interest groups. In electoral politics, as in other areas explored in connection with the abortion dispute, there is less reason to be worried about the distortion of the American system than some observers of the system may think to be the case. A divisive issue is not necessarily a destructive issue.[57]

In fact, considering the paucity of information most voters have about congressional candidates,[58] ideological PACs may be enhancing democratic representation by providing voters with more information on candidates. One can decry the quality of the information provided, but charges that the campaign rhetoric of ideological PACs is akin to propaganda only add to the problem in their own rhetorical way. After all, bemoaning the fact that campaigns in America are based on propaganda rather than reasoned debate is not new.[59] Even granting that recent approaches used by some ideological PACs in campaigns are deceptive, inflammatory, or erroneous, the remedy for such evils ought to be *more* information rather than the silencing of ideological PACs. The flourishing of sources of information enhances the basis on which voters decide who should represent them in Congress. In a similar vein, one can argue that the strong-arm tactics that liberal and conservative PACs use to hold legislators accountable to their constituents also reinforce the functioning of representative government rather than undermine it. Quite possibly, while some of the activities of ideological PACs may be cause for concern, others may prove to be positive influences in American politics.

In short, the activities and growth of ideological PACs may have important implications for American politics beyond who wins and loses specific elections. The normative criticisms leveled against liberal and conservative PACs are more than the "sour grapes" of those interests temporarily disadvantaged by political developments. The defenses ideological PACs offer for their activities are more than rationalizations for pragmatic decisions. But neither the attacks against nor the praises of ideological PACs are prima facie true. To evaluate these claims requires a sound theoretical exposition of how representative democracy in America should function, coupled with reliable information on how ideological PACs actually operate in American politics. The former is beyond the scope of this study, but the latter is precisely what I have attempted to provide. Since there is every indication that ideological PACs will be increasingly active in future elections, we do well to try to understand their operations better in order to assess both their electoral influence and their broader impact on democracy in America.

## Notes

1. For example, see Bill Peterson, "Democrats Claim Rout of the Commandos of the New Right Once and for All," *Washington Post,* November 5, 1982.
2. For a few noteworthy examples, see Senator Dennis DeConcini's remarks in the *Congressional Record,* December 20, 1982, S15773; Elizabeth Drew's two-part series, "Politics and Money," in the *New Yorker,* December 6 and 13, 1982; and Walter Isaacson's "Running with the PACs," in *Time,* October 25, 1982.
3. This definition begs the question of what "liberal" and "conservative" mean in the context of contemporary American politics. Well-respected scholars, encountering the same difficulty, have simply concluded that although the terms are generally meaningful in structuring political attitudes, which positions are considered liberal or conservative vary widely from decade to decade, and few Americans apply the terms with conceptual vigor. See Angus Campbell et al., *The American Voter* (New York: Wiley, 1960); and Norman H. Nie et al., *The Changing American Voter* (Cambridge, Mass.: Harvard University Press, 1976).
4. This description of the interests of ideological PACs is based on Jeffrey M. Berry's definition of public interest groups in *Lobbying for the People* (Princeton: Princeton University Press, 1977), 7.
5. Edward Roeder, in his reference book on PACs, compiled a listing of ideological PACs in many different categories including general liberal or conservative, foreign and military policy, civil liberties and individual rights, and economic issues. According to his list, there are about 160 PACs sponsored by other organizations and 470 unsponsored PACs that clearly concern a liberal or conservative issue or issues. I have discounted Roeder's figures by one-third to correct for duplicate references under different categories of PACs. Roeder's list may not be exhaustive or totally accurate, but it is the best list compiled in the literature to date. See *PACs Americana: A Directory of Political Action Committees (PACs) and Their Interests* (Washington, D.C.: Sunshine Services Corporation, 1982).
6. PACs tied to specific candidates have included, for example, President Reagan's Citizens for the Republic, Senator Helms's Congressional Club, and Senator Kennedy's Fund for a Democratic Majority.
7. Prior to 1977, PACs other than corporate and labor PACs were joined together in residual categories that changed from year to year.
8. Frank J. Sorauf relies on the distinction between PACs with "parents" and those without them in a provocative paper, "Accountability in Political Action Committees: Who's in Charge?" (paper presented at the 1982 annual meeting of the American Political Science Association).
9. The actual cost of mail fund raising depends on many factors, explained well in Larry J. Sabato, *The Rise of Political Consultants* (New York: Basic Books, 1981), 220-63. For data on the direct mail fund-raising programs of selected liberal and conservative PACs, see Margaret Latus, "Ideological PACs and Political Action," in *The New Christian Right,* ed. Robert Liebman and Robert Wuthnow (Hawthorne, N.Y.: Aldine, 1983).
10. *Federal Election Commission et al.* v. *National Right to Work Committee et al.* 51 Law Week 4037, 4039 (December 13, 1982).
11. The full implications of this ruling are still to be felt. Justice Rehnquist, writing for the unanimous Court, expanded on the inadequacy of the NRWC definition

Assessing Ideological PACs: From Outrage to Understanding

of membership in words that clearly suggest that sponsored PACs will need to re-assess the status of those they solicit as members: "[W]e think Congress did not intend to allow the 267,000 individuals solicited by NRWC during 1976 to come within the exclusion for 'members.' Although membership cards are ultimately sent to those who either contribute or respond in some other way to respondents' mailings, the solicitation letters themselves make no reference to members. Members play no part in the operation or administration of the corporation; they elect no corporate officials, and indeed there are apparently no membership meetings. There is no indication that NRWC's asserted members exercise any control over the expenditure of their contributions. . . . We think that under these circumstances, those solicited were insufficiently attached to the corporate structure of NRWC to qualify as 'members' under the statutory proviso." Ibid., 4039-40.

12. See "3 PACs Formed after Court's Ruling," *PACs and Lobbies,* January 5, 1983, 2-3.
13. Joseph E. Cantor, *Political Action Committees: Their Evolution and Growth and Their Implications for the Political System* (Washington, D.C.: Congressional Research Service, Report No. 82-92 GOV, November 6, 1981, updated May 7, 1982), 125.
14. 2 U.S.C. 431 (17).
15. 424 U.S. 1 (1976).
16. Figures from Federal Election Commission, *Reports on Financial Activity, 1979-1980* (Party and Non-Party Political Committees), vol. 1, summary tables, Final Report, pp. 116 and 125.
17. Federal Election Commission, *Index of Independent Expenditures, 1981-82* (September 1983).
18. John (Terry) Dolan, chairman of the notorious NCPAC (National Conservative Political Action Committee), has claimed, "A group like ours could lie through its teeth and the candidate it helps stays clean." Myra MacPherson, "The New Right Brigade," *Washington Post,* August 10, 1980, F1.
19. For example, in a NCPAC letter to Congressman Les Aspin on July 23, 1981, Dolan wrote: "If you will make a public statement in support of the President's tax cut package and state that you intend to vote for it, we will withdraw all radio and newspaper ads planned in your district." Letter reprinted in Theodore Sorensen, "Liberty or Loophole: Independent Expenditure Committees in Federal Election Campaigns" (report from the Democratic National Committee Task Force on Independent Expenditures, July 29, 1982), 63.
20. 424 U.S. (1976), 45.
21. Ibid.
22. In a written statement submitted to the House Administration Committee Task Force on Elections, July 28, 1982, Robert F. Bauer, general counsel for the Democratic Senatorial Campaign Committee, asserted "that the constitutional edicts of the Supreme Court [on independent expenditures] are to be respected, but that the virtual butchery of those principles in practice cannot be tolerated without ultimately facing the collapse of our entire effort to regulate federal campaigns with a view toward purging the corruptive influence of big money." U.S. House of Representatives, Committee on House Administration, Task Force on Elections, 97th Cong., 2d sess., *Hearings on Contribution Limitations and Independent Expenditures,* June 10 and July 28, 1982, 272.
23. See especially Sorauf, "Accountability in Political Action Committees," 20-26. Dolan

169

has asserted: "Ten independent expenditures groups, for example, could amass this great amount of money and defeat the point of accountability in politics." Quoted in MacPherson, "New Right Brigade," F1.

24. Elizabeth Drew discusses this matter at length in "Politics and Money II," and it is a major objection in the DNC Task Force on Independent Expenditures report.

25. See Joseph E. Cantor, *The Evolution of and Issues Surrounding Independent Expenditures in Election Campaigns* (Washington, D.C.: Congressional Research Service, Report No. 82-87 GOV, May 5, 1982), 46. Decrying the independent expenditure campaigns of conservative PACs in his 1982 reelection bid, Senator Dennis DeConcini warned that "present trends, if continued, will inevitably debase the quality of American politics." Statement in *Congressional Record,* December 20, 1982, S15775.

26. Personal interview with John (Terry) Dolan, November 12, 1982.

27. Senators George McGovern, Birch Bayh, John Culver, and Frank Church.

28. Figures from the Federal Election Commission, *Index of Independent Expenditures, 1979-1980,* November 1981, and the Federal Election Commission printout of the *Index of Independent Expenditures, 1981-82,* May 1983.

29. The relationship between national trends and local influences is explored in Gary C. Jacobson and Samuel Kernell, *Strategy and Choice in Congressional Elections* (New Haven: Yale University Press, 1981). Their argument is important for understanding how PAC contributions and especially tactics such as candidate recruitment or independent expenditures may influence national trends in elections. The thesis is "that politically active elites—candidates and those who recruit and finance them—provide a crucial connecting link between national-level phenomena and individual voting decisions" (ibid., 2). The leading ideological PACs examined in this study are clearly among these elites in certain cases.

30. According to Elaine Hartman, former CSFC fund raiser, in telephone interview, February 1, 1983.

31. Personal interview with Paul Weyrich, June 2, 1981.

32. According to a personal interview with CSFC executive director, Bob McAdam, November 16, 1982.

33. Personal interview with John (Terry) Dolan, November 12, 1982.

34. Personal interview with Cheryl Bendis, Dolan's personal assistant, August 9, 1982.

35. Personal interview with Lisa Dudley of the National Conservative Foundation, August 9, 1982.

36. Data on NCEC is from the November 16, 1982 report to the NCEC board of directors.

37. According to the American Security Council's 1982 President's Report.

38. Telephone interview with executive director, Richard Sellers, August 4, 1982.

39. Figures from Council for a Livable World press releases.

40. Saundra Saperstein, "Lack of Finances Causes Hogan to Curtail His Television Ads," *Washington Post,* October 16, 1982, C1.

41. Personal interview, November 18, 1982.

42. Personal interview with LAPAC's field director, Judy Parsons, September 20, 1982.

43. Telephone interview, November 5, 1982.

44. Personal interview with Paul Brown, September 20, 1982.

45. Personal interview with GOACC field representative Sam Paradez.

46. Telephone interview with Judy Parsons, August 18, 1982.

47. Information and quotations from telephone interview, January 27, 1983.
48. For further discussion on the idiosyncrasies of PAC targeting decisions, see Larry Light, "The Game of PAC Targeting: Friends, Foes and Guesswork," *Congressional Quarterly Weekly Report,* November 21, 1981, 2267.
49. For a preliminary analysis, see Larry J. Sabato, "Parties, PACs, and Independent Groups," in *The American Elections of 1982,* ed. Thomas E. Mann and Norman Ornstein (Washington, D.C.: American Enterprise Institute, 1983), 99-103.
50. Personal interview with CSFC's Bob McAdam, November 16, 1982.
51. Letter of November 10, 1982.
52. "When Campaigns Get Mean," *Washington Post,* October 31, 1982, C7.
53. Thomas J. McIntyre with John C. Obert, *The Fear Brokers* (Boston: Beacon Press, 1979), 336.
54. From a stenciled handout introducing the Center for Responsive Politics, January 1983.
55. "Political Big Bucks: Sin Against the Constitution," *Washington Post,* October 31, 1982, C1
56. "Nov. 7 Vote Turnout was 37.9%, Lowest Since '42," *New York Times,* December 19, 1978, A13.
57. Gilbert Y. Steiner, ed., *The Abortion Dispute and the American System* (Washington, D.C.: Brookings Institution, 1983), 92.
58. Scholarly evidence on how little voters know or care about congressional candidates discourages unwavering faith in how voters select their representatives to Congress. Barbara Hinckley notes that "in a 1978 national survey, for example, only 49 percent of the *voters* in *contested* House elections reported having 'any contact' with or 'learning anything about' the two candidates contesting the election" (emphasis mine). She adds that, according to a 1972 study, "a large number of people who did not care much about the congressional race and paid little or no attention to it still managed to vote in the contest." See her chapter, "Voters and the Context of Information," in *Congressional Elections* (Washington, D.C.: Congressional Quarterly Press, 1981), 17-35. For additional information on how issues and attitudes may affect voting in congressional elections, see Thomas E. Mann, *Unsafe at Any Margin* (Washington, D.C.: American Enterprise Institute, 1978), 25-47.
59. Stanley Kelley, Jr., addresses this assertion in *Political Campaigning: The Problems in Creating an Informed Electorate* (Washington, D.C.: Brookings Institution, 1960).

RUTH S. JONES

# 6. Financing State Elections

The role of money in the electoral process has been addressed in a number of excellent, comprehensive discussions.[1] Nevertheless, one of the curiosities of the study of money in politics generally, and campaign funding particularly, is that although there are many more elected state officials than federal officials, the majority of the attention given to the role of money in politics has focused on federal offices.[2] The lack of information about what has been happening in the states leaves an incomplete picture of election financing in the United States.

As a step toward filling this void, the following discussion provides an overview of (1) trends in the magnitude of campaign costs and expenditures, (2) different sources of campaign money and patterns of contributions, and (3) the nature of funding for ballot-issue campaigns in the states.

The information and tentative conclusions are presented with a sense of trepidation because there are good and sufficient reasons for the paucity of research on the role of money in state elections. First, the sheer magnitude of the number of state elections overwhelms the scholar and requires relatively arbitrary decisions as to how to manage any study more elaborate than a single-state case study. Second, it is a basic political fact that state campaign financing is governed by state law and hence any comparative analysis is complicated by the presence of 50 different sets of campaign funding regulations. Unlike studies of congressional or presidential elections, which are governed by a single set of federal laws, it is extremely difficult to find common units of analysis for the study of state-level election funding.

But the greatest obstacle to systematic inquiry about state campaign funding is the absence of comparable data. There is, for the states, no counterpart to the Federal Election Commission. There is no single repository, processor, or archive of state election funding records. Although the FEC clearinghouse has done a great deal to assist individual states in developing their electoral programs and has greatly facilitated communication and exchange among state election officials, standardized, reliable summary reports of campaign contributions and expenditure data are not available.

Although most states have made major changes in campaign reporting and disclosure laws during the last decade and now require some form of financial accounting from state candidates, the reform legislation too seldom mandates that the data be analyzed, summarized, or published. Some states have rather extensive reports, others have minimal summaries, and some have no reports. Even among existing reports, the data presented differ in fundamental ways so as to preclude easy or direct comparison. For example, each report may include information on expenditures and contributions, but the definitions of "expenditure" and "contribution" differ widely.

Consequently, the discussion that follows must be read with the understanding that in an attempt to make the data comparable across years within a state as well as between states, it is unavoidable that some distortion from the states' original reporting categories has occurred. The hope is that the distortions neither compromise the integrity of the comparisons that have been made nor distort the general conclusions of each individual state's report.[3] The 1980 election provides the most comprehensive and complete data base for state-level analysis, and therefore the primary emphasis will be on this election. Wherever data permit, information on the 1981 and 1982 elections has been included to provide an up-to-date overview of campaign financing at the state level.

## Campaign Costs

To compare the financing of campaigns for all candidates across all states is clearly an impossible task. However, a selective review provides consistent support for the notion that candidates for state offices in the 1980s were confronted with the task of raising and spending larger sums of money than ever before.

The California Fair Political Practices Commission estimates that the total campaign costs for all state, federal, and local offices in California between 1979 and 1981 exceeded $150 million. The cost of the 1980 gubernatorial campaign in Washington was up 85 percent from 1976; in the rematch between Governors Bond and Teasdale in Missouri, 1980 expenditures ($6 million) were up 241 percent from their 1976 gubernatorial contest. In the 1982 rematch in Arkansas between Governors White and Clinton total expenditures increased from $1.1 million in 1980 to $3.2 million in 1982. Governor Thornburgh of Pennsylvania spent $1.8 million in 1978 to develop the name recognition necessary to win the governorship; in 1982, as an incumbent, he had to spend $3.2 million in a battle to return to office. In California, George Deukmejian and Tom Bradley's 1982 battle for the governorship more than doubled the $8.2 million spent by their counterparts in 1978.

Total expenditures for partisan statewide candidates in Oregon in 1980 were up 40 percent over 1976, while expenditures for nonpartisan statewide races more than doubled. Six weeks prior to the 1982 general election, candidates for statewide and legislative races in California had spent over $51 million, which was $8 million more than the total record spending for the same offices in 1978. Gubernatorial candidate John D. (Jay) Rockefeller IV's expenditure in 1980 of over $9.5 million (almost all of it his own funds) to win 54 percent of the West Virginia vote, and the unsuccessful 1982 campaigns of New York's Lewis Lehrman ($11 million expenditure, over $8 million of his own funds) and Texas Governor Bill Clements ($12 million expenditure) are, at present, clearly exceptional cases. They illustrate, however, that the cost of gubernatorial campaigns are escalating and involve staggering amounts of money. These races represent a sharp deviation from the traditional patterns of campaign spending for state-level office, and if they are a trend of the future, there may be reason to be concerned about the changing nature of gubernatorial campaign politics.

Yet the contrast of the Rockefeller, Lehrman, and Clements campaigns with the successful efforts of Montana's Ted Schwinden or Frank White in Arkansas, each of whom spent only about $500,000 in 1980, or with South Dakota's Bill Janklow, who spent only $116,000 in his successful 1982 campaign, also illustrates the great variation in the cost of gubernatorial campaigns, as well as the idiosyncratic nature of statewide campaigns generally.

Campaign financing for nongubernatorial statewide offices reflects the unique political context of the various state elections, differences in the experience of candidates, and variations in the prestige of the offices at stake. For example, in Washington total expenditures for gubernatorial campaigning in 1980 were close to $3.5 million, whereas only $30,000 was spent in the campaigns for auditor. Missouri's secretary of state, a 75-year-old patriarch of the state's Democratic party, was the biggest vote getter in the state in 1980 and spent only two cents per vote, whereas the two gubernatorial candidates each spent over $1.25 per vote. In contrast, the Arizona treasurer spent 15 cents per vote in 1982 to win 51 percent of the vote, whereas the governor spent over $3.00 per vote to win 62 percent of the vote. Such variation in campaign expenditures within and between states virtually precludes any useful summary statements about campaign financing for statewide state offices other than the obvious conclusion that in any given year in any particular state for any specific office, the cost of a statewide campaign is highly dependent on the immediate electoral context of that election.

## LEGISLATIVE CAMPAIGNS

If one focuses attention on state legislative races, it becomes somewhat easier to make general comparisons about campaign financing in state politics. First, the costs of legislative campaigns seem to have increased more rapidly and more sharply than most other campaigns. "Record breaking" and "unprecedented spending" for state legislative races was reported in state after state in 1980 and again in 1982. In California, a record of $35.8 million was spent on state legislative campaigns in 1980—a 71 percent increase over 1978 expenditures. This increase occurred despite the fact that the amount spent on state Senate and Assembly seats in California had increased 1248 and 1427 percent, respectively, between 1958 and 1978. The cost of gubernatorial campaigns over the same period of 1958-78 increased only 633 percent.[4] In the 1982 California legislative primaries, the candidates spent a combined total of $19.7 million for a 104 percent increase over 1978. In Washington, a record spending of $4.3 million in legislative races was reported in 1980 and was followed by $5.5 million in 1982. In Minnesota, the 1980 record $4.4 million was more than double the 1976 expenditure level and the progression of increased spending continued in 1982.

TABLE 6.1.
AVERAGE COST PER LEGISLATIVE SEAT

|  | 1974 | 1976 | 1978 | 1980 |
|---|---|---|---|---|
| House | | | | |
| Alaska | $15,241 | $35,844 | $32,319 | $60,778 |
|  | (12,001)[a] | (24,550) | (19,470) | (29,504) |
| Colorado | 5,385 | 8,219 | 12,280 | 17,403 |
|  | (4,243) | (5,629) | (7,398) | (8,489) |
| Minnesota | 8,256 | 9,694 | 11,813 | 15,882 |
|  | (6,501) | (6,640) | (7,116) | (7,709) |
| Oregon | 10,413 | 17,765 | 27,133 | 31,773 |
|  | (8,199) | (12,168) | (16,345) | (15,499) |
| Senate | | | | |
| Alaska | $20,325 | $27,446 | $41,612 | $61,213 |
|  | (16,003) | (18,798) | (25,068) | (29,715) |
| Colorado | 14,362 | 15,809 | 16,464 | 23,423 |
|  | (11,262) | (10,828) | (9,918) | (11,426) |
| Minnesota | N.A. | 18,200 | N.A. | 34,264 |
|  |  | (12,466) |  | (16,630) |
| Oregon | 20,160 | 15,832 | 33,576 | 27,470 |
|  | (15,874) | (10,884) | (20,226) | (13,400) |

SOURCE: Average cost figures were computed from the official election finance reports of the individual state agencies and include primary and general election expenditures.

*a.* Figures in parentheses are costs reported in constant 1970 dollars.

These increases in total legislative expenditures mean that in recent years, the average cost of a legislative seat has doubled or tripled in almost every state for which there are records. The most dramatic example of the ultimate impact of these increases in 1980 was provided by California where the *average* amount spent by all candidates was $353,000 per Assembly seat and $379,000 per state Senate seat! More typical are the expenditure patterns shown in table 6.1, which indicate a steady increase in average costs per seat, especially for the lower house of state legislatures. These increases are not simply an artifact of inflation, for even in constant dollars there is a steady, albeit less sharp, increase in average costs per legislative seats.

## TABLE 6.2.
### HIGHEST TOTAL CAMPAIGN EXPENDITURE BY A SINGLE LEGISLATIVE CANDIDATE, SELECTED STATES 1980

| State | House | | | | Senate | | | |
|---|---|---|---|---|---|---|---|---|
| | Expenditure | Party | Status | Outcome | Expenditure | Party | Status | Outcome |
| Alaska | $49,838 | Republican | Incumbent | Won | $101,122 | Democrat | Open | Lost |
| California | 700,703[a] | Democrat | Incumbent | Won | 775,573 | Republican | Open | Won |
| Colorado | 34,299 | Republican | Challenger | Lost | 33,653 | Republican | Open | Won |
| Hawaii | 80,682 | Democrat | Incumbent | Won | 274,300 | Democrat | Incumbent | Lost |
| Idaho | 10,677 | Republican | Challenger | Won | 21,694 | Republican | Incumbent | Won |
| Iowa | 16,026 | Democrat | Incumbent | Won | 27,827 | Republican | Open | Lost |
| Minnesota | 24,759 | Democrat | Incumbent | Won | 77,933 | Republican | Challenger | Won |
| Missouri | 55,926 | Republican | Open | Lost | 51,807 | Democrat | Open | Won |
| Washington | 51,684 | Republican | Challenger | Won | 62,191 | Democrat | Incumbent | Lost |

SOURCE: Official reports of the individual states.

a. This includes $355,220 in transfers to other committees; the highest candidate expenditures with average transfers of funds was $369,554 by a Democrat who won an open seat.

As total legislative expenditures and average costs per seat soared, individual legislative candidate expenditures also reached all-time highs in 1980. At the extreme, 86 percent of California's successful Senate and Assembly candidates in 1980 spent over $100,000; over half spent in excess of $200,000. In 1982, the nationally known activist Tom Hayden spent over $1 million to win a seat in the California Assembly. Table 6.2 illustrates that winning the once lowly regarded state legislative seat can be a very costly venture. In the early 1970s, $15,000 was viewed as a relatively expensive legislative race in most states; by 1980, it was generally perceived as a bargain. As an observer in Colorado commented, "It isn't unusual these days in urban districts to find Democratic and Republican candidates spending $30,000 to $50,000 to win offices that pay $14,000 a year."[5]

*Expenditure patterns.* As in congressional races, there is a general pattern in state legislative campaigns of winners outspending losers, of challengers spending more than the incumbents they defeat, and of open seats being high expenditure races.[6] In 1980, for example, Alaska's winners spent an average of $7300, or 20 percent, more than the average loser. In Iowa, there was little difference in House races, but in Senate races challengers, on average, spent almost one-third again as much as incumbents and then spent twice as much per vote received. In California's 1982 legislative primary incumbents outspent challengers by a ratio of 25 to 1, and winning Senate incumbents outspent challengers by 45 to 1. As a review of some of the more expensive state legislative campaigns indicates, big spenders were not always winners, they were not always challengers, and they were found in both major political parties. In Colorado, only three state legislative incumbents lost in 1980, but all three were significantly outspent by their challengers; at the same time, in contests for 13 open seats, *all* of the highest spenders lost.

A look at individual state experiences suggests several factors important to understanding state-level campaign expenditures. First, total expenditure figures blur distinctions in expenditure patterns for primary and general election campaigns and hide the importance of money spent in the primaries. The limited number of reports that separate the costs of the two elections preclude an extensive examination, but there are numerous examples of greater expenditures for primary than general elections. For example, in the 1980 elections in Oregon, primary expenditures in both partisan and nonpartisan statewide races were greater than for the general election, and nonpartisan primary costs exceeded general election costs by a ratio of nine to one. Oregon's nonpartisan state races in 1980 provide an example where even the *average* primary expenditure was more ($8000) than the average general election expenditure. In Missouri, 27 percent more was spent on legislative primaries in 1980 than in general election campaigns. And in Colorado, where the key seemed to be incumbency, the primary losers generally outspent the winners, whereas in the general election winners outspent the losers. In Missouri, the average expenditure for winners in the 1980 Senate primaries was double the average expenditure for the general election winners ($20,500 and $8900); and for losers, the primary expenditures were almost three times as great as expenditures of losers in the general election.

The Missouri experience raises a second point in that it illustrates the importance of electoral competition in analyzing campaign expenditures. It was not win/lose or incumbent/challenger that differentiated primary campaign expenditure patterns in Missouri but whether one was looking at the dominant party (Democratic) or the minority party (Republican) campaign expenditures. The average Senate primary expenditure was $21,600 for Missouri Democrats, but it was only $4300 for Republicans. The high primary expenditures, which contributed significantly to the total average costs of legislative seats in this state, were the result of *intra*party, not *inter*party, competition. Competitiveness of elections does seem to be related to cost of campaign, and in one-party or dominant one-party states, distinguishing between intra- and interparty competition is important to the interpretation of "average" and "total" campaign costs.

Another characteristic of state legislative election financing is the wide variation in the cost of legislative campaigns. For example, in Michigan, where the average expenditure for a house seat in 1980 was about $30,000 (even though almost 90 percent of the seats were regarded as relatively safe for the incumbent party), spending in 16 targeted races exceeded $50,000, and two of them involved expenditures in excess of $100,000. As political parties and other organizations perfect the strategy of targeting state legislative districts, the standard deviation for campaign expenditures is likely to increase as the campaign costs of "targeted" seats accelerate.

*Debts and surpluses.* Along with all the evidence of increasing costs of state elections, it is not surprising to find evidence of increasing campaign deficits. As legislative campaign costs in California went up 71 percent in 1980, campaign deficits increased 69 percent over 1978 levels. While the general pattern is one in which losers, both in primary and general elections, amass the largest debts, elected officials frequently incur campaign debts as well. The object lessons provided by unsuccessful candidates struggling to pay off old campaign debts combines with the uncertainty of how expensive the next race might be to create an almost continuous cycle of legislative campaign fund raising. Incumbent state legislators in California, for example, raised $12.4 million in 1981 in anticipation of their 1982 campaigns.

Increased deficits seem predictable when campaign costs are escalating, but it is also true that numerous candidates in 1980 legislative campaigns accumulated large surpluses, some as large as $100,000 but most in the range of $2000 to $10,000. In Alaska, half of the 1980 legislative candidates broke even or had a surplus, with $17,000 being the largest surplus; only eight had deficits of more than $4000. In Arizona, the average surplus for winning Senate candidates in 1980 was $2268, but losing Senate candidates also had a modest average surplus of $870, which shows that even losing candidates do not always spend all they collect.

The big "savers" generally were incumbents who had little difficulty raising money and faced only token opposition. State laws vary on how surplus campaign funds must be handled. In many states they must remain segregated as campaign funds; in other states they may be transferred to "officeholder expense accounts" or used at the discretion of the candidate as long as they are reported as income. Saving funds for the next campaign cycle seems compatible with the spirit of a campaign contribution appeal; paying personal on-the-job expenses may be somewhat less compatible with the assumptions made by a contributor when the gift is made; using campaign contributions to pay for a new car, a ski trip, or a set of dentures seems rather remote from the original solicitation/contribution intent. But the fact remains that under the rubric of "campaign contributions," there is every incentive for candidates to raise as much money as possible rather than raise only what is projected as necessary to wage a successful election campaign. Surely this serves to fuel the fire of campaign cost escalation, as well as to divert potential resources from campaigns that could effectively use them.

*Implications.* A focus on the general trend of increasing campaign costs has led to speculation that the pool of available candidates will be inversely related to the costs of campaigning. This in turn leads to the expectation that more and more money will be spent by fewer and fewer candidates. As of 1980, there was only occasional evidence to suggest that this was happening in state legislative elections. As costs of legislative campaigns increased, the number of candidates running for the Minnesota Senate did indeed drop from 164 in 1976 to 148 in 1980; the number of House candidates dropped from 333 to 218 over the same period.

These trends were reversed in 1982, however, when 440 candidates ran for legislative seats. In Alaska, there also was a decrease in the number of candidates running for Senate in 1980 but the average number of candidates running for state House seats in elections since 1974 had increased. In Oregon, the number of candidates for both houses remained relatively constant; in Washington, the number of candidates for House and Senate increased in 1980 and again in 1982.

There seems to be no consistent relationship between the costs of campaigns and the number of candidates actually involved in campaigning. It seems clear that factors other than money play an important role in determining the pool of candidates for state legislature. As an Ohio party official said, "Legislative races are getting more expensive . . . but the costs are not driving good candidates away."

*Summary.* Although there was great variation in the costs of campaigning within a single state as well as between states, there is no doubt that 1980 was a record-breaking year in terms of money spent on state election campaigns. And when the final figures for 1982 are analyzed, it is almost certain that they will show a continuation of this upward spiral. The sharpest increases in campaign costs in 1980 were generally experienced by state legislative candidates, especially candidates for the lower house; and the increases were real rather than simply a by-product of inflation. To understand specific state campaign expenditure patterns one must differentiate between primary and general election costs, winners and losers, challengers and incumbents, and factor in both the partisan nature of the campaign and the effects of targeting. Nevertheless, the conclusion of the chairman of the California Fair Political Practices Commission describes the situation in virtually all the states: "What we have here is akin to an arms race. . . . No one knows just how high it will go."[7]

## Sources of Campaign Funding

The costs of state elections are of interest because of their dramatic increase in recent years. Given the amounts of money spent, it is feared that exceedingly high campaign costs will alter the nature of the electoral process by influencing who chooses to run, how campaigns will be conducted, and who will win. But increased election costs also raise questions about where the money comes from, what various contribution patterns mean for equity among candidates, and the bias of access or influence that might accompany contributions.

At both state and federal levels, the nominal categories for campaign reporting and disclosure are individual contributor, political party, and organized nonparty group, primarily political action committees (PACs). The individual citizen has traditionally been the central figure in discussions of financing democratic elections. Applying the logic of "he who pays the piper calls the tune" to election financing, the assumption is that individuals ought to be heavily involved in funding campaigns if a participatory democracy is to be maintained.

To the extent that political parties provide institutional representation for broad-based constituencies, they too have been viewed as integral parts of the democratic election process.[8] Political parties have played a traditional role in electoral campaigns by aggregating and articulating multiple interests and providing party-nominated candidates with the resources necessary to wage campaigns. Although the contemporary role of parties has been the subject of considerable debate, the concept of party remains central to state elections, and political party organizations are certainly involved in the electoral process.[9]

Nonparty organizations (particulary labor groups) have been active in U.S. electoral politics for a long time, and much discussion and many reform efforts have concentrated on limiting their influence. Recent changes in election laws have resulted in greatly expanded electoral involvement by an increasing number of organizations, PACs in particular. Unlike political parties, which are inclusive umbrella organizations, PACs tend to be exclusive, special-interest (usually labor, professional, corporate, or ideological) organizations. However, PACs, too, are compatible with a pluralist view of democratic politics insofar as they provide a legitimate mechanism for interest representation in the political process.

The mix or balance among these three sources of campaign money (individuals, parties, and PACs) provides one important focus for concern about the financing of elections. Changes in the campaign funding role played by the individual contributor, the partisan representation of broad group interests, or specific group representation of special interests could signify a fundamental change in the representative nature of the electoral process. Because these categories of individual, party, or PAC contributions are meaningful both for democratic theory and practical politics, they provide the framework for the discussion that follows. Several important caveats must accompany such a discussion.

First, as figure 6.1 on page 182 illustrates, these three categories are not totally discrete. Individuals contribute to candidates directly, but they also contribute to both parties and PACs. PACs and other nonparty organizations get the majority of their funds from *individual* contributors with the remainder coming from other organizations, and they give to political parties and other organizations, as well as to candidates. Political parties also get the majority of their funds from individuals, but they in turn contribute to other party organizations, as well as to candidates. When contributions from individuals or organizations are thus passed through other individuals or organizations, it is difficult to trace in detail the complete flow of money in political campaigns.

The second proviso is that state regulations of political contributions are far more diverse than even the regulations governing political expenditures. Consequently, the specific flow of campaign funds outlined in figure 6.1 will vary from state to state depending on a state's particular campaign finance laws. Specific state regulations of who can give how much to whom are important not only for their influence on *direct* contributions by individuals, parties, and PACs but also because these laws greatly influence the amount of *indirect* financing that may occur within a state. For example, in one state an individual may be limited to a $500 contribution to an individual candidate but permitted to make unlimited contributions to the political party that is also contributing to the candidate. In another state, the individual contributor may have no limitation on what can be contributed to a candidate as long as it is reported. In the former case, the contributor may make a $500 contribution directly to the candidate and then choose to make another $500 contribution to the party, which in turn will contribute the $500 to the candidate. In the second case, the contributor may give $1000 directly to the candidate. In both cases the individual contributor has made $1000 available for the funding of a single campaign. But in one state the record shows one direct contribution by the individual to the candidate, one direct contribution by the individual to the party, and one direct contribution by the party to the candidate. In the other state, it is recorded as a single $1000 contribution by the individual contributor to the candidate.

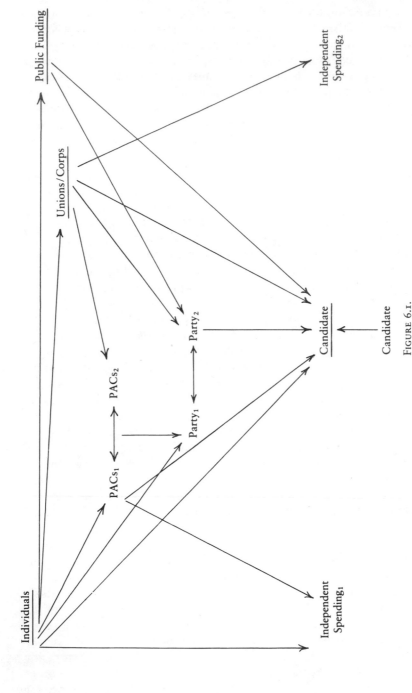

FIGURE 6.1.

THE FLOW OF CAMPAIGN CONTRIBUTIONS IN STATE LEGISLATIVE ELECTION CAMPAIGNS

NOTE: Subscripts indicate that there is an organizational hierarchy or relationship between political groups and that organizations may work in concert or independently.

The patterns of contributions to parties and PACs as well as directly to candidates are clearly important to a full explanation of campaign financing and constitute important areas of inquiry for future research. The state-by-state variations in laws governing contributions doubtless influence how contributors have chosen to channel their funds to state election campaigns, and they make it difficult to trace the flow of money in a manner than can be compared among states. Because state laws and reports vary so widely in the detail in which different patterns of contributions are presented, the following discussion of sources of campaign funds is limited to direct contributions made by individuals, parties, and PACs to individual candidates and candidate committees.

TABLE 6.3.
SOURCES OF CAMPAIGN CONTRIBUTIONS,[a] 1980

| State | Percent of Contributions[a] | | |
| --- | --- | --- | --- |
| | Individuals[b] | Party | PACs |
| California | | | |
| Legislative[c] | 17 | 19 | 73[d] |
| Iowa | | | |
| Legislative | 53 | 12 | 34 |
| Missouri | | | |
| Statewide | 64 | 2 | 23[d] |
| Legislative | 48 | 1 | 30 |
| Nebraska | | | |
| All candidates | 73[e] | 3 | 24 |
| Washington | | | |
| Legislative | 34 | 8 | 37 |
| Wisconsin | | | |
| Statewide | 58[f] | 31 | 8 |
| Legislative | 47 | 8 | 24 |

SOURCE: Official reports of the individual states.

a. These data are estimations based on reports of the various individual states. Differences in state reporting conventions make exact comparisons impossible, and although every effort has been made to keep the three sources comparable, these estimates must be interpreted with caution. Rows do not total 100 because other sources of contributions (loans, public funding, etc.) were not always identifiable.

b. Included in this category are contributions from fund raisers not reported as party or committee contributions, candidates' personal contributions, and contributions not itemized under the states' thresholds for reporting.

c. Figures are for the general election contributions only.

d. Includes funds contributed directly by corporations, businesses, or labor unions.

e. Includes all reported contributions under $200 (62% of total), some of which may have been from parties, PACs, or business or labor groups.

f. Represents the contribution residual after payment of carryover debt.

## INDIVIDUAL CONTRIBUTIONS

The most important and widely shared common denominator of campaign funding lies in the fact that contributions from individuals (rather than political parties or other organizations) continue to provide the majority of state campaign funds. Moreover, in 1980 the percentage of total contributions coming from individuals increased in several states. These increases were primarily the result of gubernatorial election campaigns, however, and the fact that candidates for statewide offices, especially gubernatorial candidates, received the overwhelming majority of their funds from individual rather than party or group contributions. Legislative candidate campaigns, especially primary and unsuccessful campaigns, also relied heavily on individual contributions. For example, individual contributions made up 63 percent of the total contributions to those defeated in the Iowa Senate primary races in 1980.

The 1980 campaigns in California provide a unique example of a marked decline in individual contributions. Contrary to the pattern in several other states, individual contributions dropped 30 percent in the primary and 58 percent in the general election compared to 1978, and they constituted just 5 percent of the total 1980 campaign contributions of over $100 reported to the California Fair Political Practices Commission by legislative candidates.[10]

Although 1980 was not a gubernatorial election year in California, which normally would generate more individual contributions, the decline in the percentage of individual contributions is noteworthy because it underscores the concern that there may be "an alarming and steady diminution of the importance of the private individual as a force in the political process . . . it may portend an undermining of a basic principle of our type of democracy."[11] A decline in the percent of individual contributions indeed may indicate a diminution of broad-based, rank-and-file citizen support and involvement in the electoral process. Such a conclusion, however, would have to rest on observations that fail to distinguish between number of contributions and percentage of contributions, that mistakenly equate "individual" and "small" contributions, and that ignore the fact that both parties and PACs have, as their basic source of funding, contributions from individual members.

The importance of these distinctions is illustrated by the state of Washington where, for example, the percentage of total campaign contributions identified as "individual contributions" declined 8 percent in 1980 but where there were 5000 *more* individual contributors in 1980 than in 1978. Indeed, more individual contributors each gave more money to the campaigns, but their total financial role declined. The number of contributors increased by 13 percent, and the average individual contribution rose a little more than one dollar; at the same time the size of the average political action committee contribution rose over $100, and the number of PACs nearly doubled.

On the other hand, the initial assumption that individual contributions represent the involvement of typical citizens is challenged when the size of contributions is examined. Alaska reports show that over half the funds received by legislative candidates who spent over $20,000 in the 1980 campaign were contributions of $100 or greater; in Minnesota, over half of all contributions to 1980 state campaigns came in amounts of $50 or more; in Washington, only

12 percent of legislative contributions were for $25 or less, and 31 percent were over $500; over half the Arkansas gubernatorial contributions were for $250 or more. Each state has its own definition of a "large" or "small" contribution based on election finance experience in the state, but it is obvious that the "average" contribution to electoral campaigns is far greater than the political funding budget of the average American voter.

Our analysis is limited to direct contributions and therefore our data do not permit a full discussion of indirect individual contributor involvement in campaigns through their funding of parties and PACs. As a by-product of our inquiry, however, it appears that both parties and PACs depend extensively on individual rather than group contributions. Thus it seems that individuals not only continue to participate directly in the financing of elections but that individual contributors remain central indirectly as well.

Two rather minor but interesting variations in the role of individual contributions involve candidates' use of their personal money to finance their campaigns and their use of money contributed to their campaigns to finance other candidates' election campaigns. Most states record the contributions of candidates to their own campaigns, and it is clear that Governor Rockefeller's and Lewis Lehrman's lavish, self-funded campaigns are exceptions rather than the rule. Most gubernatorial candidates contribute only limited amounts to their campaigns, and personal funding provides a very small percentage of total gubernatorial campaign receipts. For example, in the 1980 gubernatorial campaigns in Missouri and Washington, candidate contributions amounted to less than .5 percent of total contributions.

In state legislative races, although there was great variation within as well as between states, the percentage of total campaign contributions provided by the candidates themselves was much greater than in statewide races; nevertheless, it still constituted a relatively small part of the total campaign budget. For example, only 3 percent of Hawaii's 1980 Senate campaign contributions came from the candidates themselves. Among those 1980 legislative candidates in Alaska receiving over $20,000, 11 percent of Senate and 17 percent of House candidates' contributions were personal funds, although two senators contributed more than $20,000 of their own funds, and one House candidate provided $40,000 (84 percent) of his total campaign funding.

In states where it is possible to distinguish sources of contributions to primary or general and incumbent or nonincumbent campaigns, more self-funding occurs in primary races. Self-funding apparently plays an insignificant role in the campaigns of incumbents, a larger role in open-seat contests, and constitutes a sizable portion of the total contributions to challengers. Although some statewide candidates, like Rockefeller and Lehrman, are relatively heavy investors in their own political futures, the vast majority of candidates for state offices rely on others to fund their campaigns, and there is little evidence that state elected offices are reserved for those with enough personal wealth to fund their own campaigns.

Similarly, relatively few candidates contribute significant sums toward funding other candidates' races. In most states, these transfers of funds make up less than 1 percent of total contributions to legislative campaigns, and they tend to be idiosyncratic to time and place. There has been a noticeable increase in candidate transfers in several states, and in California there was an all-time high of over $2 million in transferred funds in 1980 state legislative campaigns. Two dramatic instances involved incumbent California Assembly candidates engaged in an intraparty battle for the Speakership, each spending in excess of $1 million during the campaign, although neither was in any electoral difficulty. Each would-be Speaker's expenditures included more than $350,000 transferred directly to other legislative candidates. In one very competitive race, an Assembly candidate received $111,500, or one-third of his total election budget, from one of the two aspirants to the Speakership; in another Assembly race, the *other* potential Speaker contributed 43 percent of one candidate's campaign expenditures. Although California was unusual in terms of the large amounts of money being transferred, it is illustrative of the fact that the dominant pattern is one in which funds are transferred from established legislative leaders to candidates of lesser status or position.

For the time being, candidate transfers are usually rather modest and limited to isolated races. Candidate transfers such as occurred in California grossly distort the notion that individual contributions always represent broad-based or rank-and-file citizen involvement, however. If candidate transfers, especially by the legislative leadership, become more commonplace, they may raise questions not only about mass versus elite involvement but also about the subsequent autonomy of individual legislators and about the process of recruitment and election of political leaders.

## PAC CONTRIBUTIONS

Even a cursory overview of state campaign funding in the 1980s suggests that the amount of campaign funds coming from nonparty political organizations continues to grow markedly and accounts for the majority of the increase in total campaign contributions. The recent growth in state PACs was prompted in some states, as at the federal level, by legislation restricting or prohibiting a direct financial role for labor and corporate organizations in state election campaigns. In other states, the growth of PACs has paralleled the desire of specific interest groups to maximize the return on the political contributions of their membership and to create a more effective and efficient means by which their interests are identified and heard in the electoral marketplace.

Although the growth of PACs in the states has lagged behind PAC development at the federal level, PACs represent a source of significant amounts of new money in state campaign funding and are thus a focus of political controversy. Proponents of PACs argue that PACs are mass-based membership organizations that legitimately aid in linking specific interests of citizens to the political and policy-making process. In financing political campaigns, either directly or indirectly, PACs also facilitate and improve the electoral process because increased campaign funds enable greater campaign activity and thus more information for the voters.

Opponents of PACs argue that by combining the contributions of individual members for the purpose of advancing a single special interest, the total amount of money a PAC contributes has an impact on the electoral process disproportionate to the size and importance of its membership and the issue being represented. Opponents also feel that candidates who wage expensive campaigns and receive large portions of their campaign budgets from a few special-interest PACs become obligated to the PACs and their interests. Because not all political interests in the society can effectively organize PACs that in turn provide large sums of campaign money and command candidates' attention, critics of PACs see the bias PACs interject into the electoral process as one that exacerbates the divisions in society caused by the unequal allocation of political resources, especially money.

The issues raised by PAC activity at the state level, then, are not unlike those raised in relation to PACs at the federal level. They involve changes in the balance among the traditional sources of campaign funds, the likelihood that PAC funds consistently advantage some interests and candidates and disadvantage others, and the potential for PAC money to have a disproportionate influence on election outcomes and subsequent governmental policy. These are serious issues and provoke questions about the viability of state electoral processes. It is important, however, to keep in mind that prior to the recent growth in PACs, state elections were scarcely paragons of political equity and mass representation. Thus the critical question about PACs is not whether they have interjected bias into the system but whether they have altered the traditional biases in state electoral systems, and if so how and to what effect.

A definitive determination of the significance of PACs in state-level campaigns and elections is as premature as it is impossible at this stage in state election research. The following discussion can provide only an overview of state PAC activity by suggesting trends of PAC growth in the states, identifying some of the sources and recipients of PAC funds, and discussing some strategies used by state PACs in financing electoral campaigns.

*PAC growth.* There is no question that there were more PACs, more PAC money, and larger PAC contributions in the 1980 and the 1982 state elections than ever before. In Oregon, for example, with no change in requirements for reporting, there were 36 committees in the 1970 general election reporting total campaign spending of slightly under $200,000; by 1980 there were 151 committees reporting total expenditures of just under $1 million in the general election. In the state of Washington, there were 114 PACs in 1978 with receipts of $2.0 million; in 1980 there were 200 PACs with total receipts of just over $4.3 million. Even in Idaho where, between the 1978 and 1980 election cycles, the total number of PACs reporting campaign expenditures decreased by more than

20 percent due to the consolidation of groups, total PAC campaign contributions increased by 20 percent. Between 1976 and 1982, the number of PACs involved in California campaigns more than tripled. In the 1980 Arizona legislative races, there were 2985 PAC contributions of over $100 compared to 1068 individual contributions of over $100, and while total contributions to winning legislative candidates increased 300 percent overall between 1974 and 1980, special-interest contributions in amounts of $100 or more increased 1218 percent. [12] The average Arizona PAC contribution to winners in the 1974 campaign was less than $3000; by 1980 it was more than $11,500; and by 1982 there was a noticeable increase in the number of state legislative candidates who received over 90 percent of their campaign funds from PACs.

PAC activity in the states has not been identical across all interest groups in the society. As at the federal level, some state PACs represent large concentrations of campaign money and are highly visible throughout the state; other PACs are less well financed and operate on a much more modest scale. For example, PAC contributions in Texas in 1980 ranged from $850 from the El Paso Beer Wholesalers to $467,000 from TREPAC, the real estate PAC; in Michigan, the fledgling Right to Life PAC contributed $25,000, whereas the established Michigan Education Association provided $254,000 to campaigns; in Oregon, auto enthusiasts reported contributing $600 to campaigns, while government employees contributed over $51,000.

Recent state PAC growth has been disproportionate among business and professional interests. In Kansas, for example, where PACs doubled their contributions to state legislative campaigns between 1978 and 1980, the number of business PACs increased by 121 while the number of labor PACs decreased by one. In neighboring Missouri, a more labor-oriented state, labor PACs held their own and even slightly increased their proportion of total campaign receipts. But the number of business PACs in Missouri increased sharply; of the state's 20 highest-spending continuing committees in 1980, ten were corporate or business PACs, five were labor PACs, and five were party organizations.

It is not clear how much the contributions from these new PACs, especially business and corporate PACs, actually represent money from new sources and how much of it is money that heretofore simply would have been given directly by individuals or corporations. But a comparison of PAC and corporate giving patterns in states where direct corporate giving is permitted suggests that PACs are more than new vehicles for established corporate contributors. The California Fair Political Practices Committee reported that although the number of business PACs has grown, the number of direct business contributions has also increased. [13] The same pattern seems to be emerging in Maryland. In Missouri, direct business contributions were legalized in 1978, and since then corporate and business PAC development has increased along with the introduction of direct corporate contributions.

If corporate PACs and direct corporate giving have continued to grow in tandem, the contribution patterns of the corporations and their PACs are often markedly different. Seventy-two percent of all direct Missouri business contributions in 1980 went to the gubernatorial campaigns, and only 11 percent went to legislative races. In contrast, 67 percent of all business PAC contributions went to legislative candidates, and only 11 percent went to gubernatorial candidates. In Washington there is evidence that corporate and new PAC contributions may be parallel (or competing) sources of funding. There, midway through the 1980 campaigns, PAC funding diminished significantly as corporate contributors, bypassing their own PACs, began making direct contributions.

*PAC recipients.* The fear of a bias in who receives PAC contributions is a large part of the concern that surrounds the growth of state PACs. Our observations, based primarily on the 1980 elections, suggest that, as in Missouri, state PAC contributions are targeted on state legislative races rather than statewide campaigns. In California, where PAC growth has been unusually heavy, much of the financial activity reported by PACs in 1980 involved ballot-issue campaigns rather than legislative or statewide races.[14] However, as in other initiative states, when ballot-issue funding is set aside, the principal focus of PAC campaign funding is clearly on state legislative races rather than statewide candidate campaigns.

PAC funds also most frequently go to incumbents rather than challengers, to winners rather than losers, and to established legislative leaders rather than freshmen. This bias, creating an incumbency advantage, is visible in many states. In Washington, where PAC contributions made up 37 percent of all legislative contributions, PACs provided 47 percent of all funds raised by incumbents, 33 percent of the total funds in open races, and only 24 percent of challengers' contributions in 1980. In Iowa, House incumbents received 40 percent of their total funds from PACs, whereas their challengers received only one-fourth of their funds from PACs. The average Kansas incumbent received half of all campaign funds from PACs in 1980, while nonincumbents received only a quarter of their funds from Kansas PACs. Business PACs in Kansas, however, are increasingly funding challengers; between 1978 and 1980, they increased contributions by 335 percent to nonincumbents and only 168 percent to incumbents.

Concentration on funding incumbents also means that PACs generally have a good win/loss record. In Texas, for example, of the 238 legislative contributions made by the medical TEXPAC, the largest spending Texas PAC in 1980, 77 percent of the funds went to successful candidates. Between 1975 and 1980, California Medical PAC contributed over $1.1 million to legislative candidates and had a win/loss record of 365 wins and only 50 losses. Georgia PACs followed the general pattern of giving to incumbents, but when they did give to challengers, they gave to successful ones; winning challengers got 31 percent of their funds from PACs, whereas losing challengers got only 9 percent of their total funds from PACs.

A spinoff of funding incumbents is that PAC money goes disproportionately to legislative leaders; or, as Binford concluded from his study of Georgia

PACs, "PACs favor powerful legislators over less powerful ones."[15] In 1980, for example, 57 percent of the average total contribution to the Kansas legislative leadership came from PACs; and in Iowa, the chairman of the Senate Commerce Committee, the Speaker of the House, and the minority leader of the House each received over half their contributions from PACs.

The general partisan trend among state PACs seems to be that Democrats are advantaged by PACs that are few in number but traditionally represent large, mass memberships; Republican candidates benefit from the proliferation of new PACs that tend to represent smaller numbers of people and that make somewhat smaller total contributions per group. The actual partisan distribution of PAC funds within a single state, is, of course, highly skewed in dominant one-party states such as Georgia, North Carolina, or Kansas and is more evenly distributed in the more electorally competitive states. As one New York Democrat put it: "Big-business money and big-labor money go to the same places because both are pragmatic."[16]

It would appear, however, that when incumbency is held constant, the growth of business and professional PACs has favored state Republican legislative candidates. The only "growth" PACs that seemed to share a common Democratic orientation in 1980 were the teacher/education and public employee PACs. In states like Alaska, where labor organizations continue to be a strong political force, the Democrats benefited from labor contributions that exceeded business PAC contributions by 50 percent. In Iowa and Wisconsin, the single largest contributing PACs in the 1980 legislative races were labor PACs, but in both states, this generally Democratic advantage was countered by the presence of numerous business PACs each spending considerably less per PAC but all contributing more to Republicans than Democrats. There are indications that some specific PAC contributions are becoming much more partisan. For example, the principal business PAC in Washington gave 34 percent of its money to Democrats in 1974, 26 percent in 1976, 22 percent in 1978 and only 5 percent in 1980. At the same time, contributions from state employee PACs to Democrats went from 83 percent in 1974 to 92 percent in 1976, to 93 percent in 1978, and to 99 percent in 1980.

*PAC strategy.* How PACs actually go about making contributions to campaigns is influenced, in part, by the specific election laws of the state as well as by a reasoned choice of political strategies. State laws determine the legality of direct political contributions from corporations, labor unions, or governmental employees; set contribution limits; and define legitimate campaign expenses. Therefore, whether a group gives directly or indirectly and how much it gives are decisions of political strategy and choice only within the constraints set by election law.

In states such as Montana, where PACs are limited in how much they can contribute to each candidate directly, PACs chose to make the maximum direct contribution and then to contribute indirectly by managing voter canvasses and get-out-the-vote drives and by providing technical assistance to candidate committees. In Wisconsin, many PACs chose to engage in direct political campaign activity rather than transfer funds to another party or candidate committee. In contrast, 69 percent of all Alaska PAC expenditures in 1980 provided cash directly to the candidates.

The question of when contributions are received is certainly important to campaign strategy, and therefore the choices made by PACs as to when to contribute are relevant to how influential such contributions may be. PACs must decide, for example, if they are going to give to primary or general election campaigns, whether contributions should be early or late in the campaign, whether they should be the reward for past performance or an encouragement for future behavior. The pattern seems to be that state PACs are becoming more and more active in primary campaigns, that they are cautious about excess publicity for their gifts, and that they continue to reward incumbent candidates but are increasingly willing to encourage and support future friends as well.

In Oregon, for example, PACs spent almost $700,000 in the 1980 primaries compared to $80,000 in 1970; in California, business PACs alone contributed over $13.5 million in 1980 primaries compared to $5.1 million in 1978. In 1982, 71 entities, compared to only 16 in 1978, each made contributions of $100,000 or more to California primaries.[17] Primary money is clearly early money, and according to conventional wisdom, early money speaks the loudest. Nevertheless, PACs also frequently chose a wait-and-see strategy, as in Michigan where members of one PAC wrote their checks early in the year but had the group's lobbyist hold the checks until the legislature recessed for the election campaign. In Missouri, there was a clear pattern of PACs contributing just after the deadline for filing preelection contribution reports. This meant that the complete scope of PAC activity was not known until after the last reporting deadline, which was 30 days after voters had cast their ballots. An extreme example of "timed" PAC contributions occurred in Georgia where three months after the 1980 election, five legislators received "belated" campaign contributions from a bank PAC on the day of a critical vote on a banking bill.[18]

The Georgia bank PAC behavior exacerbates the sensitive issue of the impact of PAC contributions on the behavior of officials, generally state legislators. Although the PAC officials explained that they had planned to make a contribution during the campaign but, because of an oversight, had not, the situation drew much criticism about buying legislative favors, especially since the controversial measure passed only on reconsideration.

Legislators in several states have commented that they are often reminded at propitious times of a particular group's past campaign contributions or their funding plans for the future. Yet few PACs are as blatant as an ideological Texas PAC in 1980 that wrote to legislators stating that the group was prepared to reward its "helpful friends" with campaign contributions and in-kind services in return for appropriate consideration of legislation the group was promoting.

PAC leaders readily acknowledge that they hope their contributions will provide them "access" to elected officials, and some even admit that "when we say 'access,' we mean 'influence.' " Yet it is difficult to comment with certainty on how much any PAC or special-interest contributions influence state legislation because research on the relationship of contributions to legislative votes is just beginning, and preliminary efforts have yielded conflicting results.[19] In their preliminary analysis of a limited set of bills, Eisenstein and Karapin found no significant relationship between PAC contributions and legislative votes. Binford, on the other hand, found a "substantial connection" between receiving contributions from bank PACs and voting in favor of the PACs' legislative position. Although it may well be that candidates' positions attract PAC money, rather than the other way around, Binford found a stronger correlation between PAC contributions and legislative votes than between PAC contributions and the candidates' self-identified legislative agenda priorities.[20]

*Future of state PACs.* Because widespread PAC involvement in state campaigns is relatively new, it is difficult to predict the future of state PACs. Nevertheless, based on our examination of recent state experiences, two conclusions seem appropriate. First, state PAC activity will continue to be determined largely by state law, and modifications in campaign finance law may dramatically alter the role PACs will play in future elections. PACs are well aware of their vulnerability to election law change and will, no doubt, be alert to any proposed changes in regulations of who can give or how much can be given or under what conditions direct and indirect campaign contributions may be made.[21]

Second, most PACs expect to be around for a while. The emotions connected with the 1980 victories and defeats were still strong when state PACs began collecting funds and organizing for the 1982 campaigns. PACs also are refining their contribution strategies as, for example, in the development of supra PACs or PACs that operate as PACs' PACs. In Texas, BACPAC (Businessmen Are Concerned) received a majority of its funds, not from single *individuals* as group members, but from *other PACs* representing service and service-delivery interests who constitute the "membership" of BACPAC. Similarly, United for California and United for Washington tend to be "umbrella" PACs that serve as auxiliary units for corporate contributions above and beyond their own PACs or individual, corporate contributions.

Variations of the supra PAC approach are Colorado's Public Affairs Council and the Maryland PAC, which were both organized by leaders of the states' chambers of commerce to make a forceful presence for business qua business interests. Both limit their activity to state legislative campaign funding and serve in lieu of PACs for individual business organizations. Those who view PAC activity as simply another legitimate way for recognized interests to participate in the electoral process view the emergence of supra PACs as an advance toward efficient and rational political behavior. Those who see the general growth of PACs as evidence that more and more campaign money is being controlled by fewer and fewer people view supra PACs as threats to mass-based participatory democracy.

*Summary.* PAC money constitutes a growing proportion of state election campaign funding, especially for legislative races. The most rapid growth is by corporate PACs, which tend to favor Republican candidates; but like more established PACs, they tend to contribute most heavily to incumbents and legislative leaders, thus partially obscuring the partisan bias associated with PAC funding. In 1982, state PACs continued to support incumbents generally, and legislative leaders more specifically, although there was slight movement toward targeting districts and successfully funding challengers, even some in the primary campaigns. PACs are developing sophisticated strategies in order to maximize the return on their contribution dollars—strategies of when to give and whether to contribute direct cash or in-kind services or to do the campaigning themselves. It is obvious that most state PACs intend to replicate if not expand their recent campaign activities. They are establishing continuing committee structures rather than ephemeral, single-election organizations, and it appears that PACs intend to regularize if not institutionalize their role in state elections.

## PARTY CONTRIBUTIONS

Contrary to the notion that parties generally are on the wane as forces in American electoral politics, state party organizations were very active in many state campaigns in 1980. Based on 1980 experiences, state parties are still centrally involved in the basic functions of nominating candidates and mobilizing electoral support. But parties clearly ranked a poor third when compared to individual or PAC contributors to electoral campaigns. Nevertheless, this "lesser" role should not be equated with an "insignificant" role. In fact, there was an increase over past years of party activity and party money in state campaigns in 1980. Parties primarily used their resources for indirect funding of legislative campaigns, and showed they were able to maximize their financial role in the campaign process through skillful management of party resources.

*Party involvement.* The increase in financial activities of political parties was illustrated in the state of Washington where, in the face of the increase in funding noted above, party contributions went from 4 percent of total contributions in 1978 to 8 percent of total contributions in 1980. The Washington Republican State Committee almost tripled its contributions to legislative campaigns, and among party organizations it was the largest single contributor to state legislative races. Similarly, California provides an example where, when contributions to ballot-issue campaigns were factored out, the two top contributors to general election campaigns in 1980 were party organizations: the Republican Assembly PAC and the National Republican State Elections Committee.

As California illustrates, a primary explanation for the increased availability of party funds for state campaigns in 1980 was the infusion of funds from

GOPAC, a state-oriented, national, Republican-affiliated political action committee, and the Republican National Committee.[22] Because the Democratic party had no significant comparable national party programs in 1980, the preponderance of state-level party financial activity occurred within Republican organizations. For example, in Republican Vermont, the state committee contributed approximately $37,000 to Governor Snelling's campaign alone, while the Democratic state committee reported total contributions of only $3000 to all statewide candidates.[23] The role of national party funding to facilitate state organization activities was clearly illustrated in Nebraska where the Republican state committee matched $15,000 from the national organization and thereby took an active financial role in targeting and funding campaigns for that state's *nonpartisan,* unicameral legislature.[24] Albeit a limited effort, it was a success because party organizations helped fund six successful primary candidates, and five of the eight general election candidates receiving party money were elected.

Not all growth in party financing activity was the direct result of national party activity; the state and local organizations of both parties have also been hard at work. The number of party organizations reporting financial activity in Oregon increased from 63 to 87 between 1976 and 1980, and the total partisan expenditures in campaigns almost doubled. In Idaho, total Republican contributions in 1980 increased 25 percent, and total Democratic contributions increased 37 percent; Republican increases were at the state committee level, whereas the bulk of the Democratic increases came at the level of county and local party organizations.

Between 1978 and 1980, the total number of individual contributors to the Washington Republican party increased 270 percent, but the average gift remained about $36. Over this same period the number of contributors to Washington's Democratic party declined by 50 percent, but the average contribution almost doubled. In part, the Washington Democratic party's contribution pattern was influenced by that party's bitter, candidate-oriented gubernatorial primary campaign and serves to illustrate the importance of specific campaign environments in shaping electoral financing patterns.

*Use of funds.* Obviously, the funding strategies adopted by a party are related to its needs and to the funds it has available. A comparison of the total amount of party money spent in state campaigns indicates that Republican organizations have been clearly and consistently better funded and thus more active in the campaign process. Wisconsin Republicans, for example, outspent Democrats three to one; Alaska Republicans outspent their Democratic rivals two to one; and Oregon Republicans had over 25 percent more money to spend than did the Democrats. The parties also differed in how they chose to use campaign funds they had, and the diversity makes any attempt at generalizations risky. Nevertheless, three patterns of party activity in 1980 can be identified.

First, state political party organizations were more extensively involved in state legislative campaigns than in any other campaigns. This focus was largely motivated by the upcoming legislative and congressional redistricting decisions state legislatures would make, but also by the growing realization that party units could significantly help to offset the increasing costs of state legislative elections by taking advantage of economies of scale to provide services basic to all campaigns. As one party official explained, "We can't raise enough money to be a force in federal or statewide campaigns—they are too expensive. But state legislative campaigns are in our ballpark and the things that are driving up the costs of legislative campaigns are things we can help with."[25] The parties' legislative focus in 1980 and 1982 normally took the form of targeting certain races, although several parties were active in candidate recruitment more generally.

In Iowa, for example, Democrats successfully sought to stem the Republican tide they saw growing by actively recruiting candidates for the state legislature and then working more closely with them than they had done in the past. As a result, the party spent more money on state legislative campaigns than ever before, and after the election was left with a $110,000 debt costing $70 a day in interest. The payoff was that they held their ground at the polls and had only two fewer members of the legislature than before the election. In Michigan, even with an extra $20,000 provided by the state committee, the Democrats' counterattack was not as successful as in Iowa, and the Republican's targeting of 33 of 75 house races paid off handsomely.

It is difficult to prove that the GOP's gain of 271 state legislative seats in 1980 was primarily the result of national party committee involvement or state party committee targeting efforts. Although targeting by both parties increased, in state after state, from Vermont to Michigan to New Mexico to California, the well-financed Republican party was able to provide considerably more assistance to their targeted campaigns, and the electoral returns generally were in their favor.

Similarly, in 1982, with redistricting issues generally settled, national GOP efforts concentrated on maintaining senatorial and congressional seats, and it is difficult to document how much the GOP losses at the state level reflected the decrease in national party involvement in state races discussed by Adamany elsewhere in this volume.

A second general pattern, especially prominent in legislative funding, was the emphasis on in-kind services rather than direct financial support. Parties within a particular state could vary in this strategy. In Alaska, for example, total partisan contributions were evenly divided between direct contributions (donations to candidates and political advertising) and indirect contributions (fund-raising and organizational activity); but Democrats emphasized direct contributions, while Republicans directed two-thirds of their spending to indirect contributions. In a reversal of party roles, Minnesota's Independent-Republican party spent over $700,000 directly on state legislative campaigns in 1980, whereas Minnesota's Democratic Farmer Labor party spent its money on voter identification and general promotion of the party and left the funding of legislative candidates to the candidate and PAC committees. In North Carolina, where Jesse Helms's Congressional Club effectively replaced the Republican state party organization, the only state candidate in 1980 to receive substantial direct assistance from the "party" was the gubernatorial candidate. More typical was the Iowa Democratic party, which devoted less than 10 percent of its budget to direct cash contributions to candidates; and the Ohio Republican state committee, which budgeted approximately 45 percent of its funds to a get-out-the-vote program, 10 percent to operational expenses, 30 percent to in-kind assistance to candidates, and only 15 percent to direct cash contributions.

A third pattern of party activity related to the extent to which political party organizations were systematic in assessing the probabilities of successfully maximizing returns of the funds they invested. In Idaho, for example, the Republican party targeted legislative districts but withheld direct campaign contributions until the candidate's campaign strategy had been reviewed and judged to be sound. Although targeting is the primary example of such assessment behavior, a similar strategy was evident in increased party financial activity in primary elections and an increased readiness to support new recruits. In Oregon, for example, between 1976 and 1980 the number of party committees reporting activity in primary campaigns doubled. As an example of support for new recruits, one Iowa state party leader whose sole task was to orchestrate the party's state legislative campaigns reported that his rule of thumb for aiding candidates was, first, to provide strong competition for open seats (recruitment), then recruit strong challengers who realistically could be expected to win, then support vulnerable incumbents, give support to "regular" incumbents, and finally give a token nod to the "unwinnable" seats. In Iowa, party contributions made up 9.5 percent and 8 percent of the total contributions to winners in the House and Senate respectively but constituted 19 (House) and 11 (Senate) percent of the total funding of winning challengers.

*Future activities.* Our review of party activities suggests two potentially significant changes in political parties' approach to state campaign financing. One is the explicit recognition by numerous party leaders of a limited direct financial role for formal party organizations but a great potential to enhance the party through diversification of function and horizontal integration with other political organizations. Although most prominent in the Republican party, leaders of both major parties encourage a more flexible organizational structure for campaigning and at the same time have begun to assume the role of a management firm that delegates much of its fund-raising responsibilities. In many states this simply means formally acknowledging the party's legislative leadership's control over their respective House and Senate campaign finance committees. In other states it means, for example, the establishment of separate finance committees, as in Ohio, or an explicit understanding with traditionally supportive nonparty organizations, as in Minnesota, or, as in Iowa, establishing an independent Lincoln Club. In each state, to the extent that the party and its array of auxiliary or adjunct committees are openly aligned and co-ordinated, the candidates seem to make little distinction between assistance directly from party organizations and assistance provided by their other organizational allies—all contributions have a clear partisan label.

The other hint of a change in the party's approach to financing campaigns comes from experiences in several states where, rather than being the nemesis of parties, PACs have become partners with parties to the mutual benefit of both organizations. As one state party executive director put it, "The PACs have always been a threat to parties for they have the ability to undermine the party at any time. We'd rather work with them than have that happen!"

The cooperation between party and PACs in 1980 took two distinct forms. First, party leaders were able to capitalize on the fact that many new state-level PACs are being managed either by attorneys or accountants who specialize in finance law but not electoral politics, or by lobbyists who are experts in the legislative process but are not equally conversant with statewide legislative electoral campaign strategies. Enterprising party leaders could, therefore, carefully match their candidates to PAC interests; make a case for the candidate with the appropriate PAC; indicate what kind of support would be needed to produce a win; and, as an indication of the party's commitment to the race, suggest a dollar figure the party would provide if matched by other funding. In these situations the PACs were made aware of the party's candid assessment of candidates, were apprised of the larger legislative electoral picture, and were introduced to "friendly" candidates worthy of their support. The party thus got new funds into its legislative campaigns that carried the imprimatur of the party at no direct expense to party coffers. Both Republican and Democratic party organizations successfully employed this approach and, in fact, used it to obtain funding from groups not generally aligned with the party but in harmony with an individual candidate's position or interest.

Party/PAC cooperation was also achieved through coordination of services-in-kind. A few PACs expressed a willingness to support certain campaigns that were identified by the party as winnable, but only on the condition that the PAC would hire the staff and oversee the management of the campaign. In such cases, the party, PAC, and candidate had to reach an accord on lines of authority and responsibility; but once this was achieved, a team concept emerged in which it was clear that the party was the initiator of the arrangement, the PAC was the financial facilitator, and the candidate was the focal point of the entire enterprise.

More flexible and broader organizational involvement by parties and direct cooperation with PACs may be momentary flourishes in the overall pattern of state campaign funding by political parties. These shifts in party activities may, on the other hand, be harbingers of future funding strategies. Regardless, based on the 1980 experiences of such diverse states as Iowa, Montana, Ohio, and Washington, these are certainly dimensions of state electoral funding that deserve close scrutiny.

## PUBLIC FUNDING

A fourth, and unique, source of campaign money potentially available in only 17 states is money generated through the use of income tax check-off or add-on programs comparable to the Presidential Election Campaign Fund.[26] As policy makers address the issues raised by the increasing costs of election campaigns, state-level public campaign financing programs continue to gain attention as experiments in election campaign funding. Even though five of the 17 states that have direct public campaign financing did not use the funds in 1980, over $2,875,000 in public funds were involved in the 1980 election campaigns in the other 12 states.[27] Although there have been occasional slight increases or decreases in the number of taxpayers participating in the public financing programs, the overall picture, state by state, is one of relatively constant percentages of taxpayers supporting these programs year after year. The taxpayer participation rates for tax year 1979, which provided funds for the 1980 elections, ranged from 7.5 percent to 41 percent in the tax check-off states and from .5 percent to almost 3 percent in the add-on states.[28]

Among the states in which taxpayers designate a partisan preference for their contributions, the partisan balance in tax year 1979 shifted slightly to increase the Republican percentage of the contributions in Minnesota, Oregon, and Utah. However, only in Utah was the actual dollar amount received by the Republican party greater than the amount received by the Democratic party. Party allocations remained relatively equal in Iowa and Idaho; elsewhere, the pattern of a Democratic advantage persisted.[29]

*Party control.* The role played by public funds in the 1980 elections seems to have depended on whether state policy specified allocation of funds to political parties or directly to individual candidates. There was, of course, great state-to-state variation in the magnitude of public funds available to the parties, as well as in the party use of these funds. In the eight states included in table 6.4 in which the political parties received a combined total of approximately $1.5 million in public funds, the major effect of the public financing program was to enable both major parties to pursue more actively the full range of party electoral activities.

Public funds were used exclusively for organizational headquarters and staff maintenance in Rhode Island. In Oregon and Utah, a portion of the public funds went directly to party county organizations where the money was generally used for organizational and office maintenance with occasional small direct contributions to political candidates. The complex North Carolina public funding program calls for funds to be allocated differently depending on whether it is a presidential election year, a state election year only, or a non-election year. The law stipulates which candidates are eligible to receive public funds but specifies that "the allocation of funds among the several candidates shall be determined solely in the discretion of the special party committee." In 1980 both state parties used half the funds for party operational costs and

TABLE 6.4.
ALLOCATIONS OF PUBLIC CHECK-OFF FUNDS: ALLOCATIONS TO POLITICAL PARTIES

| State Party | 1982 | Percent | 1981 | Percent | 1980 | Percent |
|---|---|---|---|---|---|---|
| Idaho[a] | | | | | | |
| Democratic | $66,980 | 43.3 | | | $60,170 | 48.7 |
| Republican | 76,697 | 49.6 | | | 54,412 | 44.0 |
| American | 4,895 | 3.2 | | | 5,234 | 4.2 |
| Libertarian | 2,027 | 3.9 | | | 3,798 | 3.0 |
| Total | $154,600 | | | | $123,614 | |
| Iowa[b] | | | | | | |
| Democratic | $123,768 | 50.9 | $112,832 | 47.1 | $115,603 | 50.3 |
| Republican | 119,205 | 49.1 | 126,948 | 52.9 | 114,280 | 49.7 |
| Total | $242,973 | | $239,780 | | $229,883 | |
| Kentucky | | | | | | |
| Democratic | $134,411 | 69.0 | $143,222 | 66.8 | $116,521 | 72.9 |
| Republican | 60,328 | 31.0 | 71,225 | 33.2 | 61,929 | 27.1 |
| Total | $194,739 | | $214,447 | | $228,450 | |
| Maine | | | | | | |
| Democratic | $1,923 | 58.4 | $1,777 | 54.8 | $2,049 | 62.2 |
| Republican | 1,367 | 41.6 | 1,463 | 45.2 | 1,240 | 37.8 |
| Total | $3,290 | | $3,240 | | $3,289 | |
| North Carolina | | | | | | |
| Democratic | $193,058 | 69.5 | $79,816 | 69.0 | $262,624 | 73.5 |
| Republican | 81,545 | 29.3 | 35,884 | 31.0 | 90,671 | 25.4 |
| Libertarian | 3,275 | 1.2 | | | 4,123[c] | 1.1 |
| Total | $277,878 | | $115,700 | | $357,418 | |
| Oregon[d] | | | | | | |
| Democratic | | | $125,644 | 55.5 | $130,072 | 60.8 |
| Republican | | | 98,632 | 43.5 | 83,464 | 39.1 |
| Other | | | 2,275 | 1.0 | 106 | .1 |
| Total | | | $226,551 | | $213,642 | |
| Rhode Island | | | | | | |
| Democratic | $56,028 | 67.8 | $82,535 | 74.3 | $82,649 | 73.1 |
| Republican | $26,677 | 32.2 | 28,387 | 25.6 | 30,135 | 26.7 |
| Independent | | | 179 | .1 | 264 | .2 |
| Total | $82,705 | | $111,101 | | $113,048 | |
| Utah | | | | | | |
| Democratic | $63,340 | 38.4 | $52,157 | 34.7 | $61,895 | 41.5 |
| Republican | 97,281 | 58.9 | 97,525 | 64.9 | 78,895 | 52.9 |
| American | 4,460 | 2.7 | 569 | .4 | 8,270 | 5.6 |
| Total | $165,081 | | $150,301 | | $149,190 | |

TABLE 6.4. *(Continued)*

*a.* Idaho allocates election campaign funds every two years.

*b.* The General Fund option was first used in Iowa in the 1980 tax year. The check-off money in the fund is divided evenly between the established political parties ($30,802.50 in 1980).

*c.* These figures represent $117,259 transferred to the political parties from their respective Presidential Election Year Campaign Funds generated by 50% of the check-off designations for each party in a nongeneral election year (Democratic $85,232.56, Republican $30,602.93, Libertarian $1,423.48).

*d.* The Oregon public funding program was discontinued as of 1982.

divided the rest in equal portions between congressional and statewide candidates. In Iowa, because the public funds account was the only state party committee account that clearly qualified as a "pure" account under the federal law governing campaign contributions, both parties drew heavily on the state check-off money to contribute directly to federal election candidates.

Some state party officials are more positive about the role of public funding than others, but regardless of personal preferences or specific uses of public funds in 1980, there was widespread agreement with the Idaho party official who concluded that, at a minimum, "it has simplified fund raising and given us a cushion." To party officials in 1980, these were two very important benefits.

*Candidate control.* In the four states shown in table 6.5 in which public funds were directly given to individual candidates in 1980, there is less agreement on what public financing meant to the 1980 election process. In Montana, both major-party gubernatorial candidates received slightly over $61,500 in public funds. Since this was about 12 percent of their total campaign budgets, it contributed significantly to the fund-raising and campaign strategies of the candidates. The other half of the Montana election fund was divided among eight nonpartisan candidates for state supreme court justice ($15,390 each) and constituted from 21 to 88 percent of their individual campaign budgets. Although there was no indication that the presence of public money had increased the field of candidates for governor, one public official commented that the $15,000 available to judicial candidates had encouraged a few "loony tunes," "people right off the wall," to run for the supreme court.

At the other extreme, only 18 of the 400 eligible candidates in Hawaii applied for and received public funding in 1980 and only .5 percent ($1000) of the $186,000 available public funds were actually allocated. Almost two-thirds of these public funds went to nonpartisan candidates for Board of Education and the Office of Hawaiian Affairs; no Republican candidates used public money in any race. The general explanation for the rejection of public funds was that the amount available to legislative candidates, only $50 per election, was so small that it did not warrant meeting the fund-raising prerequisites and accepting the expenditure limits that must accompany the use of public funds. In 1982, legislative candidates again rejected public funds, but candidates for governor and lieutenant governor accepted almost $425,000 in public funds to finance their campaigns.

TABLE 6.5.
ALLOCATIONS OF PUBLIC CHECK-OFF FUNDS:
ALLOCATIONS TO POLITICAL CANDIDATES[a]

| State Party/Year | | Percent |
|---|---|---|
| Hawaii (1982) | | |
| Democratic | $172,983 | 40.5 |
| Republican | 77,722 | 18.2 |
| Independent Democrat | 176,641 | 41.3 |
| Others | 150 | .03 |
| Total | $427,496 | |
| Massachusetts (1982) | | |
| Democratic | $261,421 | 53.4 |
| Republican | 228,489 | 46.6 |
| Total | $489,910 | |
| Michigan (1982) | | |
| Democratic | $2,989,571 | 52.3 |
| Republican | 2,720,165 | 47.7 |
| Total | $5,711,876 | |
| Minnesota (1982) | | |
| Democratic | $1,034,735 | 65.6 |
| Republican | 533,985 | 33.9 |
| Other parties | 8,147 | .5 |
| Total | $1,576,867 | |
| Montana[b] (1980) | | |
| Democratic | $61,561 | 25.0 |
| Republican | 61,561 | 25.0 |
| Nonpartisan | 123,123 | 50.0 |
| Total | $246,245 | |
| New Jersey (1981) | | |
| Democratic | $5,029,530 | 57.3 |
| Republican | 3,744,031 | 42.7 |
| Total | $8,773,561 | |
| Wisconsin[c] (1982) | | |
| Democratic | $826,610 | 62.0 |
| Republican | 631,371 | 38.0 |
| Total | $1,457,981 | |

a. Maryland and Oklahoma allocated no funds.
b. The Republican and Democratic gubernatorial candidates each received one-fourth of the money in the campaign fund; the other half was distributed equally to eight nonpartisan candidates for Supreme Court justices.
c. 21% of Republican and 30% of Democratic candidates for state legislature (26% of total) accepted public campaign funds.

Of the approximately $4 million spent by Wisconsin candidates for state offices in 1980, only 15 percent came from public funds. The only statewide candidates to accept public funding were three nonpartisan supreme court candidates; the remainder of the public money used in 1980 went to 30 percent of the state legislative candidates. More Democratic than Republican, more state Assembly than Senate, and more challengers than incumbent candidates chose to use public funding. While the 1980 experience represented an increase over the 1978 level of candidate participation in the public funding program, it falls far short of the expectations of advocates of public funding and indicates that public financing is still not an integral part of the Wisconsin electoral finance process.

In Minnesota, 66 percent of the candidates for the legislature accepted a total of $617,099 in public funds during the 1980 general election campaign. Compared to Wisconsin, this appears to be a successful program. When 1980 is compared to the 1978 and 1976 Minnesota experience, however, in which 88 and 91 percent, respectively, of eligible candidates used public money in their campaigns, the clear impression is that the public funding program is losing support among candidates and thus is losing its effect on the electoral process.[30] The suggested reason for this decline in use of public funds in Minnesota, as in Hawaii, was the small amount of money that a candidate stood to gain in return for agreeing to the expenditure limitations that accompanied the public funds. The Minnesota public funding program was modified in 1980 to make more public money available to candidates and raise the expenditure limitations. As a result, the number of legislative candidates participating in the 1982 public funding program increased markedly to approach the 1976 level of participation. Also indicating a revitalization of the public funding program was the fact that twice as many candidates for constitutional offices used public funds in 1982 than in 1978. However, in 1982, as in 1978, the Republican gubernatorial candidate did not participate in the public funding program, did not sign the agreement, and did not adhere to expenditure limitations.

In no state, with the possible exception of Montana, did the allocation of public funds directly to individual candidates play a major role in the financing of the 1980 state elections. In marked contrast, public funding dominated the 1981 New Jersey gubernatorial election campaign. Sixteen primary and two general election campaigns used approximately $8.6 million in public funds, and the consensus is that the availability of public funding encouraged a large field of candidates and stimulated a very expensive campaign.

Similarly, the availability of public funding for the 1982 Michigan gubernatorial primary campaign clearly encouraged the 11 candidates who entered the contest and, some observers claim, was an important factor in the outcome of the Republican primary. And, because the flat grant of $750,000 to the two major-party candidates represented 75 percent of their total campaign budgets, public funding was a major factor in the general election campaign as well. In stark contrast, the $500,000 of public money divided among 15 different statewide races in Massachusetts played a very minor role in that state's 1982 campaigns.

To date, it would appear that public funding plays a significant, consistent, and stabilizing role in the financing of election campaigns in those states that allocate the public money to political parties. In states that allocate funds directly to candidates, the record is mixed and, apparently, the importance of public funding depends on how much is available to whom. When ample funds can be concentrated on only a few campaigns or a few candidates, as in New Jersey or Michigan, public funding has a significant impact on the election campaign process. When the funds are less than adequate to give a strong financial base to the array of qualified candidates, public funding seems to play but a minor part in the overall campaign process. In these cases, public funding seems to be more important to legislative candidates than statewide candidates, more important to House candidates than Senate candidates, more important to Democratic than Republican candidates, and more important to challengers than incumbents.

The fact that a ceiling on expenditures accompanies the use of public funds has not resulted in reduced campaign spending. To the contrary, the large field of primary candidates stimulated by public funding in New Jersey and Michigan produced record total spending by gubernatorial candidates in those two states. Similarly, expenditure ceilings apply only to the candidates' committees, so the reports of record spending do not include money spent by political parties on campaign efforts such as get-out-the-vote drives. When the parties in a state have markedly unequal resources, any equity achieved by imposing expenditure limits on the individual candidates can be undermined by the ability of the well-funded party to provide substantial indirect assistance to its candidates.

*Future.* In spite of the mixed record of state-level public funding programs, public campaign financing continues to attract attention and receive support from those concerned with the increasingly large sums of money needed to wage viable election campaigns. In 1982, the Kentucky public funding program was modified to increase the amount of money taxpayers can designate to political parties via the tax check-off and to provide for the allocation of check-off funds to county as well as state political party organizations. For policy makers contemplating public financing, the experiences of the 17 states, each of which has adopted a very different public funding program, have doubtless provided useful information that will facilitate the drafting of legislation to address what otherwise would seem to be new issues. But these same policy makers continue to expand and refine the variety of responses to shared problems.

For example, a bill introduced in California calls for partial public financing of state legislative campaigns on a matching-fund basis. In Missouri, a proposed program includes no expenditure limitations and allocates 10 percent of the public campaign fund to political parties and the remainder to statewide candidates. The direct refund program established in Alaska is one of the more innovative attempts to address the issues of increased campaign costs. Having abolished the state income tax and thus the opportunity for a check-off program, the state has replaced the old tax credit for political contributions with a direct refund to match political contributions dollar for dollar up to $50 ($100 in tax year 1981). In 1980, 6907 individuals got an average refund of $44 for the total $307,269 claimed in political contributions; in 1982, more than twice as many people filed claims that totaled $1,253,575 in political contributions. Although it is too early to determine the impact Alaska's refund program is having on the electoral campaign process, it clearly represents an alternative method of stimulating political giving among a wide segment of the state's electorate.

Not all change is in the direction of *adding* new public funding programs. Oregon's public funding legislation had a three-year sunset provision, and after review during the 1981 legislative session, the program was not renewed. The Maryland add-on program was adopted in 1974, but no money from the Fair Campaign Financing Fund was ever allocated to candidates. In 1982 the legislature repealed the public funding act, and the almost $1 million that accumulated during the seven-year life of the program remains in limbo. The Oklahoma Supreme Court effectively upheld an attorney general's opinion invalidating the public funding portions of the Oklahoma Campaign Finance Act passed by the Oklahoma legislature in 1979.

In contrast to the public funds spent in the 1980 presidential campaign, the $2,875,000 in public funds spent at the state level certainly did not play a dominant role in the overall funding of state elections in 1980. Yet, within individual states, especially where the funds went to political party organizations, public funds did influence the pattern of campaign contributions and expenditures and thus touched at the very heart of campaign financing.

## Ballot-Issue Campaigns

The foregoing discussion has been limited to the expenditures and contributions for candidates seeking public office. But state elections increasingly include ballot issues as well as candidate contests. There were over 200 propositions presented to voters in 1980 and again in 1982; at least one issue was on the ballot in 42 different states.[31] The subject matter of initiatives and referenda ranged from legalized Bingo, fur trapping, and the Equal Rights Amendment (ERA) to reapportionment, local tax limitations, and nuclear development. This great diversity of ballot issues limits comparisons of the various campaigns, but it does appear that there is more diversity among the states in expenditure patterns than in contribution patterns for ballot-issue campaigns. It also may be that money had a more discernible impact on ballot-issue election outcomes than it did on the selection of state legislative or statewide officeholders.

EXPENDITURES

As with candidate elections, there is great variation in the expenditure patterns within and among states when it comes to financing ballot-issue campaigns. Ballot-issue campaigns for six issues in Nebraska reported a total of approximately $100,000 in campaign expenditures; four issues generated campaigns that accounted for a total of $2,375,300 in expenditures in Missouri; and over $23,000,000 was spent on 22 California ballot issues in 1980.

The total expenditures for ballot-issue campaigns clearly vary from year to year in a given state depending on how many highly controversial measures are on the ballot. Therefore, in contrast to the steadily increasing trend-line of costs associated with candidate election campaigns discussed above, the total costs of ballot-issue campaigns have a very irregular pattern when charted within a state over time.

There was also considerable variation in expenditures within a single state depending on the issue. For example, the 1982 California ballot-issue campaign for changing the calculation of the value of condemned property stimulated little campaign activity and consequently little campaign expenditure; less than $1000 was spent on the campaign. In contrast, $6.4 million was spent in the two campaigns for and against the Peripheral Canal.

Expenditures on similar issues also varied greatly across states. Proposals to limit nuclear development or to regulate the handling of nuclear materials were on the 1980 ballot in several states. A comparison of contribution and expenditure totals shown in table 6.6 on page 206 for nuclear issues in five of these states reveals a spending range from slightly over $100,000 in Montana to almost $2 million in Missouri. However, in each state the opponents of nuclear regulation spent more than those favoring regulation; in four of the states, the ratio of spending was almost three to one in opposition to regulation.

This illustrates a more general point. Big spending is usually negative spending. The largest sums spent in 1980 were in opposition to the legislation submitted for voter approval, as in the case of nuclear power regulations, smoking restrictions, or tax limitations. A notable exception was the Colorado lottery where the big spending was in support of the proposed legislation. Similarly, the 1982 nuclear arms freeze initiative, which had a national clearinghouse to coordinate nine statewide and 30 local ballot-issue campaigns, represents a clear case where proponents of the initiatives were the dominant spenders. Unofficial figures indicate proponents spent over $2.5 million, while opponents spent less than one-fifth that amount.[32] Even in Arizona, the only state to reject the nuclear freeze initative, proponents outspent opponents by more than three to one.

CONTRIBUTIONS

The nuclear power ballot issues in 1980 also illustrate three other features of ballot-issue campaign financing that have received relatively little attention. Those who advocate the use of the initiative and referendum often do so because they think it will facilitate grass-roots politics through increased individual

TABLE 6.6.
REPORTED EXPENDITURES FOR BALLOT ISSUES RELATED TO
NUCLEAR POWER REGULATION, 1980

| | Total Spending[a] | Favor Restrictions | Oppose Restrictions | Issue Outcome |
|---|---|---|---|---|
| Maine | $880,000 | $250,000 | $630,000 | Failed |
| Missouri | 1,953,531 | 61,160 | 1,892,371 | Failed |
| Montana | 128,544 | 2,268 | 126,276 | Passed |
| Oregon | 634,862 | 37,814 | 597,048 | Passed |
| Washington | 149,204 | 72,508 | 76,696 | Passed |

a. Spending figures for Maine based on a statement by Common Cause to the Maine Committee on Election Laws, March 24, 1981. Data for other states taken from public documents published by the states' agencies responsible for processing reporting and disclosure reports.

citizen participation. An analysis of initiative and referendum efforts in 1980 and 1982 suggests a very different experience. Contrary to the expectations of mass, individual citizen involvement, the sources of campaign contributions are frequently (1) a very few, large contributors, (2) who are highly organized groups rather than single individuals, and (3) who frequently represent out-of-state interests. For example, 92 percent of opposition money in the Missouri nuclear regulation campaign in 1980 came from a single corporate source, the Union Electric Company's "No on 11" Committee, whereas less than one-third of 1 percent of contributions to oppose the measure came from individuals or in small contributions of $50 or less. Although more than $600,000 was spent by "Oregonians Against Banning the Nuclear Option," half the funds of this group came from one source, Portland Electric (which also spent $16,500 directly to defeat the measure). The majority of the remaining contributions to Oregonians Against Banning came from out-of-state committees.

Almost 75 percent of the 1980 contributions to groups opposing nuclear regulation in Washington came from outside the state. The amount contributed from out-of-state corporations to the "Committee to Save Maine Yankee" was two and one-half times as much as was spent by indigenous Maine proponents and opponents combined.

But the dominance of large, organizational contributions from out-of-state contributors was not confined to nuclear power issues. In Colorado, $90,000 of the $93,000 reported in expenditures supporting the establishment of a state lottery came from a single out-of-state firm that designs and administers state lottery programs. With these out-of-state funds, spending in favor of the lottery was almost twice that of the opposition. In 1980, opponents successfully spent about two and one-half times as much as proponents of a California antismoking proposition, and 97 percent of the contributions to oppose the issue came from four out-of-state tobacco companies. In Iowa, the largest contributor to the successful effort to defeat ERA was STOP ERA—Iowa Division of Alton, Illinois.

The 1982 initiative to limit interest rates on consumer loans stimulated record-breaking opposition spending of $1,508,000 in the state of Washington and 40 percent of the opposition's funds were provided by J.C. Penney Co. of New York and 20 percent by the Sears chain. In Montana, a proposal for bottle deposit and glass recycling reportedly had wide public support early in 1980, but major glass and bottle interests from out of state waged an extensive media campaign (costing almost $600,000), and the November vote on the bottle issue was 65 to 35 *against* requiring deposits and recycling. Similarly, out-of-state beverage interests were heavy contributors in 1982 to the successful bottle bill opposition campaign in Arizona and to the $6 million campaign that defeated a bottle bill in California.

## FUNDING IMPLICATIONS

Contributions and expenditures in 1980 initiative and referendum elections apparently produced no general pattern in terms of the relationship of the total amount or the ratio of pro-to-con spending to the success or defeat of ballot issues. For example, in Maine and Missouri, the big-spending opposition won and thus defeated the proposed restriction on nuclear development, whereas in Montana and Oregon, the big spenders lost. In Washington, where spending by proponents and opponents was almost even, 76 percent of the votes were in favor of regulation; in Montana, where spending was greatly skewed in opposition to regulation, the restrictive measure barely passed.

As spending on the nuclear issues suggests, large campaign expenditures do not ensure victory. However, seasoned observers of the electoral process feel that money has an important role in these elections primarily because most of the money spent on issue campaigns goes into sophisticated media appeals and advertising. In Maine, the majority of the out-of-state money went "to fund a sophisticated saturation media campaign . . . $400,000 of the corporate campaign money went to advertising firms in New York and Los Angeles, most of it used to buy space and time in Maine media."[33]

In 1980, ballot-issue media campaigns ranged widely. There was the low-key, positive appeal that suggested a state lottery could provide revenue for popular activities such as parks and recreation; and there was the direct, hard-sell approach, such as on the branch banking issue in Colorado, which bombarded voters with conflicting information about the benefits and liabilities of branch banking; and there were the veiled, negative appeals such as those implying that passage of ERA in Iowa would threaten the continuation of that venerable Iowa institution—girls' basketball. Whether or not the campaigns were always persuasive and successful, it is possible that expenditures to publicize ballot issues may have been a key factor in establishing the quality or the informed nature of the ballot-issue vote.

Expenditures also seem to have had a bearing on the numbers of votes cast on ballot issues. Although voter turnout in initiative states is generally higher than in noninitiative states, cursory analysis of the 1980 campaigns indicates that the number of voters participating in specific ballot-issue elections within a single state was closely related to the amount of money spent on the campaign. In Missouri, for example, 12 percent more voters cast ballots on the issue that involved the most expensive campaign than in the least expensive ballot-issue campaign; in Colorado, the difference was 7 percent.

Apparently, based on an analysis of the 1980 campaigns, one impact of the financing patterns of ballot-issue campaigns is to create three different kinds of ballot-issue elections. The rarest kind of election involves a competitive ballot-issue campaign that provides the voters extensive and relatively balanced information via media. Such campaigns—the 1980 Colorado branch banking issue or the 1982 California Peripheral Canal, for example—pit two well-organized and well-financed corporate interests against each other. The campaign is media intensive and very expensive, but each side makes its case to the voters, and a high voter turnout is stimulated. The second kind of ballot-issue election shaped by the mix of interests and resources is the noncompetitive, generally public-interest, ballot-issue election, such as one limiting valid petition signatures to registered voters only. Few if any resources are expended, the campaign and relevant publicity are virtually nonexistent, and voter turnout wanes.

The most common kind of ballot election is one in which two active and concerned interests compete, but the competition is very unequal. One side, most often a corporate or private interest and frequently one from out of state, is well organized and well funded; the other side, usually a citizens' lobby or public interest group, is less elaborately organized and less adequately financed. In these campaigns (e.g., nuclear development, bottle recycling, lotteries), expenditures are sizable but skewed, media campaigns are highly biased, and voter turnout is much more volatile and unpredictable.

It would appear that the openness and equity of ballot-issue campaigns are as heavily dependent as, if not more heavily dependent than individual candidates' campaigns on the resource capacity of the specific interests involved. If this is true and the majority of ballot-issue campaign expenditures continues to be negative and extremely high or very unequal, or reliant on out-of-state funds, a reassessment of the viability of the initiative and referendum as vehicles for local, grass-roots policy making is in order.

## Summary

Our necessarily limited review of state election campaign financing suggests certain trends in the costs of state election campaigns, the sources of campaign contributions, and the financing of ballot-issue campaigns. State election campaign costs, especially for legislative races, are rapidly escalating beyond any increases that may be related to inflation; costs of campaigns for state legislative races are highly influenced by incumbency status, type of election, and competitiveness; and total expenditures are important, but they are not always sufficient for predicting election outcomes.

The sources of campaign funding remain individual contributors, political parties, and organized groups. Variations in state law, subsequently reflected in conscious electoral strategies, are primary determinants of the role each funding source plays in state election financing. Overall, the balance among these three sources has shifted to a proportionally less prominent role for direct individual contributions, a modified role for political parties emphasizing indirect contributions, and a proportionate as well as absolute increase in the role of other groups, especially PACs. Public funding provides a new source of campaign funds in one-third of the states. Public funding had its greatest impact in 1980 when funds were allocated directly to political parties; in the 1981 New Jersey and 1982 Michigan gubernatorial campaigns, public funding to individual candidates clearly helped shape these campaigns.

Ballot-issue campaigns are becoming more common and involve sizable campaign expenditures. The most prominent sources of funds in the majority of ballot-issue campaigns are organized groups, usually PACs, which frequently represent out-of-state interests and often serve as virtually the sole financers of a campaign.

There is great variation in spending on ballot issues within a single state during a single election cycle, within any state over time, and on similar issues across states in any given year. Although money is perhaps more influential in shaping ballot-issue campaigns than candidate campaigns, the relationship between spending and election outcome is even less predictable for ballot-issue elections.

Two factors relevant to future analyses of campaign funding in the states emerge from this initial inquiry. First, it is impossible to overstate the importance of the fact that state election financing is governed by *state* law. Although this aspect of federalism presents opportunities for ready-made, semiexperimental research designs to facilitate further study of the impact of various election finance laws on the campaign and electoral process, it also makes comparative analysis extremely difficult. It demands a breadth of knowledge of individual state political systems that probably can be found only in multimember, collaborative research efforts. Because such research efforts are demonstrably possible, there is a basis for optimism and excitement about further studies of state campaign financing.

Nevertheless, the second factor to emerge from our inquiry greatly tempers any such optimism. As recognition of the need for more comprehensive, comparable state-level data has increased, the likelihood of more quality data being made available has decreased. In fact, all the evidence suggests that there will be *less,* not more, data available to assist future systematic study of state-level campaign funding.

In state after state, agencies that prepare and publish the official reports that now provide the best data sources for systematic analysis are under attack. For example, both in Missouri and Minnesota budget and personnel cuts have threatened the ongoing publication of particularly useful, high-quality reports. The mere publication of a legally mandated, 22-page book listing only totals for campaign contributions and expenditures of each state officer elected in 1980 threatened the continuation of the Montana Commission on Political Practices, which produced the report.

Similarly, the likelihood of additional states beginning systematically to process, summarize, and publish election finance data seems more remote than ever before. In Michigan, which has one of the most efficient and best-organized systems for collecting and processing campaign finance reports, there is neither the mandate nor the resources needed to analyze and report the data, and there is virtually no possibility that either a new authorization or a new budget line will be forthcoming soon. With the threat of cuts in key personnel, it is also unlikely that the Iowa Campaign Finance Disclosure Commission will expand its role to include analysis and publication of summary data based on the contribution and expenditure reports they already process. Contact with numerous other state agencies that currently do not publish an official campaign contribution and expenditure report revealed not one state in which plans were under way to initiate such reports.

Thus, at the very time that more and more attention is being focused on the role of states, and more and more critical decisions are being made by elected *state* officials, we are likely to learn less and less about how the election campaigns of these state officials are financed. To the research community this situation is discouraging; to the advocates of an open electoral process, it is deplorable. The remedy is obvious but not easily attained, for it requires that state legislatures provide the legislative mandate and appropriate adequate resources both to collect campaign contribution and expenditure data (which most states already do) and make these data readily available to the public in a form that is informative and useful. Without such legislative commitment and action, it appears that, if money indeed talks, it will be extremely difficult in the future to determine whose voices are being heard in state elections.

# Notes

1. Alexander Heard, *The Costs of Democracy* (Chapel Hill: University of North Carolina Press, 1960); Herbert E. Alexander, ed., *Political Finance* (Beverly Hills, Calif.: Sage, 1979); David Adamany and George Agree, *Political Money: A Strategy for Campaign Financing in America* (Baltimore: Johns Hopkins University Press, 1975); and Michael J. Malbin, ed., *Parties, Interest Groups, and Campaign Finance Laws* (Washington, D.C.: American Enterprise Institute, 1980).

2. Noticeable exceptions to the national orientation are David Adamany, *Financing Politics: Recent Wisconsin Elections* (Madison: University of Wisconsin Press, 1969); Herbert E. Alexander, ed., *Campaign Money: Reform and Reality in the States* (New York: Free Press 1976); and Herbert E. Alexander and Jennifer W. Frutig, *Public Financing of State Elections* (Los Angeles: Citizens' Research Foundation, 1982).

3. The presence or absence of official reports is largely responsible for the regional imbalance in the use of examples in the text. Although they differ greatly in the inclusion, analysis, and presentation of funding data, Alaska, California, Colorado, Hawaii, Idaho, Minnesota, Missouri, Nebraska, Oregon, Washington, and Wisconsin are among the states that publish reports; noticeable in the list of states that do *not* publish formal reports are Connecticut, Florida, Illinois, Massachusetts, Michigan, New York, Ohio, Pennsylvania, and Texas. In addition to official records, the following discussion relies on information obtained from personal and telephone interviews with election officials, political party and interest-group leaders, and from newspaper reports.

4. Fair Political Practices Commission, *Campaign Costs: How Much Have They Increased and Why?* (Sacramento, Calif.: The Commission, January 1980), 1.

5. Charles Roos, "$1.5 Million Spent on State Campaigns in '80," *Denver Post,* January 19, 1981, 3.

6. Gary C. Jacobson, *Money in Congressional Elections* (New Haven: Yale University Press, 1980).

7. Fair Political Practices Commission, *Campaign Costs,* 1.

8. Leon D. Epstein, *Political Parties in Western Democracies* (New York: Praeger, 1976); E.E. Schattschneider, *Party Government* (New York: Holt, Rinehart and Winston, 1967); and Maurice Duverger, *Political Parties* (New York: Wiley, 1954).

9. Everett C. Ladd and Charles D. Hadley, *Political Parties and Political Issues: Patterns of Differentiation Since the New Deal,* vol. 1, Sage Professional Papers in American Politics (Beverly Hills, Calif.: Sage, 1973); Walter Dean Burnham, *Critical Elections and the Mainsprings of American Politics* (New York: Norton, 1970); Cornelius P. Cotter and John F. Bibby, "Institutional Development of Parties and the Thesis of Party Decline," *Political Science Quarterly* 95 (1980): 1-27.

10. Fair Political Practices Commission, "November General Election Report Available" (press release, May 28, 1981).

11. Ibid., 2.

12. Keith Bagwell, "Group Urges Vote Financing," *Scottsdale Progress,* October 20, 1981, 2.

13. Fair Political Practices Commission, *The California PAC Phenomenon* (Sacramento, Calif.: The Commission, May 1980), 8.

14. State ballot issues in 1980 are discussed more extensively in the text that follows.

15. Michael B. Binford, "PAC Campaign Contributions and the State Legislature: Impact on Legislators and the Legislative Agenda" (paper presented at the meeting of the Southern Political Science Association, Memphis, Tenn., November 5-7, 1981), 10.

16. E.J. Dionne, Jr., "Power Persuasive in Political Giving," *New York Times,* January 18, 1981, 2, 26.

17. Timothy D. Schellhardt, "Corporate PACs Turning Attention to the States as Deregulation Gains," *Wall Street Journal,* October 28, 1982, 33.

18. Binford, "PAC Campaign Contributions," 15.

19. Two case studies tracing this relationship are ibid. and James Eisenstein and Roger Karapin, "The Relationship Between Political Action Committee Contributions and Roll Call Votes in the Pennsylvania House of Representatives: A Preliminary Analysis" (paper presented at the meeting of the Pennsylvania Political Science Association, University Park, Pa., March 28, 1981).

20. Binford, "PAC Campaign Contributions," 15.

21. For example, a description of the interaction between political parties and PACs follows in the discussion of political parties as sources of campaign financing.

22. M. Margaret Conway, "Political Party Nationalizaton, Campaign Activities and Local Party Development" (paper presented at the meeting of the Midwest Political Science Association, Cincinnati, Ohio, April 16-18, 1981); Larry Light, "Republican Groups Dominate in Party Campaign Spending," *Congressional Quarterly,* November 1, 1980, 3234-39; and Christopher Buchanan, "National GOP Pushing Hard to Capture State Legislatures," *Congressional Quarterly,* October 25, 1980, 3188-92.

23. William David Deiss, "The Regulation of Campaign Finance Law in Vermont: More Loophole Than Law," *Vermont Law Review* 6 (Spring 1981): 243.

24. Malcolm E. Jewell, *Comparative State Politics Newsletter* 2, no. 1 (1981): 8.

25. Personal interview with anonymous party official from Iowa, June 1981.

26. See Ruth S. Jones, "State Public Financing and the State Parties," in *Parties, Interest Groups, and Campaign Finance Laws,* ed. Michael J. Malbin (Washington, D.C.: American Enterprise Institute, 1980), 283-321; and Jack L. Noragon, "Political Finance and Political Reform: The Experience with State Income Tax Checkoffs," *American Political Science Review* 75 (September 1981): 667-87.

27. The Maryland and Oklahoma programs did not allocate funds; Massachusetts, Michigan, and New Jersey fund candidates for offices that were not involved in the 1980 campaigns.

28. A check-off collection procedure is comparable to the federal program and does not increase the taxpayer's tax liability; an add-on is a voluntary addition to one's tax liability that is earmarked for funding political campaigns. The add-on system generates very limited amounts of money so that the public financing programs in Maine, Maryland, and Massachusetts have limited opportunity to influence the election process in these add-on states. Montana used a check-off system until 1979 when it switched to an add-on collection procedure; therefore, although there was a sizable public fund for 1980 campaigns, the dropoff in taxpayer participation from 18.3% in 1978 to 2.7% in 1979 suggests that public funds will play a decreasing role in future elections in Montana.

29. For a more detailed description of the partisan nature of public financing programs, see Ruth S. Jones, "State Public Campaign Finance: Implications for Partisan Politics," *American Journal of Political Science,* May 1980, 342-61; and idem, "Patterns of Campaign Finance in the Public Funding States" (paper presented at the

Midwest Political Science Association meeting, Milwaukee, Wisconsin, April 28, 1981).

30. A comprehensive discussion of public funding in Minnesota can be found in Ruth S. Jones, "Public Campaign Finance: The Minnesota Experiment" (paper presented at the Western Political Science Association meeting, Denver, Colo., March 26-28, 1981).

31. Austin Ranney, "Referendums, 1980 Style," *Public Opinion,* February/March 1981, 40; and Harrison Donnally, "Year of the Initiative," *Today,* November 19, 1982, 9.

32. Patrick B. McGuigan and Julie Ingersoll, "The Nuclear Weapons Freeze," *Initiative and Referendum Report,* January 1983, 9.

33. Joseph Steinberg, Statement of Common Cause to the Committee on Election Laws, Augusta, Maine, March 24, 1981, 1.

RICHARD SMOLKA

# 7. The Campaign Law in the Courts

The 1974 Federal Election Campaign Act (FECA) got off to a rocky start when, in January 1976, the U.S. Supreme Court in *Buckley* v. *Valeo* ruled unconstitutional certain sections of the act, including the method of selection of the Federal Election Commission itself.[1] Subsequent congressional legislation attempted to deal with what courts, parties, candidates, and Congress regarded as defects in the law. Supreme Court decisions and federal court rulings before, during, and after the 1980 campaign have clarified the law a bit more. Nevertheless, the law and its possible consequences have caused political participants and observers much concern.

That this should happen was no surprise. In his separate opinion in *Buckley*, Chief Justice Warren Burger noted that the court, by "dissecting the Act" failed "to recognize that the whole is greater than the sum of its parts." Burger argued that Congress had intended to regulate all aspects of federal campaign finances, "but what remains after today's holding leaves no more than a shadow of what Congress contemplated. I question whether the residue leaves a workable program."

As the courts have continued to scrutinize the law and its operation in the light of First Amendment rights, sections of the law, as well as some attempts to enforce it, have been struck down or rendered ineffective. The more the courts look at the law, the less they see that can pass constitutional muster. What is left may not be sufficient to achieve the law's primary objective: to limit the influence, or apparent influence, of money in campaigns, thereby reducing the likelihood of corruption of elected officials. Regardless of congressional efforts to be comprehensive, the First Amendment has been found to protect freedom of speech and political association in areas that the law sought to regulate. As a result, Congress has been left with a law that conforms to no one's idea of sound public policy but that candidates, parties, and groups seek to exploit for their political advantage.

A campaign finance study group at the Harvard University Institute of Politics in January 1982 made 16 recommendations for changes in the law as it affects presidential campaigning.[2] The group predicted that if these changes were not implemented, the act "will increasingly become harmful and ineffective as contradictory as that may sound." The report, echoing Chief Justice Burger, concludes that parts of the law that seek to curtail the amount of money in presidential politics "will become increasingly ineffective while the practical effects of the Act will become increasingly harmful as the contenders are unable to mobilize adequate campaigns while unrestrained amounts are spent through less accountable channels."

Among the most difficult issues posing a conflict between the law and the First Amendment during the 1980 election cycle was that of "independent expenditures"—spending by individuals or groups for or against candidates but independently of candidate or party organizations. Another issue with potentially significant consequences concerns the regulation of "draft committees"— groups working to persuade someone who is not a candidate to become one. The courts were also confronted with interpreting the law as it might regulate certain press activities, the disclosure of financial information by unpopular political parties, and the degree of freedom political parties have to structure their financial activities and contributions in an efficient manner. In each controversy discussed below, the law was arguably in conflict with First Amendment rights.

## Independent Expenditures

One question that begged for quick resolution was whether expenditure limits ruled unconstitutional in *Buckley* v. *Valeo* would be sustained if they were also a condition of receiving public funds. A footnote in *Buckley* seemed to indicate that this was the case, despite a more general principle that Congress is prohibited from doing indirectly as a condition of receipt of public funds that which it is prohibited from doing directly.[3]

The Republican National Committee (RNC) filed a suit in 1978 charging that a candidate should not be required to surrender constitutional rights to unlimited spending in order to receive the campaign subsidy. The committee added that the contribution limits prohibiting the candidate from receiving private contributions gave unfair advantages to labor unions, which are permitted to spend unlimited amounts to communicate with their members.

In holding the act constitutional, a three-judge panel noted that the candidate retained a right to refuse the public funds and to engage in unlimited spending.[4] Perhaps even more important, the court said that the rights of supporters who may have wished to contribute to a candidate receiving public funds were sufficiently protected by the right of such persons to make independent expenditures in support of the candidate. Without this right of supporters to spend unlimited funds, the limit on spending by candidates receiving public funds may have been viewed as unconstitutional. There is little doubt that the strong statement of the court regarding the right to make independent expenditures greatly encouraged independent groups to exercise this right. The Supreme Court affirmed the ruling of the lower court.[5]

Independent expenditures present one of the most difficult challenges to the law. The Supreme Court, in *Buckley,* ruled that limits on individual independent expenditures were unconstitutional. The Court equated such spending with political expression guaranteed by the First Amendment. But questions remained about whether the same reasoning would apply to a narrower section of the FECA that applied only to publicly funded candidates.

Prior to 1980, several committees were organized independently of candidates, and several indicated plans to spend large sums of money on behalf of presidential candidate Ronald Reagan. One provision of the public funding sections of the FECA limits uncoordinated expenditures to $1000 if they are made by nonparty committees, during the general election, and in support of a publicly funded candidate. Common Cause and the FEC filed separate suits in 1980 that sought to enforce these provisions. A three-judge federal panel in the District of Columbia ruled five weeks before the election that there was no substantial difference between the independent expenditure limits held unconstitutional in *Buckley* and the narrower ones involved here.[6] Altogether, some 73 committees spent more than $12 million supporting Reagan's candidacy.

More than 14 months after the election, the Supreme Court, by a 4-4 vote, affirmed the lower court ruling.[7] Justice Sandra O'Connor took no part in the *per curiam* decision. The lower court had referred to the right of individuals and groups to make unlimited independent expenditures as "a constitutional pillar of election laws." How substantial that pillar is, however, remains open to question and to further litigation. Senator Harrison "Jack" Schmitt (R-N.M.), chairman of one of the independent groups, Americans for Change, called the decision "a victory for individual rights and free speech." But Common Cause chairman Archibald Cox said that "the decision leaves the basic constitutional questions concerning independent committee expenditures in a presidential race unresolved. The statute still forbids them."[8]

The isssue will come up again in 1984. On May 12, 1983, the Federal Election Commission issued an advisory opinion saying that the commission intended to enforce the $1000 general election independent expenditure limit for publicly funded presidential candidates. Within days of the advisory opinion, the Democratic National Committee filed suit against the National Conservative Political Action Committee and the Fund for a Conservative Majority before a three-judge federal district court in the Eastern District of Pennsylvania. The DNC asked the court for a declaratory ruling on the constitutionality of the $1000 limit and for an injunction that would prohibit independent expenditures in excess of that amount. The Federal Election Commission intervened on behalf of the DNC in that suit and filed its own suit against the same two political action committees. On December 12 the district court unanimously held the independent expenditure limit unconstitutional.[9] Three days later, the FEC said it would appeal the decision to the Supreme Court.

In addition to questions of constitutionality, independent expenditures present other questions of law. To be classified as an independent expenditure, funds must be spent with no coordination between the independent committee and the candidate or campaign committee. The law will function as intended only if there is a way to determine, in a timely manner, whether prohibited coordination took place. The procedures necessary to investigate a complaint of illegal coordination and at the same time protect the rights of those participating in the campaign require a due process and therefore may take some time. Because the election date is fixed and cannot be postponed pending the outcome of such an investigation, the voting may be over long before coordination is established.

Under the best of circumstances, coordination is no easy matter to prove. Politics, by nature, requires social interaction, and not all communication can be regarded as coordination. Moreover, campaign decisions and possible strategies are widely disseminated by the media. Both independent groups and candidate committees can easily be aware of the well-publicized plans of the other. They may, without any coordination, become aware of decisions that receive little or no publicity.

## Draft Committees

A second area often cited as a loophole in the law relates to draft committees — committees formed in support of a person not yet a "candidate" to urge that person to become a candidate. When the Supreme Court, by denying a *writ of certiorari,* let stand a lower court ruling that held "draft committees" outside the scope of the FECA,[10] readers of the *Washington Post* were told that the decision "may have opened another multimillion dollar loophole in the laws limiting fund raising and spending for presidential and congressional aspirants."[11] The reason for the statement may be seen from the facts in the case.

During 1979, Senator Edward M. Kennedy said that he was not a candidate for President and that he expected President Jimmy Carter to be renominated. Notwithstanding Kennedy's statements, several committees seeking to draft him began working to make him the party nominee.

On October 4, 1979, the Carter-Mondale presidential campaign committee filed a complaint with the FEC against these committees, charging that they were "affiliated" within the meaning of the FECA and that they therefore were subject to a single $5000 limit on the contributions they could receive from any one multicandidate committee. The complaint charged that the Machinists Non-Partisan Political League (MNPL) had given contributions to the draft committees far in excess of $5000. The MNPL admitted that it had given approximately $30,000 to "draft-Kennedy" committees in seven states.

On November 5, 1979, the commission issued a sweeping subpoena to MNPL ordering production of all documents relating to communication between MNPL and other "draft-Kennedy" groups. It asked for minutes, notes, memoranda, and records of telephone conversations whereby the MNPL or any of its subunits decided to support or oppose any presidential nominee. The MNPL was asked to provide a list of every official, employee, staff member, and volunteer of the organization together with each person's telephone number.

The MNPL was one of three such groups that resisted the FEC subpoenas. They challenged FEC jurisdiction over their activities, arguing that the FECA definition of a "political committee" was restricted to a group whose major purpose was to influence the nomination or election of a *candidate*. At the time of the complaint, Kennedy was not a candidate.

The FEC responded by filing and winning four separate suits to compel the enforcement of its subpoenas.[12] One committee, Wisconsin Democrats for Change in 1980, complied with the federal court order. Other committees, the Florida for Kennedy Committee, Citizens for Democratic Alternatives in 1980, and the MNPL appealed, setting the stage for a major decision on the FECA.

The appellate court ruled, contrary to the district court ruling, "that the commission lacks subject matter jurisdiction over the draft group activities it seeks to investigate through this subpoena."[13] The court used strong language, vigorously attacking the *range* of the FEC inquiry, even though it obviously could have reached the same decision without commenting on what the subpoenas sought. The court called the FEC legal action "an unprecedented assertion of subject matter jurisdiction" and said the subject matter of the materials demanded by the FEC represents the very heart of the organism that the First Amendment was intended to nurture and protect: political expression and association concerning federal elections and officeholding. It continued: "Release of such information to the government carries with it a real potential for chilling the free exercise of political speech and association guarded by the First Amendment."

In a speculative footnote worth repeating, the court commented that the ratification of the Constitution itself was carried on by men who sought anonymity.

> One can only imagine what the Founding Fathers would have thought of a federal bureaucracy demanding comprehensive reports on the internal workings and membership lists of peaceful political groups. It bears remembering that Elbridge Gerry, Oliver Ellsworth, Roger Sherman, Spencer Roane, Noah Webster, James Iredell, and others all sought anonymity while they conducted the most important political campaign of their lives, the campaign to ratify the federal constitution."

The note emphasized that the *Federalist Papers* were published anonymously and that fear and resentment of royal administrative control over politics generally, and elections particularly, was a key element in the opposition political culture of England during the eighteenth century.

Unable to find a specific reference to draft committees in the statute, the court was unwilling to rule that they were within FEC jurisdiction. And finding no jurisdiction, the court was unwilling to enforce the subpoena. Moreover, its reasoning raised substantial doubts that even an act of Congress regulating draft committees would pass constitutional muster.

The appellate court noted that in *Buckley* the Supreme Court had justified regulation of political activity precisely on the "narrow aspect of political association where the actuality and potential for corruption have been identified." Draft committees, it found, do not fall within the Supreme Court's definition of political committees nor has their potential for corruption been identified by Congress.

The implications of the decision for incumbents, especially members of Congress, were substantial. The ruling, it appeared, created two classes of political committees. Candidates identified as such would be legally constrained in fund-raising activities, but "potential" candidates would not be subject to the same limitations. Within a month the Democratic Senatorial Campaign Committee (DSCC) and the Democratic Congressional Campaign Committee (DCCC) attempted to intervene in the suit. The decision, it was feared, invited potential candidates to allow draft committees to raise and spend substantial sums in their behalf prior to a declaration of candidacy, while incumbents, who could not logically be "drafted," would be hampered by contribution limits. For this reason, many members of Congress believe that draft committees should be treated as candidate committees, but the constitutionality of such legislation will surely be tested in the courts.

## Unpopular Political Parties

The Federal Election Commission has attempted to ensure that all political parties comply with the disclosure and recordkeeping requirements of the FECA but has been frustrated by judicial insistence that not all parties are the same when it comes to the First Amendment. The *Buckley* Court had refused to strike down disclosure requirements as overbroad, solely because they apply to minor parties and independent candidates, before the commission tried to apply the requirements in an actual case. But the Court said minor parties must have an opportunity to make a case for exemptions. The burden of proof suggested by the Court was not great: "a pattern of threats or specific manifestations of public hostility may be sufficient."

Beginning in 1976, the FEC attempted to require the presidential election committee of the Communist party, the Hall-Tyner Election Campaign Committee, to comply with the disclosure provisions of the FECA. Ultimately, the FEC brought suit to enforce compliance. Its efforts thus far have been rejected. The lower court and the appellate court, in exempting the Communist party from disclosure, relied on the *Buckley* standard of a "reasonable probability that compelled disclosure of the names of contributors will subject them to threats, harassment or reprisals from either government officials or private parties."[14]

The U.S. Court of Appeals for the Second Circuit considered evidence "documenting the history of government surveillance and harassment of Communist party members" and received affidavits indicating the desire of contributors to the party to remain anonymous. In its opinion, it emphasized, among other First Amendment precedents, the famous *NAACP* v. *Alabama* case[15] in which the Supreme Court ruled that the NAACP could not be compelled to deliver the names of its members to the Alabama attorney general. The appellate court concluded that "because compelled disclosure can seriously impair the right of privacy of association and belief, it is permissible only upon a showing of compelling state interest."[16]

The appellate court exempted the Hall-Tyner campaign committee not only from the law's disclosure provisions but also from its recordkeeping section. The court pointed out that if the records must be kept but never disclosed, then "there is little government interest served." It added: "The impact on the right of privacy of association by the recordkeeping requirement is as severe as that caused by the disclosure provisions."

The Federal Election Commission appealed the decision to an unsympathetic Supreme Court. There were strong indications that the Court was unlikely to reverse. In a case involving similar issues, the Supreme Court on December 8, 1982 exempted the Socialist Workers party from the disclosure provisions of Ohio law.[17] Ohio attempted to make the case that however unpopular the Socialist Workers might be elsewhere, there had not been significant evidence of harassment or government surveillance in Ohio. A unanimous court, however, ruled that the Socialist Workers did not have to disclose contributions, although only five justices agreed that they did not have to disclose expenditures. Finally, on January 17, 1983 the Supreme Court refused to hear the Communist party case, ending, for a time at least, the FEC's seven-year effort to enforce compliance.[18]

This enforcement proceeding reveals the difficulty of attempting to regulate speech to accomplish a limited objective. The major objective of campaign reform legislation that courts have permitted to restrict free speech is to reduce the likelihood of political corruption. If the individuals or groups regulated are not in positions of power and are not likely to achieve positions of power, this reason offers little justification for regulating their activity. But trying to regulate campaigns so that they are "fair" or "equitable" has also been an objective of the law. To those bound by the reporting requirements of the law, it appears clearly unfair to allow others to be exempt, thereby permitting them to ignore all its provisions.

If existing court decisions are an accurate guide, courts are unwilling to support regulations aimed at preventing corruption if they intrude upon the fundamental rights of persons or groups with so little political strength that the potential corruption bears little relationship to the policy process.

## Freedom of the Press

The Federal Election Campaign Act has also raised questions about the role of the press and political commentary. The issues surrounding freedom of the press are quite different from those discussed above. In this area, it would seem obvious that the intent of Congress was *not to regulate*. The definition of *press* is not self-evident, however, and the FEC felt compelled to make some decisions about activities generally associated with the press that affected campaigns. But how far can the FEC go in its investigations of what is a proper press function?

In response to complaints, the FEC has sought information relating to charges that certain publications were acting in a manner that could bring them under the jurisdiction of the act. The nature of the subject matter being investigated and the range of the FEC investigation quickly became controversial. The courts wasted no time in making it abundantly clear that the FECA was not intended to *chill* freedom of the press.

Although there has been no Supreme Court decision on FECA-press issues, the legal controversies of 1980 appear to have solidified the special status and exemptions granted to the press by the law. Courts have consistently supported the constitutional right of freedom of the press.

The drafters of the FECA took into account the First Amendment rights of the press and other media in debate and in statutory language. For example, the House Report accompanying the 1974 bill stated that it "was not the intent of Congress in the present legislation to limit or burden in any way the First Amendment freedoms of press and association. Thus the exclusion assures the unfettered right of the newspaper and other media to cover and comment on political campaigns."[19]

The statute excludes from its definition of a contribution or expenditure "any news story, commentary or other editorial distributed through the facilities of any broadcasting station, newspaper, magazine, or other periodical publication unless such facilities are owned or controlled by any political party, political committee or candidate. . . ."[20]

Thus it was surprising that one of the more important legal developments of 1980 was precipitated by the activities of a major magazine, *Reader's Digest,* and a much smaller and less known but nonetheless established political newsletter, the *Pink Sheet on the Left.* In both instances, in response to a complaint, the FEC posed a wide range of questions to the publishers. Both publications claimed exemptions under the act as well as First Amendment rights and at some point in the proceedings refused to comply with FEC requests.

The *Reader's Digest* controversy involved an article, "Chappaquiddick, the Still Unanswered Questions," that described circumstances surrounding Senator Edward M. Kennedy's much-publicized 1969 auto accident. The article included a computer study of the speed at which Kennedy's car was traveling when the accident occurred and a study of the tides and currents in the area at the time. The net effect of the article was to raise doubts about the truth of the Kennedy version of the event. The article received widespread media attention, much of it promoted by videotapes of computer reenactments produced by *Reader's Digest* and distributed to the mass media.

In August 1980 the FEC received a complaint that the *Reader's Digest* had violated the Federal Election Campaign Act (FECA) by making "an illegal corporate expenditure to negatively influence" the presidential election. The complaint cited eight points as evidence that the *Reader's Digest* had the intent of disparaging Senator Kennedy's campaign by using corporate funds. It charged that the results of the computer study were falsely reported, that the corporation knowingly approved the use of false figures, and that it purchased and distributed videotapes to all major media outlets, some of which used them just two weeks before the New Hampshire presidential primary. It charged further that the article carried an extremely anti-Kennedy bias; that the study was commissioned at the time Senator Kennedy announced his entry into the race; that the *Reader's Digest* used the testimony of a discredited witness; that it assigned control of the content and timing of the story to Melvin R. Laird, its chief counsel, who had been personal counselor to President Nixon when Nixon was conducting an anti-Kennedy campaign on the same subject; and that the *Reader's Digest* published the results of these studies just prior to the New Hampshire primary when it would have the maximum negative political impact on Senator Kennedy. The complaint also said that there was an abundance of evidence that the *Reader's Digest* could have used, if it wished to do so, without commissioning any new studies.[21]

The *Reader's Digest* declined to respond to the charges, stating simply that the article was protected by the First Amendment and that this privilege was expressly incorporated into the FECA.

The FEC reacted on December 18 with a letter stating that "there is reason to believe" that the *Reader's Digest* violated the law by making expenditures to disseminate to other media outlets videotapes of the computer reenactment of Senator Kennedy's accident. It directed the publisher within ten days to answer 15 questions regarding the content, distribution, and use of the videotapes as well as the names of the persons responsible for the uses made of the videotapes. After first requesting an extension of time to provide the answers, the *Reader's Digest* went to court seeking an injunction against the FEC to prevent the investigation from continuing.

The court ruled that the FEC should follow a two-step process when pursuing complaints against the media. In the first stage, the FEC must determine whether the acts complained of are covered by the press exemption in the law. Only after it has found that the acts are outside the exemption may the FEC inquire into such factors as "sources of information, research, motivation, connection with the campaign, etc."[22]

On this basis, the court found that about half the questions the FEC asked were outside the scope of the inquiry permitted. The court also pointed out that the most relevant question had not been asked: "Was the distribution of the tape publicity for the Chappaquiddick issue" of the magazine? If the answer to that question was in the affirmative, the court said, there would be no further basis for investigation.

The court refused to grant an injunction, warning the FEC that it should confine its investigation to the limited scope outlined and inviting the *Reader's*

*Digest* to reapply for an injunction if the FEC strayed too far. *Reader's Digest* appealed the decision. It did not matter. The FEC, recognizing the clear mandate of the court and the facts in the case, dropped its action.

The *Reader's Digest* was also involved in a minor issue when Jon Epstein complained that the publication's advertisement placed in the *Washington Post* constituted an illegal corporate contribution to the campaigns of two congressmen, one Republican and one Democrat, whose excerpted articles appeared in the ad. The FEC had no difficulty defining this issue and dismissed the complaint. Its position was confirmed by the U.S. District Court for the District of Columbia.[23] Critical to the ruling was the FEC determination that the expenditure had a purpose "other than the assistance of political candidates." The court ruled that the major purpose of the ad was "to promote the organization paying for the publicity." and said that it "did not serve a partisan purpose."

The other issue of freedom of the press involved a much more political publication but one not regarded as having a major impact on the general public. The *Pink Sheet on the Left* is a newsletter intended for readers with conservative political preferences and makes no claim to being neutral toward political figures, candidates, or issues.

The Kennedy for President Committee, on March 18, 1980, filed a complaint with the FEC charging that the firm had made an illegal corporate contribution by disseminating "a communication containing express words of advocacy for the defeat of Senator Edward M. Kennedy. . . ." The words were contained in a promotional publication soliciting subscriptions and contributions for subscriptions.

The FEC found "reason to believe " that a violation of the law had occurred because of certain language included in the promotional material mailed to potential subscribers and contributors. The phrases cited included:

> We must stop Kennedy before he seizes the Presidency.
>
> You can help with this effort to stop Teddy Kennedy.
>
> You learn how you can use this valuable information to help defeat Teddy Kennedy's drive for the Presidency.
>
> You can actually help combat Teddy Kennedy and advance the cause of conservatism in America.

The material distributed, however, was clearly soliciting subscriptions and did so in explicit language:

> Will you reconsider your decision not to subscribe?

> Yes, I want to stay informed and do more to stop Teddy Kennedy's drive for the Presidency. Please enter my subscription to *The Pink Sheet* at the special new subscriber rate.

For over eight years, *The Pink Sheet* has reported to its subscribers the behind the scenes activities of Teddy Kennedy and all other left-wingers both here in Washington and across the country.

When you subscribe to *The Pink Sheet,* you'll be getting the only newsletter in America which explains how you, the individual citizen, can take action and have an impact.[24]

Some of the questions to which the FEC sought answers were clearly within the scope of its jurisdiction. For example, directly related to its legal mandate, it asked the publisher, "Has Phillips Publishing Inc. ever been owned or controlled by a political party, political committee or federal candidate?"

Other questions went far beyond this basic inquiry. "Who paid for all costs in connection with the mailing of the letter? In this connection, please identify each account from which disbursements were made (i.e., describe each account by account number, the name and address of the financial institution at which the account is or was maintained, the name of the account, the type of account, all persons who had legal access and control of each account, the date each account was opened, and if applicable, the date each account was closed)."

Also, moving rather far afield, the FEC asked: "How was the money used which was received as a result of the mailing of the letter?"

The FEC also requested and received copies of the *Pink Sheet on the Left* for the months of January, April, August, and December 1979 and the issues of January, February, March, and April 1980, as well as the promotional mailing.

In June the FEC "found reason to believe" that Phillips Publishing had violated the law. This conclusion was reached after the FEC had determined that the promotional mailing was "not a news story, commentary, or editorial" and that therefore the exemption of the law did not apply. The FEC determined as well that the communication was not distributed through the facilities of a periodical publication, a determination "based on a facial comparison of the questioned communication to a copy of the periodical," the *Pink Sheet on the Left*. The salutation "Dear Friend" on the promotional letter was also cited as distinguishing the addressees from "Dear Subscriber," the salutation printed on the *Pink Sheet* publication.

The references to Kennedy were regarded by the *Pink Sheet* as a commentary or editorial, and it asked the FEC why it did not view the text of the promotional letter as such. Must a publication, in promoting sales or subscriptions, omit references, whether positive or negative, to candidates or potential candidates in order to avoid the time and expense involved in responding to a complaint? To what extent can such complaints, based on candidate references, be used to harass publishers and to "chill" First Amendment freedoms?

After engaging in a series of Freedom of Information requests regarding the process by which the FEC arrived at its decision, the *Pink Sheet* refused to respond to FEC interrogatories regarding the ownership, operation, and promotion methods of the newsletter beyond disavowing any connection with a political party or candidate. It turned instead to the federal courts, where its position was vindicated.

The court had little sympathy for the FEC position. Citing the *Reader's Digest* decision, it said: "If the press entity is not owned or controlled by a political party or candidate, and it is acting as a press entity, the FEC lacks subject matter jurisdiction and is barred from investigating the subject matter of the complaint."[25]

It was noted that as early as April 1980, the FEC had received responses from Phillips Publishing stating that there was no connection with any political committee and that the firm "does not solicit or receive any political contributions or make any contributions to any candidate." And the court also pointed out that there was no evidence, "or even a theory suggesting that *The Pink Sheet* was owned or controlled by any political party or candidate."

The court read the law exactly as Congress had written it. It pointed out that if the *Pink Sheet* had been established for the sole purpose of supporting or opposing a candidate, or if the FEC had some *evidence* (emphasis added) linking the *Pink Sheet* with a political organization or candidate, an FEC enforcement request could be considered. This case narrowly held that no further fact finding was necessary to show that the FEC did not have jurisdiction.

Ironically, the only case that seems remotely related to the press issues of 1980 occurred in 1976 when *Penthouse* magazine paid for an advertisement appearing in newspapers prior to the presidential election. The advertisement was critical of Jimmy Carter and warned readers not to vote until they had read the article on Carter in the November *Penthouse*. An internal inquiry was raised within the FEC and dismissed after the general counsel termed the ad "a commercial venture—namely the selling of a magazine with a controversial ad regarding Mr. Carter."[26]

If the FEC approach that included a rather wide-range inquiry into news production and into development, promotion, and distribution practices of publishers had been ruled acceptable, then the very nature of media relationships, sensitive internal affairs, and corporate affairs could become the targets of "official curiosity." Any statement, positive or negative, regarding a political candidate might have been sufficient to trigger an FEC investigation. Perhaps even neutral commentary providing exposure for a lesser-known candidate might also have rendered a publication subject to a complaint.

## Political Party Expenditures

Although the issue of internal transfer of funding authority received less attention than many other areas of controversy, the importance of this conflict was emphasized by a Supreme Court decision. Whether the ruling in *FEC* v. *Democratic Senatorial Campaign Committee* (DSCC) is regarded as affirming the law or creating another loophole, the FEC and ultimately the Supreme Court of the United States were unanimous in their liberal interpretation of the law regarding certain relationships between political parties and their constituent units.

During 1980, certain Republican state committees had designated the National Republican Senatorial Committee as their agent for expenditure purposes. The NRSC, which is authorized to make contributions to candidates, has no authority to make expenditures. The state committees, by entering into agency agreements, allowed the NRSC to spend on their behalf. This efficient use of campaign funds was challenged when the Democratic Senatorial Campaign Committee (DSCC) filed a complaint with the FEC. The FEC, citing precedents, dismissed the complaint by a vote of 6-0.[27]

The federal district court upheld the FEC. The court of appeals, which granted NRSC leave to intervene in the suit, reversed the lower court. It ruled that the "plain language" of the law precluded agency agreements.[28]

The Supreme Court agreed with the appellate court that the law did not permit the NRSC to make expenditures in its own right but said that "it does not follow that the NRSC may not act as an agent of a committee that is expressly authorized to make expenditures. . . . To foreclose such an arrangement on the grounds that the named agent is not one of the authorized spenders under Sec. 441.a(d)(3) would foreclose all agency agreements regardless of the identity of the agent and regardless of the terms of the agency."[29]

The Supreme Court read the law the same way as the FEC and the district court had read it. Even though the law is not specifically permissive, nothing in it prohibits committees from acting as agents of committees expressly authorized to make expenditures.

The Court concluded its brief and decisive opinion with the observation: "It is hardly unreasonable to suppose that political parties were fully capable of structuring their expenditures so as to achieve the greatest possible return. Agency agreements may permit all party committees to benefit from fund raising, media expertise, and economies of scale. In turn, effective use of party resources in support of party candidates may encourage candidate loyalty and responsiveness to the party. Indeed, the very posture of this case betrays the weakness of respondent's argument—an argument that, at bottom features one of the two great American political parties insisting that its rival requires judicial assistance in discovering how a legislative enactment operates to its benefit."

## What Next?

If all the issues had been resolved by these cases, at least it would be possible to make some guesses about what might achieve certain limited ends of campaign finance regulation and what First Amendment rights are clearly beyond the reach of such regulation. Such is not the case. Of the subjects discussed above, only the ruling protecting unpopular political parties from disclosing their contributors and expenditures seems secure. The other subject matters remain open for further litigation. Efforts will undoubtedly be made to curtail independent expenditures by groups and individuals. The equally divided court in *Common Cause* v. *Schmitt* almost ensured another round of litigation on the subject. Although the FEC did not pursue appeals of the *Reader's Digest* and the *Pink Sheet* decisions, its comments left no doubt that it disagreed with the decision. Another publisher on another day may be put to the same tests. The majority party was clearly displeased that the Republicans were able to take advantage of the party finance provisions to put money into campaigns where it was needed, and if they are able to muster the votes, they may try to write laws to prevent this flexibility while avoiding a direct First Amendment challenge. Finally, many regard the draft committee decisions as creating an unintended loophole, and some attempt to regulate citizens in this precampaign phase of politics is very likely. Yet, any or all of these proposed actions stands a good chance of being ruled unconstitutional. Hence, continuing uncertainty.

At the same time, if the continuing calls for reform have any justification, the law has not limited the impact of money in political campaigns nor diminished to any appreciable extent the appearance of potential corruption. More change is surely on the horizon. The long-range prospect is for more legislation, litigation, and lack of coherent public policy dealing with political campaigns.

What new tests may arise? Assuming the objective of the law is to prevent corruption or the appearance of corruption of elected officials, what justification is there for a limitation on contributions to noncandidate committees? Presumably there may be a secondary influence, but how far down can a trickle-down theory of political corruption be sustained? Any attempt to achieve equity in political debate by limiting the resources available to communicate is clearly impossible as long as there is a free press. When newspaper, radio, and television commentators are free to comment extensively and specifically on candidates and issues, as they have every right and obligation to do, anything approaching equality in political communication will be purely coincidental. To restrict contributions to noncandidate committees grants the corporate press even greater power. This is even more true because the "political press"—party and candidate publications and brochures—is effectively limited by various financial and spending limitations in the law. How much money does it take to offset the negative impact of a critical press commentary or the endorsement of an opponent by a leading publication? Is the only certain way to be able to communicate a political message to be the purchase of a newspaper or television station?

A further area of legal controversy might arise from different treatment on income tax credits between positive and negative independent expenditures, or from other proposals to regulate negative campaigns. Why should the public support through tax credits only "positive" arguments and not arguments stated from the negative position? Even formal debate begins with the presumption that the negative side is not, by definition, evil.

The assumption regarding limitations of negative campaigns is based on two concepts. First, it is assumed that negative campaigns are false campaigns, lies and distortions, or at least more likely to be so than "positive" campaigns. Second, it is assumed that there are two candidates in the race and that a negative campaign against one is a benefit, or is intended to be a benefit, to the opponent.

Although there are a multitude of examples of both phenomena, there is "no reason to believe" (FEC phraseology) that the assumptions are necessarily true. Negative campaigns can be "brutally honest," and positive campaigns may contain total fabrications. And in situations where more than two candidates are in a race, it is not always certain who the beneficiary of the negative campaign will be. On occasion, it may even be the candidate being attacked. It is impossible to confine political debate to candidates for public office without severely restricting speech, and it is just as impossible to confine political statements to positive sentiments without obstructing the choice of expression. Public debate should not be suspended merely because a campaign for office is in progress. Nor can public debate easily deal with public policies without mention of persons responsible for those policies — for example, "Reaganomics." It is at times of political choice, above all times, that a multitude of voices, including negative ones, should have an opportunity to be heard.

One of the most impressive negative political statements in human history was the Declaration of Independence. King George was attacked with a barrage of passionately negative statements employing an imaginative variety of verb usages that reveals the vacuity of contemporary political verbal assault. He had — refused, dissolved, endeavored to prevent, obstructed, erected, combined, quartered, cut off, imposed, deprived, abolished, suspended, abdicated, plundered, constrained, excited, ravaged, burnt, destroyed — and ultimately sent mercenaries "to compleat the works of death, desolation and tyranny." And if that is not enough, his character "is marked by every act which may define a Tyrant."

Almost every campaign against an incumbent is in part a negative campaign. Has anyone ever listened to the keynote addresses at the national conventions of either political party, especially when out of power, without understanding that they take a somewhat negative view of the incumbent administration and prevailing political party? Turning to issues, is the law an appropriate tool to disadvantage certain groups, whether antiwar, antinuclear, or antiabortion, that choose to express their political viewpoints logically in a negative way?

Positive but noncampaign-related activities may also be suspect under the law. From the beginning, the definition of what is or is not a political contribution has presented the FEC with difficult decisions, as illustrated by a recent example. The commission on January 20, 1983 unanimously ruled that the American Society of Mechanical Engineers (ASME) and member corporations may sponsor a congressional fellowship program.[30] The ASME fellows serve one-year terms and are compensated by their employers and by ASME. The FEC unanimously ruled that unless the intern participates in campaign-related activity, the ASME may pay the interns for their congressional work. This is well and good, but incidentally, it just may free one of the regular office staff, who may be far more valuable back home, to "take a leave of absence" and campaign. There is no doubt that this practice is both legal and an excellent way of assisting an incumbent congressman with his campaign. Whether it gives the corporation "influence" equal to or exceeding that presumed by the law to be derived from a campaign contribution is another question. Attempts to segregate political activity, using "political" in the broadest sense, from campaign activity are not easy.

There is yet another political factor that serves to undermine coherent public policy in this area. Not everyone who is subject to the law reacts in the expected manner. Some, rather than attack the law, use the courts and lawsuits to gain competitive advantages. For them, it is not always necessary to win in court. On occasion it is sufficient to delay, to distract, to cause one's opponent to expend resources and energy, and perhaps to counter negative publicity, regardless of the final outcome of the lawsuit. In a very perceptive law review article, David Ifshin, legal adviser to Walter Mondale's 1984 presidential campaign committee, pointed out that there is political benefit in using lawsuits or threats of lawsuits against opponents. Ifshin cited the range of 1980 cases to support his conclusion that "presidential campaigns were shaped to a considerable extent by legal counsel who included a variety of litigation efforts in their arsenal." In the business of politics, he said, "it presents unprecedented problems."[31]

Ifshin continued: "The plethora of complex legal issues that arose in the 1980 campaign, the continued lack of resolution of those issues, and the absence of an expeditious method of resolution suggest that the 1984 presidential election may repeat the 1980 experience. If so, we may be well on the way to finding litigation to be an institutionalized element of presidential campaigns."[32]

The current situation is hardly what the law was intended to produce, but very like what Chief Justice Burger, in his partially concurring and partially dissenting opinion in *Buckley,* suggested it would be. Congress, he said, intended to regulate all aspects of federal campaign finances, but what remains leaves no more than a shadow of what Congress contemplated. Those who now support major amendments to the law bear witness to the prescience of Burger's words. Moreover, unless the First Amendment is redefined, the likelihood of successful comprehensive campaign finance regulation is as remote as ever.

# Notes

1. 424 U.S. 1 (1976).
2. *Financing Presidential Campaigns: An Examination of the Ongoing Effects of the Federal Election Campaign Laws upon the Conduct of Presidential Campaigns.* Research report by the Campaign Finance Study Group, Institute of Politics, to the Committee on Rules and Administration, U.S. Senate (Cambridge, Mass.: John F. Kennedy School of Government, Harvard University, January 1982).
3. ". . . the overall effect of the contribution and expenditure limitations enacted by Congress could foreclose any fair opportunity of a successful challenge. However, since we decided in Part I-C, *infra,* that the ceilings on independent expenditures, on the candidate's expenditures from his personal funds, and on overall campaign expenditures are unconstitutional under the First Amendment we need not express any opinion with regard to the alleged invidious discrimination resulting from the full sweep of the legislation as enacted." *Buckley* v. *Valeo,* 424 U.S. 1, 31 (1976) fn. 33.
4. *Republican National Committee* v. *FEC,* 487 F.Supp. 280 (S.D.N.Y.).
5. Ibid., *aff'd mem.* 445 U.S. 955 (1980).
6. *Common Cause* v. *Schmitt,* 512 F.Supp. 489 (D.D.C. 1980).
7. Ibid., *aff'd per curiam* by an equally divided court, 455 U.S. 129 (1982).
8. *Campaign Practices Reports* 9, no. 2 (February 1, 1982).
9. *Democratic Party and Mezvinsky* v. *NCPAC,* No. 83-2329 (E.D.Pa.); *Federal Election Commission* v. *NCPAC,* No. 83-2823 (E.D.Pa.). See *Campaign Practices Reports* 10, no. 24 (December 19, 1983).
10. *FEC* v. *Machinists Non-Partisan Political League,* 655 F.2d 538 (D.C.Cir. 1980).
11. *Washington Post,* October 14, 1981.
12. *FEC* v. *Wisconsin Democrats for Change in 1980,* No. 80-C-124 (W.D.Wis. April 24, 1980); *FEC* v. *Citizens for Democratic Alternatives in 1980,* No. 80-0009 (D.D.C. February 29, 1980); *FEC* v. *Machinists Non-Partisan Political League,* No. 79-0291 (D.D.C. January 3, 1980); *FEC* v. *Florida for Kennedy Committee,* 492 F.Supp 587 (S.D.Fla. 1980).
13. *FEC* v. *Machinists Non-Partisan Political League,* 655 F.2d 380 (D.C.Cir. May 19, 1981). On August 2, 1982, the U.S. Court of Appeals for the Eleventh Circuit issued an opinion overturning a ruling of the U.S. District Court for the Southern District of Florida in *FEC* v. *Florida for Kennedy Committee* (Civil Action No. 80-6013), 681 F.2d 1281 (11th Cir. 1982). The appeals court ruled that the FEC lacked jurisdiction over the draft committee and reversed the district court's order enforcing the subpoenas that the commission had issued to the committee. An FEC petition for a rehearing of the case was denied October 8, 1982. Additional details can be found in the *FEC Record* 8, no. 2 (1982): 6.
14. *FEC* v. *Hall-Tyner Campaign Committee,* Civil Action No. 78 Civ. 3508 (S.D.N.Y.).
15. *NAACP* v. *Alabama,* 357 U.S. 449 (1958).
16. *FEC* v. *Hall-Tyner Campaign Committee,* U.S. Court of Appeals for the Second Circuit, No. 81-6229, dec. May 6, 1982.
17. *Brown* v. *Socialist Workers '74 Campaign Committee,* 81-776, dec. December 8, 1982.
18. *FEC* v. *Hall-Tyner Election Campaign Committee* (S.Ct. No. 82-198).
19. House Report 93-943, 93rd Cong., 2d sess., p. 4, 1974.

20. U.S.C. Sec 431 (9)(B)(i).
21. *The Reader's Digest Association, Inc.* v. *FEC,* Civil Action No. 81 Civ. 596 (PNL) (S.D.N.Y.), dec. March 19, 1981.
22. Ibid.
23. *Jon Epstein* v. *FEC,* Civil Action No. 81-0336.
24. Promotional mailing by the *Pink Sheet on the Left.*
25. *FEC* v. *Phillips Publishing Company,* Civil Action No. 81-0079 (D.C.D.C.), dec. July 16, 1981.
26. Cited in ibid.
27. FEC vote, July 11, 1980.
28. *Democratic Senatorial Campaign Committee* v. *FEC,* Civil Action No. 80-1903 (D.C.D.C.).
29. FEC v. *Democratic Senatorial Campaign Committee* and *National Republican Senatorial Committee* v. *Democratic Senatorial Campaign Committee,* 454 U.S. 27, 33 (1981).
30. FEC Advisory Opinion No. 1982-60.
31. David M. Ifshin and Roger E. Warin, "Litigating the 1980 Presidential Election," *American University Law Review* 31, no. 3 (Spring 1982): 485-550.
32. Ibid., 550.

MICHAEL J. MALBIN

## 8. Looking Back at the Future of Campaign Finance Reform: Interest Groups and American Elections

A decade of campaign finance reform has resulted, as the previous chapters have shown, in wide-ranging consequences for both electoral politics and government in the United States. Strategy and tactics have been altered in presidential, congressional, and state politics, with different legal provisions working to the advantage of some candidates and the disadvantage of others. Political parties, political action committees, and other politically influential organizations have also had their relative and absolute importance changed in foreseen and unforeseen ways. The effects of the law have not remained constant, however, and will not remain so even if Congress leaves the statutes unchanged. Legal decisions, for example, strike some provisions and modify others, thus changing the impact of the ones left untouched. Similarly, changes in nonfinancial aspects of either the rules or the political environment can bring different facets of the campaign finance law into sharper focus.

The indirect effects of court decisions have been treated in several of the preceding chapters. A good example of the potential implications of changing rules that do not obviously control finance can be seen by looking at presidential delegate selection. The Democratic National Committee's 1981-82 Commission on Presidential Nominations, chaired by North Carolina Governor James B. Hunt, tried to favor candidates with national reputations and experience by shortening the nominating season. By making New Hampshire and Iowa begin selecting delegates later in 1984 than they did in 1980, the commission hoped to decrease the bonus a small state victory could give to a dark horse candidate.

But the commission could not change the role that the media play in lending credibility to plurality winners in early contests, and it refused to add weight to the role of later primaries and caucuses by freezing states in their 1980 dates, or by creating incentives or bonuses for states that choose delegates in May or June. [1] As a result, more states felt pressured to hold early primaries in 1984, and still more entered the field with nonbinding straw polls in 1983. Add to this the AFL-CIO's decision to endorse a candidate for the Democratic presi-

232

dential nomination in October 1983, and one can readily see why presidential candidates felt compelled to spend a lot more money in 1983 than in 1979. The 1984 nominating season is longer than 1980's, despite the commission's rules changes.

The campaign finance law's overall spending limits have not been changed since 1980, however, except for an inflation adjustment. Therefore, if no candidate sews up the nomination early, despite the rules favoring an early decision, the candidates who remain will have to run in such late, large states as Ohio and California on very tight budgets. This presumably could give a boost to the candidate who has spent less in the early months. Depending on the circumstances, it could easily end up favoring a candidate who started out behind and chose his early contests carefully, while hurting a front-runner who felt compelled to take on all comers everywhere. If so, this aspect of the campaign finance law could produce an effect that was directly opposite to the one intended by the Hunt Commission, which was trying to engineer rules that would favor nationally established figures over such former outsiders as Jimmy Carter.

The example just offered was not meant as a prediction of the 1984 presidential race. The leading candidates were well aware of the problem in early 1983 and began planning accordingly. In addition, such other aspects of the law as the $1000 limit on individual contributions hurt candidates who depend on late fund raising. The example does, however, illustrate the difficulties of predicting the consequences of reform. The impact of almost every provision in the campaign finance law is shaped by case law, by other provisions of campaign finance law, by other rules governing elections, and by a constantly changing political environment. Nelson W. Polsby aptly described this situation in his book on the presidential nominating system:

> Reform is a process that involves more than the enactment of prohibitions and requirements. Requirements and prohibitions newly enacted in the course of reform are added to an ongoing corpus of customs and regulations, producing a pattern of incentives to which different political actors, though they may vary in their comprehension, in their vulnerabilities, and in their resources, can nevertheless be expected to respond. It is not always easy to anticipate the behavior of actors as they learn how to operate over the newly contoured terrain that reform creates. It is certain, however, that the intentions of reformers will not comprehensively determine their behavior. Thus the assessment of reforms in operation is bound to take into account at least some unanticipated activity. . . .
>
> Implicit both in reformers' conceptions of reform and in the conceptions of critics is the assumption that political actors can and do learn to change their behavior with fair rapidity in response to changed rules of the game. This applies not merely to that part of their behavior evoked by the desire to evade criminal penalties but also to strategic and tactical behavior, activities designed to take advantage of new rules and regulations and to avoid adverse impacts upon actors' plans and ambitions. . . . Yet it is apparent that in the wave of reform we have been examining only rudimentary thought was given to such matters.[2]

What Polsby said about presidential selection applies equally well to campaign finance. Reformers who promoted the campaign finance act of 1974, in the aftermath of Watergate, portrayed it as if it would weaken the political role of "special interests." Eight years later, after the 1982 election, many were heard to say that the situation was worse than ever. At the heart of their complaints were some very obvious numbers, but also some simplistic assumptions about causal relationships, about how interest groups work, and about the purpose of elections. Since many of the assumptions of 1974 continue to be found in some proposals for further reform, they deserve more careful investigation. Therefore, the remainder of this chapter tries to sort out for both policy makers and future researchers at least some of the issues that relate to interest groups and congressional elections.

## Reform Efforts After 1974

The Federal Election Campaign Act Amendments of 1974 provided public funding for presidential candidates; established contribution limits for individuals, political parties, and nonparty political committees; freed labor unions and corporations to form nonparty committees by lifting the existing political restrictions on government contractors; and created the Federal Election Commission. The law also tightened disclosure provisions adopted in 1971 and included limits on expenditures by congressional candidates, on what a candidate may contribute to his or her own campaign, and on independent expenditures. The last three limits were all declared unconstitutional by the Supreme Court in *Buckley* v. *Valeo*.

Common Cause, the major organization that lobbied for the 1974 law, was never satisfied with it. Its original bill had included public funding for congressional elections, using a matching-grant system similar to the one adopted for presidential primaries. The Senate passed the proposal twice, in 1973 and 1974, but the House killed it, and Common Cause has blamed that action ever since for what has happened to congressional campaign finance. According to Common Cause, public financing drove special-interest money out of the presidential race, and that money sought a new home by playing an ever increasing role in congressional races.[3] It is true that contributions from nonparty political committees, or PACs, made up an increasing proportion of congressional campaign contributions between 1974 and 1982. To equate PACs with "special interests" is overly simplistic, however, as I argue below. In addition, the implied cause and effect needs further analysis. Does it really make sense to argue that special interests have disappeared from presidential races, that they would disappear from publicly funded congressional races, or that what is happening in congressional races simply represents an increase of interest-group activity? I argue later that the answer to all these questions must be *no*. But that is neither Common Cause's answer nor that of its many supporters in Congress.

Feeling that they had left their work only half finished, reformers pushed again in 1977 for publicly financed congressional elections. The odds looked good. Wayne Hays—the implacable foe of public financing who had chaired the House Administration Committee—was no longer in the Congress. Frank Thompson, the new chairman, favored public financing, and a reform-minded Democrat was now in the White House. Jimmy Carter had endorsed the public financing of congressional elections during the 1976 election campaign and included it in a package of five proposals for election reform that he announced on March 22.

The major House and Senate bills for 1977 differed in details, but both included matching grants for small contributions and limits on personal expenditures and on overall expenditures for publicly funded candidates. *Buckley v. Valeo* had declared mandatory expenditure limits and limits on personal spending unconstitutional, but permitted them in presidential elections as conditions for accepting public funds. Therefore, although public financing and expenditure limits are conceptually distinct, and have different practical effects, the issues have been linked ever since.

Despite the bright initial prospects for passage, public financing did not become law in 1977-78. The bill was filibustered in the Senate, where supporters were unable to gather more than 52 votes for cloture, eight short of the required 60.[4] In the House, opponents of public financing followed a more indirect strategy. In an October 25 markup by the House Administration Committee, they successfully added an amendment to the bill that would have extended its coverage to primaries, knowing that the expansion would kill the bill on the House floor. All eight Republicans on the committee voted for the amendment. Democrats were split 7-8, with many fearing that public financing would stimulate challengers to enter races that now go largely uncontested. After the vote, Thompson decided to drop the bill. Efforts to revive it on the House floor were defeated.

Public financing, this time given the symbolically significant designation of H.R. 1 by the Democratic leadership, was again defeated by the House in 1979. The House Administration Committee voted 8-17 on May 24 not to report the bill, with eight of the committee's 16 Democrats joining all nine Republicans in opposition. Two weeks later, the leadership announced that its whip count showed there were not enough votes for the measure to bring it directly to the floor.

Later in 1979, on October 17, the House voted 217-198 to add new PAC limits to the FEC authorization bill. Sponsored by public financing supporters David Obey (D-Wisc.) and Tom Railsback (R-Ill.), the bill would have reduced the amount that any one PAC could give a candidate and placed a new ceiling ($70,000) on the total amount of contributions a candidate could accept from all PACs over a two-year cycle. Although the bill applied only to House elections, the threat of a filibuster led Democratic Majority Leader Robert C. Byrd (D-W.Va.) to keep it off the Senate floor in 1980.

Efforts to revive the PAC limitation bill in the 97th Congress (1981-82) got nowhere.[5] The bills foundered on the practical argument that limits on PAC contributions would simply stimulate such other forms of PAC activity as independent expenditures, and on the constitutional concern that they would amount to a quasi limit on candidate expenditures.[6] Although hearings were held in the House Administration and Senate Rules and Administration Committees, no votes were taken. Neither did the committees mark up any of the other major campaign finance bills of 1981-82, including one supported by the Republican leadership that would have increased the role of political parties, and a public financing bill that was essentially similar to ones defeated previously.

The 1982 election saw a heavy increase in the level of coverage the press gave to PAC contributions. Perhaps most important for Washington readers was Elizabeth Drew's lengthy, two-part series, "Politics and Money" in the December 6 and 13 issues of the *New Yorker* (later reprinted in book form). A broader audience was reached with a *Time* magazine cover story, a series of CBS-TV Evening News special reports narrated by Bill Moyers, and prominently featured articles in *Newsweek, U.S. News and World Report,* the *New Republic, Business Week,* the *Washington Post,* and the *Wall Street Journal,* to name just a few. Their themes were almost monotonously repetitious: PACs have grown beyond all historic proportions, they are successfully using election money to buy legislative influence, and the problem could be resolved through reform of campaign finance laws.

Armed with this press coverage, supporters of PAC limits and public financing tried to put the issue high on the legislative agenda of the 98th Congress. Common Cause President Fred Wertheimer used a February 1 speech to the National Press Club to "declare [or, more accurately, redeclare] war on PACs." While few of Wertheimer's supporters in Congress saw much chance for a bill to become law with the Republicans in control of the Senate and White House, they hoped to use 1983-84 to build a sustained drive in the House that would create a political issue for the 1984 election and then carry over into sessions of the mid-1980s. Extensive hearings were held during 1983 on a staggering variety of legislative proposals. Observers could not help but be struck, however, by the skepticism and lack of consensus that continued to prevail among Democrats on the House Administration Committee and in other leadership positions.

## Four Different Approaches

While many specific bills were introduced in 1983, the major legislative alternatives were included in four bills.

1. Representatives Mike Synar (D-Okla.) and Beryl Anthony (D-Ark.) and Senator David Boren (D-Okla.) proposed placing limits on a candi-

date's receipts from political action committees and increasing individual contribution limits.

2. Representatives David Obey, Dan Glickman (D-Kan.), and James Leach (R-Iowa), acknowledging the previous criticisms of simple PAC-limit bills, gathered 72 other co-sponsors and introduced comprehensive legislation that would do the following:

   a. Provide public matching grants for small, individual contributions to congressional candidates in general elections.
   b. Limit general election expenditures to $200,000 for candidates accepting public financing.
   c. Remove the spending ceiling and double the matching grant for candidates facing opponents who do not accept public financing.
   d. Put a $90,000 limit on the amount candidates may receive from PACs during a two-year election cycle.
   e. To counter the argument that PAC limits might increase independent expenditures, give candidates faced with independent expenditures on the electronic media a choice between free response time or a federal grant equal to the value of the expenditure, and give candidates faced with other independent expenditures worth more than $5000 a public grant equal to their value.

3. The third major bill of 1983, introduced by Representative Bill Frenzel (R-Minn.) and Senator Paul Laxalt (R-Nev.), included a number of provisions to increase the role of parties, including one that would remove all limits on coordinated expenditures by the national party committees.

4. Finally, Representatives Matt McHugh (D-N.Y.) and Barber Conable (R-N.Y.) dropped their previous sponsorship of a broad public finance and expenditure limit package in favor of a simple tax credit bill drafted by Richard Conlon, executive director of the liberal Democratic Study Group. The bill would replace the existing 50 percent tax credit for contributions to all candidates and political committees with a 100 percent credit (of up to $50 for an individual and $100 for a joint return) for contributions to House and Senate candidates from the contributor's own state and a 50 percent credit for contributions to political parties. No tax credits would be given for contributions to other candidates or PACs.

Speaking broadly, with some oversimplification, these four bills represent four alternative approaches to shaping the future role of PACs. The first, or Synar bill, tries to limit PACs directly and replace part of the money lost to campaigns by increasing the contribution limit for individuals. The second, or Obey bill, would limit PACs directly, create public financing to replace the lost money, and use public finance as a legal precondition that would permit the government to reduce independent expenditures and limit overall spending. The third, or Laxalt-Frenzel bill, would leave PACs alone, but seeks to limit their importance by building up their main organizational competitors, the political parties. The fourth, or McHugh-Conable bill, also leaves PACs and candidate spending untouched, but would modestly decrease an individual's incentive to give to PACs by repealing the existing tax credit for such contributions. More important, the McHugh-Conable bill tries to reshape the incentives for candidates. Believing that candidates now hold receptions for PACs and engage in other forms of national fund raising because these activities are economically efficient, the bill's sponsors try to use a 100 percent tax credit to increase the economic efficiency of looking for small, in-state individual contributions. To the extent such an approach succeeds it would, like the political party bill, indirectly reduce the importance of PACs by increasing the importance of an alternative source of funds.

UNINTENDED CONSEQUENCES

*Simple PAC limit bill.* Before we consider the assumptions underlying these four legislative approaches, it would be worthwhile to comment on some unintended consequences associated with each one. The major consequence of the Synar bill remains the same as it was four years ago when its sponsors were Obey and Railsback. PACs are not simply conduits for money. While most do remain small and decentralized, as Eismeier and Pollock have shown, a substantial number have become institutionalized, with professional staffs that have a career stake in their own and their organization's continued efficacy. Prohibiting or limiting PAC contributions will not make these career professionals fold up their tents and run. If they thought it was in their interest to influence elections or curry favor with incumbents, they will continue trying to do so within the new rules. For some that may mean independent expenditures, but not for all. It takes more organizational expertise to spend money than to give it, and some organizations may not want the attendant publicity. Encouraging independent expenditures, therefore, would tend to favor the largest and most politically professionalized organizations over smaller ones. It is no accident that the National Association of Realtors and the American Medical Association, the two largest trade association PACs in 1981-82 with receipts of $3.0 million and $2.6 million, were also the only two economic interest groups among the top ten independent spenders. We may assume that other large associations will join the picture if the bill passes. Some umbrella groups—such as the Chamber of Commerce or Business-Industry Political Action Committee —may even set up, and accept corporate PAC contributions for, ad hoc independent spending committees in closely contested districts in which the favored candidate has reached the PAC limit. In other words, the Synar bill would, in the name of reducing the role of special-interest groups, create an easily circumvented regulation that would work strongly to the advantage of large, powerful organizations and the disadvantage of smaller ones.[7] One suspects this is not what the bill's authors had in mind.

*Comprehensive public finance bill.* The Obey bill is more complicated, and so are its problems. The bill tries to respond to the issue just described by including provisions on independent expenditures along with its limits on PACs. It proposes two methods for discouraging independent expenditures. The first would require radio and television stations to make free air time available to candidates who have been targets of independent advertising. This would, in effect, tell broadcasters that they either must charge double for independent expenditures or functionally accept half the going rate—since running an ad will mean giving away free time. The practical result inevitably will be to keep independent expenditures off the airwaves. Supporters of this approach believe there are no constitutional problems because the Supreme Court has ruled that issue advertisers do not have a right of access to the airwaves against a broadcaster's wishes. However, the cases so far have dealt with instances in which the broadcaster has limited access on its own instigation. The situation could well be different if the broadcaster is responding to congressionally mandated economic disincentives. The First Amendment does say, after all, that "*Congress* shall make no law . . . abridging the freedom of speech."

The bill's second mechanism for dealing with independent expenditures involves public grants. These would seem to raise no constitutional difficulties. Whether they would be desirable may be another matter. Margaret Ann Latus, in the conclusion to her chapter, questions the common assumption that independent expenditures are simply harmful. Even if one believes they are harmful, one should be aware that compensation may not be as straightforward as it first appears. It is wrong to assume that negative independent expenditures are made just to benefit the candidate who is not attacked. Independent expenditure groups often are trying to control the substantive agenda by raising issues both candidates prefer to ignore. The groups' agendas, and their interests, are not the same as those of the candidates they may prefer. Independent advertising often forces supposedly favored candidates to spend unwanted time or money dealing with, and sometimes distancing themselves from, positions espoused in the ads, just as it forces the attacked opponents to respond. By compensating the attacked candidates, therefore, the bill could end up adding to the burden of the candidates supposedly favored.

The public grants approach to independent spending is a small part of the Obey bill's overall public finance package. The bill also contains general election matching grants and an expenditure limit. Gary Jacobson has shown in his chapter, and in his previous work cited there, that the amount of money raised by a challenger tells one more about an election's likely outcome than the amount raised by an incumbent. This is because incumbents are known to their constituents; challengers have to spend a lot of money to become known and begin competing. Therefore public financing, unencumbered by spending limits, would tend to foster competition by giving challengers some needed help to get started. It would have its greatest effect in the least competitive districts, where challengers have the hardest time raising seed money. Spending limits work the other way. In the aggregate, with some exceptions that grow out of the peculiarities of individual races, spending limits would favor incumbents and would be felt most heavily in the most competitive districts. Mixing public financing with expenditure limits would have unpredictable consequences that might depend upon exact dollar figures. It is possible that combining the two could increase competitiveness nationally, if public financing were generous enough, by making more challengers viable and making more districts subject to national forces. On the other hand, a spending limit low enough to be supported by most members of Congress would probably decrease competitiveness by cutting off some promising challengers late in their campaigns.

These comments about spending limits are meant to be general. Two specific features of the Obey bill, however, would increase the pro-incumbent effect. First, because the bill provides public financing only for the general election, its spending limits can cover only the same time period. Most public financing bills are written this way to save the government from underwriting frivolous primary campaigns. To understand the effect of the spending limit, however, one must realize that most vulnerable incumbents stimulate primaries in the opposition party, but not in their own. A general election spending limit, therefore, would affect challengers and incumbents differently. Incumbents could spend unlimited amounts during the primary season pursuing a general election campaign strategy, while the challenger is still trying to win a contested primary.

Second, the Obey bill's $90,000 cap on the total amount candidates may accept from PACs applies to the full two-year election cycle, but the overall spending limit applies only to the general election. It is true that incumbents and challengers could both raise their PAC money before the overall spending limit applies, but that is like saying the law equally prohibits the rich and the poor from sleeping under bridges. Most PACs do not give money to challengers until after their primaries, but have no similar compunctions about giving early to incumbents. That means that a challenger's limited PAC contributions would be raised at a time when they would count against his or her general election spending limits, but an incumbent's probably would not. Most incumbents would be able to raise all of their PAC contributions before the primary and still raise as much as the spending limit will allow in matchable, individual contributions for the general election. Because PAC contributions would not be matched, the bill would tend to provide more federal money for incumbents than challengers.

*Party bill.* The most important unintended consequences of the final two bills are simpler to explain. The Laxalt-Frenzel bill contains a number of provisions that would benefit parties directly without producing unrelated side consequences foreseeable by this author. Included among these would be provisions: (1) to triple to $15,000 per election (primary or general) the amount party committees could contribute to House candidates and to increase from $17,500 to $30,000 per election cycle the amount they could contribute to Senate candidates; (2) to expand the present law's provision permitting unlimited state and local party expenditures for registration and get-out-the-vote drives in presidential election years to permit similar efforts in midterm elections; and (3) to increase by 50 percent the amount that national party committees could spend on behalf of presidential candidates.

More problematic would be two provisions that would permit unlimited expenditures by the national party committees. One would extend the provisions for unlimited expenditures on registration and get-out-the-vote drives from state and local to the national parties. The other would remove all limits on national and state party expenditures coordinated with Senate and House candidates. The latter expenditures, known as 441a(d) expenditures after the section of the law in which they appear, are now computed on an inflation-adjusted 1974 base of $10,000 for most House candidates and two cents times the voting-age population (or a minimum of $20,000) for Senate elections or House elections covering a whole state.

In 1982, the inflation-adjusted 441a(d) limits, which are equal for national and state or local parties, amounted to $18,400 for most House elections and a maximum of $685,874 for Senate elections. As Gary Jacobson and David Adamany explained in their chapters, combining the maximum national, state, and local direct party contributions and the two sets of 441a(d) party expenditures produced maximum party limits in 1982 of $66,880 for House elections and Senate limits that ranged from $101,260 for the smallest states to $1,399,248 for California.

As these numbers indicate, the existing limits for party spending are hardly penny-pinching. They have not prevented the Republican party from increasing its role markedly since 1974, as both Jacobson and Adamany have shown. Nevertheless, one could make an arguable case for increasing the limits to give the parties an even greater voice than they now have. This author does not agree with Adamany's contention that the law at present gives the parties a legal advantage over other participants in the process. Others may spend unlimited amounts on indpendent expenditures. The parties may also spend unlimited amounts, but only for limited purposes. Therefore, it may well be desirable to counter the efforts of independent spending groups, assuming one places no direct limits on them, by extending unlimited *state* and *local* party registration and get-out-the-vote efforts to midterm congressional elections or by increasing the spending limits on coordinated *national* party efforts.

In the short term, any increase in party limits would favor Republicans and will therefore be opposed by Democrats. But even if the parties become financial equals, removing all limits on *national* party activities could have some serious and not fully predictable consequences for the future relationships between the legislative and executive branches of government. A President still can exercise a great deal of control over national party committees. As Adamany's chapter indicated, the Democratic National Committee was essentially a Carter committee during the last administration, and during the first years of this one President Reagan controlled the choice of the chairmen of the Republican National Committee and Republican Senatorial Campaign Committee. While the willingness of these committees to exercise influence over the legislative behavior of incumbents now operates within severely constrained boundaries, the situation could change if the national party could spend unlimited amounts to elect congressional candidates. One's position on unlimited national party expenditures, therefore, should be dictated ultimately by one's views about legislative-executive relations. Anyone who wants to promote party discipline between the branches should view this as an important weapon to add to the President's arsenal. I personally would like to see the party made somewhat stronger in Congress. But, particularly when I think about the presidential selection process, I believe that the nation is well served by a system in which the Congress is able to maintain its independence. For that reason, I tend to look cautiously on reforms that would greatly strengthen the national parties' financial role.

*Tax credit bill.* Compared to the other three, the McHugh-Conable bill is a model of simplicity. It adds no new limits and removes none. Since only about 4 percent of all taxpayers now use the existing 50 percent tax credits, limiting their use to parties would not directly hurt presidential campaigns or political action committees. A 100 percent credit for contributions to congressional candidates, however, would be a lot easier for people to understand than a 50 percent credit and therefore would almost surely stimulate more small, individual in-state contributions to House and Senate races. For that reason, it would also change the incentives for congressional candidates, giving them a reason to look harder for local contributors. The bill thus could reduce the importance of PAC's indirectly by reducing their proportional significance to candidates.

One potential loophole may work against this. Organizations could always tell their potential contributors to write checks directly to local candidates instead of to the organization's PAC. The checks could then be collected by the PAC and forwarded to the candidate with a letter from a PAC officer. Under the precedent established by the Washington-based Council for a Livable World, described in Latus's chapter, the checks would count as individual contributions eligible for a 100 percent tax credit. Whether this device would be used primarily by local or national PACs cannot be predicted with confidence, but well-organized national PACs could turn it to their advantage. The McHugh-Conable bill thus might not have much effect on the relative strength of national and local groups, but it could affect the distribution of power between groups and individuals. It also would clearly benefit challengers, since it would be a form of public financing without expenditure limits.

## The Limits of Limits

Congress may not use any of these four bills as a vehicle for legislative action. The bills nevertheless were worth a detailed examination, both because they exemplify the major approaches Congress is likely to consider and because they serve as examples of our opening observations about the difficulties of predicting the consequences of reform. From the specifics, we now turn to a more general look at some underlying assumptions.

Two of the four approaches try to limit the role of PACs directly. Three basic assumptions seem to underlie many of the arguments commonly advanced on their behalf:

1. The electoral role of interest groups has expanded beyond all historic proportions or, in Elizabeth Drew's words, "the role that money is currently playing in American politics is different both in scope and nature from anything that has gone before."[8]
2. The expanded role of interest-group money in the electoral process brings with it an expanded control over the legislative process.
3. The political role and legislative influence of interest groups can be reduced significantly by limiting election contributions from PACs.

INTERESTED MONEY, THEN AND NOW
Political action committees obviously are new forms of political organizations.[9] The PAC phenomenon began with the Congress of Industrial Organizations in the early 1940s, but nonlabor PACs did not really sprout until the new campaign finance law took effect in 1975. In the years since then, the role of PACs has grown steadily. PACs make up an increasing proportion of all campaign funds, having grown from 22 percent of all funds received by general election House candidates in 1976 to 30 percent in 1982 (see appendix, table A.7). The percentages vary greatly with different kinds of candidates, of course. Senate Republican challengers received only 11 percent of their funds from PACs in 1982 and 21 percent from their party; House Democratic incumbents, in contrast, received 38 percent from PACs and only 1 percent from their party (see appendix, table A.8). Still, the general trend for PACs is upward. Moreover, PACs clearly have been bringing new people into the process, increasing the total amount of organized-group money in congressional elections. Despite this, it is not possible to argue that the *proportional* role of special-interest money is greater now than it was in the past.[10] Some PACs, such as the ideological and issue groups, do not represent "special interests" at all, and many economically motivated contributors are individuals and not PACs. We do not know much about interested giving in the days before disclosure began on April 7,

1972, and never will. Nevertheless, everything we do know gives us good reason to believe the "special interests" were present in force from the beginning, but covertly.

*Early examples.* The campaign role of people with special economic interests dates back to the earliest days of the Republic. For example, George Thayer's *Who Shakes the Money Tree?*[11] describes how Aaron Burr worked in the late 1790s to set up an anti-Federalist state bank that would lend Democrats money to buy property, thus qualifying them to vote. He did this because Federalist banks had been refusing loans to known Democratic partisans in order to control access to the electorate.

One early source of special-interest money is particularly noteworthy. In the second and third quarters of the nineteenth century, the United States had what might be thought of as an indirect form of partial public financing. During this period, the primary source of campaign funds appears to have been kickbacks from bureaucrats in patronage positions. After the Pendleton Civil Service Reform Act of 1883 dried up the kickbacks, the country moved into the age of the trusts. Corporations had been giving money to congressional and presidential candidates for years, but moved to the forefront after 1883. Mark Hanna, an Ohio businessman and early McKinley supporter, systematized the participation of corporations when he was chairman of the Republican National Committee during the 1896 campaign. According to Thayer, most of McKinley's $6 million to $7 million in campaign funds that year came because Hanna "levied regular assessments on all businesses of consequence throughout the country" to fight silver coinage and preserve protective tariffs.[12]

Hanna's success was followed by the Tillman Act of 1907, prohibiting direct corporate contributions to federal campaigns. The act looked good, but achieved little. Executives simply took raises for themselves and made campaign contributions as individuals. Even so, direct corporate money still found its way into political campaigns through legal and illegal subterfuges, including gifts to national party conventions, unreported in-kind contributions, and cash in suitcases.

Many of the same industries that dominated campaign finance in the 1890s continued to do so in the 1920s — even after the Tillman Act and the 1925 Federal Corrupt Practices Act. In her classic 1932 book, *Money in Elections,* Louise Overacker found that 30 percent of all Democratic money and 30 percent of all Republican money in the 1928 presidential election came in contributions of $5000 or more from bankers, stockbrokers, manufacturers, and people in mining, oil, railroad, and public utilities businesses.[13] Obviously, these same few businesses would have counted for more than 30 percent if Overacker had been able to identify the financial interests of people who contributed less than $5000.

In the 1930s through 1970s the balance of power changed, and the universe of active interest groups expanded as organized labor began to participate aggressively alongside the business community. In the past few years, the balance has shifted again. The shifts are politically important, but shifts in power are not automatically signs of a new process. Whatever else we may think about the campaign finance laws of the 1970s, they did not spawn something foreign to American politics when they encouraged interest groups to form political action committees.

*The Nixon campaign.* Anyone inclined to romanticize the world before PACs should be required to spend some time thinking about 1972, the last presidential election in what campaign finance buffs may think of as the *ancien régime.* In the three years after that election, 21 different corporations were found guilty of having illegally contributed $958,540 in corporate funds to the 1972 presidential candidates, $842,500 to President Richard M. Nixon.[14] We have no way of knowing how many in-kind or cash contributions escaped prosecution in 1972 or previous years, but we do know they existed and were substantial. In addition, in the noncorporate business world, the investigations of the Senate Watergate Committee chaired by Sam S. Ervin (D-N.C.) uncovered a milk producer pledge of $2 million and actual contributions of $632,500 made to the President's reelection effort, allegedly in exchange for favorable treatment on dairy price supports.[15]

On the legal side of the table, the Finance Committee to Reelect the President (FCRP) also engaged in what the Ervin committee described as a "systematic solicitation of contributions from corporate executive, and middle management salaried employees"[16] to bypass pre-1975 legal prohibitions on government contractors' corporate or PAC contributions. The Ervin committee's words were reminiscent of Thayer's about Mark Hanna, but some of those solicited have made the requests sound closer to extortion. Two tracks were followed for corporate solicitations. One was a "corporate conduit program" in which FCRP officials would persuade officers from the top 1000 Fortune industrials and about 900 other companies to "stimulate" their employees to contribute directly to the President's reelection. The other, which overlapped the first, was arranged by industry and concentrated on 60 major industry groups.[17]

The contributions produced by these and other solicitations were substantial. Even if one limits the analysis to large ($10,000+) contributions raised after April 7, 1972 (the date disclosure was required by the 1971 law), the large contributors accounted for 46 percent of the $23.7 million in postdisclosure money raised by Nixon, 43 percent of $11.7 million raised by Democratic nominee George S. McGovern, and 60 percent of the $1.7 million raised by Hubert H. Humphrey, McGovern's main challenger in the late primaries.[18]

As impressive as these numbers may seem, they do not begin to tell the story of the role played by large givers in 1972. According to the Ervin committee, the systematic effort to solicit large contributions was run unofficially in the early stages by Herbert W. Kalmbach, Nixon's long-time associate and personal attorney. Kalmbach did not hold a government position, but his fund

raising was conducted "under the supervision of"[19] White House chief of staff
H.R. Haldeman. The following lengthy passage from the report of the Ervin
commitee describes the importance of Kalmbach's efforts.

> In November 1970, Kalmbach was requested by Haldeman to involve himself in
> early fund raising. According to Kalmbach, on a number of occasions, before as
> well as after the November meeting, Haldeman told him to obtain cash contribu-
> tions wherever he could. Thereafter, Kalmbach sought out friends in an effort to
> obtain what amounted to commitments for campaign contributions. Kalmbach
> states that he never asked for a commitment in so many words, but rather ap-
> proached people, suggested an amount to them and asked if they would accept
> that as a "goal figure."
>
> Kalmbach acknowledged that he told contributors that there were different
> classes of contributors, and he had different "cut-off points," for example, at $25,000,
> $50,000 and $100,000. Kalmbach said that on occasions he referred to a "100
> Club"—meaning contributors who gave $100,000. He indicated that he told con-
> tributors that there were a lot of people in the $25,000 class, and if one wanted
> to be known as a major contributor, he should give more. . . .
>
> In all, Kalmbach solicited pledges of over $13.4 million. [Of these, three were
> for less than $25,000, five were for $25,000 to $49,999, fifteen were for $50,000
> to $99,999, 32 were for $100,000 to $199,999, nine were for $200,000 to $300,000,
> one was for $1 million and two were for $3 million.] In fact, a total of $10,658,000
> was given. . . . Of this total, over $8.8 million was contributed prior to April 7,
> with over $1.8 million coming after April 7, 1972. Kalmbach emphasized the im-
> portance to his solicitation efforts of being able to assure potential contributors
> that their contributions would remain confidential if made before April 7. Kalm-
> bach was also concerned about having his own solicitation role disclosed. In fact,
> Kalmbach resigned his position with FCRP when the new disclosure law went in-
> to effect on that date. . . .
>
> Kalmbach's efforts thus amounted to a commitment for one-third of the total
> campaign budget, virtually all of which was committed prior to April 7, 1972.
> Most significant was the proportion of contributions in the highest ranges listed
> by Kalmbach. Of anticipated contributions of $100,000 or more, which constituted
> $22.5 million of the $40 million budget, Kalmbach solicited pledges of $12.725
> million, or over 57 percent of the budgeted amount. . . . In terms of actual contribu-
> tions, Kalmbach was responsible for about $9.69 million of the total of $22.5 million
> required from contributors of $100,000 and over, or 43 percent of the amount
> sought.[20]

What emerges from the sordid record of the 1972 campaign is a picture
of semicoercive fund raising, under-the-table cash contributions, and financial
dominance by a handful of large givers most of whom had an interested ax
to grind. It seems almost ludicrous, therefore, to suggest that the growth of
PACs has somehow reduced the dignity of the process. The 1974 law was a
direct reaction to the practices of 1972 and has in fact achieved many of its
original purposes. Interested money still is contributed, but the amount any
one person may give is limited, and all contributions are disclosed. PACs have

increased their proportionate share, but to do so they have had to disclose their activities and involve more people, most of whom contribute relatively small amounts.[21] Some might think the country would be better off if there were no interested money in politics or smaller amounts of it. Whatever one may think, it takes a large set of blinders to miss the fact that the emergence of PACs represents an improvement over what went on before.

## PACs and Legislation

Interested money may not be new, but PACs are. I examine some of the organizational consequences of PACs later, but first I want to look at the assumed connection between PAC contributors and legislative results. The two issues are related because professional political organizations normally can be expected to focus their contributions more systematically than a scattering of like-minded individuals.

*Logical fallacies.* The assumption that PAC contributions relate directly to policy is made not only by journalists and supporters of public finance but by many PAC representatives. In its most common form, the argument suffers from both a lack of evidence and faulty causal logic. Two simple logical errors recur frequently. The first has to do with what correlations mean. Common Cause regularly publishes examples of parallel contribution and voting patterns to support the claim that money influences votes. But simple correlations cannot say anything about causal direction. Therefore they cannot help one choose between Common Cause's interpretation and the opposite one offered by House Democratic Whip Thomas Foley: "Money follows votes and not the other way around."[22]

The second logical fallacy, which we learned in school as Ockham's Razor, can be found in Elizabeth Drew's book, in which she claimed that the Democratic party was selling its soul for campaign funds. Her major example was the omnibus tax bill of 1981. In her opinion, the Democratic members of the House Committee on Ways and Means added tax breaks to the bill for independent oil producers to help the party regain campaign contributions it had lost during the 1970s.[23] From her quotations, it appears that at least one lobbyist and two Ways and Means Democrats linked campaign contributions with the party's position on the tax bills. The views of the two Democrats who were central to the process were given shorter shrift. The picture they drew was a lot simpler and more persuasive. The House Democrats desperately wanted a victory on the tax bill after they were humiliated by President Reagan on the budget in May 1981. They did, as Drew said, engage in a bidding war with the Republicans. The main prizes sought were not campaign contributions in a year and a half, but the immediate floor votes of oil state members of Congress on the omnibus tax bill. Both elements may have been involved, but as Ockham might have said, the simpler and more direct explanation seems weightier.

*Recent research.* Political scientists and economists who have used more sophisticated quantitative models to examine the connection between contributions and legislative floor votes have come up with a mixed picture that would lead one to dismiss Common Cause's one-dimensional view of the world, but not to dismiss the possibility that there is some connection worth examining. Two studies that looked at a large number of floor votes found that when they controlled for other factors, the members' general ideological outlooks were much better predictors of floor votes than were campaign contributions or just about anything else.[24] On the other hand, three studies that looked at individual, narrow economic regulation bills did see a relationship between contributions and votes, although a weaker one than might be expected from the popular conception.[25] The reason for the relationship was explained this way by the authors of one of the specific studies:

> Votes are linked so strongly to PAC contributions on this issue precisely because other forces are not operating as strongly as they normally do. Trucking deregulation in 1980 was not a clearly partisan or ideological issue, and for most Senators it was difficult for them to calculate the issue's relevance to their constituencies. In sum, the forces that normally structure legislative voting only slightly predisposed Senators in one direction or the other in this case.[26]

When supporters of stricter PAC limits are being less rhetorical, this is also the serious core of their case. Representative Dan Glickman seemed to be making essentially the same point when he testified on behalf of his own bill:

> I do not think any member of Congress votes because of how a PAC gives him money on El Salvador, or the MX missiles, or some of what I call the broader, abstract national issues. But those are not the ones I am really worried about. The ones I worry about are the specialty issues on which nobody is on the other side. . . . Where was the public last year before the dramatic rate increases that we are now seeing as a result of divestiture of the telephone company? The public wasn't there; AT&T [The American Telephone and Telegraph Company] and CWA [Communications Workers of America] were there. Where has the public been on dairy legislation when we raise dairy price supports, which come before my committee? The public generally is not there; the dairy lobby is there. Where is the public on banking policy? On pharmaceutical legislation? Usually, when you talk about specialty legislation, the public is not there. The public doesn't know, and I think the smaller specialty issues, where no one is on the other side, are the heart of the dramatic problem of special interest contributions.[27]

Representative Glickman's argument can be supplemented, and often is, in a way that brings into question the utility of roll-call analyses for studying the role of contributions. As little as the public may not "be there" when "specialty issues" come up for votes on the House or Senate floor, still less is it there in the crucial formative stages of legislation, whether in open committee sessions or in closed private meetings that produce the agendas and bills on which committees act.

Therefore, if the correlations between floor votes and contributions are weak, they might turn out to be stronger if the focus shifted to aspects of the legislative process that are less amenable to study. No one can say for sure; the claim is worth analyzing, but the research has not been done. Before one simply assumes, however, that committees are systematically more friendly than the floor to interest groups, one should bear in mind that committees are used by members who want to sit on, and thus kill, special-interest bills, as well as by members who want to advance them.

*PACs and interest groups.* Glickman does have a point. Interest groups tend to be more successful on bills that do not capture the public's attention than on ones that do. The problem is not that Glickman's argument is wrong but that it does not go far enough. Everything he has said about campaign contributions can be applied to interest groups more generally. Every one of the issues he mentioned (telephone rates, dairy price supports, banking, and pharmaceuticals), and all three specialty issues analyzed by the political scientists mentioned above (trucking deregulation, cargo preference, and dairy price supports again), involve groups that not only give campaign contributions but also maintain sophisticated Washington lobbying operations. As Eismeier and Pollock point out, most PACs do not fit this model. Even if one confines oneself to Washington-based PACs, it is difficult to separate the importance of PAC contributions from the lobbying efforts they are supposedly meant to enhance.

Some people suggest there is a connection between the growth of PACs that has occurred since the mid-1970s and the increased success of business in Congress. There are several problems with this. First, if business is so powerful, why, as President Carter's former White House aide in charge of regulatory policy pointed out, did business fail in almost every one of its major 1981-82 efforts to bring about the regulatory changes it most wanted?[28] Second, where business did have some success, it is necessary to separate the general effects of public opinion, and the messages members of Congress read into the election returns of 1978 and 1980, from the effects of interest-group activity. Finally, once the issue has been narrowed to interest-group activity, it is then necessary to separate out the changes in Washington lobbying before attributing too much to the role of campaign contributions.

The 1970s were years of explosive growth for the Washington lobbying community. The scope of federal regulation increased dramatically, bringing the federal government more directly into more aspects of more people's lives. (The *Federal Register* grew steadily from 20,036 pages in 1970 to 77,497 pages in 1979.)[29] As regulation grew, more corporations and associations thought it important to open Washington offices. About twice as many (or about 500) corporations had Washington offices in 1980 as in 1970; and corporate employees in Washington tripled over the same period.[30] Associations with their national headquarters in Washington also grew in number over the decade from about 1200 to 1739, a growth rate of about one per week.[31]

The corporate[32] and association[33] growth curves flattened in the early 1980s, during the recession, but the number of association employees continued to increase from about 40,000 in 1979 to an estimated 50,000 in 1983.[34] In addition, businesses without Washington offices tended to rely more heavily on Washington lawyers to handle their governmental affairs; membership in the D.C. Bar increased from 16,800 in 1973 to 32,200 in 1980[35] and 39,212 in 1983.[36] None of this even begins to document the growth in state and local governments with offices in Washington,[37] or nonprofit and citizen groups, whose growth curves rose even more steeply during the 1970s than those for the private sector.[38]

At the same time as the number of Washington offices and employees has increased, so too has their productivity. Good lobbyists learn quickly that an argument made by a Washington representative is not nearly as effective as the same argument made by a legislator's own constituents. Washington lobbyists are important for getting early information; knowing the technical issues; knowing who are the important members of Congress, congressional staff, and agency staff on particular issues; knowing which people are most open to what kinds of arguments; knowing the real possibilities for compromise or damage control; and synthesizing all this into presentations that are appropriate for each person to be persuaded. Generally, lobbyists present their arguments directly. But on crucial issues, they have discovered it is much more effective to turn back to the grass roots. Grass-roots or indirect lobbying is "the only lobbying that counts," says Richard L. Lesher, president of the U.S. Chamber of Commerce; "the growth area of lobbying," according to Common Cause lobbyist Michael Cole.[39]

The communication revolution has helped lobbyists in almost every aspect of their work, but particularly in their ability to present technical arguments to individual members and to activate the grass roots. Computers let lobbyists tell individual members how particular options—down to the numbers used in formula grants[40]—will affect their own districts. Computers also can generate targeted mail that will stimulate a lobbying organization's members to write to their representatives or senators. (Three different commercial firms sell lists or computer tapes matching zip codes with congressional districts.[41] These lists are then further broken down by interest groups to match their members' zip codes with members of Congress arranged by subcommittee, issue area, and specific positions.)

When mail would be too slow, the changes in telecommunication—from cheap long-distance telephone rates to teleconferencing and the Chamber of Commerce's $5 million satellite television network[42]—facilitate the process. For example, when President Reagan gave a television address on July 27, 1981, two days before the House voted on his tax bill, business groups, primed by the White House, used their communication networks to stimulate an immediate flow of letters and mailgrams to Congress, often written by people who had contributed to the member's last election campaign.[43]

The amount of money spent on the new lobbying techniques dwarfs the amount given directly in campaign contributions. No reliable figures are available, but a few anecdotal stories from the press give an idea of the order of magnitude. Labor law reform was killed by a filibuster in the Senate in 1978 supported by a business and right-to-work grass-roots lobbying campaign whose cost was estimated at about $5 million.[44] On the other side of the same bill, Victor S. Kamber, who coordinated labor's efforts, said his budget for the fight was about $2.5 million.[45] That comes to $7.5 million for one bill!

More recently, AT&T reportedly spent $2 million to oppose a bill that would have overturned the antitrust and divestiture settlement it reached with the Justice Department in 1982.[46] The Health Insurance Association's advertising campaign against President Reagan's proposals to curb hospital reimbursements for Medicare reportedly cost another $2 million,[47] the Savings and Loan Foundation spent $4.5 million to publicize its industry's problems and lobby for the short-lived All-Savers' Certificates of 1981,[48] and the industry-backed Committee for Fair Insurance Rates spent about $800,000 to oppose unisex pension and life insurance rates and benefits in 1983.[49] The insurance campaign also employed a new technique that shows what money can buy these days; each of its letters contained a pretyped return letter with varying texts, complete with laser-printed personalized letterheads on different colors of stationery, for the recipient to sign and return to his or her member of Congress. The mailings, produced by the Targeted Communications Corporation for a pricey 50 to 75 cents per piece, have also been used by the Motion Picture Association on the Home Recording Act of 1982 and by AT&T on the divestiture bill.[50]

None of these examples is offered to suggest that the burden of analysis should simply shift from campaign finance to lobbying expenditures. For one thing, concentrating on lobbying expenditures may be just as problematic as concentrating on campaign finance. As James Q. Wilson has pointed out, there may be some large gaps between resources or expenditures and political power.[51] If this were not true, it would be difficult to explain the continued success environmental groups have had defending clean air and clean water acts from well-funded industry attacks. For another, it would be premature simply to rule out the possibility that campaign finance does have at least some independent influence over legislative decisions.

We know some lobbyists and members think that campaign finance influences legislation and some lobbyists time their contributions to coincide with crucial committee votes.[52] Others tell members that they use "report cards" of their votes on key issues to decide on their contributions.[53] On the other hand, members of Congress can and do defend themselves by taking organizational mailing lists and putting them on their own computers. When this happens, the members can turn something that started out as pressure to their own advantage, making themselves less, instead of more, dependent on a group's leaders for the group's members' electoral support.[54]

*Conclusion.* In summary, the view that PAC contributions influence policy can neither be fully accepted nor fully rejected out of hand. The evidence offered to support the conclusion tends to be weak or irrelevant. Common Cause's correlations defy logic, and the complicated quantitative methods used by political scientists and economists have failed to separate the financially modest role of campaign contributions from the much larger lobbying world within which they are assumed to fit. Moreover, even if you could separate the effects of lobbying and contributions, the fact that a contributor intends his money to have a certain effect does not mean that it was received in the same spirit, even if the recipient behaves as the contributor might have wished. The world is too complicated to be encapsulated by such simple analyses. Anyone who wants to say something precise about the independent effect of contributions will have to pursue a different line of research from the ones we have seen so far.

INFLUENCING ELECTIONS WITHOUT CONTRIBUTIONS
Although we cannot speak precisely about the current independent effect of contributions on legislation, we do know enough to reject the claim that limiting contributions will bring about a significant reduction in the importance of interest groups to elections. One reason has been mentioned already: PACs are organizations with ongoing professional staffs that have a stake in organizational maintenance. If their ability to contribute to candidates is limited by legislation, they will still have an interest in, and ability to, seek other outlets for expressing their electoral support.

*Presidential elections.* This general point can be best understood by looking at what happens in presidential elections. Common Cause and its supporters often say that their aim is to make congressional more like presidential campaign finance. They note that PACs contributed only 1.4 percent of the amount candidates raised directly in the 1980 prenomination period,[55] and they played no role at all, of course, in the public funds that went to the two major-party candidates in the general election. If they think that groups and individuals pursuing special interests did not play a significant role in the 1980 presidential election, however, they are dead wrong.

Herbert Alexander's chapter identified four sources of campaign spending in the 1980 general election that were open for interest-group participation:

1. Groups were permitted to contribute toward the legally unlimited compliance funds of the major candidates, each of whom raised $1.5 million for this purpose in 1980.
2. State and local party expenditures on behalf of the ticket were also unlimited and amounted, according to Alexander, to $15.0 million for President Reagan and $4.0 million for President Carter. National party expenditures amounted to another $8.5 million. PACs could con-

tribute directly to these funds. There was a $15,000 annual limit for PAC contributions to the national party, but limits for PAC contributions to state and local parties, where they existed, varied by state and 30 states permitted direct corporate and labor treasury, as well as PAC, contributions.

3. Independent expenditure groups accounted for another $10.6 million spent on President Reagan's behalf.

4. Corporations and labor unions are both permitted to spend unlimited amounts on internal communication, voter registration, and get-out-the-vote drives. Registration and turnout drives must ostensibly be nonpartisan, but groups are permitted to coordinate these activities with candidates and focus on neighborhoods they think will do their candidate the most good. In 1980, corporations and associations spent $1.5 million, mostly on internal communication, in Reagan's behalf; labor, mostly the Teamsters and Longshoremen, spent another $1.5 million to support the Republican candidate. President Carter, according to Alexander, was the beneficiary of $15 million in labor expenditures, mostly in unreported registration and get-out-the-vote activities. This compares with $11 million that I had estimated in labor expenditures for Carter in 1976,[56] a figure subsequently confirmed as approximately accurate in court depositions.[57]

*Groups in the primaries.* As revealing as these general election figures may be, the full range of interest-group possibilities does not become apparent until the focus shifts to the prenomination period. Consider the following 1980 examples:

1. The Iowa Democratic caucus meetings of January 21 were described by both the *Washington Post* and the *New York Times* as essentially battles between the United Auto Workers (UAW), which supported Senator Edward M. Kennedy (D-Mass.), and the National Education Association, which supported President Carter. The UAW had 50,000 members in Iowa; the NEA had 35,000. In 1976 the UAW supported Carter in Iowa and was able to get 4000 of its members to attend the caucuses, or about half of Carter's total caucus support. (Carter's 29 percent showing at a time when the 1976 national polls still showed him at only 1 percent was responsible for gaining him the recognition that eventually won him the nomination. In a time-honored political tradition, the UAW's president ended up during the Carter administration with the country's top diplomatic post in China.) In 1980 the UAW hoped to double its 4000 turnout of four years before, but its support was concentrated geographically around automobile factories. The NEA, in contrast, was geographically well distributed, a major political plus. Its 1.8 million national members in 1980 were distributed among 12,000 affiliates, an average of 6000 members per congressional district. The teachers had 26 staff members working in the

field in Iowa in 1980, and 6700 telephones devoted to turning out the vote for Carter. The goal was to get 10,000 teachers to turn out. On January 21, Carter won the caucus vote handily, thanks in large part to the NEA.[58]

2. The NEA's efforts in Iowa and other states eventually resulted in 302 NEA members being named delegates to the Democratic National Convention, or about 9 percent of the 3331 total convention delegates; another 162 were named alternates. (The total of 464 compares with a total of 265 NEA delegates and alternates in 1976.) Since most of the 1980 NEA delegates were among Carter's approximately 1900 at the convention, however, their influence was even greater than their numbers might indicate. Eight of the 34 members of the platform committee's task force on human needs were NEA delegates, and they were able to write education planks into the platform that were virtually identical to the ones advocated by the organization. When the NEA delegates decided to break with Carter on the convention floor on a platform amendment that would have prohibited party aid to candidates who refused to endorse an Equal Rights Amendment to the Constitution, the Carter staff backed away from a fight and let the amendment be adopted by a voice vote.[59]

3. The NEA was hardly the only interest group represented in force at the 1980 Democratic National Convention. The AFL-CIO and its affiliated unions (not counting such then-unaffiliated unions as the UAW and United Mine Workers) had 405 delegates divided among the Carter and Kennedy camps. The National Organization for Women claimed 200 members among the delegates and alternates, without counting nonmember delegates affiliated with the National Women's Political Caucus and other feminist organizations. Both groups were able to win convention platform fights against Carter's wishes on the issues it considered central.[60]

4. Some interest groups did not have to go as far as the convention to achieve what they wanted. According to a *National Journal* article written before the February 26, 1980 New Hampshire primary, leading chiropractors in that state wrote letters to their colleagues urging them to vote for President Carter. They followed up with phone calls in which they asked their colleagues to write similar endorsement letters on their own stationery to their patients. In this way they hoped to reach 40,000 chiropractic patients in the state. The reason for this unusual behavior was made clear in the article. Senator Kennedy wanted to exclude chiropractors from national health insurance coverage. President Carter included chiropractors in the plan his administration made public in September 1979, but only in those rare cases when patients are referred by medical doctors. On October 19, after a visit to New Hampshire by Chip Carter, the head of the New Hampshire Chiropractic Political Action Committee wrote in a letter to the President's son that "the removal by your Dad of the mandate 'ordered by a physician' would surely generate chiropractic support throughout the nation, beginning most emphatically here in New Hampshire." On January 2, 1980, White House domestic policy adviser Stuart E. Eizenstat wrote letters to the presidents of two leading chiropractic associa-

tions and to the chairman of the New Hampshire PAC, promising to delete the referral requirement. On January 21, the day of the Iowa caucuses, the Department of Health and Human Services forwarded its new legislative language to Congress. The chiropractors claim to have influenced some 15,000 voters on Carter's behalf in the Iowa caucuses.[61] None of the chiropractors' activities had to be reported as a PAC contribution.

5. The Republican 1980 prenomination process was less dominated than the Democrats' by interest-group activity, but both parties found that the new delegate selection and campaign finance rules had left them open to remarkably similar campaigns by prolife and stop-ERA forces on the Republican side and by gay rights and antinuclear activists on the Democratic side. In all four instances, a poorly funded, ad hoc organization with a network of grass-roots volunteers was able to win major concessions in one of the party platforms. Local volunteers would confront candidates at citizens' forums in the early primary states; long-distance telephone calls would alert volunteers of the candidates' answers so they could be asked follow-up questions at their next stop, sometimes a thousand or more miles away; if the answers were satisfactory, volunteers would work for the candidate in the primaries; after the primaries, the groups worked hard to get its supporters named first as delegates to the national convention and then as members of the platform committees; once on the committees, both parties' practice of permitting people to choose their subcommittees let the activists play a disproportionate role on the subcommittees that handled their issues; after the activists had convinced either the subcommittees or full platform committees to endorse language that Carter or Reagan initally opposed, the candidates were faced with the choice of fighting a battle that they might not win, and even if they won, would alienate some supporters who had showed they could mobilize volunteers for the fall election. In each case, the candidate gave in to most of the groups' demands.[62]

*Conclusion.* The examples of interest-group activity in the 1980 presidential election could be expanded almost at will. Enough have been given to show the main point. Neither public financing nor strict expenditure limits nor even the complete exclusion of private contributions from the general election can eliminate interest groups from the electoral process. The rules do not eliminate but transform interest-group politics, working to the advantage of some groups and disadvantage of others. Groups that can mobilize dispersed networks of volunteers—single- or multi-issue groups, labor unions, and a few professional associations—have been made more important in presidential elections. Groups whose members are reluctant to volunteer and in the past relied on Washington representatives and monetary campaign contributions—corporations and trade associations—have become less important because candidates are less willing to use their limited money to pay for such things as phone banks that can be staffed less efficiently, but more cheaply, with volunteers. It would be difficult to argue that an organization is less of a "special interest" because it relies on one set of resources rather than another. Whether they know it or not, therefore, people who say they want to use public financing to make congressional more like presidential elections are just saying they prefer some kinds of interest groups to others.[63]

The examples also suggest another line of thought. The rules of campaign finance seem to encourage a situation in which Presidents and members of Congress come to office with systematically different interest-group electoral bases. It is possible—we can only speculate at this stage—that this could help explain some of the difficulties Presidents have in working with Congress.[64] Legislative-executive relations might be improved somewhat if the branches' electoral bases were made more similar. (Of course, this is an argument that could be made to eliminate presidential public financing as well as extend it.) On the other hand, it may be beneficial to have a system that gives different groups better access to each branch. But whichever view of legislative-executive relations one might prefer, the separation of powers and the permeability of the system both rest on foundations that would change only slightly with new rules of campaign finance.

## PACs and the Organizational Perspective

The thrust of this chapter so far has been reactive. Proposals have been examined for unintended consequences, assumptions have been refuted, and some of the limits of our knowledge have been indicated. The aim has been to clear away underbrush fertilized by a decade's worth of rhetorical mulch. It will not do to leave matters in this state. In the remaining pages, I first look at PACs as organizations to see how it might help policy makers to think about organizational imperatives as they consider PAC legislation. I conclude the chapter by proposing some changes of my own.

Reformers who want to limit the electoral influence of PACs often seem to assume that a change in the law will produce similar effects across the full spectrum of organized interest groups. Our discussion of presidential elections discloses the fallacy of such thinking. It is impossible to predict how an organization would react to a change in the legislative environment without considering the organization's needs on its own terms. PACs, as we have noted several times, are ongoing organizations, or parts of ongoing organizations, that among other things seek to maintain themselves.[65] The perspective that informs this statement should be explored further by politicians who want to change the way organizations function politically.

The organizational perspective is a familiar one to political scientists.[66] It leads one to expect that the precise nature of an organization's political activities will generally be chosen with an eye toward maintaining the organization's health and that the relationships between organizational maintenance and political activity will almost always be more complex than they appear on the surface. The lack of understanding among members of Congress on this point is no particular surprise; the connections between maintenance and PAC behavior have not yet been explored adequately by anyone in published research.

Some of the needed work has begun. Handler and Mulkern, for example, have examined the effect that differences in chief executive officers, Washington vice-presidents, and PAC decision-making processes may have on a corporate PAC's political activities.[67] Edwin M. Epstein, also focusing on corporate PACs, has looked at the relationships between company size, industry grouping, and political behavior.[68] Industry grouping was also important in Eismeier and Pollock's contribution to this volume, as were PAC size and Washington location. Finally, Frank Sorauf has looked at some differences between independent PACs and PACs with parent organizations.[69] In each case, the authors found political decisions importantly influenced by organizational factors usually missed in the reformers' "who benefits?" model of legislative causation.

*Independent PACs.* Sorauf's work points directly at some questions that need further examination. He argues that among the independent PACs, there is a possibility for unaccountable, self-aggrandizing behavior by staff that would not be tolerated in a PAC that had to justify its activities to an ongoing, parent organization. Many independent PACs are "one-man" operations, with paper boards, whose geographically scattered donors exercise little control over policy. "Exits [decisions by members to drop out] are not apt to change PAC policy," Sorauf writes, "beyond forcing the drafting of a new direct mail appeal. When a 2 to 5 percent return on a mailing to a list is considered 'good,' exit ceases to have much meaning."[70] The lack of accountability, Sorauf suggests, helps explain why *Miami Herald* reporter Robert D. Shaw, Jr., found in 1981 that 79 percent of all money raised by selected New Right PACs in 1979-80 was spent on fund raising and overhead.[71] The hints contained in Shaw's two 1981 articles were explored at great length by the *Baltimore Sun's* Robert Timberg in an eleven-part series published between July and October 1982. Timberg's articles were filled with examples of PACs on the right and left whose fund-raising practices, contractual relationships with old friends, internal decision-making processes, and low level of direct or indirect campaign expenditures made them look suspiciously as if they existed for the personal benefit of PAC directors and their vendors.[72]

Neither Timberg's nor Shaw's articles have been refuted, as far as I know. I would suppose, therefore, that they are at least partly true. But let us think about how an independent, ideological PAC might behave if it operated without the slightest hint of impropriety. Vendors would still probably be chosen from among the friends and associates of the PAC directors because directors would want letters and advertisements to be cast in ideological terms, and activist ideological soulmates tend to work and socialize together in Washington. PAC directors probably would also continue to spend substantial proportions of their money on fund raising and overhead, for three reasons. First, the law makes it harder for independent groups than associations, corporations, or labor unions to raise administrative funds. Second, direct mail is a very costly way to raise money, but the best way for a group that is not part of an existing organization. Finally, expenditures for overhead that may look extravagant at first glance may seem less so when you consider organizational objectives and resources.

Independent PACs, by definition, are not created with ready-made public identities. No one in the press will pay much attention to them until they earn it. A lack of attention might not bother most corporate PACs, but it could destroy a new ideological PAC. The objective of most of these PACs is not only to help favored candidates win elections but also to influence the terms of public debate. To achieve this, it is crucial for them to gain some attention both in and outside of Washington, for themselves, and for their issues. (Such attention, not coincidentally, also helps with fund raising.) The need for attention means that these PACs must maintain a presence in Washington, either physically or through the press, and support enough of a staff to spread that presence outside. If they fail to gain attention, and fail therefore to influence the content of the substantive agenda, they will have failed as organizations. They literally have no other reasons for being and no other way to maintain themselves. Because of this, we can predict that independent PACs would react aggressively to sustain their political activities in the face of any change in the law. We can also predict that the simple internal structure of most independent PACs would facilitate their ability to adapt when they have to.

Consider now the very different, multifaceted world of PACs with parent organizations. As mentioned, little work has been done on their varying organizational imperatives. If I were planning such research, I would begin by thinking about some differences in the political interests of the parent organizations themselves. In no particular order, the following speculations come to mind. Each relates directly to the way different groups would respond to legislative limits on their activity.

*Labor PACs.* Labor unions rely on a broad base of very small contributors who belong for reasons that have little to do with politics. We know from James Q. Wilson's work that this produces a relatively high degree of autonomy for the professional staffs to pursue noneconomic legislative interests. The level and kind of activity, and the amount of internal decentralization, vary with a union's structure and history, but a high level of staff autonomy from the membership seems present across the board.[73] This, in turn, permits close coordination between electoral and legislative activities.

Plenty of conflict exists among unions, of course. The American Federation of Teachers sticks to a more purely educational agenda than the National Education Association, while the Steamfitters and Steelworkers disagree with the United Auto Workers on such nonindustrial issues as U.S. relationships with the Soviet Union. The different agendas produce different levels of willingness among unions to use contributions to reward or punish members of Congress for a few votes on pure labor issues, such as labor law reform, or industry-specific issues, such as auto emissions standards or common situs picketing. Construction trade unions, for example, were more willing to withhold funds from Democrats who voted against their position on common situs than was the UAW on emissions standards.

These policy considerations may have a great deal of effect on any union's willingness to concentrate on its members' purely economic interests, but they seem to have little effect on a union's ability to maintain itself as an organization. We would expect researchers to discover relatively little institutionally based conflict within any particular union that would divide top management, legislative directors, and political directors. If there is conflict, it would probably stem more from individual political outlooks than from any differences in perspective inherent in the different jobs. We would also expect, therefore, that if the legal rules of the game were changed, the three levels of union management might disagree about tactics, but they ultimately would be able to coordinate new strategies without having to trim their decisions to resolve internal conflicts of institutional interest. The process would be more complicated than for independent PACs, but simpler than for most other PACs with parent organizations.

*Corporate PACs.* Corporations are more varied than labor unions. Handler and Mulkern argued that the degree of corporate diversification, the industrial or nonindustrial character of the parent corporation, and a corporation's regulatory environment all affect a PAC's political decisions.[74] Epstein showed that political behavior is also affected by whether a corporation is a government contractor.[75]

For our purpose of assessing the potential effects of reform, some other aspects of organizational maintenance are worth keeping in mind. Corporations exist, first and foremost, to sell products or services. For this reason, we would expect that chief executive officers could not afford to let corporate political activities alienate potential customers, create interdivisional conflict, or weaken employee morale. Concern over employee morale is known, for example, to affect solicitation patterns in many companies and to lead some to permit contribution decisions to be made by politically inexpert local employees, even if they may not reflect a Washington view of how best to mesh contributions with immediate lobbying strategy.[76] Decentralizing contribution decisions can help lobbying over the long term, of course, by getting more of a company's employees to become politically active, but that is not why many companies choose this approach. The choice seems more often to reflect a difference between Washington lobbyists and corporate headquarters over the importance of consulting employees.

We also know from interviews that some corporate officers worry about the effects of political activity on public opinion, [77] and presumably therefore on sales. Such a concern does not show up as clearly in aggregate-level research.

In fact, even though most people, and therefore most potential customers, support their incumbent House members, companies that sell products directly to the public seem to give higher percentages of their budgets to Republicans, and less to incumbents, than those selling services regulated by the government, who have an obvious stake in protecting their friends in Congress (see Eismeier and Pollock, table 4.8). Thus we have to be very tentative at this stage about the role of public opinion, employee morale, and the like because most of the research so far has not looked enough at individual corporations. Obviously, we are dealing with complex sets of interrelated interests. How corporate officers balance the partially conflicting interests of their organizations may well vary on an individual basis. So, too, would corporate reactions to future legislative curbs on PACs. In general, we can predict that internal conflicts of interest would restrain most corporations from reacting as forthrightly (e.g., with direct independent expenditures) as independent PACs, unions, or trade associations.

*Association PACs.* Associations, like corporations, come in many shapes and sizes. Borrowing from Jack Walker's recent classification, some groups have occupational and professional requirements for membership, and others have none. Among groups with occupational requirements, some have members in the profit-making sector, such as most trade and professional associations; others fall in the not-for-profit sector; and others are mixed.[78] Because of tax rules governing nonprofit entities, most politically active associations are either trade groups, occupational groups for people in the private sector, or nonoccupational groups. The latter tend to be issue groups; when they engage in electoral politics, they are similar to ideological organizations but without the freedoms and constraints of the independent groups. Professional associations range in their political behavior from ones that are similar to the most active trade associations, such as the American Medical Association and the Association of American Trial Lawyers, to others that engage in no direct political activity, such as the American Bar Association. Trade association PACs themselves vary in their level of political activity from the Direct Mail Marketing Association (1981-82 receipts: $1760) to the Realtors' Political Action Committee (1981-82 receipts: $2,991,732).

As a preliminary observation, it would appear that the relationships between organizational maintenance, on the one hand, and legislative or political activity, on the other, are more straightforward among associations than corporations. That is because the association needs to satisfy only one constituency, its members; the corporation has to look at employees, stockholders, and customers. For that reason, associations are better able to coordinate their electoral and legislative strategies, or engage in independent expenditures, than are corporations.

This is not to say that associations need not worry about maintenance when they get involved in politics. The character of an organization's membership base clearly affects what it does. The AMA, for example, has a large number of small individual contributors, much like a labor union, and behaves in almost an equivalent, though ideologically opposite, manner. The U.S. Chamber of Commerce has a large number of mostly small corporations as members. Traditionally, the chamber's membership has not allowed as much staff independence as a union's or the AMA's. Generally this produces operation by consensus. In recent years, it has led to support for Republicans, as the chamber has staked out broad positions about what its members believed would be good for business as a whole. Most of the chamber's political activities are indirect, but of the $16,967 the chamber contributed directly to House and Senate candidates in 1981-82, all but $736 went to Republicans, and 59 percent went to nonincumbents. In contrast, the American Bakers' Association is funded by a few large corporations with highly focused legislative interests. Its political arm, Bread PAC, contributed all but $4600 of its $50,910 in 1981-82 House and Senate contributions (or 91 percent) to incumbents; 55 percent of its money went to Democrats. Like the AMA, Bread PAC probably would be better able to respond quickly to changes in campaign finance laws than the chamber, which in turn would be in a better position than many corporations.

*Conclusion.* In summary, an interest group's political behavior will vary both with the professional staff's independence of its supporting members and with the particular interests, and maintenance needs, of the parent organization. Some of the distinctions among parent organizations correspond roughly to the Federal Election Commission's four largest nonparty groupings (labor union, corporation, trade/member/health, no connected organization). But these distinctions are far from airtight. Corporations run by ideologues, for example, may behave politically almost as if they were ideological PACs. (Dart and Kraft, Inc., to mention one, gave 89 percent of its $125,584 in 1981-82 House and Senate contributions to Republicans and 52 percent to nonincumbents.) In addition, the variations within each major category are far too rich to be encompassed by facile generalizations. I have chosen in this section, therefore, to present some guidelines and suggestions for future researchers who want, to borrow a phrase from Latus, to move beyond outrage to understanding. Until we have such understanding, we must reiterate that legislative proposals designed to curb PACs in fact would affect groups differentially in ways that we cannot foresee, but that undoubtedly would be related to a PAC's or parent group's own organizational needs. If those needs require political involvement, then political involvement there will be. In a country that protects the freedoms of association and speech, the rules may channel or shape a group's political activity, but they cannot eliminate it.

## Groups and Elections

My discussion of organizational maintenance, like much that went before, focused on predicting the consequences of reform. In this section, I turn to more basic questions. In what precise ways have elections, and the political-governmental environment, been affected by the professionalization of interest-group electoral participation stimulated by the campaign laws of the 1970s? After addressing this question, I consider ways in which PACs and interest groups may help further, or work against, the purposes elections are meant to serve. Finally, I indicate the kinds of legislative changes that might preserve the benefits of the present system while alleviating some of its costs.

I stated earlier that even if the existence and role of interested money is not new to elections, the proliferation of formally organized, professionally staffed groups is. What difference does it make if money is channeled through PACs instead of being given directly to candidates by interested individuals? The differences are significant, affecting actual contribution patterns, other political and lobbying activities of a PAC's parent organization, and perhaps the behavior of members of Congress. Each of those effects contributes to a concluding evaluation of the role of PACs.

*PACs and challengers.* It is vitally important for a representative government to preserve a serious threat of competition in legislative elections. Since 1950, however, approximately 90 percent of all incumbent members of the House who have sought reelection have won. Since 1968, more than 70 percent have won with at least 60 percent of the two-party vote.[79] Competition in House races was at a low level before the PAC phenomenon, in other words, and has stayed that way. Nevertheless, if it can be shown that the role of PACs significantly adds to the advantage of incumbency in this uncompetitive climate, that would be a strong argument on the side of those who see PACs as harmful.

It is well known that PACs contribute more, on the whole, to incumbents than nonincumbents. But when the distribution of PAC contributions (see appendix, tables A.16-A.21) is measured against the distribution of candidates by party and candidate status (line 1 of the tables), it becomes clear that what is called a pro-incumbent bias in fact covers several phenomena. Labor's money is almost entirely Democratic; it tilts toward Democratic incumbents, but a fair share also goes to Democratic challengers. Very little labor money goes to Republican incumbents or challengers. Corporate PACs, in contrast, give Democratic incumbents about as much as one would expect from a random distribution of funds, but give almost as much on these terms to Republican challengers and more to Republican incumbents. Reversing labor's partisanship, corporations tend not to give to Democratic challengers. Thus, as Eismeier and Pollock also argue, it would not be accurate to treat PAC contributions merely as if they favor incumbents. The pro-incumbent bias of the aggregate numbers results from trade associations, and from the fact that labor's partisanship exceeds that of corporate PACs.

PACs are more cautious in their contribution patterns than individuals, however, even if they are not simply pro-incumbent. We can see this by looking at the timing of 1977-82 contributions of PACs, by category, compared with non-PAC contributions (see appendix, tables A.24-A.26). As the tables show, few PACs outside the ideological group give early seed money to nonincumbents. Contributions to nonincumbents pick up after the primary season, as it becomes possible for professionals to identify the most promising challengers and open-seat candidates. At no time during 1981-82, however, did nonincumbent giving by any group of PACs, including the ideological PACs, match that for non-PAC givers. The picture was different in 1980. That year, many PACs increased their giving to nonincumbents by substantial amounts after June 30. The 1980 election was one in which conservative and business groups saw good opportunities for challengers. In 1982, a Democratic year, these same groups tried to protect incumbent Republicans. Corporate PACs, for example, gave 32 percent of their House contributions to Republican incumbents and 29 percent to Republican nonincumbents in 1980; in 1982 the figures were 45 percent for Republican incumbents and only 18 percent for Republican nonincumbents (see appendix, tables A.17-A.18).

At first glance, the figures seem to support the common assertion that economic PACs, seeking access for lobbying, reinforce the political advantages of incumbency. Some other considerations point in the opposite direction, however. First, while PACs may not provide seed money to new people, they do seem to weigh in with significant amounts of money for nonincumbents later in the race. Second, we know that when we separate candidates by the competitiveness of their race, most nonincumbent PAC money is concentrated in close races while incumbent money is spread more broadly (see appendix, tables A.22-A.23). Finally, Jacobson's work tells us that marginal dollars tend to mean more for nonincumbents than for incumbents. On balance, therefore, we suspect that the effects of PAC giving may vary with the calendar. Early in the election cycle, when the bulk of organized giving goes to incumbents, the effect may be to help incumbents scare off good challengers or otherwise solidify their position. Later, when strong challengers have been identified, the overall effect may be the opposite. By concentrating their resources on close races, PACs may help to increase the net number of incumbent defeats in a campaign's closing weeks — but only after they have helped reduce the number of potentially vulnerable incumbents in earlier months.

*PACs and lobbying.* If PACs are not simply seeking to improve their lobbying position by reinforcing incumbents, perhaps having a PAC helps lobbying in other ways. I argued earlier that it is difficult, when talking about legislative influence, to separate direct campaign contributions from the other electoral and lobbying activities in which interest groups engage. In fact, the activities tend to reinforce each other within the group. When a group organizes itself to solicit employees or members, it is better able to stimulate its employees or members to engage in other activities, and the contributing employees or members are more likely to respond. Two business PAC representatives made this point in 1982 hearings before the House Administration Committee's Task Force on Elections. The first was Gregg Ward, director of governmental affairs for the Sheet Metal and Air Conditioning Contractors National Association:

> Simply writing a check doesn't constitute, in and of itself, much in the way of participation in the process. What we have found is that only begins their interest in the process, and to a neophytic group, an unsophisticated one largely like the one I am with, they now see that they can be involved.
>
> They want to know what has happened with their money. We try to keep them informed as to what we are doing with it, but beyond that, it stimulates and generates an interest factor. That interest factor generally then translates into them doing something about it in other manifest ways.[80]

Don V. Cogman, vice-president of MAPCO Inc. for governmental affairs, and president of the National Association of Business Political Action Committees, expanded upon Ward's point by describing some of the specific programs his company uses:

> I can tell you that coming from the political side of this game, and now being on the corporate side, that in my opinion the individual involvement, the people involvement, the volunteer involvement, is more important than money and I think you are finding in the corporate community particularly a new awareness of that. Our counterparts in the labor movement have understood that for decades. The business community has not. I think you are finding that they are beginning to understand it.
>
> In my company specifically we have a program called the citizenship involvement program, which tries to educate, promote, motivate and get involved our employees in all phases of the political system. The PAC is just part of it. I think there is a growing awareness in the corporate community of that fact.[81]

In short, forming a PAC helps a corporation or association get its members or employees active in other aspects of politics and it helps them get members or employees to respond when it is time for grass-roots lobbying. It is possible, therefore, that legislation sharply curbing PAC contribution activity would affect these other programs. My own guess is that the effect would not be substantial and would be most felt by those organizations, a large majority, that do not as yet have a PAC or any form of ongoing political organization. Those with PACs would presumably continue soliciting, if only to involve people in other activities. Those that do not yet solicit will be encouraged through ongoing programs run by the Chamber of Commerce and others to become active in whatever way the law will permit. The campaign laws, therefore, may well have stimulated or facilitated other forms of electoral and lobbying activity when they legitimized direct campaign contributions through PACs, but PAC contributions are not necessary for those activities to continue. Thus, even though a change in the law historically may have been responsible for something, it does not follow that changing the law back will reverse what has happened. The new techniques, once learned, will not be so readily forgotten.

*PACs and members of Congress.* The indirect connection between PACs and lobbying is an easy one to understand. Far more complicated is how the growth of PACs may have affected the direct relationships between interest groups and members of Congress. Here we must be even more speculative than we have been so far. I suspect that members of Congress and lobbyists both tend to look at the issue from the wrong end. Both speak of contributors directly pressuring members, using scorecards and other similar devices to get members to behave or vote *against* their inclinations. I frankly do not believe this happens very often. Direct conversion of an opponent is the most difficult of lobbying techniques, tried only in desperation and with rare success. Even when it is successful, or when it results in a slight tempering of a legislator's attitude, we would still have to separate the effect of contributions from lobbying.

But there are more subtle relationships that may be worth further thought and investigation. We know that incumbents proportionally rely more on PAC money than nonincumbents (see appendix, tables A.8, A.22, and A.23). This is usually interpreted by referring to what PACs hope to achieve, but would be worth considering from the members' perspective. Unless something like the McHugh-Conable tax credit bill (described above) becomes law and changes the incentives for members, PAC money is and will remain the easiest money for most incumbents to raise. Tens of thousands of dollars typically change hands in any of the hundreds of Washington fund raisers held every year.[82] Far from being events at which lobbyists hold the whip hand and buy favors from members, these fund raisers normally are attended by people who either want to reward their friends for past behavior or are afraid of turning down "invitations" from members whose committees have jurisdictions over their organizations' futures. The members, clearly on top of the situation, use the events to raise $250 or so in quasi-tribute fees from people who might not otherwise support them, in modest latter-day versions of the reverse pressure techniques perfected by Herbert Kalmbach in the 1972 Nixon campaign.[83]

If PAC contributions do not convert legislators, and if fund raisers represent reverse more than direct lobbying pressure, what effects might the current fund-raising process have on members? If we leave aside the significant changes that may come from replacing incumbents with more sympathetic freshmen, the most important effects may be very subtle and hard to trace. Opponents of the current campaign finance system like to say that contributions do not buy votes, but do buy access—that is, they help a lobbyist gain entry into a member's office to present a case. I am skeptical that a lobbyist who attends a fund raiser gets any more access than the same lobbyist would if there were no fund raisers—although I concede that when fund raisers are common, refusing an invitation can have a negative effect. I also believe that specialty bills, of the sort discussed earlier, bring out business lobbyists who are opposed to each other. Trucking bills bring out the railroads, cotton subsidies bring out the chemical manufacturers, and so forth. Whatever course the member may choose, there are plenty of PACs around to lend their support at campaign time.

What fund raisers may do is not change members' minds but change the way they spend their time. Congressional campaign costs have risen dramatically over the years, particularly for House races. As the value of incumbency grows, and elections become less subject to national or party swings, challengers have to spend increasing amounts of money in order to win.[84] In protective reaction, incumbents raise more to preserve their safety (see appendix, tables A.1, A.4-A.6). The result is that incumbents, never fully secure in their own minds despite the odds in their favor, devote more time and effort to raising early money.

The need to raise funds in turn means that members spend more of their personal time at fund raisers. If lobbyists do not "pressure" members at fund raisers, the members might still be affected by their conversations at these events. Talking with lobbyists might get the members to see and understand the problems of the people they meet and thus help shape their outlooks or their agendas. It would be difficult to prove this point. For one thing, despite their need for funds, most members do not spend all that much of their personal time at Washington fund raisers. A half dozen per year would be a good guess, and those nights are spent more on quick handshakes than on extended conversations. Let us assume, however, that Washington fund raisers play at least a small role in helping form or cement the relationships that make up Washington's many "issue networks."[85] If so—and I think this is the most that can plausibly be claimed for them—it would mean that this aspect of campaign fund raising helps reinforce the nationalization of interest-group politics that followed the expansion of the federal government's role. That is not earthshaking, but it is not insignificant either.[86]

*Groups and the purposes of elections.* The nationalization of interest-group activity and of a part of campaign fund raising brings us to the most basic issue: the relationship between campaign finance and the purpose of elections. During the debate over the Bill of Rights in the First Congress, a motion was made by Thomas Tudor Tucker of South Carolina to add a clause to what is now the First Amendment that would have given people the right to instruct their representatives on specific issues.[87] The motion was rejected then, as it was repeatedly over the the next few decades, because it was based on the view that the ideal representative should mirror the wishes, feelings, and interests of his or her constituents. The alternative view, which prevailed, was that representation in an extended, diverse republic required members to come together and deliberate in a central place—talking directly to one another, sharing opinions, compromising, and thereby reaching a national consensus that would transcend the local concerns from which members would most likely begin.[88] If the decisions displeased constituents, the constituents could change their representatives at the next election.

One assumption in the discussion of 1789 is striking for our purposes. The members of the First Congress, and most of the active Federalists in the two-year period before then, saw the national legislature as a place where members would be several steps removed from the clamor of special interests, most of which were assumed to have local bases. Today, in contrast, reformers yearn for a more locally based campaign finance system in the hope that this will help legislators escape a different sort of nationalized, interest-group clamor. The hope is fruitless. The only way to escape the current clamor would be to return to the government, policies, and environment of almost two hundred years ago. Failing that, a complex age calls not for nostalgia but for a sophisticated understanding of the multiple objectives that have to be balanced, and compromises that have to be made, to keep elections and representative institutions serving their purposes at least reasonably well.

The main purpose of elections, as mentioned, is to give voters a chance to react to government policy by replacing the people who govern them. As a corollary, elections should also serve to confer legitimacy upon those who assume office. Finally, an election system that works well should help facilitate the process of government—not necessarily by making governmental actions easier, as supporters of parliamentary regimes would wish, but by giving the elected members a sense of institutional and personal self-interest that helps each branch perform its proper function.

When we take this broad view, we can begin to see that the problems of campaign finance in the modern communications age do not lend themselves to easy solutions, for at least two reasons. First, there was always an inherent, and healthy, tension between the desire for accountability and the desire to preserve freedom for members of Congress to think about the national interest. The tension has been exacerbated in recent years. The complexity of government makes it all but impossible for voters to follow individual issues. In addition, a legislator who wants to serve the national interest cannot possibly learn about the potential effects of proposed legislation without the reaction of organized groups. In this situation, the wishes of groups should not be seen merely as nuisances. They also help confer and sustain support for people in government, and they help facilitate the process of both government and opposition by keeping the governors and governed informed.[89]

If interest groups are not merely nuisances, neither has their proliferation been just a blessing. It may be important for people to organize on a national level, especially as the role of government expands. The proliferation of a multiplicity of interests also has some important benefits, as James Madison argued in *Federalist No. 10*. But I am not one of those twentieth-century pluralist misinterpreters of Madison who believes the public good is simply the sum of, or a compromise among, interest-group claims. Group conflict does sometimes produce legislative stalemate, and groups do sometimes win special benefits, at the expense of the general public, when the public is not looking.

It would be misleading, however, to treat campaign finance, or even lobbying, as if they were the fundamental causes of legislative outcomes. They do make a difference, but only at the margins. Lobbyists can win when their activities generally go along with what the public wants, when public opinion is divided, or when the public has no particular opinion. Lobbyists can also help lighten the burden of defeat when the public is against them. Campaign finance may modestly help reinforce the effects of lobbying. But to address the contemporary role of interest groups fully, in its most basic aspects, would force one ultimately to look broadly at the reasons institutional power has been decentralized and at the public philosophy elected members tend to believe or, at least, act upon. These considerations go well beyond the scope of this chapter. Suffice it for now to say that the problem *exists* because most people, in part of their souls, want the government to look after their special, intensely felt desires and needs. It is *perceived* as a problem by most of these same people because, in another part of their souls, they want the government to listen to their more general, less intensely felt, needs and desires when they conflict with the special desires of others. Politically, there is no easy solution because, as Aaron Wildavsky has noted, the Pogo Principle applies: "We have seen the enemy and they are us."[90] All of us react strongly to our own particular concerns, and a fair number of us are likely to let those special concerns determine our vote. As long as that is true, organized interests will continue to play an important role in electoral politics, whatever the rules of campaign finance.

The second reason there are no easy solutions has to do with another by-product of modern government and communication: the advantages of incumbency, especially for members of the House. The communication resources available to incumbent members, the fractionalization of the congressional policy process, and the long-term weakening of the importance of party to voters all make it hard to defeat incumbents without spending a great deal of money. But a system within which a lot of private money is available almost assuredly is a system in which special interests will participate on an individual or group basis. Interest-group participation may not be all that bad, therefore, if it is a necessary condition for assuring there will be enough money in the system to make the threat of subsequent accountability real.

*Proposals for change.* Having said this, we are now prepared to look again at some proposals for changing the law. The benefits and problems interest groups bring to the *legislative* process would not be affected greatly if groups could not contribute to candidates. The benefits they bring to *elections* would be lost, however, unless the money they provide challengers toward the end of a campaign could be replaced. In theory the job might be done by full public financing, if it were sufficiently generous to cover the country's most expensive districts. Such a form of public financing might eliminate whatever reinforcement contributions now give to lobbying, while substituting for the needed money that now comes from interested contributors. There are two problems with this approach. First, as was argued earlier in connection with presidential elections, eliminating direct contributions would not and could not eliminate the electoral role of interest groups. It would only introduce new forms of bias into the system. Second, even if the idea were good in theory, it would stand little chance of being adopted. Members of Congress are not likely ever to give their opponents enough money, solely from public funds, to permit serious challenges in expensive districts. Incumbents cannot be expected to think first about the system's need for electoral insecurity as they design the rules for their own reelection campaigns.

We return, therefore, to the real world of political practice, where some form of interest-group participation is accepted, however unhappily, as inevitable, and where the level of electoral competition and the fragmentation of the legislative process are both causes for legitimate concern. In that real world I, for one, come back to the third and fourth of the legislative approaches analyzed earlier. To the extent that fragmentation is caused partly by the role of groups, but more basically by the splits within our selves, the institutional remedy logically seems to call for building up those political institutions and organizations that can counter our particularized interests in the name of our more general ones. In practical terms, this means increasing the role of parties.

Parties should not be considered panaceas. Excessively strong national committees could weaken Congress, as we saw. In addition, one cannot simply assume that turning all power back to the parties would weaken the power of interest groups The strong parties of the late nineteenth century, and the national conventions of today, hardly leave one sanguine on that score. Instead of a lesser role for groups, a system in which parties were dominant could just mean better access for fewer groups. But parties are a long way from being dominant today. A great deal can be done to strengthen their role in elections without granting the unlimited spending authority Republicans might wish. Spending limits can be raised, and state and local party volunteer activities can be encouraged, as they would be in other parts of the Laxalt-Frenzel bill.

In addition, the government could reclaim some of the air time it now gives freely to federally licensed radio and television stations. The stations could then be required to make 60 minutes or so of free prime time available to each party to be used in blocks of at least five minutes. In some local areas, the parties might turn the time over to candidates. In most, however, they would probably increase their generic advertising. This advertising, described in Adamany's chapter, would make the parties more important for both candidates and voters, nationalizing the election in a manner that would go a long way toward countering the decentralizing effects of individualistic, candidate-centered campaigning. To the extent this happens, it would heighten the sense that elections produce mandates, adding weight to the inclinations of those members who want to resist particularized pressures in the name of a more general interest.

The second approach that deserves serious consideration is exemplified by the McHugh-Conable tax credit bill: public financing unencumbered either by spending limits or limits on a candidate's PAC receipts. As noted, public financing without limits works to the benefit of challengers, especially challengers who have not yet managed to establish themselves as serious competitors. In this respect, it serves as a perfect complement to the existing finance system, in which PACs avoid commitments to challengers in the early stage, but flock to the most serious ones at the end.

Public financing without limits also would decrease the importance of PACs by giving candidates other places to look for their funds. Not all forms of public financing would be equal in this respect, however. Matching grants would do nothing to change the mix of private givers or their importance. Flat grants —whether in cash or in such in-kind forms as postal subsidies, the frank, or free media—would decrease the importance of private money but not the mix. Of all of the bills proposed so far, only a 100 percent tax credit or voucher would change the incentives for candidates in a way that would broaden the base of participants. Interest groups would continue to play an important role, but their proportionate influence would be reduced in a way that would also reduce, rather than increase, the biases inherent in the current system.

In short, many steps can be taken to reduce the costs of interest-group participation while preserving the benefits. Nothing can be done, however, with a strategy of limits that fails to recognize that the fundamental source of interest-group power has little to do with campaign finance. Interest groups are what they are in the United States because parties, governmental institutions, communications and human nature are what they are. Any attempt to deal with what is essentially a surface symptom, the contemporary electoral role of organized groups, solely through direct regulations and limits can do little more than shift group power around and weaken electoral competition. The supposed reforms might also make a few regulators feel good for a while—but only until they glance backward at the unintended consequences of some past reforms and realize that they are looking at their own future.

## Notes

1. Michael J. Malbin, "The Democratic Party's Rules Changes—Will They Help or Hurt It?" *National Journal,* January 23, 1982, 139, 165.
2. Nelson W. Polsby, *Consequences of Party Reform* (New York: Oxford University Press, 1983), 131-32.
3. For example, John Gardner, then chairman of Common Cause, wrote in December 1976 about that year's election that "the money-heavy special interests could not buy themselves a President, so they tried to buy as many members of Congress as they could." Quoted in Rhodes Cook, "Prospects Improve for Public Financing of Congressional Races," *Congressional Quarterly,* April 16, 1977, 709.
4. *Congressional Quarterly,* August 6, 1977, 1681; Senate Vote 320.
5. For a description of bills introduced in the 97th Congress, see Joseph E. Cantor, *Political Action Committees: Their Evolution and Growth and Their Implications for the Political System* (Washington, D.C.: Congressional Research Service, Report No. 82-92 GOV, November 6, 1981, updated May 7, 1982), 194-210.
6. See the analysis by University of Illinois law professor John Nowak, inserted in Ex-

tension of Remarks by Representative Guy Vander Jagt in *Congressional Record,* September 25, 1979, E4745. Cited by Cantor, *Political Action Committees,* 201.

7. These points were made explicitly by business PAC managers and consultants in 1982 congressional testimony. Gregg Ward, director of governmental affairs for the Sheet Metal and Air Conditioning Contractors National Association, told the House Administration Committee's Task Force on Elections on June 10, 1982: "We believe reducing the maximum levels would have the counterproductive effect of increasing the emphasis of independent expenditures, which smaller organizations do not have ready access to." PAC consultant Michael Dunn seconded this point: "If PACs cannot contribute in a key congressional race because the candidate they support has already received the limit of PAC contributions, you can be sure that the money will be spent through constitutionally protected independent expenditures which have no limits." U.S. House of Representatives, Committee on House Administration, Task Force on Elections, 97th Cong., 2d sess., *Hearings On Contribution Limitations and Independent Expenditures,* June 10 and July 28, 1982, 74 (Ward) and 85 (Dunn). Also see Jones's chapter in this volume: "In states such as Montana, where PACs are limited in how much they can contribute to each candidate directly, PACs chose to make the maximum direct contribution and then to contribute indirectly by managing voter canvasses and get-out-the-vote drives and by providing technical assistance to candidate committees" (pp. 190-91).

8. Elizabeth Drew, *Politics and Money: The New Road to Corruption* (New York: Macmillan, 1983), 1. First published in the *New Yorker,* December 6, 1982, 54.

9. The next six paragraphs are adapted from Michael J. Malbin, "The Problem of PAC-Journalism," *Public Opinion,* December/January 1983, 15-16.

10. I have argued this point previously in Michael J. Malbin, "Of Mountains and Mole-hills: PACs, Campaigns and Public Policy," in *Parties, Interest Groups, and Campaign Finance Laws,* ed. Michael J. Malbin (Washington, D.C.: American Enterprise Institute, 1980), 152-84 and 211-16.

11. George Thayer, *Who Shakes the Money Tree? American Campaign Financing Practices from 1789 to the Present* (New York: Simon and Schuster, 1973), 26-28.

12. Ibid., 49.

13. Louise Overacker, *Money in Elections* (New York: Macmillan, 1932), chap. 6.

14. Herbert E. Alexander, *Financing the 1972 Election* (Lexington, Mass.: Heath, 1976), appendix X, 707-10.

15. U.S. Senate, 93rd Cong., 2d sess., Select Committee on Presidential Campaign Activities, *Presidential Campaign Activities of 1972—The Final Report,* SRept 93-981, June 1974, 612-21 and 743. The committee's full report on the milk fund fills pp. 579-743. Hereinafter cited as the Ervin Committee Report.

16. Ibid., 544. See also Alexander, *Financing the 1972 Election,* 469.

17. For details, see Ervin Committee Report, 544-50.

18. Alexander, *Financing the 1972 Election,* 405-7.

19. Ervin Committee Report, 505.

20. Ibid., 505-7. The figures in brackets are derived from a table at ibid., 508-10. The $40 million budget figure used by the Ervin committee was obtained from a planning document written in the spring of 1971. Actual expenditures were computed by Alexander as $61.4 million, including expenditures by the Republican National Committee and other committees. McGovern's 1972 expenditures were $42 million. See Alexander, *Financing the 1972 Election,* 271-72.

21. According to a survey of corporate PACs conducted by Edward Handler and John R. Mulkern, the average contribution to a corporate PAC is $288 per year for top managers, $137 for middle managers, and $83 for those in the lower echelons. These averages do not count employees who fail to contribute at all. According to the authors, one out of three do not give to PACs that solicit only top managers, three out of four do not give when middle management is solicited, and nine out of ten do not give when solicitations reach lower echelons. Handler and Mulkern, *Business in Politics* (Lexington, Mass.: Heath, 1982), 46 and 52.

22. Remarks before the National Capital Area Political Science Association, December 7, 1982.

23. Drew, *Politics and Money,* 38-43.

24. Candice J. Nelson, "Counting the Cash: PAC Contributions to Members of the House of Representatives" (paper delivered at the annual meeting of the American Political Science Association, September 2-5, 1982); and James B. Kau and Paul H. Rubin, *Congressmen, Constituents and Contributors* (Boston: Martinus Nijhoff, 1982).

25. Henry W. Chappell, Jr., "Campaign Contributions and Voting on the Cargo Preference Bill: A Comparison of Simultaneous Models," *Public Choice* 36 (1981): 301-12; W.P. Welch, "Campaign Contributions and Voting: Milk Money and Dairy Price Supports," *Western Political Quarterly* 35 (December 1982): 478-95; and John P. Frendreis and Richard W. Waterman, "PAC Contributions and Legislative Behavior: Senate Voting on Trucking Deregulation" (paper delivered at the annual convention of the Midwest Political Science Association, April 20-22, 1983).

26. Frendreis and Waterman, "PAC Contributions and Legislative Behavior," 28.

27. Testimony before the Election Task Force of the House Administration Committee, June 9, 1983; not published at the time of this writing.

28. Simon Lazarus, "PAC Power? They Keep on Losing," *Washington Post,* March 27, 1983, B1-B2.

29. Timothy B. Clark, "The Public and the Private Sectors—The Old Distinctions Grow Fuzzy," *National Journal,* January 9, 1980, 104.

30. Atlee K. Shidler, *Local Community and National Government* (Washington, D.C.: Greater Washington Research Center, 1980), 19.

31. Clark, "The Public and the Private Sectors," 104.

32. Conversation with Raymond L. Hoewing of the Public Affairs Council, July 12, 1983.

33. *Association Trends,* July 8, 1983, sec. 2, p. 2.

34. Ibid.

35. Shidler, *Local Community and National Government,* 20, from information provided by the D.C. Bar.

36. Information provided by the D.C. Bar.

37. Shidler, in *Local Community and National Government,* 18, said "only a few" state governments had offices in Washington in 1970 and two-thirds had them in 1980. Over 100 cities and towns were directly represented in 1980, two or three times the number in 1970.

38. Jack Walker, "Origins and Maintenance of Interest Groups in America," *American Political Science Review* 77, no. 2 (June 1983): 390-406.

39. Both quotes are in Charles Mohr, "Grass-Roots Lobby Aids Business," *New York Times,* April 17, 1978, A1.

40. See R. Douglas Arnold, "The Local Roots of Domestic Policy," in *The New Congress,* ed. Thomas E. Mann and Norman J. Ornstein (Washington, D.C.: American Enterprise Institute, 1981), 250-87.

41. "Grassroots Lobbying Ups Competition," *Association Trends,* July 8, 1983, sec. 2, p. 1.

42. The figure is from William J. Lanouette, "Chamber's Ponderous Decision Making Leaves It Sitting on the Sidelines," *National Journal,* July 24, 1982, 1298-1301. It includes $4 million to expand the Chamber's radio and television studios and $1 million for satellite transmission equipment.

43. Elizabeth Wehr, "White House's Lobbying Apparatus Produces Impressive Tax Vote Victory," *Congressional Quarterly,* August 1, 1981, 1372-73.

44. Harrison Donnelly, "Organized Labor Found 1978 a Frustrating Year, Had Few Victories in Congress," *Congressional Quarterly,* December 30, 1978, 3539-42.

45. James W. Singer, "Labor and Business Heat Up the Senate Labor Law Reform Battle," *National Journal,* June 3, 1978, 884-85.

46. Margaret Garrard Warner and James A. White, "AT&T Cranks Up a $2 Million Blitz to Defend Its Antitrust Settlement," *Wall Street Journal,* April 12, 1982, 25.

47. Robert Pear, "Critics Say Reagan Medicare Cuts Would Only Shift Hospital Costs," *New York Times,* March 3, 1982, A21.

48. "S & L Group Takes Some Credit for Its Ad's Effect on Congress," *Wall Street Journal,* June 25, 1981, 29.

49. Robert D. Hershey, Jr., "Insurance Lobbying Drive Draws Ire from 'Folks in the Boondocks,'" *New York Times,* May 20, 1983, A18.

50. Bill Keller, "Computers and Laser Printers Have Recast the Injunction: 'Write Your Congressman,'" *Congressional Quarterly,* September 11, 1982, 2245-47.

51. James Wilson, *Political Organizations* (New York: Basic Books, 1973), chaps. 15-16.

52. See Jerry Knight, "Commodity Trading PACs Gave to Tax Unit Members Before Vote," *Washington Post,* August 8, 1981, A5.

53. See James M. Perry, "How Realtors' PAC Rewards Office Seekers Helpful to the Industry," *Wall Street Journal,* August 2, 1982, 1 and 13; John F. Bibby, ed., *Congress off the Record: The Candid Analyses of Seven Members* (Washington, D.C.: American Enterprise Institute, 1983), 33-34.

54. Ibid., 34, 46.

55. "FEC Releases Final Report on 1980 Presidential Primary Activity" (Federal Election Commission press release, November 15, 1981).

56. Michael J. Malbin, "Labor, Business and Money—A Post-Election Analysis," *National Journal,* March 17, 1977, 412-17.

57. In the 1978 case of *Republican National Committee* v. *Federal Election Commission,* the RNC unsuccessfully tried to use labor expenditures as one ground for arguing the unconstitutionality of general election spending limits. 487 F.Supp. 280 (S.D.N.Y.,) *aff'd mem.* 445 U.S. 955 (1980). The case is discussed in Richard Smolka's chapter in this volume. In depositions taken for the case, the AFL-CIO stipulated that it had spent $2,978,303 in activities that benefited President Carter in 1976, the United Auto Workers stipulated $1,994,786.87, and the International Association of Machinists stipulated another $350,000.28. The total for the three was $5,323,990.15.

The interviews with union sources that formed the basis of my 1977 article were not based on the careful auditing that produced the above figures. In my article, unreported spending by the AFL-CIO and UAW were each reported by union sources as $3 million and the National Education Association as $400,000. Adding these to reported communication costs produced a figure of $8.3 million. The remainder of the $11 million was nothing more than a "guesstimate" by people in labor of the sum of all unreported activities by the IAM, Garment Workers, and others.

In 1980, reported communication costs by labor were even less revealing than they were in 1976. That is because the FEC does not require reporting unless half of a publication is devoted to advocating the election of a candidate. Many unions in 1980 devoted the front page of their newspapers to supporting President Carter, put other items on the remaining three pages, and reported nothing.

58. Francis X. Clines, "Iowa Democratic Caucus: Union vs. Union," *New York Times,* January 15, 1980, D15; and David S. Broder and Kathy Sawyer, "Teachers Union Becomes a Powerful Force in Party Politics," *Washington Post,* January 20, 1980, A7.
59. Robert W. Merry, "Teachers Group's Clout on Carter's Behalf Is New Breed of Special-Interest Politics," *Wall Street Journal,* August 13, 1980, 2; Leslie Bennett, "Teachers Show Their Strength at Garden," *New York Times,* August 14, 1980, B3; and Stephen Chapman, "The Teachers' Coup: NEA Seizes Power," *New Republic,* October 11, 1980, 9-11.
60. Michael J. Malbin, "The Conventions, Platforms, and Issue Activists," in *The American Elections of 1980,* ed. Austin Ranney (Washington, D.C.: American Enterprise Institute, 1981), 128-30; and Michael J. Malbin, "The Democrats: A Platform That Carter May Find Awkward to Stand On," *National Journal,* August 23, 1980, 1389-92.
61. Timothy B. Clark, "Carter and the Chiropractors—The Tale of a Political Deal," *National Journal,* February 16, 1980, 269-72.
62. Malbin, "The Conventions, Platforms, and Issue Activists," 105-16 and 120-26.
63. See Polsby, *Consequences of Party Reform,* 132.
64. Ibid., 139, 152-56.
65. See Wilson, *Political Organizations,* 10: "Whatever else organizations seek, they seek to survive."
66. For a recent article with citations, see Walker, "Origins and Maintenance of Interest Groups in America."
67. *Business in Politics;* and "The Governance of Corporate PACs" (paper presented at the annual convention of the American Political Science Association, September 2-5, 1982).
68. Edwin M. Epstein, "PACs and the Modern Political Process" (paper prepared for delivery at a Conference on the Impact of the Modern Corporation, sponsored by the Center for Law and Economic Studies, Columbia University, School of Law, November 12-13, 1982).
69. Frank J. Sorauf, "Accountability in Political Action Committees: Who's In Charge?" (paper presented at the annual meeting of the American Political Science Association, September 2-5, 1982).
70. Ibid., 21.
71. Ibid., 22-23, citing Robert D. Shaw, Jr., "New Right Gave Candidates Little," *Miami Herald,* March 29, 1981, 1A and 20A; and "Direct-Mail Pleas Raise Thousands for Fundraisers, Little for Causes," *Miami Herald,* March 30, 1981, 1A and 4A.

72. The following 11 articles by Robert Timberg appeared in the *Baltimore Sun* on the dates indicated: "The Political Money Machines: Fat, Fancy, Free of Curbs," July 11, 1982; "NCPAC Means Business for Friends on the Right," July 12, 1982; "Insiders in NCPAC Operate Group Like a Family Business," July 13, 1982; "Liberal PROPAC Takes Unaccountability to Audacious Limit," July 14, 1982; "Anti-Abortion PAC Sticks to Fund Raising," July 15, 1982; "PACs, Principles and Profits: This Activist Is a One-Man Band," July 16, 1982; "Hyde Says 'No Thanks' to Aid Proferred by PAC," July 17, 1982; "New PAC Follows Old Financial Game Rules," July 25, 1982; " 'PAC Factory' was a Blueprint for Profits," August 15, 1982; "PACs Could Allow Foreign Role in Elections" (co-authored by Grant Williams), August 29, 1982; "New Right Campaign Operation Bypasses Election Laws," October 17, 1982. The last article cited was about Senator Jesse Helms's National Congressional Club. For a related article, see Irwin B. Arieff, Nadine Cohodas, and Richard Whittle, "Sen. Helms Builds a Machine of Interlinked Organizations to Shape Both Politics, Policy," *Congressional Quarterly,* March 6, 1982, 499-505.

73. *Political Organizations,* chap. 7.

74. *Business and Money,* 27-32.

75. Epstein, "PACs and the Modern Political Process."

76. Handler and Mulkern, *Business and Politics,* chaps. 3-4.

77. Ibid., chap. 3.

78. Walker, "Origin and Maintenance," 392-94.

79. Norman J. Ornstein, Thomas E. Mann, Michael J. Malbin, and John F. Bibby, *Vital Statistics on Congress, 1982* (Washington, D.C.: American Enterprise Institute, 1982), 46, 50.

80. *Hearings on Contribution Limitations and Independent Expenditures,* June 10 and July 28, 1982, 89.

81. Ibid.

82. For some examples, see Thomas J. Foley, "Politicians Reach Out — But Not to Shake Hands," *U.S. News and World Report,* January 7, 1982, 39-40.

83. Consider this analysis of why people attend fund raisers from a *Washington Post* article on PACs: "Most of all, they go because they feel they can't risk not going. 'I run scared,' says William Colley, a lobbying lawyer at Patton, Boggs and Blow. 'I always worry that a member might say "Well gee, Colley used to come to my fund raisers. Why isn't he here at this one?" ' " See Paul Taylor, "Lobbyists' Success at Raising Funds Proves Costly," *Washington Post,* August 2, 1982, A9. For an account of how one incumbent, Senator Quentin Burdick (D-N.D.), used "the congressional buddy system" to raise money from people who did not come before his committee, see Tom Hamburger, "How to Fleece the PACs," *Washington Monthly,* July/August 1983, 27-30.

84. In 1982 House races, the mean expenditure for a challenger defeating an incumbent was about $300,000. This was less than 1980 but more than every year before that (see appendix, table A.5).

A great deal has been written about the fact that campaign expenditures have increased much more quickly than the general rate of inflation in the United States. There are two basic reasons for this. First, it costs a lot more every two years for candidates just to do the same old things. Advertising makes up more than half of a typical budget in a competitive race. According to one professional in the field, the price of a minute of air time has been going up about 40 percent every two years, assuming the same time slot and station. (Conversation with Larry McCarthy, vice-president for politics and public affairs for Ailes Communications, Inc., a political advertising firm, July 26, 1983.) Second, candidates are spending their money on such expensive, new, and effective tools as targeting, computerized telephoning, and tracking polls.

Some people have argued that the cost of campaigning is too high. It should be noted, on the other side, that the money is being spent primarily to communicate with voters, and the expenditures apparently work. In his study of the effect of spending on turnout, Gary W. Copeland found that more spending did mean higher turnout, once other variables were controlled. See "The Effects of Campaign Expenditures on Turnout for Congressional Elections" (paper presented at annual convention of the Midwest Political Science Association, April 28-May 1, 1982).

General election candidates for the House and Senate in 1982 spent a total of $288 million. Newspaper columnist George Will pointed out that this was about the same as McDonald's annual advertising budget, half of Procter & Gamble's annual advertising budget, and about one-fifth of the annual national bill for chewing gum. See "The Political Wars and the Burger Wars," *Washington Post,* November 18, 1982, A19. Perhaps more to the point is that although election campaigns in the United States are longer, more complicated, and more disaggregated than almost anywhere else in the world, the per voter cost of campaigns in this country is only about average when the value of state owned television and party expenditures in other countries is counted. See Howard Penniman in Malbin, *Parties, Interest Groups, and Campaign Finance Laws,* 372.

85. The term is from Hugh Heclo, "Issue Networks and the Executive Establishment," in *The New American Political System,* ed. Anthony King (Washington, D.C.: American Enterprise Institute, 1978), chap. 3.
86. Some PACs may also be said to contribute to decentralization by relying on grass-roots fund raising and volunteers.
87. *Annals of Congress,* 1st Cong., 1st sess., August 15, 1789, 733.
88. See especially the speeches of Hartley, Sherman, and Madison in ibid., 733-34. The motion was defeated by a vote of 10-41; ibid., 747. For an extended discussion of the underlying issue, see Michael J. Malbin, "What Did the Framers Want Congress to Be?" (paper presented at the annual convention of the American Political Science Association, September 2-5, 1982).
89. Polsby, *Consequences of Party Reform,* 124.
90. Aaron Wildavsky, *How to Limit Government Spending* (Berkeley: University of California Press, 1980), 58.

MICHAEL J. MALBIN AND THOMAS W. SKLADONY

# Appendix: Selected Campaign Finance Data, 1974-82

TABLE A.1.
HOUSE CAMPAIGN EXPENDITURES, 1974-82
(NET DOLLARS)

| | 1974 | 1976 | 1978 | 1980 | 1982 |
|---|---|---|---|---|---|
| **All Candidates** | | | | | |
| Total expenditures | 44,051,125 | 60,046,006 | 86,129,169 | 115,222,222 | 174,921,844 |
| Mean expenditure | 53,384 | 73,316 | 109,440 | 153,221 | 228,060 |
| | (N = 810) | (N = 819) | (N = 787) | (N = 752) | (N = 767) |
| Mean, Democrats | 53,993 | 74,563 | 108,986 | 143,277 | 213,369 |
| | (N = 434) | (N = 429) | (N = 416) | (N = 396) | (N = 411) |
| Mean, Republicans | 54,835 | 71,945 | 109,995 | 164,282 | 245,020 |
| | (N = 376) | (N = 390) | (N = 371) | (N = 356) | (N = 356) |
| **Incumbents** | | | | | |
| Mean, all incumbents | 56,539 | 79,398 | 111,159 | 165,081 | 265,001 |
| | (N = 382) | (N = 382) | (N = 377) | (N = 391) | (N = 383) |
| Mean, Democrats | 38,743 | 73,322 | 103,519 | 158,010 | 247,573 |
| | (N = 218) | (N = 254) | (N = 249) | (N = 248) | (N = 216) |
| Mean, Republicans | 80,339 | 91,456 | 126,022 | 177,345 | 287,543 |
| | (N = 163) | (N = 128) | (N = 128) | (N = 143) | (N = 167) |

|  | 1974 | 1976 | 1978 | 1980 | 1982 |
|---|---|---|---|---|---|
| **Challengers** | | | | | |
| Mean, all challengers | 40,015 (N = 323) | 50,795 (N = 335) | 74,802 (N = 299) | 121,751 (N = 277) | 151,717 (N = 270) |
| Mean, Democrats | 59,266 (N = 162) | 46,330 (N = 122) | 70,948 (N = 109) | 93,313 (N = 105) | 141,390 (N = 137) |
| Mean, Republicans | 20,644 (N = 161) | 53,352 (N = 213) | 77,012 (N = 190) | 139,111 (N = 172) | 162,354 (N = 133) |
| **Open seats** | | | | | |
| Mean, all open-seat candidates | 90,426 (N = 106) | 124,506 (N = 102) | 201,049 (N = 111) | 201,790 (N = 84) | 284,476 (N = 114) |
| Mean, Democrats | 99,743 (N = 54) | 145,497 (N = 53) | 211,871 (N = 58) | 180,312 (N = 43) | 256,004 (N = 58) |
| Mean, Republicans | 80,751 (N = 52) | 101,802 (N = 49) | 189,205 (N = 53) | 224,116 (N = 41) | 314,547 (N = 56) |

NOTE: Includes primary and general election expenditures for general election candidates who filed reports with the Federal Election Commission. The 1979 amendments to the Federal Election Campaign Act exempted low-budget (under $5000) campaigns from reporting requirements. A number of low-budget candidates who did file reports are included in the table. However, because of these amendments, the data for 1980 and 1982 are not strictly comparable with previous years.

SOURCES: Compiled from the following sources: For 1974, Common Cause, 1974 Congressional Campaign Finances, vol. 2 (Washington, D.C., 1976). For 1976, Federal Election Commission, Disclosure Series No. 9 (House of Representatives Campaigns), September 1977. For 1978, Federal Election Commission, Reports on Financial Activity, 1977-78, Interim Report No. 5 (U.S. Senate and House Campaigns), June 1979. For 1980, Federal Election Commission, Reports on Financial Activity, 1979-80, Final Report (U.S. House and Senate Campaigns), January 1982. For 1982, Federal Election Commission, Reports on Financial Activity, 1981-82, Interim Report No. 3 (U.S. Senate and House Campaigns), May 1983.

TABLE A.2.
HOUSE CANDIDATES WITH NET EXPENDITURES GREATER THAN $200,000, 1974-82

|  | Democratic | Republican | Total |
|---|---|---|---|
| 1974 | 6 | 4 | 10 |
| 1976 | 15 | 16 | 31 |
| 1978 | 60 | 68 | 128 |
| 1980 | 91 | 114 | 205 |
| 1982 | 170 | 183 | 353 |

SOURCES: Same as table A.1.

Number of Candidates

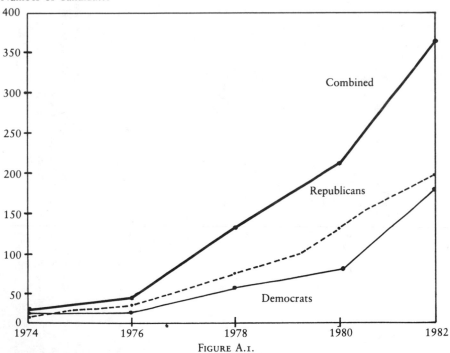

FIGURE A.1.
HOUSE CANDIDATES WITH NET EXPENDITURES GREATER THAN $200,000, 1974-82

# Appendix: Selected Campaign Finance Data, 1974-82

TABLE A.3.
HOUSE CANDIDATES WITH NET EXPENDITURES GREATER THAN $500,000, 1974-82

|  | Democratic | Republican | Total |
|---|---|---|---|
| 1974 | — | — | — |
| 1976 | — | — | — |
| 1978 | 3 | 4 | 7 |
| 1980 | 15 | 13 | 28 |
| 1982 | 31 | 36 | 67 |

SOURCES: Same as table A.1.

Number of Candidates

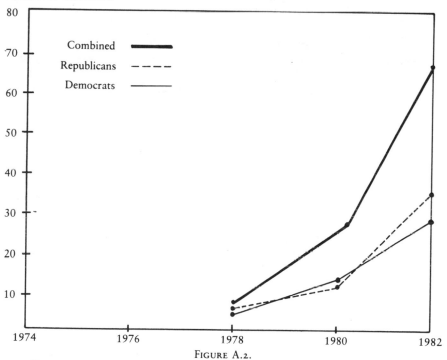

FIGURE A.2.
HOUSE CANDIDATES WITH NET EXPENDITURES GREATER THAN $500,000, 1974-82

## TABLE A.4.
## SENATE CAMPAIGN EXPENDITURES, 1974-82
### (NET DOLLARS)

|  | 1974 | 1976 | 1978 | 1980 | 1982 |
|---|---|---|---|---|---|
| **All Candidates** | | | | | |
| Total expenditures | 28,436,308 | 38,108,745 | 64,695,510 | 74,163,669 | 114,036,379 |
| Mean expenditure | 437,482 (N = 65) | 595,449[a] (N = 64) | 951,405 (N = 68) | 1,106,920 (N = 67) | 1,781,815 (N = 64) |
| Mean, Democrats | 487,775 (N = 34) | 569,902 (N = 33) | 762,831 (N = 35) | 1,170,580 (N = 34) | 1,881,379[b] (N = 32) |
| Mean, Republicans | 382,343 (N = 31) | 616,635 (N = 30) | 1,151,407 (N = 33) | 1,041,332 (N = 33) | 1,682,252[b] (N = 32) |
| **Incumbents** | | | | | |
| Mean, all incumbents | 555,714 (N = 25) | 623,809[a] (N = 25) | 1,341,942[c] (N = 22) | 1,301,692 (N = 25) | 1,858,140 (N = 29) |
| Mean, Democrats | 525,766 (N = 15) | 503,111 (N = 17) | 618,211[d] (N = 11) | 1,355,660[e] (N = 19) | 1,696,226[b] (N = 18) |
| Mean, Republicans | 600,636 (N = 10) | 891,342 (N = 7) | 2,065,674[c] (N = 11) | 1,130,792 (N = 6) | 2,123,089 (N = 11) |
| **Challengers** | | | | | |
| Mean, all challengers | 332,579 (N = 22) | 452,275 (N = 23) | 697,766 (N = 21) | 842,547 (N = 24) | 1,217,034 (N = 29) |

| | | | | | |
|---|---|---|---|---|---|
| Mean, Democrats | 390,297 (N = 10) | 645,441 (N = 8) | 830,282 (N = 11) | 557,006 (N = 6) | 1,516,015 (N = 11) |
| Mean, Republicans | 284,480 (N = 12) | 349,253 (N = 15) | 551,999 (N = 10) | 937,727 (N = 18) | 1,034,324[b] (N = 18) |
| **Open Seats** | | | | | |
| Mean, all open-seat candidates | 401,484 (N = 18) | 756,951 (N = 16) | 820,787 (N = 25) | 1,132,560 (N = 18) | 4,142,687 (N = 6) |
| Mean, Democrats | 532,691 (N = 9) | 636,295 (N = 8) | 828,127 (N = 13) | 1,188,903 (N = 9) | 4,331,959 (N = 3) |
| Mean, Republicans | 270,277 (N = 9) | 877,606 (N = 8) | 812,835 (N = 12) | 1,076,218 (N = 9) | 3,953,415 (N = 3) |

NOTE: Includes primary and general election expenditures for general election candidates only.

SOURCES: Compiled from the following sources: For 1974, Common Cause, 1974 *Congressional Campaign Finances*, vol. 1 (Washington, D.C., 1976). For 1976, Federal Election Commission, *Disclosure Series No. 6 (Senatorial Campaigns)*, September 1977. For 1978, Federal Election Commission, *Reports on Financial Activity, 1977–78, Interim Report No. 5 (U.S. Senate and House Campaigns)*, June 1979. For 1980, Federal Election Commission, *Reports on Financial Activity, 1979–80, Final Report (U.S. Senate and House Campaigns)*, January 1982. For 1982, Federal Election Commission, *Reports on Financial Activity, 1981–82, Interim Report No. 3 (U.S. Senate and House Campaigns)*, May 1983.

a. Includes one incumbent independent, Senator Harry F. Byrd of Virginia, $802,928.

b. Two candidates did not file reports with the FEC in 1982: incumbent William Proxmire (D-Wisc.) and challenger Clarence J. Brown (R-Hawaii).

c. These figures include the $7.5 million Helms reelection campaign in North Carolina. Without it, the Republican mean would be $1,526,145, and the mean for all incumbents would be $1,650,560.

d. Includes incumbent J. Bennett Johnston (D-La., $857,860), who was unopposed in the general election but faced a primary challenger who spent $327,340.

e. Includes incumbent Russell B. Long (D-La., $2,166,838), who was unopposed in the general election but faced a primary challenger who spent $142,368.

TABLE A.5.
MEAN HOUSE NET CAMPAIGN EXPENDITURES, BY ELECTION OUTCOME, 1974-82
(IN DOLLARS)

| | 1974 | 1976 | 1978 | 1980 | 1982 |
|---|---|---|---|---|---|
| **Incumbent Won with 60% or More[a]** | | | | | |
| Democratic | 35,146 | 56,937 | 85,424 | 117,773[b] | 206,670 |
| incumbent | (N = 194) | (N = 185) | (N = 184) | (N = 170) | (N = 178) |
| Republican | 12,481 | 24,865 | 32,850 | 50,213 | 110,454 |
| challenger | (N = 137) | (N = 144) | (N = 125) | (N = 95) | (N = 101) |
| Republican | 60,593 | 77,855 | 105,687 | 138,050 | 186,717 |
| incumbent | (N = 57) | (N = 87) | (N = 103) | (N = 114) | (N = 86) |
| Democratic | 25,891 | 26,606 | 36,040 | 44,120 | 36,628 |
| challenger | (N = 56) | (N = 81) | (N = 84) | (N = 75) | (N = 62) |
| Difference between | 32,023 | 42,968 | 68,031 | 101,021 | 143,277 |
| incumbents and | (N = 192) | (N = 226) | (N = 209) | (N = 170) | (N = 163) |
| challengers[c] | | | | | |
| | | | | | |
| **Incumbent Won with Less Than 60%** | | | | | |
| Democratic | 68,513 | 119,440 | 145,065 | 223,345 | 446,542[d] |
| incumbent | (N = 20) | (N = 62) | (N = 51) | (N = 50) | (N = 35) |
| Republican | 66,405 | 109,079 | 144,347 | 198,728 | 324,647[d] |
| challenger | (N = 20) | (N = 62) | (N = 51) | (N = 50) | (N = 31) |
| Republican | 83,632 | 104,465 | 204,674 | 336,046 | 361,295[d] |
| incumbent | (N = 70) | (N = 36) | (N = 20) | (N = 26) | (N = 55) |
| Democratic | 63,134 | 77,075 | 187,290 | 195,135 | 182,232[d] |
| challenger | (N = 70) | (N = 36) | (N = 20) | (N = 26) | (N = 53) |
| Difference between | 16,747 | 16,616 | 5,412 | 64,402 | 144,951 |
| incumbents and | (N = 90) | (N = 98) | (N = 71) | (N = 76) | (N = 84) |
| challengers[c] | | | | | |
| | | | | | |
| **Incumbent Was Defeated** | | | | | |
| Democratic | 64,191 | 97,874 | 189,994 | 285,636 | 353,201[d] |
| incumbent | (N = 4) | (N = 7) | (N = 14) | (N = 28) | (N = 3) |
| Republican | 71,404 | 144,883 | 226,028 | 341,499 | 373,093[d] |
| challenger | (N = 4) | (N = 7) | (N = 14) | (N = 27) | (N = 1) |
| Republican | 105,203 | 234,435 | 230,323 | 295,170 | 465,027[d] |
| incumbent | (N = 36) | (N = 5) | (N = 5) | (N = 3) | (N = 26) |
| Democratic | 103,661 | 144,491 | 192,037 | 353,855 | 292,781[d] |
| challenger | (N = 36) | (N = 5) | (N = 5) | (N = 4) | (N = 22) |
| Difference between | 1,185 | 10,055 | − 16,476 | − 56,537 | 123,361 |
| incumbents and | (N = 40) | (N = 12) | (N = 19) | (N = 31) | (N = 23) |
| challengers[c] | | | | | |

TABLE·A.5. *(continued)*

SOURCES: Same as table A.1.
   a. Percentage of the vote received by the two leading candidates.
   b. For reasons explained in the note to table A.1, a number of nonfiling candidates with low-budget campaigns are not included.
   c. Includes only races contested in the general election, both candidates filing.
   d. The number of challengers does not equal that of incumbents because of six incumbent-incumbent races in 1982 due to redistricting. The mean expenditure for Democrats in these races was $585,205; for Republicans, $592,080. The mean expenditure for winners (4 Democrats, 2 Republicans) was $600,337; for losers, $583,824.

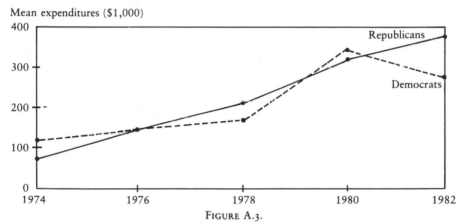

Mean expenditures ($1,000)

FIGURE A.3.
MEAN NET EXPENDITURES OF HOUSE CHALLENGERS WHO BEAT INCUMBENTS, 1974-82

## Table A.6.
### Mean Senate Net Campaign Expenditures, by Election Outcome, 1974-82 (in dollars)

| | 1974 | 1976 | 1978 | 1980 | 1982 |
|---|---|---|---|---|---|
| **Incumbent Won with 60% or More[a]** | | | | | |
| Democratic incumbent | 447,234 (N = 11) | 340,362 (N = 11) | 559,046[b] (N = 4) | 1,220,616[c] (N = 6) | 1,401,794 (N = 12) |
| Republican challenger | 222,955 (N = 8) | 171,997 (N = 9) | 56,233 (N = 3) | 332,404 (N = 5) | 807,276 (N = 12) |
| Republican incumbent | — | — | 318,749 (N = 3) | 1,075,038 (N = 4) | 2,607,983 (N = 1) |
| Democratic challenger | — | — | 38,458 (N = 3) | 265,822 (N = 4) | 424,507 (N = 1) |
| Difference between incumbents and challengers[d] | 299,321 (N = 8) | 220,202 (N = 9) | 341,750 (N = 6) | 747,967 (N = 9) | 739,686 (N = 12) |
| **Incumbent Won with Less Than 60%** | | | | | |
| Democratic incumbent | 741,729 (N = 4) | 1,237,910 (N = 1) | 586,055 (N = 2) | 796,984 (N = 4) | 2,417,100 (N = 5) |
| Republican challenger | 407,531 (N = 4) | 665,058 (N = 1) | 332,537 (N = 2) | 727,617 (N = 4) | 1,589,864 (N = 5) |
| Republican incumbent | 497,945 (N = 10) | 320,239 (N = 4) | 3,133,293[e] (N = 6) | 1,242,300 (N = 2) | 2,117,088 (N = 9) |
| Democratic challenger | 254,374 (N = 10) | 282,441 (N = 4) | 1,212,929 (N = 6) | 1,139,376 (N = 2) | 1,629,490 (N = 9) |

| | | | | | |
|---|---|---|---|---|---|
| Difference between incumbents and challengers[d] | 314,376 (N = 14) | 241,346[f] (N = 5) | 1,503,653[g] (N = 8) | 80,553 (N = 6) | 608,897 (N = 14) |
| **Incumbent Was Defeated** | | | | | |
| Democratic incumbent | — | 714,201 (N = 5) | 678,406 (N = 5) | 1,693,991 (N = 9) | 1,625,042 (N = 1) |
| Republican challenger | — | 605,153 (N = 5) | 937,244 (N = 5) | 1,367,400 (N = 9) | 981,197 (N = 1) |
| Republican incumbent | 513,456 (N = 2) | 1,319,440 (N = 4) | 1,483,203 (N = 2) | — | 1,692,204 (N = 1) |
| Democratic challenger | 679,514 (N = 2) | 1,008,440 (N = 4) | 870,079 (N = 2) | — | 1,586,245 (N = 1) |
| Difference between incumbents and challengers[d] | -166,158 (N = 2) | 198,906 (N = 9) | -9,706 (N = 7) | 326,591 (N = 9) | 374,902 (N = 2) |

SOURCES: Same as table A.4.

a. Percentage of the vote received by the two leading candidates.

b. Includes incumbent J. Bennett Johnston (D-La., $857,860), who was unopposed in the general election but faced a primary challenger who spent $327,340.

c. Includes incumbent Russell B. Long (D-La., $2,166,838), who was unopposed in the general election but faced a primary challenger who spent $142,368.

d. Includes only races contested in the general election, both candidates filing.

e. If one excludes the 1978 race between Republican Senator Jesse Helms of North Carolina and his challenger, John Ingram, this figure becomes $2,267,758.

f. 1976 Senate incumbents who won with less than 60% included one independent, Senator Harry F. Byrd of Virginia, who spent $802,928.

g. If the Helms-Ingram race is excluded, this figure becomes $690,335.

TABLE A.7.
FUNDING SOURCES FOR GENERAL ELECTION CANDIDATES
IN HOUSE AND SENATE ELECTIONS, BY PARTY, 1974-82
(INCLUDING COORDINATED PARTY EXPENDITURES)

| | Amount Raised by Candidates and Party Expenditures on Behalf of Candidates (in millions)[a] | Percentage Distribution | | | |
|---|---|---|---|---|---|
| | | Nonparty PACs | Party (contributions plus 441a[d] expenditures)[a] | Individual Contributions $500+ | Other (individuals to $500, candidate to self, and unrepaid loans)[b] |
| **HOUSE** | | | | | |
| 1974[c] | | | | | |
| All candidates | $45.7 | 17 | 4 | 15 | 64 |
| Democrats | 23.9 | 22 | 1 | 16 | 61 |
| Republicans | 21.7 | 10 | 7 | 15 | 68 |
| 1976 | | | | | |
| All candidates[d] | 66.1 | 22 | 8 | 11 | 59 |
| Democrats | 35.1 | 27 | 4 | 11 | 58 |
| Republicans | 30.5 | 17 | 13 | 11 | 59 |
| 1978[e] | | | | | |
| All candidates[d] | 93.6 | 24 | 7 | 12 | 57 |
| Democrats | 48.7 | 27 | 3 | 13 | 57 |
| Republicans | 44.2 | 22 | 11 | 12 | 55 |
| 1980[e] | | | | | |
| All candidates[d] | 127.1 | 28 | 6 | 15 | 51 |
| Democrats | 61.4 | 32 | 2 | 17 | 49 |
| Republicans | 64.6 | 25 | 9 | 13 | 53 |
| 1982[e] | | | | | |
| All candidates[d] | 191.0 | 30 | 6 | — 64 | — |
| Democrats | 94.6 | 34 | 2 | — 64 | — |
| Republicans | 96.3 | 27 | 10 | — 63 | — |
| **SENATE** | | | | | |
| 1974[c] | | | | | |
| All candidates | $28.2 | 11 | 6 | 27 | 56 |
| Democrats | 16.2 | 13 | 2 | 27 | 58 |
| Republicans | 11.6 | 7 | 13 | 28 | 52 |
| 1976 | | | | | |
| All candidates[d] | 39.2 | 15 | 4 | 27 | 54 |
| Democrats | 19.5 | 19 | 2 | 32 | 47 |
| Republicans | 18.8 | 11 | 6 | 22 | 61 |
| 1978[e] | | | | | |
| All candidates[d] | 68.9 | 13 | 6 | 21 | 60 |
| Democrats | 27.8 | 14 | 3 | 27 | 56 |
| Republicans | 40.6 | 12 | 8 | 17 | 63 |

TABLE A.7. *(continued)*

| | | | | | |
|---|---|---|---|---|---|
| 1980[e] | | | | | |
| All candidates[d] | 83.5 | 19 | 9 | 24 | 48 |
| Democrats | 42.0 | 18 | 4 | 27 | 51 |
| Republicans | 41.2 | 21 | 15 | 21 | 43 |
| 1982[e] | | | | | |
| All candidates[d] | 128.2 | 17 | 9 | — | 74 | — |
| Democrats | 64.5 | 17 | 4 | — | 79 | — |
| Republicans | 63.4 | 17 | 16 | — | 68 | — |

NOTE: The figures in this table differ from those in text table 2.1. These figures include coordinated party expenditures, and those in table 2.1 do not.

SOURCES: Compiled from the following sources: For 1974, Gary C. Jacobson, *Money in Congressional Elections* (New Haven: Yale University Press, 1980), chap. 3. For 1976, Federal Election Commission, *Disclosure Series No. 4* (National Party Committees), *No. 6* (Senate Campaigns) and *No. 9* (House Campaigns), September 1977. For 1978, Federal Election Commission, *Reports on Financial Activity, 1977-78, Interim Report No. 5* (U.S. Senate and House Campaigns), June 1979, 31-32. For 1980, Federal Election Commission, *Reports on Financial Activity, 1979-80, Final Report* (U.S. Senate and House Campaigns), January 1982, 49-50. For 1982, Federal Election Commission, *Reports on Financial Activity, 1981-82, Interim Report No. 3* (U.S. Senate and House Campaigns), May 1983, 33-34.

   a. The "amount raised" column includes the sum of what general election candidates raised from January 1 of the odd-numbered year preceding an election through December 31 of the election year plus 441a(d) party expenditures on behalf of those candidates. The 441a(d) expenditures for each year are given in table A.10.
   b. "Other" includes contributions from individuals of less than $500, contributions from the candidate to himself or herself, unrepaid loans and, for the 1974 Senate races, some funds whose sources were not identified. Because of confusion over unrepaid loans, the FEC says that it cannot specify loan amounts or candidate self-financing and that its numbers from 1976 and 1978 are unreliable. This also affects the data for small individual contributions, many of which need not be reported individually because those figures had been derived by subtracting all other categories from the total.
   c. The figures for 1974 are only for candidates who were opposed in the general election.
   d. Includes minor-party candidates.
   e. Louisiana instituted a two-step election process in 1978 in which candidates of all parties run against each other in a September primary. If no candidate wins 50% or more of the vote at that time, the top two candidates run against each other in November. In these data, candidates in a September Louisiana primary are considered "general election candidates" when the September balloting produces a clear winner with more than half the total vote.

TABLE A.8.

FUNDING SOURCES FOR GENERAL ELECTION CANDIDATES IN 1982 HOUSE AND SENATE ELECTIONS, BY PARTY AND CANDIDATE STATUS

| Party and Candidate Status | Number of Candidates | Amount Raised by Candidates plus Party Expenditures on Behalf of Candidates (in millions) | Total Party Contributions plus 441a(d) Expenditures | Percentage Distribution | | | | | | |
|---|---|---|---|---|---|---|---|---|---|---|
| | | | | Total PAC Contributions | Corporate PAC | Labor PAC | Trade/ Membership/ Health PAC | Non-connected PAC | Coop and Corp. w/o Stock PAC | Individuals Candidate to Self, and Other |
| HOUSE | | | | | | | | | | |
| All Candidates[a] | 830 | $191.0 | 6.1 | 30.2 | 9.5 | 7.6 | 8.3 | 3.6 | 1.3 | 63.7 |
| Democrats | 435 | 94.6 | 1.8 | 33.9 | 6.9 | 14.6 | 7.0 | 3.8 | 1.3 | 64.3 |
| Incumbents | 218 | 59.1 | 1.1 | 37.6 | 9.9 | 13.1 | 9.1 | 3.3 | 2.1 | 61.3 |
| Challengers | 166 | 21.7 | 3.7 | 27.8 | 0.8 | 18.7 | 2.7 | 5.0 | 0.5 | 68.5 |
| Open seats | 51 | 13.9 | 2.0 | 27.6 | 3.5 | 14.9 | 4.3 | 4.0 | 1.0 | 70.4 |
| Republicans | 395 | 96.3 | 10.3 | 26.5 | 12.0 | 0.7 | 9.6 | 3.4 | 1.0 | 63.2 |
| Incumbents | 168 | 53.3 | 7.9 | 33.0 | 15.3 | 1.1 | 12.5 | 2.5 | 1.5 | 59.1 |
| Challengers | 176 | 24.9 | 14.0 | 17.0 | 6.7 | 0.0 | 5.1 | 4.9 | 0.2 | 69.0 |
| Open seats | 51 | 18.1 | 12.1 | 20.8 | 9.2 | 0.4 | 7.0 | 3.7 | 0.4 | 67.1 |

SENATE

| | | | | | | | | | |
|---|---|---|---|---|---|---|---|---|---|
| All Candidates[a] | 66 | $128.2 | 9.5 | 16.9 | 6.4 | 3.7 | 3.8 | 2.5 | 0.5 | 73.6 |
| Democrats | 33 | 64.5 | 4.4 | 16.7 | 3.6 | 6.9 | 3.2 | 2.4 | 0.6 | 78.8 |
| Incumbents | 19 | 33.4 | 4.2 | 23.5 | 6.4 | 8.0 | 5.4 | 2.6 | 1.0 | 72.3 |
| Challengers | 11 | 17.4 | 5.2 | 11.8 | 0.3 | 7.5 | 1.0 | 2.7 | 0.3 | 83.0 |
| Open seats | 3 | 13.6 | 3.7 | 6.2 | 0.8 | 3.2 | 0.7 | 1.4 | 0.1 | 90.1 |
| Republicans | 33 | 63.4 | 14.7 | 17.2 | 9.3 | 0.6 | 4.3 | 2.5 | 0.4 | 68.1 |
| Incumbents | 11 | 25.9 | 8.7 | 24.6 | 13.1 | 1.2 | 7.2 | 2.5 | 0.6 | 66.7 |
| Challengers | 19 | 23.5 | 21.3 | 11.4 | 6.0 | 0.1 | 2.1 | 3.1 | 0.1 | 67.3 |
| Open seats | 3 | 14.1 | 14.8 | 13.1 | 7.9 | 0.2 | 2.7 | 1.6 | 0.6 | 72.1 |

SOURCE: Compiled from "FEC Releases Data on 1981–1982 Elections," Federal Election Commission Press Release, May 2, 1983. The official *Reports on Financial Activity* cited in table A.7 do not subdivide incumbents, challengers, and open-seat candidates by party. FEC press releases did not subdivide them before the 1982 election.

a. Includes minor-party candidates.

TABLE A.9.
POLITICAL PARTY FINANCIAL ACTIVITY, 1976-82

| | Adjusted Receipts | Adjusted Disbursements | Contributions to Presidential, Senate, and House Candidates | Expenditures on Behalf of Presidential, Senate, and House Candidates |
|---|---|---|---|---|
| **1976** | | | | |
| Democratic | | | | |
| National committee | $13,095,630 | $12,516,979 | $22,050 | $3,055,644 |
| Senatorial | 1,017,454 | 971,562 | 375,237 | 4,359 |
| Congressional | 937,717 | 1,011,157 | 423,200 | 500 |
| Conventions, other national | 3,164,573 | 3,062,675 | 0 | 0 |
| State/local | N.A. | N.A. | N.A. | N.A. |
| Total Democratic | $18,215,374 | $17,562,373 | $820,487 | $3,060,503 |
| Republican | | | | |
| National committee | $29,118,930 | $26,679,143 | $1,871,726 | $1,442,773 |
| Senatorial | 1,774,815 | 2,010,629 | 445,902 | 113,976 |
| Congressional | 12,207,055 | 9,243,195 | 2,071,525 | 329,853 |
| Conventions, other national | 2,605,088 | 2,143,220 | 11,343 | 0 |
| State/local | N.A. | N.A. | N.A. | N.A. |
| Total Republican | $45,705,888 | $40,076,187 | $4,400,496 | $1,886,602 |
| **1978** | | | | |
| Democratic | | | | |
| National committee | $11,314,008 | $11,455,639 | $64,307 | $68,822 |
| Senatorial | 269,981 | 893,773 | 427,000 | 0 |
| Congressional | 2,766,963 | 2,118,161 | 537,438 | 0 |
| Conventions, other national | 3,324,519 | 3,428,481 | 403,502 | 0 |
| State/local | 8,688,999 | 8,994,213 | 433,337 | 329,765 |
| Total Democratic | $26,364,470 | $26,890,267 | $1,865,584 | $398,587 |
| Republican | | | | |
| National committee | $34,221,058 | $36,016,600 | $905,244 | $366,981 |
| Senatorial | 10,882,480 | 11,107,961 | 456,110 | 2,599,290 |
| Congressional | 14,062,070 | 15,695,690 | 1,817,424 | 839,421 |
| Conventions, other national | 4,400,216 | 2,330,882 | 598,382 | 0 |
| State/local | 20,960,029 | 20,728,829 | 745,191 | 579,974 |
| Total Republican | $84,525,853 | $85,879,962 | $4,522,351 | $4,355,666 |
| **1980** | | | | |
| Democratic | | | | |
| National committee | $15,418,300 | $15,150,984 | $41,051 | $3,942,526 |
| Senatorial | 1,653,849 | 1,618,162 | 481,500 | 589,316 |
| Congressional | 2,864,088 | 2,828,184 | 614,097 | 34,686 |

TABLE A.9. *(continued)*

| | | | | |
|---|---|---|---|---|
| Conventions, other national | 8,147,837 | 6,631,517 | 132,200 | 0 |
| State/local | 9,103,520 | 8,754,177 | 384,358 | 375,660 |
| Total Democratic | $37,187,594 | $34,983,024 | $1,653,206 | $4,942,188 |
| **Republican** | | | | |
| National committee | $77,838,238 | $75,821,719 | $844,455 | $5,352,269 |
| Senatorial | 22,308,963 | 21,211,482 | 414,893 | 5,025,802 |
| Congressional | 20,287,961 | 34,790,731 | 2,005,663 | 1,229,110 |
| Conventions, other national | 6,031,367 | 6,080,735 | 482,159 | 0 |
| State/local | 33,781,069 | 32,545,199 | 781,207 | 837,292 |
| Total Republican | $161,247,598 | $170,449,866 | $4,528,377 | $12,444,473 |
| | | 1982 | | |
| **Democratic** | | | | |
| National committee | $16,466,029 | $16,547,601 | $124,574 | $144,742 |
| Senatorial | 5,622,254 | 5,568,352 | 530,000 | 1,877,245 |
| Congressional | 6,525,419 | 6,461,703 | 563,105 | 197,936 |
| Conventions, other national | 3,086,023 | 3,838,556 | 0 | 0 |
| State/local | 7,567,985 | 7,731,834 | 546,290 | 1,081,674 |
| Total Democratic | $39,267,710 | $40,148,146 | $1,763,969 | $3,301,597 |
| **Republican** | | | | |
| National committee | $84,140,281 | $85,113,252 | $1,700,178 | $232,964 |
| Senatorial | 48,879,354 | 47,680,853 | 558,327 | 8,707,537 |
| Congressional | 58,041,972 | 57,041,301 | 2,554,924 | 4,943,249 |
| Conventions, other national | 2,967 | 87,246 | 0 | 0 |
| State/local | 23,984,934 | 24,099,337 | 812,787 | 401,213 |
| Total Republican | $215,049,508 | $214,021,989 | $5,626,216 | $14,284,983 |

NOTE: N.A. = not available.

SOURCES: For 1976, compiled from Federal Election Commission, *Disclosure Series No. 4* (National Party Political Committees: Receipts and Expenditures), November 1977, 5-40. For 1978, Federal Election Commission, *Reports on Financial Activity, 1977-78, Final Report* (Party and Non-Party Political Committees), vol. 1, April 1980, 101. For 1980, Federal Election Commission, *Reports on Financial Activity, 1979-80, Final Report* (Party and Non-Party Political Committees), vol. 1, January 1982, 61. For 1982, Federal Election Commission, *Reports on Financial Activity, 1981-82, Final Report* (Party and Non-Party Political Committees), vol. 1, October 1983, 55.

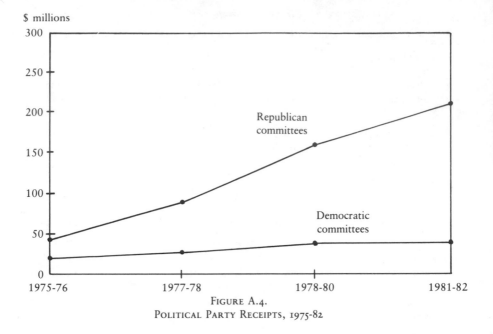

FIGURE A.4.
POLITICAL PARTY RECEIPTS, 1975-82

TABLE A.10.
COORDINATED PARTY EXPENDITURES IN CONGRESSIONAL ELECTIONS,
1976-82, BY OFFICE AND PARTY

|  | Senate | House |
|---|---|---|
| **1976** | | |
| Democrats | $4,359 | $500 |
| Republicans | 113,976 | 329,583 |
| **1978** | | |
| Democrats | 229,218 | 72,892 |
| Republicans | 2,723,880 | 1,247,079 |
| **1980** | | |
| Democrats | 1,132,912 | 256,346 |
| Republicans | 5,434,758 | 2,203,748 |
| **1982** | | |
| Democrats | 2,260,789 | 689,980 |
| Republicans | 8,715,761 | 5,276,868 |

NOTE: Coordinated expenditures are also known as 441a(d)
expenditures because the legal spending limits are
contained in U.S. Code, Title 2, Sec. 441a(d).

SOURCES: Same as table A.7.

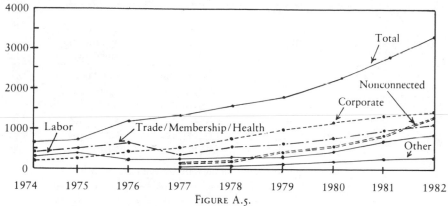

Number of Committees

FIGURE A.5.
GROWTH OF NONPARTY POLITICAL ACTION COMMITTEES, 1974-82

TABLE A.11.
NUMBER OF REGISTERED POLITICAL ACTION COMMITTEES, 1974-82

|  | 1974 | 1976 | 1978 | 1980 | 1982 |
|---|---|---|---|---|---|
| Corporate | 89 | 433 | 784 | 1204 | 1467 |
| Labor | 201 | 224 | 217 | 297 | 380 |
| Trade/membership/<br>health[a] | 318 | 489 | 451 | 574 | 628 |
| Nonconnected | — | — | 165 | 378 | 746 |
| Cooperative | — | — | 12 | 42 | 47 |
| Corporation<br>without stock | — | — | 24 | 56 | 103 |
| TOTAL | 608 | 1146 | 1653 | 2551 | 3371 |

NOTE: Data as of December 31 for every year except 1975 (November 24).

SOURCE: "PACs Increase in Numbers," Federal Election Commission press release, January 14, 1983.

a. Includes all noncorporate and nonlabor PACs through December 31, 1976.

TABLE A.12.

FINANCIAL ACTIVITY OF POLITICAL ACTION COMMITTEES, 1972-82

| Election Cycle[a] | Adjusted Receipts[b] | Adjusted Expenditures[b] | Contributions to Congressional Candidates |
|---|---|---|---|
| 1972 | N.A. | $19,168,000 | $8,500,000[c] |
| 1974 | N.A. | 25,000,000[d] | 12,526,586 |
| 1976 | $54,045,588 | 52,894,630 | 22,571,912 |
| 1978 | 79,956,291 | 77,412,860 | 34,121,356[e] |
| 1980 | 137,728,528 | 131,153,384 | 55,217,211[e] |
| 1982 | 199,452,356 | 190,173,539 | 83,620,190[e] |

NOTE: N.A. = not available. All data are for full election cycle.

SOURCES: For data on receipts and expenditures, see the sources listed for table A.13. For data on contributions, see the sources listed for table A.14.

a. The periods covered by the election cycles vary. Data for 1972 are limited for the period before April 7, 1972, the effective date for disclosure under the Federal Election Campaign Act of 1971. Until then, campaign finance disclosure was governed by the Federal Corrupt Practices Act of 1925, under which much activity went unreported. Data for 1974 cover September 1, 1973, to December 31, 1974. Data for 1976 and for subsequent years cover January 1 of the odd-numbered year to December 31 of the even-numbered year.

b. Adjusted receipts and expenditures exclude funds transferred between affiliated committees.

c. Excludes contributions to candidates defeated in primaries.

d. This is a rough estimate and does not correspond to the total in table A.13, which was thought to be too low.

e. Contributions to candidates for election in the year indicated, made during the two-year election cycle.

# Appendix: Selected Campaign Finance Data, 1974-82

TABLE A.13.
ADJUSTED EXPENDITURES OF POLITICAL ACTION COMMITTEES,
BY CATEGORY, 1972-82 (IN MILLIONS)

| Type of PAC | 1972 | 1974[a] | 1976 | 1978 | 1980 | 1982 |
|---|---|---|---|---|---|---|
| Labor | $8.5 | $11.0 | $17.5 | $18.6 | $25.1 | $34.8 |
| Business-related[b] | 8.0 | 8.1 | — | — | — | — |
| Corporate | c | c | 5.8 | 15.2 | 31.4 | 43.3 |
| Trade/member ship/health | c | c | d | 23.8 | 32.0 | 41.9 |
| Nonconnected[e] | 2.6 | 0.8 | d | 17.4 | 38.6 | 64.3 |
| Other[f] | — | 1.1 | 29.6 | 2.4 | 4.0 | 5.8 |
| TOTAL[g] | $19.2 | $20.9 | $52.9 | $77.4 | $131.2 | $190.2 |

NOTE: Adjusted expenditures exclude transfers of funds between affiliated committees.

SOURCES: For 1972-76 and for footnotes, Joseph E. Cantor, *Political Action Committees: Their Evolution and Growth and Their Implications for the Political System,* U.S. Library of Congress, Congressional Research Service, Report No. 82-92, November 6, 1981, updated May 7, 1982, 83-84. For 1978, Federal Election Commission, *Reports on Financial Activity, 1977-78, Final Report* (Party and Non-Party Political Committees), vol. I, April 1980, 139-40. For 1980, Federal Election Commission, *Reports on Financial Activity, 1979-80, Final Report* (Party and Non-Party Political Committees), vol. I, January 1982, 97-98. For 1982, Federal Election Commission, *Reports on Financial Activity, 1981-82, Final Report* (Party and Non-Party Political Committees), vol. I, October 1983, 90-92.

a. Data for 1974 do not correspond with those in table A.12, which reflects an estimated amount, because the data in this table were thought to be low.

b. This category is based on a large assumption that the majority of PACs it encompasses do indeed have a basically probusiness orientation. It is included here for the purpose of listing the data for 1972 and 1974, before the specific breakdowns were devised by the FEC for the corporate and other categories, and it is only roughly comparable to the combined corporate and trade/membership/health data in 1978-82. For 1972 it includes PACs listed by the Citizens' Research Foundation as business/professional, dairy, education, health, and rural; for 1974 it includes those PACs grouped by Common Cause under the headings of business/professional, health, and agriculture/dairy. Most of these PACs would today fall into the corporate and trade/membership/health categories used by the FEC, although some would be scattered in the nonconnected, cooperative, and corporation without stock categories.

c. Included in business-related.

d. Included in other.

e. For 1972 and 1974 this represents spending by ideological PACs, as grouped by the Citizens' Research Foundation (1972) or Common Cause (1974). After 1976 it corresponds directly to the FEC category by that name (which is dominated by the ideological groups).

f. This is a catchall category, for which only the 1978-82 figures are comparable to each other. For 1974 this represents PACs grouped as "miscellaneous" by Common Cause and includes such groups as the NEA (and affiliates), environmentalists, and some cooperatives. For 1976 it includes all PACs now grouped by the FEC as trade/membership/health, nonconnected, cooperative, and corporation without stock. For 1978-82, it combines the FEC categories of cooperatives and corporations without stock.

g. Figures in columns may not add to totals because of rounding.

TABLE A.14.
CONTRIBUTIONS TO CONGRESSIONAL CANDIDATES BY POLITICAL ACTION COMMITTEES,
BY CATEGORY, 1972-82 (IN MILLIONS)

| Type of PAC | 1972 | 1974 | 1976 | 1978[a] | 1980[a] | 1982[a] |
|---|---|---|---|---|---|---|
| Labor | $3.6 | $6.3 | $8.2 | $9.9 | $13.2 | $20.3 |
| Business-related[b] | 2.7 | 4.4 | 10.0 | — | — | — |
| Corporate | — | — | — | 9.5 | 19.2 | 27.5 |
| Trade/member-ship/health | — | — | — | 11.2 | 15.9 | 21.9 |
| Nonconnected[c] | — | 0.7 | 1.5 | 2.5 | 4.9 | 10.7 |
| Other[d] | 2.2 | 1.0 | 2.8 | 1.0 | 2.0 | 3.2 |
| TOTAL[e] | $8.5 | $12.5 | $22.6 | $34.1 | $55.2 | $83.6 |

NOTE: Data are for all congressional candidates, except for 1972, where primary losers are excluded.

SOURCES: For 1972-76, and for footnotes, Cantor, *Political Action Committees,* 87-88. For 1978, Federal Election Commission, *Reports on Financial Activity, 1977-78, Interim Report No. 5* (U.S. Senate and House Campaigns), June 1979, 94. For 1980, Federal Election Commission, *Reports on Financial Activity, 1979-80, Final Report* (U.S. Senate and House Campaigns), January 1982, 127. For 1982, Federal Election Commission, *Reports on Financial Activity, 1981-82, Final Report* (U.S. Senate and House Campaigns), October 1983, 92.

a. Contributions to candidates for election in the year indicated, made during the two-year election cycle.

b. This encompasses the Common Cause categories for business, health, and, in 1976, lawyers. This category is included here for the purpose of listing the data for 1972-76, before the specific breakdowns were devised by the FEC for the corporate and other categories, and it is based on the assumption that the majority of PACs it includes have a basically probusiness orientation. It is only roughly comparable to the combined corporate and trade/membership/health groups in 1978-82, but most of the business-related PACs would fall into those two FEC categories (some would be scattered in the nonconnected, cooperative, and corporation without stock groups).

c. For 1974 and 1976 the nonconnected category, as defined by the FEC, correlates with the ideological group used by Common Cause for those two years. Most of the ideological PACs are today listed in the nonconnected group, but the latter also includes PACs that are not ideological. Thus the data for 1974 and 1976 are not exactly comparable to those for 1978-82, in view of the different standards applied to the nonconnected and the ideological groups. (Ideological PACs in 1972 were lumped into Common Cause's "miscellaneous" group.)

d. This is a catchall category, in which the earlier figures are only roughly comparable to the later ones. For 1972-76 the data represent Common Cause's "miscellaneous" category, which included such groups as the NEA (and affiliates), environmentalists, and some cooperatives, and its agriculture/dairy category. In 1972 Common Cause included the ideological PACs under "miscellaneous," before their separate listing in 1974; thus 1972 includes more types of PACs than the 1974 and 1976 data do. For 1978-82 the "other" data equate directly with the FEC's cooperatives and corporations without stock groups. Thus the data for 1972 are not exactly comparable with those for 1978-82. The common thread is the inclusion of the major dairy PACs—ADEPT, C-TAPE, and SPACE—in "other" in all six election years.

e. Figures in columns may not add to totals because of rounding.

TABLE A.15.

POLITICAL ACTION COMMITTEE CONTRIBUTIONS, BY OFFICE AND COMMITTEE TYPE, 1978-82

| Committee Type | Number Making Contributions | Total | 1978 Contributions (in millions) | | | Number Making Contributions | Total | 1980 Contributions (in millions) | | | Number Making Contributions | Total | 1982 Contributions (in millions) | | |
|---|---|---|---|---|---|---|---|---|---|---|---|---|---|---|---|
| | | | Presidential | Senate | House | | | Presidential | Senate | House | | | Presidential | Senate | House |
| Labor | 215 | $10.3 | $0.03 | $2.8 | $7.4 | 240 | $14.2 | $0.3 | $4.2 | $9.7 | 293 | $20.9 | $0.04 | $5.2 | $15.7 |
| Corporation | 704 | 9.8 | 0.01 | 3.6 | 6.1 | 1101 | 21.6 | 1.1 | 7.7 | 12.7 | 1317 | 29.4 | 0.04 | 9.9 | 19.4 |
| Nonconnected | 122 | 2.8 | 0.00_ | 0.7 | 2.1 | 243 | 5.2 | 0.1 | 1.9 | 3.2 | 407 | 11.0 | 0.01 | 3.4 | 7.5 |
| Trade/membership/health | 400 | 11.3 | 0.001 | 2.8 | 8.6 | 490 | 17.0 | 0.3 | 4.6 | 12.1 | 524 | 22.9 | 0.01 | 5.7 | 17.2 |
| Cooperative | 11 | 0.9 | 0.009 | 0.2 | 0.7 | 31 | 1.5 | 0.04 | 0.4 | 1.1 | 46 | 2.2 | 0 | 0.5 | 1.7 |
| Corporation without stock | 22 | 0.1 | 0 | 0.03 | 0.1 | 50 | 0.7 | 0.04 | 0.3 | 0.4 | 78 | 1.1 | 0.001 | 0.3 | 0.8 |
| TOTAL | 1474 | $35.2 | $0.05 | $10.1 | $25.0 | 2155 | $60.2 | $1.8 | $19.1 | $39.3 | 2665 | $87.6 | $0.1 | $25.1 | $62.4 |

NOTE: Figures may not add to totals because of rounding. The Senate and House figures include contributions made to committees that may not have been those of candidates during the election cycle indicated, such as debt retirement committees or the committees of retiring incumbents. The figures therefore may be higher than those in tables A.14. Also, the number of committees making contributions is lower than the number registered in table A.11.

SOURCES: For 1978, Federal Election Commission, *Reports on Financial Activity, 1977-78, Final Report* (Party and Non-Party Political Committees), vol. 1, April 1980, 144-52. For 1980, Federal Election Commission, *Reports on Financial Activity, 1979-80, Final Report* (Party and Non-Party Political Committees), vol. 1, January 1982, 102-10. For 1982, Federal Election Commission, *Reports on Financial Activity, 1981-82, Final Report* (Party and Non-Party Political Committees), vol. 1, October 1983, 96-105.

TABLE A.16.

## POLITICAL ACTION COMMITTEE CONTRIBUTIONS TO HOUSE CANDIDATES, BY CANDIDATES' STATUS, 1977–78

| Committee Type | Amount Contributed | Percentage Distribution | | | | | | |
| --- | --- | --- | --- | --- | --- | --- | --- | --- |
| | | Incumbent | | Challenger | | Open Seat | | |
| | | Democrat | Republican | Democrat | Republican | Democrat | Republican | Total[a] |
| Distribution of candidates[b] | (N = 797) | 31 | 17 | 14 | 25 | 7 | 7 | 100 |
| Labor | $ 7,462,424 | 60 | 3 | 17 | 0 | 19 | 0 | 100 |
| Corporate | 6,158,069 | 35 | 28 | 2 | 16 | 7 | 12 | 100 |
| Nonconnected | 2,064,062 | 12 | 13 | 4 | 39 | 6 | 25 | 100 |
| Trade/membership/ health | 8,571,697 | 36 | 27 | 2 | 14 | 9 | 12 | 100 |
| Cooperative | 674,698 | 66 | 16 | 2 | 1 | 9 | 6 | 100 |
| Corporation without stock | 95,390 | 48 | 13 | 7 | 4 | 17 | 11 | 100 |
| TOTAL | $25,026,340 | 42 | 19 | 7 | 12 | 11 | 10 | 100 |

SOURCE: Federal Election Commission, *Reports on Financial Activity, 1977–78, Final Report* (Party and Non-Party Political Committees), vol. 1, April 1980, 149–50.

a. Figures may not add to 100 because of rounding.
b. General election candidates only. Contribution figures are for all 1978 House candidates, but most went to general election candidates.

TABLE A.17.

Political Action Committee Contributions to House Candidates, by Candidates' Status, 1979-80

Percentage Distribution

| Committee Type | Amount Contributed | Incumbent | | Challenger | | Open Seat | | Total[a] |
|---|---|---|---|---|---|---|---|---|
| | | Democrat | Republican | Democrat | Republican | Democrat | Republican | |
| Distribution of candidates[b] | (N = 738) | 34 | 19 | 13 | 23 | 6 | 5 | 100 |
| Labor | $ 8,883,834 | 69 | 4 | 16 | 0 | 10 | 0 | 100 |
| Corporate | 11,662,361 | 36 | 32 | 1 | 20 | 1 | 9 | 100 |
| Nonconnected | 2,831,209 | 21 | 15 | 5 | 41 | 4 | 12 | 98[b] |
| Trade/membership/ health | 11,215,269 | 39 | 32 | 2 | 17 | 3 | 8 | 100 |
| Cooperative | 985,177 | 59 | 26 | 2 | 3 | 3 | 7 | 100 |
| Corporation without stock | 387,740 | 47 | 30 | 2 | 11 | 2 | 7 | 100 |
| TOTAL | $35,965,590 | 45 | 24 | 5 | 15 | 4 | 7 | 100 |

NOTE: General election candidates only.

SOURCE: Federal Election Commission, *Reports on Financial Activity, 1979-80, Final Report* (U.S. Senate and House Campaigns), January 1982, 65-66.

a. Figures may not add to total because of rounding.

b. PACs not connected to other organizations also gave more than 1% of their House contributions to challengers who were neither Democrats nor Republicans.

POLITICAL ACTION COMMITTEE CONTRIBUTIONS TO HOUSE CANDIDATES, BY CANDIDATES' STATUS, 1981-82

| Committee Type | Amount Contributed | Percentage Distribution | | | | | | Total[a] |
| | | Incumbent | | Challenger | | Open Seat | | |
| | | Democrat | Republican | Democrat | Republican | Democrat | Republican | |
|---|---|---|---|---|---|---|---|---|
| Distribution of candidates | (N = 830) | 26 | 20 | 20 | 21 | 6 | 6 | 100 |
| Labor | $14,557,589 | 53 | 4 | 28 | 0.1 | 14 | 1 | 100 |
| Corporate | 18,136,407 | 32 | 45 | 1 | 9 | 3 | 9 | 100 |
| Nonconnected | 6,886,695 | 29 | 19 | 16 | 18 | 8 | 10 | 100 |
| Trade/membership/ health | 15,901,781 | 34 | 42 | 4 | 8 | 4 | 8 | 100 |
| Cooperative | 1,650,239 | 52 | 33 | 4 | 1 | 6 | 3 | 100 |
| Corporation without stock | 771,847 | 51 | 32 | 5 | 3 | 5 | 4 | 100 |
| TOTAL | $57,904,558 | 39 | 30 | 11 | 7 | 7 | 7 | 100 |

NOTE: General election candidates only.

SOURCE: Federal Election Commission, *Reports on Financial Activity, 1981-82, Final Report* (U.S. Senate and House Campaigns), October 1983, 47-48.

a. Figures may not add to 100 because of rounding.

## TABLE A.19.

### POLITICAL ACTION COMMITTEE CONTRIBUTIONS TO SENATE CANDIDATES, BY CANDIDATES' STATUS, 1977-78

|  |  | Percentage Distribution | | | | | | |
|  |  | Incumbent | | Challenger | | Open Seat | | |
| Committee Type | Amount Contributed | Democrat | Republican | Democrat | Republican | Democrat | Republican | Total[a] |
|---|---|---|---|---|---|---|---|---|
| Distribution of candidates[b] | (N = 68) | 16 | 16 | 16 | 15 | 19 | 18 | 100 |
| Labor | $ 2,831,336 | 38 | 9 | 33 | 1 | 20 | 1 | 100 |
| Corporate | 3,616,388 | 15 | 37 | 6 | 20 | 7 | 15 | 100 |
| Nonconnected | 732,993 | 10 | 19 | 11 | 37 | 4 | 18 | 100 |
| Trade/membership/ health | 2,751,980 | 19 | 32 | 9 | 17 | 10 | 13 | 100 |
| Cooperative | 202,600 | 22 | 21 | 13 | 10 | 20 | 13 | 100 |
| Corporation without stock | 25,578 | 16 | 35 | 7 | 16 | 12 | 15 | 100 |
| TOTAL | $10,160,875 | 22 | 26 | 15 | 15 | 11 | 11 | 100 |

SOURCE: Federal Election Commission, *Reports on Financial Activity, 1977-78, Final Report* (Party and Non-Party Political Committees), vol. 1, April 1980, summary tables, 147-48.

a. Figures may not add to 100 because of rounding.

b. General election candidates only. Contribution figures are for all 1978 Senate candidates, but most went to general election candidates.

Table A.20.

Political Action Committee Contributions to Senate Candidates, by Candidates' Status, 1979-80

Percentage Distribution

| Committee Type | Amount Contributed | Incumbent | | Challenger | | Open Seat | | Total[a] |
|---|---|---|---|---|---|---|---|---|
| | | Democrat | Republican | Democrat | Republican | Democrat | Republican | |
| Distribution of candidates | (N = 66) | 27 | 9 | 9 | 27 | 14 | 14 | 100 |
| Labor | $ 3,428,404 | 65 | 9 | 14 | 1 | 11 | 1 | 100 |
| Corporate | 6,445,566 | 25 | 14 | 1 | 47 | 2 | 11 | 100 |
| Nonconnected | 1,690,574 | 22 | 6 | 2 | 53 | 2 | 14 | 100 |
| Trade/membership/ health | 3,816,424 | 37 | 17 | 3 | 32 | 5 | 7 | 100 |
| Cooperative | 325,050 | 65 | 11 | 1 | 11 | 6 | 6 | 100 |
| Corporation without stock | 214,853 | 40 | 18 | 3 | 27 | 5 | 7 | 100 |
| Total | $15,920,871 | 37 | 13 | 4 | 33 | 5 | 8 | 100 |

Note: General election candidates only.

Source: Federal Election Commission, *Reports on Financial Activity, 1979-80, Final Report* (U.S. Senate and House Campaigns), January 1982, 63-64.

a. Figures may not add to 100 because of rounding.

TABLE A.21.

POLITICAL ACTION COMMITTEE CONTRIBUTIONS TO SENATE CANDIDATES, BY CANDIDATES' STATUS, 1981-82

| Committee Type | Amount Contributed | Percentage Distribution | | | | | | Total[a] |
|---|---|---|---|---|---|---|---|---|
| | | Incumbent | | Challenger | | Open Seat | | |
| | | Democrat | Republican | Democrat | Republican | Democrat | Republican | |
| Distribution of candidates | (N = 66) | 29 | 17 | 17 | 29 | 5 | 5 | 100 |
| Labor | $ 4,830,051 | 56 | 7 | 27 | 0.3 | 9 | 1 | 100 |
| Corporate | 8,275,630 | 26 | 41 | 1 | 17 | 1 | 14 | 100 |
| Nonconnected | 3,150,309 | 28 | 20 | 15 | 23 | 6 | 7 | 100 |
| Trade/membership/ health | 4,857,841 | 37 | 39 | 4 | 10 | 2 | 8 | 100 |
| Cooperative | 427,526 | 52 | 19 | 12 | 2 | 1 | 14 | 100 |
| Corporation without stock | 262,140 | 45 | 33 | 3 | 6 | 2 | 11 | 100 |
| TOTAL | $21,803,497 | 36 | 29 | 10 | 12 | 4 | 9 | 100 |

NOTE: General election candidates only.

SOURCE: Federal Election Commission, *Reports on Financial Activity, 1981-82, Final Report* (U.S. Senate and House Campaigns), October 1983, 45-46.

a. Figures may not add to 100 because of rounding.

TABLE A.22.
RECEIPTS, PAC RECEIPTS, AND PERCENT FROM PACs, 1982 HOUSE ELECTIONS,
BY ELECTION OUTCOME

| | Number of Candidates | Mean Receipts ($) | Mean PAC Receipts ($) | Percent from PACs |
|---|---|---|---|---|
| Incumbent Won with 60% or More[a] | | | | |
| Democratic incumbent | 178 | 235,056 | 91,105 | 39 |
| Republican challenger | 95 | 119,099 | 15,960 | 13 |
| Republican incumbent | 86 | 216,938 | 72,387 | 33 |
| Democratic challenger | 57 | 40,412 | 9,176 | 23 |
| Difference between | | | | |
| incumbents and and challengers[b] | 151 | 157,431 | 80,012 | — |
| Incumbent Won with Less Than 60%[a] | | | | |
| Democratic incumbent | 35 | 453,042 | 154,547 | 34 |
| Republican challenger | 31 | 325,664 | 76,096 | 23 |
| Republican incumbent | 55 | 364,239 | 125,840 | 35 |
| Democratic challenger | 53 | 203,297 | 52,648 | 26 |
| Difference between | | | | |
| incumbents and challengers[b] | 84 | 135,589 | 73,493 | — |
| Incumbent Was Defeated | | | | |
| Democratic incumbent | 3 | 349,109 | 145,142 | 42 |
| Republican challenger | 1 | 375,519 | 169,931 | 45 |
| Republican incumbent | 26 | 469,834 | 168,301 | 36 |
| Democratic challenger | 22 | 294,094 | 100,878 | 34 |
| Difference between | | | | |
| incumbents and challengers[b] | 23 | 125,568 | 48,337 | — |

SOURCES: Same as table A.1.

a. Percentage of the vote received by the two leading candidates
b. Includes only those races where both major-party candidates filed reports with the FEC. Does not include incumbent/incumbent races caused by redistricting.

TABLE A.23.
RECEIPTS, PAC RECEIPTS, AND PERCENT FROM PACs, 1982 SENATE ELECTIONS,
BY ELECTION OUTCOME

| | Number of Candidates | Mean Receipts ($) | Mean PAC Receipts ($) | Percent from Pacs |
|---|---|---|---|---|
| **Incumbent Won with 60% or More**[a] | | | | |
| Democratic incumbent | 12 | 1,504,174 | 384,346 | 26 |
| Republican challenger | 12 | 813,003 | 142,318 | 18 |
| Republican incumbent | 1 | 2,967,802 | 585,601 | 19 |
| Democratic challenger | 1 | 424,948 | 57,068 | 13 |
| Difference between incumbents and challengers[b] | 12 | 848,937 | 263,896 | — |
| **Incumbent Won with Less Than 60%**[a] | | | | |
| Democratic incumbent | 5 | 2,516,831 | 529,422 | 21 |
| Republican challenger | 5 | 1,601,017 | 143,093 | 9 |
| Republican incumbent | 9 | 2,131,679 | 576,072 | 27 |
| Democratic challenger | 9 | 1,636,226 | 188,482 | 12 |
| Difference between incumbents and challengers[b] | 14 | 645,581 | 387,140 | |
| **Incumbent Was Defeated** | | | | |
| Democratic incumbent | 1 | 1,642,261 | 590,415 | 36 |
| Republican challenger | 1 | 1,025,847 | 250,010 | 24 |
| Republican incumbent | 1 | 1,706,963 | 601,973 | 35 |
| Democratic challenger | 1 | 1,606,965 | 308,917 | 19 |
| Difference between incumbents and challengers[b] | 2 | 358,206 | 316,731 | — |

SOURCES: Same as table A.4.

a. Percentage of the vote received by the two leading candidates.

b. Includes only those races where both major-party candidates filed reports with the FEC. See table A.4, note b.

TABLE A.24.

TIMING OF PAC AND NON-PAC CONTRIBUTIONS, 1977-78
(ALL CANDIDATES, SENATE AND HOUSE ELECTIONS)

| | January 1, 1977-June 30, 1978 | | July 1-September 30, 1978 | | October 1-December 31, 1978 | | 1977-78 |
|---|---|---|---|---|---|---|---|
| | % of 1977-78 contributions given Jan. 1, 1977-June 30, 1978 | % of Jan. 1, 1977-June 30, 1978 contributions to non-incumbents | % of 1977-78 contributions given July 1-Sept. 30, 1978 | % of July 1-Sept. 30 contributions to non-incumbents | % of 1977-78 contributions given Oct. 1-Dec. 31, 1978 | % of Oct. 1-Dec. 31 contributions to non-incumbents | % of all contributions to non-incumbents |
| Corporations | 26 | N.A. | 21 | N.A. | 52 | 54 | 41 |
| Labor unions | 36 | N.A. | 22 | N.A. | 42 | 48 | 41 |
| No connected organization | 22 | N.A. | 25 | N.A. | 53 | 84 | 74 |
| Trade/member/health | 31 | N.A. | 24 | N.A. | 45 | 52 | 40 |
| Cooperative | 54 | N.A. | 13 | N.A. | 33 | 53 | 30 |
| Corporation without stock | 33 | N.A. | 12 | N.A. | 55 | 39 | 42 |
| All PACs | 31 | N.A. | 23 | N.A. | 46 | 54 | 43 |
| Other contributors | 50 | N.A. | N.A. | N.A. | N.A. | N.A. | 66 |
| (PACs as percentage of all contributions in period) | (13) | – | N.A. | – | N.A. | – | (21) |

NOTE: Numbers may not add to 100% because of rounding. N.A. = not available.

SOURCES: Compiled from Federal Election Commission press releases: "FEC Releases Mid-Year Report on Political Committee Financial Activity," September 7, 1978; "FEC Releases Summaries of Non-Party Political Committee 1977-78 Financial Activity," November 2, 1978; "FEC Releases Final Report on 1977-78 Financial Activity of Non-Party and Party Political Committees," April 24, 1980.

TABLE A.25.
TIMING OF PAC AND NON-PAC CONTRIBUTIONS, 1979-80
(ALL CANDIDATES, SENATE AND HOUSE ELECTIONS)

| | January 1, 1979-June 30, 1980 | | July 1-October 15, 1980 | | October 16-December 31, 1980 | | 1979-80 |
|---|---|---|---|---|---|---|---|
| | % of 1979-80 contributions given Jan. 1, 1979-June 30, 1980 | % of Jan. 1, 1979-June 1980 contributions to non-incumbents | % of 1979-80 contributions given July 1-Oct. 15, 1980 | % of July 1-Oct. 15 contributions to non-incumbents | % of 1979-80 contributions given Oct. 16-Dec. 31, 1980 | % of Oct. 16-Dec. 31 contributions to non-incumbents | % of all contributions to non-incumbents |
| Corporations | 39 | 24 | 49 | 52 | 12 | 67 | 43 |
| Labor unions | 40 | 19 | 56 | 35 | 4 | 40 | 29 |
| No connected organization | 24 | 58 | 56 | 75 | 20 | 60 | 68 |
| Trade/member/health | 38 | 23 | 59 | 44 | 3 | 50 | 36 |
| Cooperative | 40 | 9 | 54 | 18 | 6 | 100 | 19 |
| Corporation without stock | 36 | 5 | 22 | 23 | 42 | 60 | 32 |
| All PACs | 38 | 24 | 54 | 47 | 8 | 59 | 39 |
| Other contributors | 54 | 58 | N.A. | — | N.A. | — | 59 |
| (PACs as percentage of all contributions in period) | (17) | — | N.A. | — | N.A. | — | (22) |

NOTE: Numbers may not add to 100% because of rounding.

SOURCES: Compiled from Federal Election Commission press releases: "FEC Reports on 1979-80 Senate and House Financial Activity," October 1, 1980; "FEC Releases New PAC Spending Figures for '80 Elections," March 29, 1981; "FEC Releases Final PAC Report for 1979-80 Election Cycle," February 21, 1982; "FEC Releases Final Statistics on 1979-80 Congressional Races," March 7, 1982."

## TABLE A.26.
## TIMING OF PAC AND NON-PAC CONTRIBUTIONS, 1981-82
### (ALL CANDIDATES, SENATE AND HOUSE ELECTIONS)

| | January 1, 1981-June 30, 1982 | | July 1-October 13, 1982 | | October 14-December 31, 1982 | | 1981-82 |
|---|---|---|---|---|---|---|---|
| | % of 1981-82 contributions given Jan. 1, 1981-June 30, 1982 | % of Jan. 1, 1981-June 30, 1982 contributions to non-incumbents | % of 1981-82 contributions given July 1-Oct. 13, 1982 | % of July 1-Oct. 13 contributions to non-incumbents | % of 1981-82 contributions given Oct. 14-Dec. 31, 1982 | % of Oct. 14-Dec. 31 contributions to non-incumbents | % of all contributions to non-incumbents |
| Corporations | 46 | 16 | 40 | 36 | 14 | 41 | 27 |
| Labor unions | 40 | 28 | 44 | 52 | 15 | 56 | 43 |
| No connected organization | 27 | 45 | 44 | 59 | 30 | 57 | 54 |
| Trade/member/health | 45 | 15 | 45 | 34 | 9 | 45 | 26 |
| Cooperative | 41 | 7 | 44 | 20 | 15 | 41 | 18 |
| Corporation without stock | 45 | 12 | 39 | 22 | 16 | 37 | 20 |
| All PACs | 42 | 21 | 43 | 42 | 15 | 49 | 34 |
| Other contributors | 52 | 55 | 30 | 65 | 19 | 58 | 59 |
| (PACs as percentage of all contributions in period) | (20) | — | (31) | — | (20) | — | (23) |

NOTE: Numbers may not add to 100% because of rounding.

SOURCES: Compiled from Federal Election Commission press releases: "FEC Releases First Full PAC Study for '82 Elections," October 3, 1982; "PAC Activity Increases," January 6, 1983; "1981-82 PAC Giving Up 51%," April 29, 1983.

TABLE A.27.
INDEPENDENT EXPENDITURES, 1977-82

| Type of Expenditure | 1977-78 | | | 1979-80 | | | 1981-82 | | |
|---|---|---|---|---|---|---|---|---|---|
| | House | Senate | President | House | Senate | President | House | Senate | President |
| For Democrats | $28,725 (N = 55) | $102,508 (N = 13) | $4,442 (N = 2) | $190,615 (N = 91) | $127,381 (N = 24) | $123,058 (N = 2) | $241,442 (N = 84) | $127,451 (N = 25) | $568 (N = 1) |
| Against Democrats | 31,034 (N = 7) | 36,717 (N = 6) | 0 | 38,023 (N = 32) | 1,282,613 (N = 15) | 737,796 (N = 3) | 862,654 (N = 39) | 3,182,986 (N = 28) | 1,394 (N = 1) |
| For Republicans | 70,701 (N = 83) | 26,065 (N = 22) | 1,726 (N = 1) | 410,478 (N = 205) | 261,678 (N = 58) | 12,537,522 (N = 3) | 492,404 (N = 164) | 298,410 (N = 46) | 91,765 (N = 1) |
| Against Republicans | 5,298 (N = 5) | 1,915 (N = 5) | 0 | 45,132 (N = 6) | 12,430 (N = 5) | 65,040 (N = 2) | 66,296 (N = 14) | 483,750 (N = 9) | 0 |
| TOTAL[a] | 143,162 (N = 164) | 168,125 (N = 48) | 6,168 (N = 3) | 684,727 (N = 321) | 1,684,102 (N = 89) | 13,746,444 (N = 15) | 1,662,796 (N = 276) | 4,092,597 (N = 90) | 93,727 (N = 2) |

NOTE: N = number of candidates.

An independent expenditure is defined as an "expenditure by a person for a communication expressly advocating the election or defeat of a clearly identified candidate that is not made with the cooperation or with the prior consent of, or in consultation with, or at the request or suggestion of, a candidate or any agent or authorized committee of such candidate" (11 C.F.R. 109.1 [a]).

The Federal Election Commission's data on 1975-76 independent expenditures were not completed or verified. On October 9, 1980, the FEC released the following information about independent expenditures during the 1975-76 election cycle: $2,033,207 was spent independently for or against 144 candidates; $1,646,540 was spent for or against presidential candidates; $198,787 was spent for or against Senate candidates; $187,880 was spent for or against House candidates.

SOURCES: Federal Election Commission Press Releases. For 1975-78, "FEC Releases Information on Independent Expenditures," October 9, 1980. For 1979-80, "FEC Study Shows Independent Expenditures Top $16 Million," November 29, 1981. For 1982, "FEC Issues Final Report on 1981-82 Independent Spending," October 14, 1983.

a. The totals include expenditures made on behalf of, or in opposition to, candidates who were neither Democrats nor Republicans. In 1979-80, $479 was spent on behalf of one such candidate for the House, $271,978 was spent on behalf of seven presidential candidates (including $199,438 on behalf of John Anderson), and $11,059 was spent in opposition to two presidential candidates. In 1977-78, $7404 was spent on behalf of fourteen candidates for the House and $920 on behalf of two Senate candidates. (In 1981-82, there were no independent expenditures for or against candidates who were neither Democrats nor Republicans.) The totals refer to total number of candidates. Because there may have been independent expenditures for and against the same candidates, the total may be less than the sum of the candidates in each column.

# About the Authors

MICHAEL J. MALBIN is a resident fellow at the American Enterprise Institute for Public Policy Research, adjunct associate professor of politics at the Catholic University of America, and contributing editor to *National Journal*. His previous books include: *Unelected Representatives: Congressional Staff and the Future of Representative Government; Vital Statistics on Congress, 1982; Parties, Interest Groups, and Campaign Finance Laws;* and *Religion and Politics: The Intentions of the Authors of the First Amendment*.

HERBERT E. ALEXANDER is director of the Citizens' Research Foundation, which specializes in campaign finance analysis, and professor of political science at the University of Southern California. The most recent of his many books on campaign finance is *Financing the 1980 Election,* the sixth in a quadrennial series that began in 1960.

GARY C. JACOBSON is professor of political science at the University of California, San Diego. He is the author of *Money in Congressional Elections* and *The Politics of Congressional Elections* and co-author of *Strategy and Choice in Congressional Elections*.

DAVID ADAMANY is president of Wayne State University in Detroit, Michigan. A lawyer and political scientist, Adamany has held numerous positions in Wisconsin state government, including the chairmanship of the Wisconsin State Elections Board. He is the author of *Campaign Finance in America* and co-author of *Political Money*.

THEODORE J. EISMEIER is assistant professor of government and director of the Term in Washington Program at Hamilton College. He is co-editor of *Public Policy and Public Choice* and author of several articles on fiscal politics in the United States.

PHILIP H. POLLOCK III is assistant professor of political science at the University of Central Florida. He has authored several articles on public opinion and political participation.

MARGARET ANN LATUS is a Ph.D. candidate in the department of politics at Princeton University writing a dissertation on ideological political action committees. She has published several articles and papers on ideological PACs. In 1982-83, she was a graduate research fellow at the Brookings Institution. She will join the political science faculty at the College of the Holy Cross in September 1984.

RUTH S. JONES is professor of political science at Arizona State University and has served on the Governor's Commission on Campaign Reform and Official Conduct in Missouri. Her chapter in this volume is one of several she has written in the last four years as part of a long-range research project on campaign finance in state elections.

RICHARD SMOLKA is professor of political science at American University and editor of *Election Administration Reports,* a biweekly newsletter for election officials. He is the co-author of *Polling and Political Campaigns* and *American Parties and Elections.*

THOMAS W. SKLADONY is a research assistant at the American Enterprise Institute for Public Policy Research and a Ph.D. candidate in political science at the University of Pennsylvania.

# Index